THE METAPHYSICAL POETS

LONGMAN MEDIEVAL AND RENAISSANCE LIBRARY

General Editors:

Charlotte Brewer Hertford College, Oxford and *N. H. Keeble* University of Stirling

THE METAPHYSICAL POETS

DAVID REID

Longman

An imprint of **Pearson Education**

Harlow, England · London · New York · Reading, Massachusetts · San Francisco
Toronto · Don Mills, Ontario · Sydney · Tokyo · Singapore · Hong Kong · Seoul
Taipei · Cape Town · Madrid · Mexico City · Amsterdam · Munich · Paris · Milan

Pearson Education Ltd
Edinburgh Gate
Harlow
Essex CM20 2JE
England

and Associated Companies around the World.

Visit us on the World Wide Web at:
www.pearsoneduc.com

First published 2000

© Pearson Education Limited 2000

ISBN 0 582 29835 0 PPR
ISBN 0 582 29834 2 CSD

British Library Cataloguing-in-Publication Data
A catalogue record for this book can be obtained from the British Library

Library of Congress Cataloging-in-Publication Data
Reid, David, 1940–
      The Metaphysical poets / David Reid.
          p. cm. — (Longman medieval and Renaissance library)
      Includes bibliographical references (p.   ) and index.
      ISBN 0–582–29834–2 — ISBN 0–582–29835–0 (pbk.)
      1. English poetry—Early modern, 1500–1700—History and criticism.
   2. Metaphysics in literature.   I. Title.   II. Series.

   PR545.M4 R45 2000
   821'.309--dc21   99–086025

10 9 8 7 6 5 4 3 2 1
04 03 02 01 00

Typeset by 35 in 11/13pt Baskerville MT
Produced by Pearson Education Asia Pte Ltd.
Printed in Singapore

For Susan

CONTENTS

LIST OF ILLUSTRATIONS

ACKNOWLEDGEMENTS

Thanks are due to the University of Stirling for a Sabbatical, during which a large part of this book was drafted.

I am particularly grateful to Neil Keeble, editor of Longman Medieval and Renaissance Library, not only for the scholarship he brought to bear on various seventeenth century matters I raised with him, but for the generous pains he took in editing the manuscript and for his encouragement. I must also thank Mary Lince, Editor, and Casey Mein, Assistant Commissioning Editor, at Pearson Education, for their care and efficiency in bringing out the book.

I am greatly indebted to my wife, Susan Reid, for taking time off from her own work to discuss some of the poems I examine and to read the manuscript. The book owes a great deal to the quality of attention and incisiveness she put into both tasks.

The publishers are grateful to the following for permission to reproduce copyright material:

Faber and Faber Limited for extracts from the poem 'Mr Apollinax' by T. S. Eliot from *Prufrock and Other Observations*; Faber and Faber Limited/ Harcourt Brace & Company for extracts from 'Little Gidding' by T. S. Eliot from *The Collected Poems* 1963.

Bodleian Library, University of Oxford for *Antiq eE. 1632.11. Deaths Duell by John Donne, 1632. Frontispiece portrait; Douce D 38. Poems by John Donne, 1635. Frontispiece portrait; Douce c 98. Poems by John Cleveland, 1653. Frontispiece portrait*; The Houghton Library, Harvard University for *MS Eng 1405*, a drawing of George Herbert by Robert White; The National Portrait Gallery, London for a portrait of Andrew Marvell by an unknown artist; The Master and Fellows of Trinity College Cambridge for a crayon drawing of Abraham Cowley.

Whilst every effort has been made to trace the owners of copyright material, in a few cases this has proved impossible and we take this opportunity to offer our apologies to any copyright holders whose rights we may have unwittingly infringed.

INTRODUCTION

When the eighteenth-century critic Samuel Johnson wrote of a 'race' of Metaphysical poets in his 'Life of Cowley', he drew his illustrations of their style from Abraham Cowley and John Donne and once from John Cleveland. He mentions others, whom he thinks of as followers not just of Donne, but of Ben Jonson: Edmund Waller, John Denham, Sir John Suckling and John Milton (in his juvenile epigrams on Hobson the carrier). For Johnson, however, 'the fashionable style remained chiefly with Cowley'.[1] The poets whom I talk about at length are, except for Donne, notably absent from this list. Johnson says nothing about George Herbert, Richard Crashaw, Andrew Marvell or Henry Vaughan; Thomas Traherne's poetry lay still in manuscript, unknown. Yet many twentieth-century discussions of the Metaphysicals treat these six poets. They are the main figures in Robert Ellrodt's essential survey of the field, *Les Poètes Métaphysiques Anglais* (1960), though he, unusually, discusses Lord Herbert of Cherbury at length as well, and, more usually, subjects Cowley to extended dismissive analysis.[2]

Behind these different selections lies a history of critical taste and ideas. For Johnson, 'Metaphysical' meant much the same as 'Gothick' did for Joseph Addison in his *Spectator* papers on wit. He was playing on a view of metaphysics as the philosophy of the medieval philosopher divines, the schoolmen, a view derived from the Renaissance humanists and Francis Bacon, which was sufficiently prevalent for 'Metaphysical' to be used as a nickname to associate its object with what was seen as the empty and fantastic philosophical culture of the Middle Ages, with ideas spun out of words rather than derived from the study of things. In that way 'Metaphysical' characterized the wit of the earlier seventeenth century as insubstantial and out of touch with human nature. Cowley was the great representative because his gifts for expressing himself with analytic precision and human warmth were easily

---

1. Johnson 1952, I, pp. 13–28.
2. Traherne is frequently left out in surveys of the Metaphysicals (e.g. in Bennett 1964 and Mackenzie 1990); for those that include him see Ellrodt 1960 and Helen White 1936. Miner 1974, p. 86, feels that Cowley deserves much more serious consideration than Traherne; see his discussion of Cowley in Miner 1969, pp. 110–17.

appreciated by the eighteenth century and at the same time he was an object lesson in how extravagance and lack of judgement might render great powers inconsequential. He was a serious, not an absurd, example of the 'Metaphysical' or 'Gothick' vice in writing. As for the twentieth-century vogue for Donne, Marvell, Herbert and Crashaw, behind that lies the extraordinary influence of T. S. Eliot's views. He spoke of the Metaphysicals as masters of the kind of poetry he wanted: difficult, complex, learned and simultaneously intellectual, sensual and feeling. Even where his ideas were rejected, his sensibility caught on. He did not praise Vaughan or Traherne.[3] But somehow they were taken along with the others. They probably owed their popularity to surviving late Romanticism and in particular the cult of Blake and the visionary and hermetic strain in Yeats. But influences are not unaccountable, and the twentieth-century interest in the Metaphysicals goes with an insight that Eliot's criticism and poetic practice helped to make current: the intellectual style of the Metaphysicals expresses a highly individual angle on the world, its playfulness intimating unease, even neurosis, but carrying these things off in a self-contained way, lightly, obliquely, ironically. Where Johnson looked for a social point of view and found it wanting, even in Cowley, the twentieth century has singled out masters of troubled interiority, and Cowley, whose extravagances usually at least nod at common sense, has been neglected.

The focus of this book and the choice of poets that goes with it follows the twentieth-century bent. The title might have been expanded: *The Metaphysical Poets, Six Studies in Seventeenth-Century Interiority*. Cowley, an interesting and fitfully excellent poet, comes in at the end, along with Cleveland, only to bring out by contrast the introspectiveness of Donne, Herbert, Crashaw, Marvell, Vaughan and Traherne. An interest in oneself is a limited thing of course, but it is these poets' interest in themselves that makes them matter to us.

Literary classifications are always fuzzy. 'Metaphysical' is a particularly fuzzy term. After all, if the poets picked up by it depend so much on point of view as the change from Johnson's selection to the twentieth-century one suggests, questions will arise about definition. I have found, though, that wrangling about formal definition and boundary disputes leads nowhere with literary classification. It is best to be content with ostensive definition, that is, with pointing to the representatives and letting the connotation of the term take care of itself. Still, before we go any further, there are two points to be made about using 'Metaphysical' as a name.

The first is that it does not point to a line of descent, as Johnson's 'race' of poets might suggest. Connections can certainly be made, but only here

---

3. Eliot 1927, pp. 260–61, 263.

and there. Marvell writes in Donneish vein in 'The Definition of Love'. Cowley's *The Mistress* is full of echoes of Donne. But both these poets could only in part be said to belong to a school of Donne. They assimilated many other writers along with him. Herbert, bound by ties of friendship to Donne and perhaps inspired by his example as a devotional poet, resembles him in his writings only in very general ways. He does not sound like Donne, though he may be closer to him than to, say, Milton. Herbert had followers. Vaughan is extraordinarily derivative of him, and yet Vaughan's parasitism allowed him to develop an entirely different poetry from anything to be found in his master. Kinship with Herbert is claimed in the title of Crashaw's volume *Steps to the Temple*, after Herbert's *The Temple*. Yet differences between Crashaw's manner and Herbert's are more striking than affinities. As for Traherne, few telling connections with earlier Metaphysicals can be made out. The six poets whom I shall be discussing are in fact all highly individual. That is one thing they do have in common. But it is hardly a basis for defining what makes a Metaphysical. It would be going too far to say that the Metaphysicals are like a constellation, the appearance of their being a group depending upon point of view rather than real connections between them, but the connections between them are certainly tenuous.

The second point about 'Metaphysical' as a classifying term is that the Metaphysicals run into other groupings. A conventional map of poetry in the earlier seventeenth century divides it into three lines of descent: the schools of Spenser, of Jonson (the Tribe of Ben, the Cavalier poets) and of Donne (the Metaphysicals).[4] But some Metaphysicals might equally well be called Spenserians. Clement Paman, for instance, wrote in 'Good Friday' (*c.* 1647?) a beautiful and personal poem, highly derivative of Herbert, and an elegy on Edward King that combines Spenserian water fantasy with conceits in the manner of Donne. Again Joseph Beaumont writes in *Psyche* (1648) a Spenserian allegorical romance of the soul's intercourse with Christ in a conceited style that he developed in association with Crashaw, playful and wilfully absurd, too recherché for Spenser.

The boundary between the Metaphysicals and the Cavalier poets is even harder to draw. Johnson classed Suckling, Waller and Denham as Metaphysicals, though twentieth-century commentators usually separate them into a Cavalier school because they are courtly and social in their concerns, more polished, less learned and far-fetched. That works up to a point as we shall see, and yet one of them, Thomas Carew, wrote more admiringly of Donne than of Jonson; his 'Elegy on the Death of Dr Donne' imitates rather hoarsely Donne's arresting couplet manner. It is from Carew, rather

---

4. E.g. in Bush 1962, pp. 76–129.

than from Donne or Herbert, that Crashaw borrows phrasing and ideas. It is Suckling, of all people, that Traherne most distinctly echoes. And Waller is more frequently felt as a presence in Marvell's verse than Donne.

With such material, it is futile to try for watertight definition.[5] Nevertheless, the Metaphysicals do have certain shared qualities. I shall point to these in the next few paragraphs; I shall be attempting, not definition, but general description with a view to bringing out some of what is remarkable about the poets I shall be discussing. I shall be painting with broad strokes; nuanced discussion may be found in the succeeding chapters.

The Metaphysical style is an extravagant style. Most early seventeenth-century poets wrote with an excess of manner over matter.[6] But the Metaphysicals write more extravagantly than the Tribe of Ben and the Spenserians. Their extravagance is not idle decoration, as the curious elaborations of Joshua Sylvester and his followers usually are. Metaphysical extravagance is expressive of singularity, of individual self-consciousness or individual estrangement from the world. It is most easily identifiable in Donne's use of paradox, conceit and what his contemporaries called 'strong lines'. 'Strong lines' are not lines of poetry but expressions made arresting and difficult through abrupt or riddling syntax or of course through paradox or conceit. 'We see we saw not what did move' (Donne, 'The Ecstasy', l. 32) is a strong line because of a certain wilful puzzle in 'we see we saw not'; 'They are ours, though they are not we, we are / The intelligence, they the sphere' ('The Ecstasy', ll. 51–52) is a strong line for a similar difficulty in phrasing as well as for its intellectual conceit on a metaphysical idea of planetary motion. Few Metaphysicals bristle so much with Metaphysical devices as Donne, but they are all marked by stylistic mannerisms that, at least in their good work, make expressive forms of interesting interiorities.[7]

The wit or extravagance of the Cavalier poets is usually a social game. In a 'Sonnet', Suckling tells Cupid that it is not beauty but appetite 'in love that makes the sport':

---

5. Strikingly Parfitt's general study of seventeenth-century poetry avoids 'Metaphysical' as a classification, finding other groupings more useful. Recent studies of poetry in the earlier seventeenth century, such as can be found in Gerald Hammond 1990, Nigel Smith 1994 and Loxley 1997, pursue interests that cut across the conventional literary categorizing of the period.
6. See Winters 1967, pp. 27–29, 72.
7. On strong lines, see Williamson 1960, pp. 120–31; on interiority as a characteristic of the Metaphysicals, see Miner 1969, pp. 3–47. Ellrodt 1960, I, pp. 42–43, with vastly more theoretical sophistication than Miner (or myself), makes Renaissance 'self-consciousness' the historical ground of his discussion of Metaphysical structures of consciousness.

> For though some long ago
> Lik'd certain colours mingled so and so,
> That doth not tie me now from choosing new:
> If I a fancy take
> To black and blue,
> That fancy doth it beauty make.
>
> 'Tis not the meat, but 'tis the appetite
> Makes eating a delight,
> And if I like one dish
> More than another, that a pheasant is.[8]

His perverse notion that he might take a fancy to a black and blue complexion, instead of a red and white one, asserts the rule of his caprice, and his ungallant analogy of women to dishes and his indelicate taste for gamey ones express bored contempt for any tie of affection or admiration. But his insolence, far from being morose or in any way Byronic, is all social banter and preening. By contrast, when Donne in 'Love's Diet' claims to have attained a state of indifference, a certain violence in his expression suggests bitterness:

> If [Love] wrung from me a tear, I brined it so
> With scorn or shame, that him it nourished not;
> If he sucked hers, I let him know
> 'Twas not a tear, which he had got,
> His drink was counterfeit, as was his meat;
> For, eyes which roll towards all, weep not, but sweat.[9]

The absurdity may be a social game, but it is a game that puts Donne outside society. Where Suckling's 'black and blue' and his pheasant play with social coinage, Donne's tears belong to a world of private feeling that Suckling is too chic to be touched by. And Donne's expressions of resentment are not elegant but suggest rather a revengeful satirist on women. Although 'Love's Diet' is a pose poem, Donne's measures to achieve indifference suggest fear of betrayal; there is no such inner turbulence in Suckling's posing.

The Metaphysicals did not have a monopoly of interiority. One need only cast one's mind over the soliloquies in Shakespeare's tragedies or some of the erotic dreamwork in *The Faerie Queene* (1590, 1596, 1609) or the dark reflections and visitings of the self in Fulke Greville's *Caelica* (late 1580s to 1628) for that to be obvious. And Metaphysical interiority is not simple.

---

8. Suckling 1953, p. 192.
9. Donne 1971.

Metaphysical wit, like the wit of the Tribe of Ben or wit as we normally think of it, is the wit of wits, a social adroitness with words. Donne, Herbert, Marvell and in his way Crashaw are all wits, university-educated men conscious of the social figure they cut and of the tone of the governing classes. They are not necessarily amusing. Donne's 'Valediction: forbidding Mourning' would not have set the table at the Devil's Tavern in a roar, nor would his sermons. But though he, of all Metaphysicals, presents himself most in the character of melancholiac, he speaks to those whose intelligence and sensibility are to some extent socially attuned and style-conscious. That this social side of wit is weakly developed or absent in Vaughan or Traherne means that their poetry is simpler and that as poets they are less intelligently present in the world. At the same time, Metaphysical wit is self-consciously freakish. In the next age a poet like John Dryden might be appreciative of Donne's flashes of mind and yet find him unfit for company because of his ill-carried learning and unpolished manner.[10] And we may agree that Metaphysical wit would sound odd as social entertainment. But it is because its play of mind is not entirely socialized that it is so expressively interesting. Its strangenesses are both cerebrally controlled and genuinely strange, shadowing the designs of the mind with emotional suggestions, sometimes quite obscure, where the mind is not so much in control as surprised. Even in the thin 'Love's Diet', the sally 'eyes which roll towards all, weep not, but sweat' intends scorn, but its extravagance suggests the grotesquely wilful obsessions of jealousy. Donne's wit involves him in ugly and shameful emotions, but manners or the rules of self-presentation he has chosen for himself in his poetry do not make that ugly and shameful stuff unpresentable for him.

The curiousness of the Metaphysical style is seized on by its finest practitioners to figure some individual intensity, and at the same time its element of play, for most of them, qualifies the personal with a dash of worldliness. Socially it is the idiom of men who have received a gentleman's education at a university but who for one reason or another are not wholly at one with their world. All six of the poets in this book were involved with the ecclesiastical polity of the Elizabethan and Stuart state, and for five of them the involvement was a troubled one: for Donne by reason of his Catholic upbringing; for Crashaw and Vaughan because of their being on the Royalist and episcopal side during the ascendancy of the Puritans; for Traherne because, however accommodating his nature, he had to accommodate himself to the shifts in Church and state between the Commonwealth and the Restoration by an extreme spiritualizing; for Marvell because of his divided loyalties during the Civil War, his anti-Court politics under Charles II and his persistent

---

10.   Dryden, *A Discourse Concerning the Original and Progress of Satire* (1693) in Dryden 1900, II, p. 19.

hostility to the rule of bishops. As for the sixth, Herbert, by birth the most fit to play the part of gentleman and servant of the state, for whatever reason – ambition, illness or deep-seated sense of unworthiness – he took orders only after long delay and his poetry is the most searching of all seventeenth-century devotional writings on the struggle between individual will and conformity.

Trouble with the state power in religion is a historical theme running through the lives of the Metaphysicals and one that matches the combination of highly personal with worldly in their use of wit. Another way in which Metaphysical interiority was historically coloured touches only some of them. In an essay on Marvell, Barbara Everett puts forward an attractive suggestion that seventeenth-century interiority may have developed with the more sophisticated interiors of upper-class houses, hangings, paintings, mirrors and all those ornaments of a gentleman's life that enlarged and reflected his mind and sensibility, from curios and scientific instruments to books, themselves often mazes of elaborate bemusement in their layout, decorations and illustrations.[11] Herbert's interiority turns to figures of fine domestic interiors, transparent rooms, cabinets, boxes within boxes. Crashaw is a poet of the book and the lady's chamber. Marvell has his microscope and picture gallery. Yet neither Herbert nor Crashaw is a more inward poet than Donne, with his ungracious or at least simple interiors, a cramped chamber or little room made an everywhere. And Marvell, like Vaughan, is not often an indoors poet, but takes his inward broodings outside to 'shaddy Woods, / Deep Meadows, and transparent Floods'. And also to gardens. These were certainly a developing feature of rich houses. And still Marvell's green worlds are not so different from the Arcadian woods to which Elizabethans retired for self-communing. The scenery is more cultivated and Marvell's expression of inward trouble is more sophisticated. But the advances of material culture were not necessary for a rich inward life and did not of course necessarily imply it. It was rather that some of the Metaphysicals drew on finer surroundings as props in the cultivation of their inner lives and that Crashaw and Marvell in particular developed from the aesthetic refinement of Caroline civilization special sensibilities or consciousnesses of their own sensations.

Some earlier literary forms of self-communing are absent from the Metaphysicals, such as the dream. And self-pleasing melancholy, which was an Elizabethan and eighteenth-century fashion, really comes in only with Vaughan. In a general way, of course, it is obviously true that Metaphysical poets express religious or love melancholy. But as far as cultural fashion goes, only the 'subtle-witted antic youth' ('Satire I', l. 63), Donne, got

---

11. Everett 1979, pp. 62–103; she does not say that a more developed material culture *explains* Marvell's interiority. See also Ferry 1983, pp. 45ff.

himself up in a melancholy hat (at least for the Newbattle portrait), and as far as the psychological condition was understood at the time neither Donne's nor any of the others' work fits well into the categories of Robert Burton's encyclopaedic treatment of it in *The Anatomy of Melancholy*.[12] Stoical withdrawal into the kingdom of the self, the form of some of Sir Thomas Wyatt's inwardness in the early sixteenth century, is adopted noticeably only by Donne in some of his verse epistles. One interesting form of self-absorption or self-recollection makes an appearance with the Metaphysicals for the first time: the poet's childhood appears as a visionary figure of the unsocialized self.[13] But this is only in the poetry of Vaughan and Traherne.

The forms in which Metaphysicals typically express their interiority are devotional and love poems. In the devotional poem (except strikingly with Traherne) the self to which they give such lively expression is, perhaps paradoxically, viewed as evil. In this they follow a venerable tradition of interiority going back at least as far as St Augustine in the fifth century.[14] Their struggle is the attempt of a guilty consciousness to be taken over and reconstituted by the divine. Praying to St Teresa as a pattern of dying to oneself, Crashaw concludes 'The Flaming Heart':

> Leave nothing of my SELF in me.
> Let me so read thy life that I
> Unto all life of mine may dy.

The only unusual thing about Crashaw's desire for loss of self is its lack of anguish. 'Heart' and 'soul' are more ambivalent terms for the inner man.[15] A heart may be as hard as iron or stone, yet from it proceeds the clamour for deliverance. A soul may be guilty of dust and sin, but a soul is also a yearning, erotic creature, immortal yet always dying. It brings out a traditionally feminine side of Metaphysical spirituality, guilty in the face of God ('a woman's place is in the wrong') yet loving.

In the love poem, the Metaphysicals took over the 'I'-centred perspective of the sixteenth-century sonneteers and perhaps accentuated the privacy of love against the public world. While Donne and Marvell do not usually turn their analyses explicitly upon themselves, their talk of love or souls

---

12. On the Renaissance fashion for melancholy, see Panofsky 1955, pp. 165–69.
13. For a discussion of childhood as a form of cultural retreat in the poetry of the mid seventeenth century, see Marcus 1978.
14. Aers 1992; on Donne, see Aers and Kress 1981.
15. These terms are in many ways interchangeable: see George Herbert, 'A true Hymne' and 'Affliction' (IV). See also Ferry 1983, for a discussion of the terms of Renaissance inwardness, though I believe she makes them a good deal more foreign to our ways of thinking than in fact they are.

displays a complex and ironic involution of mind and feeling. Love is rarely a hermitage with them, but its concerns more than make up a little world inside the big one. In this inner world of love, unlike the devotional one, neither the 'I' nor the soul is guilty. And the talk of souls expresses an absoluteness for love that plays against wit and irony, which with the Metaphysicals make, in part anyway, a masculine sort of game, guarded, though clever and parading, like fencing. Soul talk brings what one might call a certain femininity into the poetry. At least, the soul's seriousness about desire makes the resourceful 'I' of the male speaker vulnerable and equal with the loved one.

And finally, the Metaphysicals are forever treating supernatural or marvellous happenings. In the religious verse, of course, the poets are concerned with miraculous overturnings of the natural order, either in themselves or in history. Even Herbert, the most scrupulous in his use of Metaphysical extravagance, by a trick of words or verse or figure is constantly suggesting a divine intrusion into his life. Donne's and Marvell's love poetry equally overturns earthly limitations. Souls may unite lovers who are physically separate. Love performs all sorts of miracles in contracting or expanding space or time. Ecstasies and other neoplatonic or alchemical operations suspend the order of the public world and remake it according to private desire. And apart from their use of metaphysical ideas, there is something in the nature of the Metaphysical style, in its drive to paradox and the yoking of heterogeneous things together by violence, that delights in overturning socially constructed reality.

None of the Metaphysicals was mad, all were clever men and most could be hard-headed. They use a Gothic idiom. They love to surprise and be surprised. But apart from Traherne and perhaps Vaughan, their defiance of common-sense ways of seeing things is usually complicated by irony or playfulness. Is Donne serious about being canonized for love? Well, yes and no, and in a way he has been. Does Marvell really think trees a better object of platonic love than women? Who can tell? The wonder, at least, is amusing and serious. Did Herbert really think he had been touched by God's wit when he found the initials 'J. C.' in the curves of a bunch of grapes? It would be in the nature of religious hope, half creating and half receiving, to half think so. We may turn from this sort of thing to some of the poetry of Cowley and to his successors, the Augustans, pleased to find our feet so intelligently on the ground. But equally, we may respond to the peculiar power of the Metaphysicals to take us into a world of individual desire and trouble where we are not quite sure where we stand.

The plan of this book will be obvious. To each of six major Metaphysicals I devote a chapter prefaced with a biographical and historical introduction explaining the circumstances that bear on his poetry; a discussion of the forms that interiority took in his poetry follows; and each of the chapters is rounded off (except with Donne) with comparisons to other Metaphysical work. In the final chapter I discuss the poetry of Cleveland and Cowley as Metaphysical poetry without Metaphysical interiority, and compare Metaphysical wit with the Augustan sort that supplanted it. I have had to omit poets. I should have liked to deal with the work of Lord Herbert of Cherbury, Henry King, Clement Paman and Joseph Beaumont, even of Edward Benlowes, but regretfully excluded them for reasons of space. And the same consideration has kept me from taking up Metaphysical prose.

This book is an introduction to the study of Metaphysical poets. Its aim is to help the reader to get the hang of poems and enjoy them. That is why for each of the poets I examine at least one poem in detail to suggest how it works. My frame of discussion, the theme of interiority, is intended as an aid to appreciation. It breaks down into the various poets' inward master concerns. For these I make no theoretical, let alone psychoanalytical, claims. Donne's difficulties with being in the world, Herbert's terrible exactingness with himself that brings out a vivid sense of his own quickness, Crashaw's aesthetic self-immolation, Marvell's self-division, Vaughan's self-attenuation, Traherne's self-enlarging appetite for God – these are not ideas that are supposed to reduce poets or poems to a scheme. I should regard that as a betrayal of both the poetry and the expense of spirit behind it. They are offered as pointers to where the poets' turnings of their thoughts in words are peculiarly alive and also to the rich diversity and sheer exoticness of their inner lives. If they help readers to explore these things or convert enjoyment of poems and the feelings of strangeness they arouse into discovery and insight, they will have served their purpose.

As for the biographical and historical sketches, my chief concern has been to set out matters of fact that bear on the poems – dates, circumstances and, too frequently but necessarily, uncertainties and gaps in our knowledge. Interpretation and commentary that do not have an accurate grasp of these things will be fanciful. And while most of the information can be found in good editions, one of the things an introduction can usefully do is to gather it in one place. Besides, as Empson remarks, 'those who enjoy poetry must be in part biographers'.[16] The lives of the poets are a reminder that in Metaphysical poems, however obliquely, someone is speaking, and what we think a poem says must be answerable to what we think a poet might be saying either specifically from what we know about him or more generally from what we conjecture a man (they are all men) might want to say. The biographies connect the poets with their time. They supply at least a

---

16. Empson 1953, p. 242.

10

general, and sometimes a quite specific, context of utterance. It is not that history determines what Metaphysicals write, but that they speak to us strongly out of their time. Their interiority is individual and an individual is always of his time and of his place. Pure, unconditioned self-consciousness of the sort imagined by Traherne is an intellectual figment very much of his time and place. The more history and biography we have, the better we are placed to understand appreciatively what a poet is saying, as long as we do not mistake the history and biography for the appreciative understanding itself. And so as an entry to the living preoccupations of the various poets, I have set down what facts I could glean. I have shaped them according to what I see as the concerns of the poetry. But it was in plying to and fro between poems and lives that I arrived at what I thought should be said.

Throughout I have quoted from the standard Oxford English Texts editions except in the case of Donne, where A. J. Smith's Penguin edition is more convenient. I use 'Metaphysical' when I am thinking of the poets and 'metaphysical' when I am thinking of metaphysics.

ANNO DÑI. 1591.
ÆTATIS SVÆ 18.
ANTES MVDADO
MVERTO QVE

This was for youth, Strength, Mirth, and wit that Time
Most count their golden Age; but t'was not thine.
Thine was thy later yeares, so much refind
From youths Drosse, Mirth, & wit; as thy pure mind
Thought (like the Angels) nothing but the Praise
Of thy Creator, in those last, best Dayes.
Witnes this Booke, (thy Embleme) which begins
With Love; but endes, with Sighes, & Teares for sins.

Will: Marshall sculpsit.   IZ: WA:

John Donne, from an engraving by William Marshall (after a painting by Nicholas Hilliard?), the frontispiece to *Poems*, 1635. Bodleian Library, University of Oxford.

CHAPTER ONE

John Donne

Life

More is known about Donne, the man, than about any other poet before Milton, and what is known adds up to a story of someone with an uneasy relation to the world. It is not that his life was unusually hard, but that with all his exceptional social and intellectual gifts, with all his ambition to employ them in a worldly career, the circumstances and events of his life thwarted his fitting easily into public life and becoming a servant of the state like his friend Sir Henry Wotton. He was born a Catholic when Catholics were persecuted as enemies of the state; his marriage cast him out of the world into which he had managed to find an entry; after thirteen years of 'exile' from the world, he was ordained in the Church of England and there certainly became at last a pillar of the establishment, but only by an institutionalizing of his estrangement from the world and bringing the demands of another world to bear on this one. Alienation from the world is not all there is to Donne's poetry by any means. But it is a persistent feature, even the ground note of his poetry, a note always somewhere behind its peculiar intensity. In Donne, interiority takes the shape of isolation and its attendant anxieties and exaltations.

Donne was set apart from the world he later tried to join by his Catholic upbringing. He was born in 1572. His father, John Donne, was a prosperous London merchant, an iron-monger with claims to descent from Welsh gentry. He died in 1576, when Donne was four. Soon after, Donne's mother married John Syminges, a successful doctor in London. After he died in 1588, she took a third husband, Richard Rainsford, in 1590 or 1591. There is no conclusive evidence that John Donne senior or John Syminges were

Catholics. They probably were but must have been discreet about it. Donne's mother, on the other hand, came from the heroic wing of English Catholicism. Elizabeth Donne was grandniece of the Catholic martyr, Sir Thomas More. Her father, John Heywood, a writer of interludes and epigrams, went into exile in 1564 rather than make his peace with Queen Elizabeth's Protestant settlement of the English Church. Two of her brothers, Ellis and Jasper, became Jesuits. Jasper, who led a Jesuit mission to England in the early 1580s, was imprisoned in the Tower and narrowly escaped a hideous martyrdom. And there were other members of the family who suffered for their faith. After the death of Dr Syminges, Elizabeth Donne became known as a recusant, and soon after her third marriage she settled with her husband in Antwerp to escape the penalties imposed on Catholics in England.[1]

Catholics under Queen Elizabeth were at first penalized for nonconformity with the state church. They were barred from public office and fined for non-attendance at church services. For about a decade the government hoped that its measures were not so severe as to provoke desperate resistance but severe enough to push all but the firmest towards the Church of England. After the rebellion of the Northern Catholics in 1569–70 and the papal bull of 1570 excommunicating Elizabeth as a heretic and therefore a tyrant and usurper to whom no allegiance could be owed, the issue became a matter of treason. The Pope urged Elizabeth's subjects to dethrone her, and the government's response was to treat the Catholic minority as a fifth column waiting for a propitious moment. To the government anyway, propitious moments must have seemed almost continuous in the 1580s, what with plots involving Mary Queen of Scots, Elizabeth's Catholic cousin and prisoner, and with hostilities with Catholic Spain mounting to open war and attempts at invasion. In these circumstances the Elizabethan state did not show its devoutness by burning heretics but exhibited its power or its fear by hanging, drawing and quartering as traitors both Catholic priests found guilty of seducing the Queen's subjects from their obedience to their sovereign and those they seduced. Even to remain a staunchly Catholic layman was financially ruinous. Those attending Mass were fined a hundred marks; recusants, that is those refusing to attend Church of England services, were fined twenty pounds a month. The fines were a welcome source of revenue and a system of government spies, the detestable poursuivants mentioned in Donne's 'Satire IV', ll. 214–17, was set up to exact them.[2]

---

1. Bald 1970, pp. 49–50. Throughout I have made free use of Bald's biography for the details of Donne's life.
2. See also Donne 1930, pp. 74–75.

Meanwhile a Jesuit missionary campaign from the English Colleges on the Continent was bent on a heroic attempt to recover England for Rome. The campaign may have braced the resistance of some and must have sharpened the anguish of being Catholic for the community as a whole. Despite persecution, most English Catholics wished nothing more than to be loyal subjects of the Queen, and most detested the Pope's claim to depose her. Many, perhaps most, of the English Catholic community found it possible to live with attending Church of England services as demanded by law and so evade its penalties. Some of them may have found it possible to take the Oath of Supremacy and accept Elizabeth as head of the English Church. The Jesuit missionaries came to force a more rigorous faith on the conscience of Catholic England, a choice of political loyalty to the Pope rather than to Elizabeth and an end to compromise with the state religion. In doing so they aroused the hostility, not only of the patriotic and easygoing among the laity, but also of the secular priests (that is, priests who were not Jesuits or in monastic orders) who knew the temper of the Catholic community as a whole and did not think it possible to change it in the direction of heroic intransigence, and who, moreover, did not wish to give their persecutors a reason for harsher measures.

Did Donne grow up under a reign of terror? In thirty-three years of Elizabeth's reign after 1570, 250 died for their Catholicism (some from imprisonment rather than execution). This is a negligible toll by twentieth-century standards and fairly mild in comparison with the burning of 300 Protestants in five years under Mary Tudor, though the tortures used by Elizabeth's government to find out and kill its enemies rightly got it an evil name in Catholic countries. Some of the reports of those who submitted to the laws that demanded attendance at the services of the established church suggest carelessness and contempt rather than timid acquiescence, let alone fear. Whether all this implies the moderation or simply the limited power of the Elizabethan state to cow its subjects, the degree of anxiety felt among the Catholic community would depend on where one was placed, whether on the heroic wing ready for martyrdom or among the discreet, compromising or careless. It is possible that Donne's family was divided, his father and first step-father preferring to lie low, his mother, with the martyrs among her kinsmen, less willing to compromise and more willing to take risks for her faith. This is speculation, but the idea that Donne was brought up in an atmosphere of unqualified Catholic ardour with a vocation for martyrdom ignores the complexity of Catholic affiliation under Elizabeth. That being a Catholic may from the start have been a divided thing bears, as we shall see, on Donne's later dividing himself from the church he was born into and his going over to the Protestants.

Nevertheless, Donne's childhood and youth were certainly marked by a Catholicism that set itself against the religion of the Elizabethan state. For this we have Donne's own account in the Preface to his *Pseudo-Martyr*:

> I had longer work to doe then many other men; for I was at first to blot out, certaine impressions of the Romane religion, and to wrastle both against the examples and against the reasons, by which some hold was taken; and some anticipations early layde vpon my conscience, both by Persons who by nature had a power and superiority ouer my will, and others who by their learning and good life, seem'd to me iustly to claime an interest for the guiding, and rectifying of mine understanding in these matters.[3]

Before he went to university, he was educated privately by a tutor who, Bald says, we may assume 'without question' to be 'a good Catholic, perhaps a seminary priest'.[4] At Oxford, he matriculated from Hart Hall, a college without a chapel and consequently popular with Catholics because it was hard to check on attendance at services. He went up young and made out that he was even younger than he was by a year, eleven not twelve. This too was to evade the legislation meant to keep Catholics out of higher education: university statutes required that those taking degrees should swear to the Oath of Supremacy and that those matriculating at sixteen or older should subscribe not only to the Oath of Supremacy but also to the Thirty-Nine Articles of belief imposed by the Church of England. By entering young and lying about his age, Donne might gain a university education, if not a degree, without renouncing his Catholicism.[5]

According to his seventeenth-century biographer Izaak Walton, Donne was transplanted from Oxford to Cambridge at fourteen, and then at seventeen went up to Lincoln's Inn to study law.[6] The records show, however, that he entered Lincoln's Inn in 1592, when he was twenty, and would according to the prescribed course have entered Thavies Inn a year earlier. Bald, noting the discrepancy, suggests that Donne may have gone on his travels to Italy and Spain between 1589 and 1591.[7] According to

---

3. Preface to Donne 1610, sig. B2ᵛ–B3.
4. Bald 1970, p. 39.
5. Flynn 1989, pp. 308–9, cites a letter from Heywood to Claudio Aquaviva in which he reports that during the early 1590s 'the Privy Council . . . had ordered the heads of Oxford colleges to require the Oath of Supremacy from selected students from as young as twelve years of age' and thinks that Donne could not have stayed longer than one term 'before he would likely be required, as a member of a noted Catholic family and nephew of a now imprisoned Jesuit missionary, to swear to the Oath of Supremacy'. From this he argues against Walton and those who follow him with modifications that Donne went abroad after one term at Oxford in the train of the Earl of Derby.
6. Walton 1927, 'Life of Dr Donne', p. 24.
7. Bald 1970, pp. 50–52.

Walton, again, when Donne entered the Inns of Court, his mother 'and those to whose care he was committed, were watchful to improve his knowledge, and to that end appointed him Tutors in the *Mathematicks*, and all the *Liberal Sciences* to attend him. But with these Arts they were advised to instil particular principles of the *Romish Church*.'[8]

In spite of all these precautions, Donne began to move away from Catholicism during his time at the Inns of Court. It is probable that as a student at Oxford and Cambridge he had already entered a freer, more worldly society than that in which he had been brought up, if some of the friendships of his later life, such as those with Henry Wotton and Henry Goodyer, were begun then.[9] About the Inns of Court, there is no doubt. These were conspicuously an upper-class society. Some of its members, it is true, prepared themselves for a career in the law. But Donne separates himself from that sort of student in 'Satire II' in Coscus, a caricature of drudgery and small chicane. He must have aligned himself with the sons of gentry who prepared themselves for a career in government service with a training in the law. He would have found it easier to support that character when in 1593 he came into the inheritance left by his father and so was freer of his mother's influence. The Inns of Court, gathering together those 'of study and play made strange hermaphrodites' ('An Epithalamion Made at Lincoln's Inn', l. 30), were also a school of wit, smart, citified, satirical, scabrous. It was in this company that Donne invented himself as Jack Donne, the author of the first and second Satires, of many of his Elegies and 'An Epithalamion Made at Lincoln's Inn', and of some of the early verse letters that carry on the business of friendship by means of complimentary poems about his correspondents' poems. Outside his poetry, the character of Jack Donne comes over in the description in the *Chronicles* of his contemporary Sir Richard Baker: 'not dissolute but very neat; a great visiter of Ladies, a great frequenter of Playes, a great writer of conceited verses'.[10] 'Dissolute' here means slipshod. Jack Donne was a dandy.

While Donne was finding himself as an entertaining companion and fine spirit among those who expected to play a part in the world, he was naturally much occupied with the Catholicism that kept him out of it. A dreadful reminder of that was the death in prison of his younger brother, Henry, in 1593. He had gone up to Oxford with Donne and followed him to the Inns of Court. Henry had been caught harbouring a priest; the priest

8. Walton 1927, 'Life of Dr Donne', p. 24.
9. See Walton 1927, 'Life of Sir Henry Wotton', p. 106; Bald 1970, p. 47.
10. Cited Bald 1970, p. 72; Donne, wishing to dismiss his scapegrace youth, wrote to Sir Robert Ker in 1619 that *Biathanatos* was a book 'written by Jack Donne, and not by D. Donne' (Gosse 1889, II, p. 124).

was executed in the usual vile manner, while Henry died in prison before he was sentenced. At the same time, Donne was deep in the study of the controversies between the English and the Roman Churches.[11] Clearly this had to do with the search for true religion he speaks of in 'Satire III', a personal inquiry that he felt concerned his own salvation. And clearly Donne undertook the inquiry with exceptional thoroughness, laying the foundation of a knowledge for which he would be consulted as an authority later in life and which suggested to some the otherwise not very obvious idea that he should become a churchman. But there must have been practical reasons as well for his interest in the confessional dispute. Bald suggests, for example, that he may have had to give the Dean of Gloucester an account of his beliefs after the arrest of his brother. If Donne had made it clear to him that he was obstinately Catholic, he would have been expelled from Lincoln's Inn.[12] Besides, if his legal studies were to lead anywhere, he would have to find a way to joining the Church of England. Ambition and caution as well as religious motives and disinterested intellectual curiosity must have driven his inquiry.

It is hard to come well out of leaving a persecuted minority to join the church of its oppressors. But if on examination Donne found the intellectual case for Rome less than compelling, he would have been weak to feel obliged to 'get himself martyred to please his relations'. The poet of Songs and Sonnets and the religious poems is marked by an intense inwardness. But there is another side to his mind, which Empson has aptly characterized as 'broad and statesmanlike'.[13] That side of his mind would have found that the matter and the conduct of ecclesiastical polemic went against anything to which he could owe allegiance. As religious poet, controversialist and divine, the older Donne is always for a comprehensive position, never for the dogmatic exclusions that inspire the devout to kill and be killed. Perhaps he found the dogmatic vagueness of the Church of England's *via media* between Rome on the one hand and Calvinist Geneva on the other congenial; perhaps he helped to give it shape. At any rate, as a young man at the Inns of Court entering on the religious studies that were to produce the churchman, Donne's disengagement from a Catholicism that kept him continually thinking of martyrdom[14] need not have been unprincipled, even

---

11. See Donne 1610, sig. B2^v–B3; Walton 1927, 'Life of Dr Donne', pp. 25–26.
12. Bald 1970, pp. 69–70.
13. Empson 1993, pp. 84, 162.
14. 'I haue beene euer kept awake in a meditation of Martyrdome, by being deriued from such a stocke and race, as, I beleeue, no family (which is not of farr larger extent, and greater branches) hath endured and suffered more in their persons and fortunes, for obeying the Teachers of the Romane Doctrine, then it hath done' (Donne 1610, sig. 1A).

if at the same time it opened up to him the opportunity of a worldly career, for which his talents were eminently suited.

I cannot agree with John Carey that the religious references in Donne's secular poetry show the neurotic guilt of someone who was not strong enough to break with his background.[15] Incongruous religious references crop up in the Satires in a way that might suggest obsession. Coscus, in 'Satire II', turns from a student into a lawyer, who draws up deeds

> So huge, that men (in our time's forwardness)
> Are Fathers of the Church for writing less.
> These he writes not; nor for these written pays,
> Therefore spares no length; as in those first days
> When Luther was professed, he did desire
> Short *Pater nosters*, saying as a friar
> Each day his beads, but having left those laws,
> Adds to Christ's prayer, the power and glory clause.

(ll. 89–96)[16]

Here the analogies to Church Fathers and to Luther's changing from the shortened version of the Lord's Prayer he used as a friar as he told his rosary to the lengthened one he prescribed as a reformer irrupt into the text and certainly show that Donne's theological studies were on his mind while he was a law student. They would have occurred to no one else. But they are not necessarily evidence of bad conscience about religion. They may suggest that Donne was disturbed by his theological reading or obsessed by religion, but the whole passage also suggests that at the same time he is very much in control, that he has got hold of the art of turning personal matter, even anguish, into burlesque comedy. One is struck by the exuberant heaping up of analogy, by the wild yet logical stitching of Luther and Coscus together, by the surprising felicity that yokes together legal and theological scribbling. This may fall short of great satire, it may not be *The Dunciad*, but it makes spirited fun of the solemn paperwork that binds our lives and of two professions that live on the authority of written words, imagining with energetic absurdity that both businesses come down to crooked and pettifogging calculations. We have to deal, not with someone who is expressing a sneaking consciousness of being a turncoat by a compulsion to jeer, but rather with someone who is turning a clever, sceptical eye on the authority of learned corporations.

---

15. Carey 1990, pp. 1–45, esp. pp. 21–22.
16. All quotations from Donne's poetry are from A. J. Smith's edition, Donne 1971.

At this stage in his life, Donne was able to make his awkward position in the world into aggressive intelligence as a writer. Distinctly, however, his rebellion against the world in which he found himself never tended in the direction of active social criticism and it actually removed him from the sphere of Catholic grievance and plotting. His quarrel with the world ran to libertinism, scepticism and melancholy, personal, not political, disaffection.

In 1596, Donne left the Inns of Court to join the Earl of Essex's expedition against Spain. This sacked Cadiz and the success inspired an abortive second expedition to intercept the Spanish treasure fleet in the Azores. Donne's military service would not be an irrevocable step away from a career at the Bar, but certainly he was trying a more adventurous course. He joined a crowd of gentlemen volunteers under the command of Essex, the most dazzling gentleman in England. In doing so, he was joining a raid against the chief Catholic power, the enemy of the English Protestant state and the hope, if not the very present aid, of intransigent English Catholics. It is hard to say if, in addition to cutting a social dash, Donne meant to make an anti-Catholic gesture; he was certainly making a patriotic one. Neither of these motives is mentioned by Donne in 'The Calm' among the hopes he lists to a friend at the Lincoln's Inn with elegant vagueness about what might have prompted him to take part in the second expedition:

> Whether a rotten state, and hope of gain,
> Or, to disuse me from the queasy pain
> Of being beloved, and loving, or the thirst
> Of honour, or fair death, out pushed me first,
> I lose my end.

> (ll. 39–43)

Yet Donne did find his end on the voyage, though it was not any of the ones he mentions. He had been companion of Thomas Egerton, son of Lord Egerton, Master of the Rolls, and a fellow student, perhaps friend, at Lincoln's Inn. In late 1597 or early 1598, soon after he returned from the Azores, Lord Egerton took Donne on his son's recommendation as secretary. Since the appointment was not a public one, it did not require Donne to take the Oath of Supremacy and publicly renounce his Catholicism. But Egerton himself was a distinguished example of someone who had moved from Catholicism to the Church of England and whose public career had flourished. And a private secretaryship in a great man's service was a recognized first step toward a public career. If Donne had not entirely made up his mind how he stood on matters of religion, the course he had embarked on was more or less making up his mind for him.[17]

Donne remained Egerton's secretary for four years. 'Nor did his Lordship . . . account him to be so much his Servant, as to forget he was his Friend; and to testifie it, did alwayes use him with very much courtesie, appointing him a place at his own Table, to which he esteemed his Company and Discourse to be a great Ornament.'[18] But this promising start came to a sudden end in December 1601 when Donne, now twenty-nine, secretly married Ann More, a girl of sixteen or seventeen. She was Egerton's niece and had been brought up in his household from her fourteenth year. Her father, Sir George More, had a famous temper. While Donne was poor, George More was very rich. He could not have been expected to consent to the match. But to marry a minor without her parents' consent was an offence against canon law. When the news was finally broken to him, More had Donne imprisoned together with the friend who read the service and the other friend who gave the bride away. He attempted to have the marriage annulled and got Egerton to dismiss Donne from his post. But since the marriage was judged valid, all he achieved was that his daughter married a man without prospects: '*John Donne, Anne Donne, Un-done*'.[19] More changed his mind, but Egerton would not hear his entreaty that Donne should be taken back as secretary, and for thirteen years Donne was out of a job, reduced to the position of hanger-on in a world in which he had hoped to play a conspicuous part, and forced to court the great in efforts to find the patronage and job he hoped would provide for his growing family as well as give himself scope. As a law student and as Egerton's secretary he had been free to satirize the ways of the world at the same time as he was making towards a career in it. Now he was no longer free. He had to find a career in the world, where his marriage stood against him; no one seems to have considered that he should make a living as a lawyer, and he was forced to apply himself to arts that must have gone against his self-respect. A verse letter written to Sir Henry Wotton ('Sir more than kisses') with the disdainful rectitude he could afford as Egerton's secretary sounds like an unwitting prophecy of what was in store for him. Whether in court, city or country,

17. He had probably made up his mind by the time of his marriage since he had to clear himself to Sir George More of the charge of attachment to 'a corrupt religion' (cited Gardner, in Donne 1965, p. xxv). But see Klause 1994, p. 212, for the view that his indecision was more protracted.
18. Walton 1927, 'Life of Dr Donne', p. 27.
19. Walton 1927, 'Life of Dr Donne', p. 29.

> if men, which in these places live
> Durst look for themselves, and themselves retrieve,
> They would like strangers greet themselves, seeing then
> Utopian youth, grown old Italian.

(ll. 43–46)

Italians were supposed to be machiavellian schemers. To someone so pre-occupied with himself and the image he projected, one of the humiliations of these years must have been to find himself a stranger to the self he had set up when young.

Donne was now excluded from the world, not by reason of religious allegiance or a divided sense of how he stood to the Elizabethan state. He had excluded himself by a choice of action that turned out to be disastrous, partly by bad luck, partly probably by miscalculation. He may have thought that he could advance himself by marrying money. That calculation would not mean that he did not marry for love; nothing is simple with Donne. But if he did calculate, then he overestimated his value to Egerton, who parted with him with regret but firmly. Walton speaks of Donne's marriage as 'the remarkable error of his life', thinking of it as a moral error.[20] Donne was not above sometimes abjectly sounding as though he took Walton's view, except that it is a worldly rather than a moral error that seems uppermost in his mind. He writes to Lord Hay about 1608: 'I have been told, that when your Lordship did me that extreme favour of presenting my name, his Majesty remembered me by the worst part of my history, which was my disorderly proceedings, seven years since, in my nonage'.[21] What Donne is regretting is that his marriage has got him a name in court circles as an unsound man for patronage or pushing into a job.

But Donne was capable of feeling more courageously. Excusing himself from paying a visit because it would mean leaving his wife alone with the children, he wrote in 1614, 'We had not each other at so cheap a rate, as that we should ever be weary of one another'.[22] That sounds a note of tender consideration that is hard to find in his love poetry. But it also sounds a note much closer to some of the Songs and Sonnets, where the values of the little world of the lovers are asserted in despite of the big world; the 'each other' and 'one another' fairly ring out with a mutual doing to which he is resolved to be true. We cannot give dates to the Songs and Sonnets, but it is unlikely that some of them were not written out of the

---

20. Walton 1927, 'Life of Dr Donne', p. 60.
21. Gosse 1889, I, p. 201.
22. Gosse 1889, II, p. 48.

experience of his love for Ann, the need for secrecy before marriage and for cheering themselves up afterwards.

Ann died in 1617, worn out after giving birth to the twelfth child in the fifteen years of their marriage. Donne did not marry again.

Most of Donne's religious poetry was written in the period between his marriage and his ordination. During this time, his letters speak of his sense of being nothing, of being in a prison, a grave. He suffered from depression and frequent illness. These are the general circumstances in which he seems to have written most of the Holy Sonnets where he tries to focus his trouble about himself and clamour for deliverance. To this period too belong poems of extravagant praise of women written to gain favour and money. Such are the verse letters to Lucy, Countess of Bedford, and the two 'Anniversaries' commemorating Elizabeth Drury, which Donne wrote to recommend himself to her parents. In these poems, the women he praises are celebrated as more angel than human, compounded of unearthly virtue and purity. If they are not angels, it is because they have bodies, but bodies of such a refined make as the rest of humanity can only hope for at the resurrection. It is hard to imagine what the Countess of Bedford, who was at least praised for intelligence, or the Drury parents made of these extraordinary poems. It is also painful for an admirer of Donne to see what he could force his gifts to. At the same time, the exalted notion of purity and virtue there, at once utterly above and yet vulnerable to 'this rotten world' ('The Second Anniversary', l. 49), clearly picks up in a strained way his own anguished relation to the world, his sense of being involved in its corruption and fears for his immortal soul.

In January 1615, Donne was ordained in the Church of England. All his angling for employment in the service of the state, his making up to the great and frequently corrupt figures at the court of James, had come to nothing. He had put his knowledge of the Roman Church and its controversies with the Church of England to effective use in the tracts of 1610 and 1611, *Pseudo-Martyr* and *Ignatius his Conclave*. There he defended the supremacy of King James by attacking and ridiculing the claims made for papal supremacy as well as those who most formidably upheld it, the Jesuits. In doing this, he had certainly caught the King's eye, but convinced him that he was better fitted for a place in the Church than for the sort of courtier's job in the service of the state that he was looking for. Donne had already turned down an offer of advancement in the Church in 1607 on the grounds, according to Walton, that he could not be sure that he had a religious vocation and that his earlier life might cause scandal in a churchman.[23] But another

---

23. Walton 1927, 'Life of Dr Donne', pp. 32–35.

reason must have acted as a powerful dissuasion. In his excellent verse letter 'To Mr Tilman after he had taken orders' (1619?), Donne asks,

> Why doth the foolish world scorn that profession,
> Whose joys pass speech? Why do they think unfit
> That gentry should join families with it?
> As if their day were only to be spent
> In dressing, mistressing and compliment;
> . . .
>
> What function is so noble, as to be
> Ambassador to God and destiny?

(ll. 26–38)

To be an ambassador to God would not have been smart enough for a man who hoped to be ambassador to Venice. For someone who was the companion of courtiers, the Church would be socially dowdy. It was a part of Donne's achievement as a churchman and preacher to give social gloss to his profession. In this among other things he was followed by George Herbert.[24]

Some of the ways in which Donne reconciled the claims of the world with his otherworldly calling are supple, to say the least. He took orders only when he failed to secure the post of ambassador to Venice through the patronage of the King's favourite, Somerset. This is hard to square with his earlier scruples about entering the Church. And he did not commit himself before making sure that James would make the light of his countenance to shine upon him. The King's favour was shown immediately in his appointing Donne a Royal Chaplain, a post that would keep him in touch with the court, and in his requiring Cambridge University to make Donne Doctor of Divinity in the face of protests from the Vice-Chancellor about sons of darkness 'who come in at the windoe, when there was a fayre gate open'.[25] Within a year the King had given him the rectory of Keyston as a living, and his old master, Egerton, now Lord Ellesmere, added the rectory of Sevenoaks, a sinecure. Holding two benefices was allowed to Royal Chaplains. Pluralism was, in any case, widely practised and, given the wretched salaries of most of the clergy, the only way to make a career in the Church an attractive proposition to able and educated men. Even so, Donne's amassing of these and other offices was greedy. There is a stanza in 'A Litany', probably written in the winter of 1608–9 during illness at a time

---

24. See Novarr 1980, pp. 108–15, on the connection of this poem with Herbert.
25. John Chamberlain, *Letters*, I, 591; cited Bald 1970, p. 308.

when Donne had no mind to become a clergyman, which is interesting for its attempt to strike a balance between worldliness and unworldliness; a Christian did not have to be a monk:

> From being anxious, or secure,
> Dead clods of sadness, or light squibs of mirth,
> From thinking, that great courts immure
> All, or no happiness, or that this earth
> Is only for our prison framed,
> Or that thou art covetous
> To them whom thou lov'st, or that they are maimed
> From reaching this world's sweet, who seek thee thus,
> With all their might, Good Lord deliver us.

(ll. 127–35)

The exposure of false reasons for renouncing the world is acute and, quite reasonably for a courtier, leaves plenty of room for enjoying the goods of the world. Six years later, his behaviour at the time of his ordination seems to be guided by the same principles; he seems to have thought he could combine in himself the courtier and the churchman. The worldly strain runs through his career in the Church. He took the royal supremacy as a maxim of sound divinity. Preferments followed. He was elected Dean of St Paul's in 1621 and was in line for a bishopric when he died in 1631. His literary talents went chiefly into preaching and he took care to have his sermons published. He was an enormously fashionable preacher at court, at the Inns of Court and at St Paul's, though it goes without saying that he created his own fashion, one that combined his wit, his power to impress and astonish in words, his theatrical talents, with inwardness, a life of prayer and meditation, above all on the themes of death and resurrection.

In this way, he was able to make of his troubled relation with the world, half in, half out, a religious profession that gained him a very comfortable place in the world. He had now become what he calls in his verse letter 'To Mr Tilman', 'a blessed hermaphrodite', a creature combining two natures, secular and sacred, human and ghostly. He most strikingly realized that hermaphroditism in the extraordinary theatre that he made of his dying. Among the several acts recorded by Walton by which Donne willed his death is his rising from his terminal sickbed to preach his last sermon on the text 'To God the Lord belong the issues from death'.

And, when to the amazement of some beholders he appeared in the Pulpit, many of them thought he presented himself not to preach mortification by a living voice: but, mortality by a decayed body and a dying

> face. . . . Many that then saw his tears, and heard his faint and hollow
> voice, professing they thought the Text prophetically chosen, and that
> Dr. Donne *had preach't his own Funeral Sermon.*[26]

The performance as Walton describes it, at once intensely inward and shamelessly public as great acting must be, is a way of anticipating death, of speaking as if already beyond life, of joining this world and the next.

Donne brought out no collected edition of his poems. The first edition was in 1633, followed by several others with additional poems, including the edition of 1650 collected by his son.

This account of Donne's life in terms of his negotiations with the world needs a note on the Church in which he found a career. If James himself had a consistent ecclesiastical policy, it was his insistence on the royal supremacy and the rule of bishops. That set him firmly against Puritan opposition to episcopal government and those ceremonies and vestments that had been taken over from the unreformed Church in Elizabeth's time. His position on those matters was clearly laid down at the Hampton Court conference of 1604 when the Millenary Petition of the Puritan wing in the Church of England was rejected. At the same time, the character of the bishops whom James inherited from Elizabeth and at first tended to promote was predominantly Calvinist. Calvinism in theology did not mean in their case a leaning to Geneva as a model of church government. In theology, James's own predilections were probably Calvinist. From time to time Calvinist supplements to the Thirty-Nine Articles were published, as for instance the Canons of the Synod of Dort. But they were never finally adopted as articles of belief. In his later years, James gave more support to the anti-Calvinists (Arminians such as Richard Montague, Lancelot Andrewes and the coming man, William Laud), churchmen who rejected the Calvinist doctrine of predestination to heaven or hell and emphasized the importance of ritual in church services.

While James was resisting Puritan encroachment on the government of the Church, he had also to deal with the Catholics. His policy was more conciliatory here. He professed to seek reconciliation with Rome, if only the Pope would surrender his claims to be able to excommunicate and depose monarchs. Meanwhile the penal laws against Catholics remained in operation. The apparent contradiction between persecution and promises of conciliation exasperated a handful of Catholics to enter upon the Gunpowder Plot of 1605. That provoked harsher legislation including the imposition of an Oath of Allegiance, which abjured the authority of the Pope to depose

---

26. Walton 1927, 'Life of Dr Donne', p. 75.

kings. Most Catholics were appalled at the Gunpowder Plot and many, following George Blackwell, the Archpriest or head of the Catholic clergy in England, were prepared to take the Oath. The Pope, however, condemned the compromise, and there followed ten years of pamphlet warfare of Catholic against Catholic and Catholic against Protestant. It was in support of the English Church's defence against Rome that Donne weighed in with his *Pseudo-Martyr* and *Ignatius his Conclave*.

When Donne became a Protestant, he would have found in the Elizabethan and Jacobean Church what could be represented as rational moderation, a mean between the extremes of Rome and Geneva. Its doctrinal vagueness might also have seemed reasonable. As early as 'Satire III', Donne seems to have been in search of what one might call an Erasmian tradition of Christian practice and to have distrusted doctrinal vigour and rigour in matters where vigour and rigour were not to be had but simply beside the point.[27] And the vagueness could also be made out to be comprehensiveness, tolerance of many shades of Christian opinion, even Catholic and Puritan, if only they would shed their exclusiveness. The royal supremacy may have appeared to Donne a means of safeguarding this reasonableness and comprehensiveness, though his support for it would not have harmed his career.[28] At any rate his interest in the Gallican movement in the French Church is consistent with a view that kings should curb the power of Rome while preserving as much continuity of tradition and teaching as possible. Probably for the same reasons he shared with Sir Henry Wotton an interest in Paolo Sarpi, the adviser of Venice in its quarrel with Rome and the author of a *History of the Council of Trent* that exposed the dangers of leaving the government of the Church to churchmen.[29]

Perhaps as early as 1604, at the time of the Millenary Petition's request that the sign of the cross should be dropped in baptism, Donne wrote a plea for its retention in Christian worship, 'The Cross'. He consistently ranged himself against the Puritans. Calvin is one of the most frequently discussed authorities in his sermons. But though Donne treats his views with respect, he deals with him freely, not as a disciple. With the doctrine most notoriously associated with Calvin and most eagerly taken up by Puritans, predestination to heaven or hell, he distances himself. In a sermon of 1629, he deprecates

27. Donne, however, never cites Erasmus as a theological authority, though there is no reason to suppose from his other references that his jibe at Erasmian indefiniteness in points of doctrine in *The Courtier's Library* was more than a passing vivacity.
28. Donne need not have been an uncritical supporter of James's authority; see Norbrook 1990b; Patterson 1991, pp. 255ff.
29. Walton 1927, 'Life of Dr Donne', p. 68, and 'Life of Sir Henry Wotton', p. 120; Baker-Smith 1972, p. 225; see also Bald 1970, pp. 222, 255, on the nature of Donne's move from Rome.

Men that will abridge, and contract the large mercies of God in Christ,
and elude, and frustrate, in a great part, the generall promises of God.
Men that are loth, that God should speak so loud, as to say, *He would have
all men saved*, And loth that Christ should spread his armes, or shed his
bloud in such a compasse, as might fall upon *all*. Men that think no sinne
can hurt them, because they are *elect*, and that every sin makes every other
man a *Reprobate*. But with the Lord there is *Copiosa redemptio*, plentifull
redemption, *and an overflowing cup of mercy*.

(*Sermons*, IX, 119)

This shows the comprehensiveness of Donne's churchmanship, his rejection
in the name of God's generosity of exclusive formulations. It also shows his
support of royal policy. The sermon was preached at a time of Puritan
complaint about the rulings that predestination should not be preached or
discussed from the pulpit by anyone under the rank of Dean or not a
learned man at a university.[30] This and other pronouncements make Donne
an Arminian in a loose sense. But there is no reason to think that he was
one of an Arminian alliance in the Church of England; he was not particularly close to Lancelot Andrewes, John Buckeridge, Richard Montague or
William Laud.[31] Perhaps the best side of his churchmanship is his opposition to the spirit of clerical faction in any form.

On the other hand, there is a great deal that is unattractive about Donne's
career as a churchman and establishment figure. His social attitudes to
beggars, for instance, are heartless, as Carey notes.[32] His vision of a comprehensive church went with a willingness to punish those who rejected
comprehensiveness as offenders against social order.[33] But an eye to pleasing the King and his advisers was not his only guide. His Arminianism, his
stress on comprehensiveness, his championship of the royal supremacy
hang together as a consistent set of principles. They allowed him to think
that he could leave the Church of Rome without deserting the religion
of his ancestors and that the Church of England was a reasonable teacher
of the 'easy ways and near' to heaven, made hard by more rigorous
churches.[34]

---

30. Tyacke 1990, p. 182.
31. See Tyacke 1990, pp. 103, 182, 261, and Oliver 1997, pp. 44–47, for Donne's
    Arminianism; also Strier 1996. For more strict views of what constitutes an 'Arminian',
    see Julian Davies 1992.
32. Donne 1990, p. xxx.
33. For his condemnation of Sectaries and Catholics, see *Sermons*, VI, 245, 283, VII, 157;
    cited by Carey in Donne 1990, p. 114; see also Donne 1990, pp. 264, 291.
34. 'Satire III', l. 14.

Some general characteristics of Donne's poetry

Donne has more range than other Metaphysicals such as Herbert, Vaughan or Crashaw. Obviously his Elegies differ vastly in genre from his Holy Sonnets. He also evolved different manners for the different sorts of poems he wrote. And still he always sounds like himself.

> Sir; though (I thank God for it) I do hate
> Perfectly all this town, yet there's one state
> In all ill things so excellently best,
> That hate, towards them, breeds pity towards the rest.
> Though poetry indeed be such a sin
> As I think that brings dearths, and Spaniards in,
> Though like the pestilence and old fashioned love,
> Riddlingly it catch men; and doth remove
> Never, till it be starved out; yet their state
> Is poor, disarmed, like papists, not worth hate.   10
> One (like a wretch, which at Bar judged as dead,
> Yet prompts him which stands next, and cannot read,
> And saves his life) gives idiot actors means
> (Starving himself) to live by his laboured scenes;
> As in some organ, puppets dance above
> And bellows pant below, which them do move.
> One would move love by rhymes . . .

and so on until line 39,

> But these punish themselves; the insolence
> Of Coscus only breeds my just offence.

('Satire II', ll. 1–17; 39–40)

Compare that with the opening of 'The Second Anniversary':

> Nothing could make me sooner to confess
> That this world had an everlastingness,
> Than to consider, that a year is run,
> Since both this lower world's and the sun's sun,
> The lustre, and the vigour of this all,
> Did set; 'twere blasphemy to say, did fall.
> But as a ship which hath struck sail, doth run
> By force of that force which before, it won:
> Or as sometimes in a beheaded man,

> Though at those two red seas, which freely ran, 10
> One from the trunk, another from the head,
> His soul be sailed, to her eternal bed,
> His eyes will twinkle, and his tongue will roll,
> As though he beckoned, and called back his soul,
> He grasps his hands, and he pulls up his feet,
> And seems to reach, and to step forth to meet
> His soul; when all these motions which we saw,
> Are but as ice, which crackles at a thaw:
> Or as a lute, which in moist weather, rings
> Her knell alone, by cracking of her strings: 20
> So struggles this dead world, now she is gone;
> For there is motion in corruption.

('The Second Anniversary', ll. 1–22)

In the first passage, Donne's satirical manner is self-consciously rough and difficult. The syntax, involved in parentheses, is both elaborate and head-long and at least occasionally wrenches the couplets into violent enjamb-ment ('I do hate / Perfectly'; 'and doth remove / Never'). The passage conveys an extravagant outburst of spleen by heaping up vile bodies of poets for execration, and surges, or tumbles, on until the verse paragraph is completed and at last we learn what 'one state' 'In all ill things' is 'so excellently best, / That hate, towards them, breeds pity towards the rest', namely those legal drudges whom Coscus represents.

By contrast, the course of the first two sentences of 'The Second Anni-versary' is less wilfully contorted. The versification is smoother; the syntax falls into couplets without much strain. The one striking enjambment, 'And seems . . . to step forth to meet / His soul', catches the macabre running into each other of the two selves, body and soul, where the enjambments of the first passage wrench for crashing emphasis. Partly because the array of examples of motion in corruption all illustrate the same idea, the rhetorical trajectory of the long second sentence, in spite of the rather elaborate syntactical suspensions, is clear. Donne has in fact mastered a forceful expository style, less nimble than his earlier manner, but with a good long stride.

Yet though the manners differ, we are obviously dealing with the same poet. One of the first things we become aware of in a poem by Donne is the control exerted by thought. We have to follow him if we are to make anything of his poetry. The control may take the form of argument. But there are no arguments here. The wiry evolving of thought has to do with the sentences, the elaborate string of clauses that subjects and orders things according to the direction of the mind at play.

Control is also exerted in the piling up of examples in each passage. This is a display of power of invention, and at the same time it calls attention to the ability of the speaker to keep so much in play without the thought folding up. Donne's mind runs to analogy in a way that only the twentieth-century poet William Empson can equal for fertility and surprise. With Donne, analogies have to be grasped by an analytic act of intellection; the resemblances do not lie ready to be picked up by a wise passivity but have to be found out by looking round corners and an active making of connections. So, for example, the starving poet playwright in 'Satire II' may give actors a means to live by his plays, as a condemned criminal may give the prisoner next him a means to live by prompting him so that he seems to be able to read and consequently can plead benefit of clergy and escape hanging. Then, as if that weren't far-fetched enough, like the small orange growing in a navel orange, another analogy grows out of the former one: the playwright (and altruistic criminal prompter) gives life to actors (or an illiterate fellow prisoner) as bellows animate puppets on some ingenious organs (as well as producing the blast of air that sounds in the pipes). What is striking here is the mental energy that yokes the three heterogeneous sets of things by violence together. The notion of giving life is not so much a pre-existing ground of comparison between them as something struck out of them by the thought. The astonishing spilling forth of analogies in 'The Second Anniversary' is less arbitrary. The impetus that drives a sailing ship when the wind has dropped, the twitchings of a beheaded man, the cracking of ice in a thaw and the twanging of lute strings in damp weather are all examples of movement in unliving things, like the persistence of the world now that (according to Donne) its principle of life, Elizabeth Drury, has gone. And yet their sheer proliferation and the disparate areas of experience from which they are drawn again impress on us the thought that keeps it all from falling apart. Johnson was not impressed by such passages: 'Who would imagine that in a very few lines so many remote ideas could be brought together?'[35] He expects us to agree that they are absurd, but we are more likely to be taken by their remarkable flow of invention.

That touches one of the most celebrated aspects of Donne's style, his flair for bizarre compounds: 'a sundial in a grave' ('The Will', l. 51), 'God is . . . a multiplied elephant',[36] and the inevitable example, 'A bracelet of bright hair about the bone' ('The Relic', l. 6). 'Who but Donne would have thought that a good man is a telescope?'[37] Noting his penchant for incongruity,

---

35. Johnson 1952, I, p. 20.
36. Donne 1990, p. 390.
37. Johnson 1952, I, p. 20; he is referring to 'Obsequies to the Lord Harrington', ll. 35–39.

Carey makes the suggestion that Donne was so much possessed by death because death brings about transformation, dissolution, above all the metamorphosis of resurrection: 'How witty's ruin!' ('The First Anniversary', l. 99). Like Lewis Carroll's rabbit hole or looking glass, death in Donne is the entry to a counterworld where the imagination can sport freely, released from the rules of life. This theory at least calls attention to the play of surrealistic invention in the Epicedes and Anniversaries and in his Sermons, even if it does not entirely account for the way death comes into the earlier work. Mismatchings, which are also cunning matchings, bring up in a striking way how Donne breaks up and remakes the world. Everything has to go a process through his mind, to be dissembled and reassembled. One never has a sense of a world, a coherent order of Nature, to which he holds up a mirror. His creativity goes into the odd angle, the astonishing fragment that only he could come up with.

Because Donne breaks up the outlines of things, his descriptive verse letters, 'The Storm' and 'The Calm', are not so much descriptions as congeries of observations in the form of witty turns. They have some superb notation of detail: 'The south and west winds joined, and, as they blew, / Waves like a rolling trench before them threw' ('The Storm', ll. 27–28), or

> And all our beauty, and our trim, decays,
> Like courts removing, or like ended plays.
> The fighting place now seaman's rags supply;
> And all the tackling is a frippery.
> No use of lanthorns; and in one place lay
> Feathers and dust, today and yesterday.

> ('The Calm', ll. 13–18)

That last line and a half was particularly admired by Ben Jonson;[38] the hidden exactness of the comparison of waves to a rolling trench deserves equal admiration. But these things are untypical and most of 'The Storm' and 'The Calm' sounds like 'Lightning was all our light, and it rained more / Than if the sun had drunk the sea before' (ll. 43–44). A rattling series of witticisms such as that makes one quickly see how Samuel Johnson could say of the Metaphysicals in general (and of Donne by implication): 'Their attempts were always analytick; they broke every image into fragments: and could no more represent, by their slender conceits and laboured particularities, the prospects of nature, or the scenes of life, than he, who dissects a

---

38. 'Conversations with William Drummond', Jonson 1975, p. 463.

sun-beam with a prism, can exhibit the wide effulgence of a summer noon.'[39] Of course, 'The Storm' and 'The Calm' are not typical of Donne's work, or his best. But they do make clear that Johnson had a point, a point that applies also to poems that come off triumphantly. The splendid 'Air and Angels', say, or 'Love's Growth', does not 'represent . . . the prospects of nature, or the scenes of life'. It subjects the world to the designs of Donne's thought and fancy. One might say that in doing so it 'dissects a sunbeam with a prism': it analyses states of love with extraordinary fineness and make us feel that it is with Donne as he said it was with the Elizabethan miniaturist, Hilliard, in comparison with those who attempted vast ambitious historical paintings: 'a hand, or eye / By Hilliard drawn, is worth an history' ('The Storm', ll. 3–4). Fragments of that quality are worth an epic.

Fragmentariness as a style can be seen even in the arrangement (or derangement) of the love poems as we have them. The Elegies and Songs and Sonnets do not make up a coherent, if sketchy, history of an emotion as, say, Sidney's or Shakespeare's sonnets do. They are bewilderingly various in tone and content.[40] A helpful comparison in this connection is the early poetry of T. S. Eliot, who did so much to create the twentieth-century taste for Donne's poetry. If a collection like *Prufrock and Other Observations* coheres by virtue of a prevailing Laforguian mood, the mood is corrosive of coherence, turning any attempt to connect self and world to bafflement, inconsequence, self-reflexive irony. The mind fixes on startling combinations: 'In the palace of Mrs Phlaccus, at Professor Channing Cheetah's / He laughed like an irresponsible foetus', or 'Midnight shakes the memory / As a madman shakes a dead geranium'. It is true that whereas in Donne's conceits the mind is active and the remoteness of his comparisons starts up an agile course of connective thought, in Eliot's the mind withdraws dismayed and unsettled from the task of making a thought out of rational grounds of comparison. Metaphysical and Laforguian modes are only partially comparable. But the resemblance between Donne's and Eliot's conceits is not entirely accidental. Eliot's ask one to enter an alienated state of mind, a state of spleen, where one might see an evening as a patient etherized upon a table, and Donne's too have a Laforguian tendency to take one inside an extraordinary head, set apart from ordinary thoughts by what men of the sixteenth and seventeenth centuries would have diagnosed as melancholy. One recalls that, in Dürer's engraving, 'Melencholia' sits among instruments and tools suggesting in their disorder the 'heap of broken

---

39. Johnson 1952, I, p. 15.
40. Gardner's Donne 1965 proposes a chronological arrangement that tells a story of sorts but no one seems to have accepted it.

images' that Donne, as well as Eliot, makes play of. What the comparison with early Eliot brings out, then, is that the fragmentariness of Donne's extraordinary style is not just cerebral and clever but expresses a feeling of anomie and displacement that would go with his uneasy position in the world. Eliot's early poetry is, of course, witty as well as *distrait*. His Mr Appollinax, the voice of one laughing in the wilderness, the man of many wiles, is after all a fragment of himself among other things. And it would be even more absurd to forget the play and high jinks of Donne's poetry because its tone is introverted.

A further general way in which Donne's poetry removes us from the world and takes us inside his head is his use of what Johnson called 'enorm-ous and digusting hyperboles' – John Donne, Overdone.[41] If he weeps, there is a sea of tears:

> You which beyond that heaven which was most high
> Have found new spheres, and of new lands can write,
> Pour new seas in mine eyes, that so I might
> Drown my world with my weeping earnestly.

('I am a little world made cunningly', ll. 5–8)

Hyperbole, like paradox, characterizes the language of the Bible and con-sequently seems natural enough in a prayer for repentance. But Donne's tears as a lover are also seas. In the quatrain from the Holy Sonnet above, Donne's repentance requires a cosmic disaster to express itself sufficiently. But a merely lunar disaster in the following lines manages a grief beyond grief even more hyperbolically:

> O more than moon,
> Draw not up seas to drown me in thy sphere,
> Weep me not dead, in thine arms.

('A Valediction: of Weeping', ll. 19–21)

The ordinary moon draws the tides up at most forty feet above their lowest point (in the Bay of Fundy). Donne's lover is more than the moon because she draws seas of salt tears right up into the heaven of her arms where he lies weeping with her. The reason why this example of the 'confused magnificence' Johnson says Metaphysical hyperbole may achieve works so well is that Donne has built up a chain of conceits involving his grief with

---

41. Johnson 1952, I, p. 21.

the world.[42] Tears become pregnant, then one swells to become a world flooded with a new deluge of her tears, and now he casts beyond the universe we know. All, the whole world, is not enough to make pictures of his grief, so he fantastically cancels and improves on the shape of the universe to give himself to the melodrama of parting.

Hyperbole goes with a general habit of extravagant expression: 'Sir; though (I thank God for it) I do hate / Perfectly all this town . . .', and yet he hates something beyond perfect hate. Death is his regular figure for screwing experience up to a pitch of infinite intensity. The coldness of his lover is death, parting is death, orgasm is death – all small change of Elizabethan verse but somehow in Donne becoming an expression of an emotional temper that lives outside the ordinary world.

The surprising thing is that the high pitch does not become tedious. This is partly because Donne in his overgoings has the talent to astonish freshly, unlike the hero of Christopher Marlowe's Elizabethan tragedy *Tamburlaine*, whose strivings for the illimitable are doomed to repetitiousness, and partly because, at least in most of Donne's secular poetry, there is an element of playfulness in his extremity and we make allowance for the transcendental humour he adopts. We enjoy, for example, Donne's ham acting at the beginning of 'The Canonization', where he presents himself as a doting decrepit, so playing up to his critic's idea of him and making it absurd:

> For God's sake hold your tongue, and let me love,
> Or chide my palsy, or my gout,
> My five grey hairs, or ruined fortune flout.

(ll. 1–3)

Extravagance with Donne gives him freedom for ironic manoeuvre. Similarly in the Satires and Elegies, where exaggeration runs to caricature, we are as amused by the performance of the caricaturist as with the caricature itself. 'The grim eight-foot-high iron-bound serving-man' in 'The Perfume' (l. 31) is funny not just because it is too much and yet hits something off by exaggerating, but also because the perfumed cad who is speaking is making a spectacle of his cravenness and takes us along with him as he does so.

Donne is conscious of having an extraordinary manner. He knows how to use it for games-playing or role-playing. Even where he is doing neither, he seems to be conscious of his effect. His voice with its various inflection is produced by art. There is nothing in the least colloquial about his famous

42. Johnson 1952, I, p. 15.

openings: 'Nature's lay idiot, I taught thee to love / And in that sophistry, oh, thou didst prove / Too subtle', 'Busy old fool, unruly sun', 'Thou hast made me, and shall thy work decay?' Only Donne talks in that emphatic, arresting manner; even when he is being quiet, he is so penetratingly:

> So let us melt, and make no noise,
>   No tear-floods, nor sigh-tempests move,
> 'Twere profanation of our joys
>   To tell the laity our love.

('A Valediction: forbidding Mourning', ll. 5–8)

Talking like other people can have its own way of being impressive: 'Now I am here, what thou wilt do with me / None of my books will show' ('Affliction' [I], ll. 55–56). But plain speech with its resources of directness and flatness that Herbert draws on here is never cultivated by Donne, for all his avoidance of poetic diction.

Evidence for Donne's consciousness of his making an effect lies in an early verse letter in which he encourages Samuel Brooke to write poetry: 'I sing not, siren like, to tempt; for I / Am harsh' ('To Mr S. B.', ll. 9–10).[43] Obviously he cultivated harshness in his satires, mastering jarring sounds and various ways of making morose music:

>   words, words which would tear
> The tender labyrinth of a soft maid's ear,
> More, more, than ten Sclavonians scolding, more
> Than when winds in our ruined abbeys roar.

('Satire II', ll. 57–60)

This is not a description of his own practice as a satirical poet but of the wretched Coscus, this time at his wooing. Partly the effect here is owing to the combination of heaped up analogy and strong syntactical control that we noted at the beginning of this general account of Donne's poetic manner as a form of self-assertion. The strident repetitions ('words, words'; 'more, more') pile on the stress, and there is an odd random play of rhyme with internal rhyme and half-rhyme going on in the second couplet that sounds more derisive than musical (like the absurd harping on 'ee' sounds in the third and fourth lines of 'The Flea'). But above all there is the rough

---

43. Cf. 'Haste thee harsh verse', 'To Mr T. W.', l. 1.

handling of the iambic pentameter. It is always hard to manage a trochaic substitution in the fourth foot as in 'words which would tear'. Close by, one has to sort out the jamming together of strong stresses in 'a soft maid's ear'. This resolves, I believe, into a ladder of stress, the higher the number, the heavier the stress: a^1 soft^2 | maid's^3 ear^4. In this way the line comes out as a regularly iambic pattern of relative stress and unstress within each foot, but this and another ladder ending on a trochaic substitution in the second foot ('Than^1 when^2 | winds^3 in^1 |') tax the ear and aim at a sound, dismissive in its harshness of ordinary poetic music.[44] Donne cultivates awkward metrical effects like this not so much to accommodate speech rhythms as to make himself an artist in the jarring.

For different purposes, he could draw on his mastery of harsh sound outside his satire – for an ugly jeer in 'Love's Alchemy':

> Ends love in this, that my man,
> Can be as happy as I can; if he can
> Endure the short scorn of a bridegroom's play?

> (ll. 15–17)

or for a violent prayer for violence against himself:

> That I may rise, and stand, o'erthrow me, and bend
> Your force, to break, blow, burn, and make me new.

> ('Batter my heart', ll. 3–4)

But discordance is not his only skill. The lines that I have already discussed from 'A Valediction: of Weeping' manage a splendid wail:

> Oh more than moon,
> Draw not up seas to drown me in thy sphere,
> Weep me not dead, in thine arms, but forbear . . . .

> (ll. 19–21)

One is struck by the skilful use of alliteration, assonance and half-rhyme. Donne can produce a considerable range of inflection on the remarkable instrument of his voice. He can even sound sweet:

---

44. On Donne's scansion, see Bradshaw 1982, pp. 338–60.

Sweetest love, I do not go,
For weariness of thee,
Nor in hope the world can show
A fitter love for me.

('Song', ll. 1–4)

But this, it must be said, is untypical. With its trim, untroubled metricality and trim sentiments, it is a rather good example of the sort of Elizabethan poetic manner Donne breaks with to establish his own moody, wayward, fantastic manner.

Donne always slighted his poetry. He would not publish it but allowed it only to circulate in manuscript. When he did publish two poems, the 'Anniversaries', he spoke disparagingly of 'my descent into printing'.[45] He wanted to maintain the character of a gentleman who wrote with ease rather than the socially unglamorous one of a professional writer such as Drayton or Jonson. Besides, quite apart from the scandalous content of some of his elegies, he felt that to be known as a poet would be undignified and perhaps damage his chances in finding a career.[46] It does not fit with this embarrassed and dismissive attitude that in his early verse letters Donne eagerly encourages his friends' talents in a way that shows more enthusiasm for poetry than can be accounted for as just spreading the itch of a literary coterie. To judge from a remark in one of his sermons, he was a careful craftsman, studious of his effects and how to work them into a design: 'In all Metricall compositions, . . . the force of the whole piece, is for the most part in the shutting up; the whole frame of the Poem is a beating out of a piece of gold, but the last clause is as the impression of the stamp, and that is it that makes it currant' (*Sermons*, VI, 41).[47] If this has a bearing on his own poems, his talk of his poems as evaporations, exhalations from a heated brain, is misleading, whether from social anxiety or, as Ricks would have it, from a deeply divided attitude to his poems.[48] The spontaneity and improvisation in his poetry is, like the modulation and inflection of his voice, a work of art. But that does not mean that he wrote poems like a *grant rhetoriqueur* applying techniques and artifices to given themes. The occasions of Donne's poetry are mostly

---

45. Donne 1990, pp. 233–34.
46. For fear of scandal, see Donne 1990, p. 67, and for fears for his gravitas, p. 197. Ricks 1996, pp. 35ff., thinks that Donne's dismissive attitude to his poems was not really a pose and that he despised his poetry in a self-debilitating way.
47. Compare also the finish Donne gives to the observation of a stream's movement in the elegy, 'O let me not serve so', ll. 21–34, with the unfinished translation of verses on the same subject in *Ignatius his Conclave*, p. 9.
48. Donne speaks of his poetry in his letters as 'light flashes' and 'evaporations' (Gosse 1889, I, pp. 171, 197).

his own and what he made of those that were not is quite unconventional. His sermons more nearly tended toward rhetorical exercises. But they (and how much more his poems) speak in so distinct a voice with such odd or striking turns of thought that they express at the very least an intensely personal involutedness and grasp of their matter. Donne's manner is an expression of an interiority that is also consciously and deliberately a public performance. We never overhear Donne speaking to himself. His monologues are always addressed to someone. He comes over like a character in a play, even if the play is his own and he has neglected to give other people parts and in fact writes only scenes.[49] Though Donne's is an utterly singular voice, though it gives expression to his singularity, his feelings of isolation, his self-centredness, his poetry puts a public face on these things and not just by making poetry of them (a trivial point) but by stamping them with so extravagant and unconvivial a personality.

Satires and moral verse

Donne's satires, it is fairly certain, were written between 1591 and 1601. He wrote the first three probably while still a student at Lincoln's Inn, the fourth some time in late 1597 or early 1598 after his return from the Azores expedition, and the fifth during his employment as Egerton's secretary. 'Metempsychosis' is dated 16 August 1601, a few months before his marriage. The Satires, then, are early work and belong to a period in Donne's life when his trouble with the world had to do with his Catholic background. In 'Satire III', he is committed to a strenuous search for true religion; to that extent anyway he has left implicit faith in the religion in which he was brought up. In most of the satires, incongruous references to religious persecution and theological warfare come in. Donne is evenhanded in his jibes. He glances satirically at Luther, but equally at the Catholic historians Jovius and Surius (IV, l. 48). He talks of the Protestant Dutch as mutinous in their war against Spain (II, l. 17), but 'fires of Spain' (II, l. 24) suggests a good reason for mutiny. Religion was clearly on his mind as it was on the minds of his contemporaries; yet for a man of letters, Donne conceives the religious predicament of his time with an unusual range of international and learned reference. If he is anxious and disturbed, he is at the same time determined to take a broad, detached view. This means that satirically his religious unease does not discharge itself in partisan animus but is suspended

---

49.   There are sketches for parts for others in Satires I, II, and IV and a dialogue in 'Eclogue 1613. December 26'.

in a general feeling of absurdity. 'Metempsychosis' exaggerates this dark humour and makes scepticism about religion part of its general disaffection from the world with an antic disposition not as psychologically resonant as Hamlet's, but intellectually more interesting, for all its air of inconsequence.

Among Donne's contemporaries, it was the Satires rather than the Songs and Sonnets or the religious verse that counted. Ben Jonson, in particular, praised the satirist, and even in the eighteenth century, when there was little taste for Metaphysical verse, Pope 'translated' Satires II and IV. Few now would evaluate them so highly; at least I should not rate the Satires above the Songs and Sonnets. But they are remarkable writing all the same because of Donne's observation of the world around him and his management of the satirist's role.

In the most famous of Donne's poems one is confined to the inside of Donne's head and has only the astonishing play of mind to admire. Who would read 'The Ecstasy' for its descriptions of the country surroundings in which the lovers lie? But in the Satires, Donne shows a wonderfully sharp eye for the sights of the city. In 'Satire II', for example, Coscus's laborious, small, crooked dealings start up this comparison:

> For as a thrifty wench scrapes kitchen stuff,
> And barrelling the droppings, and the snuff,
> Of wasting candles, which in thirty year
> (Relic-like kept) perchance buys wedding gear;
> Piecemeal he gets lands.

> (ll. 81–85)

This, in its heartless way, is an unforgettable shot of a servant's life, such as even Jonson can hardly equal, and moreover just dashed off at a wild angle to the satire on Coscus. Another way in which people live off each other is caught in 'Satire IV' with the same true satirical poet's appetite for rancid detail. The pest, whose company Donne cannot escape, plagues him with knowing talk of

> who hath sold his land, and now doth beg
> A licence, old iron, boots, shoes, and egg-
> Shells to transport; shortly boys shall not play
> At span-counter or blow-point but they pay
> Toll to some courtier.

> (ll. 103–7)[50]

---

50. According to Smith's note, Donne 1971, span-counter is a sort of marbles and blow-point a 'forfeit game played with and for the . . . tags which fastened the hose to the doublet'.

Donne's cleverness comes out not just in his eye for the sordid and the defective but also in his way of representing the involvement of the satirical narrator in what he satirizes. In Satires I and IV, which both rework in an original way Horace's 'Satire IX' in Book I, the narrators are studious figures, soberly dressed and given to solitude. But at the same time, they are quite unable to resist the lively inanity of the pests who seize their company and show them the absurdities of society. They are standoffish, setting themselves up by putting others down. And yet in 'Satire I', the narrator takes measures not to be deserted by the man he despises, and in 'Satire IV' the narrator is drawn a second time to the court he fled earlier in the day when the pest drew him there. The complicity in the follies they despise comes over particularly interestingly in 'Satire IV', where the men advance on the women,

> and praise, as they think, well,
> Their beauties; they the men's wits; both are bought.
> Why good wits ne'er wear scarlet gowns I thought
> This cause: these men, men's wits for speeches buy,
> And women buy all reds which scarlet dye.
> He called her beauty lime twigs, her hair net;
> She fears her drugs ill laid, her hair loose set.

(ll. 190–96)

The narrator includes himself in this ridiculous picture of smart talk at court. Simply by recording what he thought at the time, the narrator makes himself part of the emptiness he describes, so pleased with his own wit that he cannot leave it out of the story. That is as far as Donne goes in dramatizing his narrator satirically. Normally in Satires I and IV the involvement of the narrator in the follies he describes is felt just as an implication of the style: the wild exaggeration has a kind of sympathy with the whirl of headless activity it describes. So, for example, in 'Satire I' the pest at last sees his love in a window,

> And like light dew exhaled, he flings from me
> Violently ravished to his lechery.
> Many were there, he could command no more;
> He quarrelled, fought, bled; and turned out of door
> Directly came to me hanging the head,
> And constantly awhile must keep in his bed.

(ll. 106–12)

For all the hard words, the lively motions of the writing make the pest more a young blade than the butt of satiric condemnation.

If we bring to mind the satire of Dryden or Pope, we can see immediately that Donne has not found a way to establish a persona that speaks with satiric authority. In his 'Epistle to Arbuthnot', Pope sets himself up as the friend of the great and the good. His villa and grotto at Twickenham are a materializing of his established social position as well as of his idea of true civilization. There he is secure to laugh at fools and to attack knaves, even if he pretends to be menaced by a plague of poets and madmen. Similarly Horace, jostled on the streets of Rome in 'Satire IX' (Book I), is secure from the pest who besets him, because his friendship with Maecenas makes him part of a good community where the pest's social manipulations have no place. Donne, by comparison, in his satirical persona, has no social immunity from the follies or worse that surround him. He is isolated and, in 'Satire IV', menaced by the absurd society he describes. There is no community of the good and civilized for him to appeal to except in the unsatisfactory 'Satire V'. Even his surly virtue is fragile.

As a satirist, Donne assumes the moral position of stoic aloofness from a corrupt world. But his aloofness in the Satires is complicated by a style and self-dramatizing that implicate him in the follies he derides. Even where his style shows no underhand sympathy with the object of his scorn, the very extravagance of his scorn rebounds on the scorner. The long verse paragraph opening 'Satire II', already discussed, is so fantastically splenetic that it makes the poet satirist a more extraordinary spectacle than the poets he rails at. This could be satirical ineptitude. The Latin satirists Donne imitates in a free spirit avoid self-parody.[51] But Donne is not trying to stand entirely above or outside the absurdities he satirizes. For him the satirist's alienation from the world and the contradictions of his alienation come into a picture of the world's absurdity. The way in which the revenger in Revenge Tragedies is himself corrupted by his indignation at the corruption of the world is another instance of how Elizabethans or Jacobeans might represent moral outrage in an inclusively human way. Donne may be moved to self-referential finesse because his satirical targets are close to him: in 'Satire I' idle attractions of fashionable London, in 'Satire II' the petty crookednesses of a legal career, and in 'Satire IV' the court with its ritualized subjection and parasitic life-forms, always with fear in the background. He could not attack these things at any level of seriousness without bringing himself in.[52] And so his satire expresses an ironic, ambiguous attitude to himself and the world in the form of disaffected

---

51. He imitates Horace's matter and the rough, obscure manner of Persius and of Juvenal, as the Renaissance understood him.
52. See Everett 1972, p. 6, for the pest as alter ego.

42

play. It lacks Dryden's or Pope's magisterial authority, but it has something their satire lacks, a self-aware feeling for how an alienated perspective on the world reflects on the satirist. Obviously this falls short of the terrible surprise by which the narrator himself becomes the butt of satire in Book IV of *Gulliver's Travels*; what is in question is rather a diffused awareness that the satirical point of view belongs inside the absurd world it pictures. 'Satire IV' is a particularly engaging and developed example of satire in this vein.

'Metempsychosis' shows a more general and disturbed alienation from the world. It is a curious production, which nevertheless contains some of Donne's most extraordinary writing. It is perhaps intentionally deformed. It starts out as an epic, with an epic statement of subject, epic invocation and more than epic boasts for the stupendousness of the undertaking. And yet the poem is not a mock epic. After the first seven stanzas, there are no epic gestures and the plot is simply a string of loosely related episodes. The subject of the poem is the history of a soul, which first lived in the apple that Eve plucked; as soon as that was plucked, it transmigrated to a germinating mandrake, and when Eve pulled that up, it took itself to a sparrow's egg, and so on. The poem imagines the Pythagorean doctrine of metempsychosis applied to an individual soul, running through changes of incarnation from the Creation until, according to Donne's announced plan, it would end up in some great contemporary personage (perhaps he had in mind Queen Elizabeth herself).[53] But the poem stops with its eleventh incarnation, Themech, 'Sister and wife to Cain', and already Donne's inventiveness cannot impress on the succession of lives any developing interest. His poem is *infinitati sacrum*, devoted to infinity or to endlessness. It could have gone on, if not for ever, certainly longer than Donne could write. And it does not come to an end, merely to discontinuation. The poem resists classification, even as a parodic example of a genre, and is perhaps best classified as a Renaissance grotesque, written almost to spite poetic ambition in a fit of anti-creativity. But this nihilistic spleen against poetry gives scope to a vividly morbid imagining of the world.

Yet satire is not the poem's strongest point. The satire lies in Donne's comments on his story, not in the story itself, and for that reason it is a good deal more general than in the Satires. The soul, in one of its incarnations, takes the body of a whale the size of the Peloponnese, whose stomach is an inland sea. The whale

---

53. See ll. 38–39 and 62–63 and Smith's notes in Donne 1971.

> hunts not fish, but as an officer,
> Stays in his court, as his own net, and there
> All suitors of all sorts themselves enthral.

> (ll. 321–23)

This is typical of the political satire in the poem, ingeniously sardonic, the more effective for linking the predatoriness of human power with a picture of the natural world impelled by devouring appetite. But in comparison with the city or court scenes of the Satires it is unspecific and consequently expresses feelings of nausea more than it offers critical observation. That goes with a scarcely novel misogyny: 'Man all at once was there [in Paradise] by woman slain, / And one by one we're here slain o'er again / By them' (ll. 91–93). At the same time, quite inconsistently, Donne praises the sexual libertinism of the first age and admires its greater sexual gust. Yet he reflects that the sparrow that occasions these thoughts and feelings burns himself out:

> freely on his she friends
> He blood, and spirit, pith and marrow spends,
> Ill steward of himself in three years ends.

> (ll. 208–10)

Donne's free-thinking questions about the biblical story are similarly curbed by self-preserving thoughts about the dangers of heresy (stanzas 11 and 12).

It would be easy, noting the poem's ungenerous libertinism and its distinctly cautious scepticism and political satire, to dismiss them as a parade of modish cynicism. But what lifts the poem beyond such objections is Donne's imaginative representation of the growth of the bodies in which the soul lodges.[54] His absorbed drawing of natural processes goes with his interest in the condition of the soul in the body, whether vegetable or animal. The serpent

> Broke the slight veins, and tender conduit-pipe,
> Through which this soul from the tree's root did draw
> Life, and growth to this apple.

> (ll. 122–24)

---

54. On this subject see Carey 1978, pp. 134–35.

Even the stalk of an apple excites Donne's mind to imagine the subtle capillaries through which the soul draws life into a body. Wherever he writes of soul joining body and making it alive, he writes with the sensitivity of someone to whom life in the body, which is our only way of being in the world, is strange yet fascinating. The growth of a mandrake in the earth or of a child in Eve's womb draws him to putting himself inside the physical textures and stretchings of the body that the soul quickens, at once botanist and plant, phytologist and embryo. Or consider this account of roe and milt becoming fish:

> a female fish's sandy roe
> With the male's jelly, newly leavened was,
> For they had intertouched as they did pass,
> And one of those small bodies, fitted so,
> This soul informed, and abled it to row
> Itself with finny oars, which she did fit,
> Her scales seemed yet of parchment, and as yet
>   Perchance a fish, but by no name you could call it.

(ll. 223–30)

The fry excites Donne's metaphysical imagination as a life-form just beginning to appear on this side of nothing in the transparent scales and the name that can hardly be assigned. And at the same time Donne's observation of the sandy roe and the spawning of the fish as they 'intertouch' is miraculously exact. This sort of apprehension of the organism in which the soul takes body gives imaginative resonance to the conventional cynicism of Donne's comments on the social order. Donne's trouble with the human world is grounded in an estranged yet wondering feeling for what it is to be alive in the world. And one might add that he draws the departure of the soul from the body, like lightning in its 'quick nimble haste', 'vapouring' 'thinner than burnt air' (ll. 171, 173), with equal verve. If one cannot speak of scientific observation there, one can at least say that Donne's imagination is informed by alchemy as well as an intense interest in disembodiment and escape from the conditions of life in the world.

Satire came so naturally to Donne's alienated sensibility that one wonders why he gave up writing in this form. Admittedly, the general estrangement from the world in 'Metempsychosis' looks forward to the religious estrangement from a corrupt world in his verse letters to great ladies and his Anniversaries. But in those poems one can only lament the disappearance of the feeling for the condition of incorporated minds that informs 'Metempsychosis' and of the worldly sense of the world's absurdity and the keen eye for the social scene that enliven the Satires. Carey suggests that Donne wrote satire when it was fashionable in order to catch the eye of his social superiors; once he had established himself as a choice spirit he had no further use for that sort of writing; besides, continued satire might have got him a bad name as a malcontent. But at least as plausible reasons for his abandoning the form are that with his marriage, Donne lost his satirical detachment and insouciance, however sardonic, and that he could no longer represent himself in his favourite satirical guise as a young man dismayed by the ways of the world but all the same constantly betraying his solitude to make their acquaintance. Carey remarks also that none of Donne's satires expresses serious or dangerous criticism of those in power and cites by way of contrast Donne's contemporary, Michael Drayton, as one who took risks in 'The Owle'.[55] It is true that Donne is a lightweight satirist. The nearest he comes to censor of the age is in 'Satire V'. There he does express moral indignation with the corruption of the legal system but is careful to enlist the protection of Egerton and absolve the Queen. Morally it is the most earnest and the least serious of his satires. Satires I, II and IV are more concerned with absurdity than with vice. Those for whom that is not enough should certainly read 'The Owle'.

Before leaving Donne as moralist, I should say something about 'Satire III', along with Donne's verse letters to Sir Henry Wotton and Sir Henry Goodyer. These poems moralize, not in the form of play as the Satires do, but explicitly. In various ways they try to turn alienation or withdrawal from the world to a position of moral command.

Though 'Satire III' satirizes misplaced courage and various sorts of churchmanship, it is as a moral reflection on how to live, on Christian virtue or heroism, that it impresses. The first forty-two lines are written in the contorted, ingenious manner that is the vice of Donne's style. Perhaps he intends it as a gallant attempt at railing in the face of violent mixed feelings of grief and anger, which reduce him to incoherence; that would be one way of taking the first four lines. But in spite of its laboured paradoxes ('This fear great courage, and high valour is' [l. 16]), the introduction is interesting for Erasmian ideas of Christian life as the war of virtue with vice. It is interesting also for the appearance of a dead father as an Erasmian preceptor of 'easy ways and near' to heaven. A father comes in later as the first of a series of fathers going back to the days of the primitive church before the original teachings of Christ had been distorted and overlaid by human traditions. Although this father is 'thy father', anyone's father, Donne may have in mind John Donne senior as a true Christian in the Erasmian sense of one who lived a life of heartfelt piety issuing in practical goodness

---

55. Carey 1978, pp. 63–64.

rather than a true Catholic in the heroic tradition of his mother's family. And if that is what is going on, Donne is not so much shuffling into apostasy from a Catholicism that would cost him too much as looking for a sane and central religious tradition, which he might persuade himself was the true tradition of his family.[56]

In any event, the opening discussion of a true Christian life as a heroic calling is by way of introduction to the particular heroic struggle: 'Seek true religion. Oh where?' (l. 43). From this point on the poem goes as if it had acquired a new muscle. First there comes the series of satirical vignettes of the various seekers of true religion, each pictured as a lover. Mirreus seeks her in Rome for her finery (described as rags). Crants seeks her in Geneva,

> plain, simple, sullen, young,
> Contemptuous, yet unhandsome; as among
> Lecherous humours, there is one that judges
> No wenches wholesome, but coarse country drudges.

(ll. 51–54)

And so on through the man who finds true religion in the Church of England, the one who finds her in no church and the one who finds her in all.

The satirical reduction of religious persuasions to curious tastes in love, with its libertine tone, sets off the magnificent lines enjoining the heroic search for true religion:

> doubt wisely, in strange way
> To stand inquiring right, is not to stray;
> To sleep, or run wrong is. On a huge hill,
> Cragged, and steep, Truth stands, and he that will
> Reach her, about must, and about must go;
> And what the hill's suddenness resists, win so;
> Yet strive so, that before age, death's twilight,
> Thy soul rest, for none can work in that night.
> To will, implies delay, therefore now do:
> Hard deeds, the body's pains; hard knowledge too
> The mind's endeavours reach, and mysteries
> Are like the sun, dazzling, yet plain to all eyes.

(ll. 77–88)

---

56. See Strier 1993, pp. 283–322, on Donne's religious quest in 'Satire III', and Oliver 1997, pp. 55–67, for a different account of the poem.

Notably, Donne's harsh style lends itself to the expression of unresolved difficulty, discordance, mental conflict. The lines about truth on her hill are justly famous, not only for the visionary huge hill but for the way the verse uses enjambment to convey the effort of ascent and rhymes unstressed with stressed syllables ('go / so', '[twi]light / night') for a crepuscular effect. The difficult, riddling syntax, with which the passage begins and ends, catches both the difficulty of the mental striving Donne urges and a certain stoic pride in the labour to be undertaken. Striving is necessary because the human mind, embedded in human traditions and the history of theology, puzzles over what is in fact enormously clear. The individual effort to sift the evidence dispassionately, to doubt wisely, is itself heroic. It is more so in a world of religious compulsion and persecution. The poem ends with a grim, though consoling, contrast between those who find peace in the will of God and those who make their peace with the will of earthly tyrants, Catholic or Protestant.

Most of Donne's later religious verse is devotional; he puts all the intensity of his art into his relation with God. 'Satire III' moves in a larger, less exclusively inward world, in which the problem is not himself but the contemporary state of religion. In that, there is more for his mind to grapple with.

On the whole Donne represents himself as an unreliable character, mercurial, ambivalent, self-ironizing. That is one of the fascinations of his poetry. But the moral intelligence at work in 'Satire III' brings out a surprisingly solid person, someone also seen in the friendships with men that he kept up in his verse letters over the years. A verse letter to Sir Henry Wotton ('Sir, more than kisses') written in 1598 is attractive for what he says about the importance of friendship to the life of his mind:

> Sir, more than kisses, letters mingle souls;
> For, thus friends absent speak. This ease controls
> The tediousness of my life: but for these
> I could ideate nothing, which could please,
> But I should wither in one day, and pass
> To a bottle of hay, that am a lock of grass.

(ll. 1–6)

But in spite of this attractive sociability, Donne quickly passes to stoical solitariness and aloofness from a corrupt world:

> Be then thine own home, and in thyself dwell;
> Inn anywhere, continuance maketh hell.
> And seeing the snail, which everywhere doth roam,
> Carrying his own house still, still is at home,

Follow (for he is easy paced) this snail,
Be thine own palace, or the world's thy gaol.

(ll. 48–52)

Of course the stoic self-sufficiency is courteously shared with his friend, but Donne's mind is engaged not so much with life in the world (as it is in 'Satire III') as in elaborating an idea.[57]

A letter to Sir Henry Goodyer, written between 1605 and 1610, gives better advice about how to convert withdrawal into a good life. It is perhaps the finest of his verse letters, certainly his most impressive appearance as moralist in them. Donne has brought his intelligence to bear closely on life as it is actually lived and on the ways we achieve self-control. He writes in the abrupt, difficult, sententious manner learned from the Stoics, but what he recommends is shrewd: not withdrawal into an abstract and impossible kingdom of the mind as in the letter to Wotton, but travel as a way of breaking bad habits, in particular Goodyer's extravagance:

To be a stranger hath that benefit,
We can beginnings, but not habits choke.
Go; whither? Hence; you get, if you forget;
New faults, till they prescribe in us, are smoke.

(ll. 25–28)

No one likes to be preached at, however good the advice. But Donne's concern for his friend, expressed in applying his mind seriously to Goodyer's life, is the best sort of tact. And again, as in the letter to Wotton, Donne speaks of letter writing as a way of the friends' being present to each other in absence, conversation carried on in writing (Donne wrote on horseback as he rode home from Sir Henry's to Mitcham).

Satire, by its nature, implies alienation from the ways of the world. But Donne's satires have a considerable range of ways to express alienation, from sardonic and self-ironizing fun to resolving on heroic individuality. Strikingly, this art of alienation from the world takes in the world in a more lively and immediate way than most of his other writing. Strikingly too, if studious or stoic withdrawal from the world is present as a moral point of reference, the poems are most interesting where the mind is involved in the mixed condition of life. And that applies also to the verse letters.[58]

---

57. See Aers and Kress 1994, pp. 116–17.
58. See Geoffrey Hill's discussion of Donne and Wotton, 1991, pp. 41–61.

Love poems

Dating

It is natural to wish to map out the Elegies and Songs and Sonnets on Donne's biography and so construct a love story or series of love stories or at least a history of feelings and attitudes attached to what we know of his life. But the poems have not been arranged in manuscripts or early editions to suggest any such story or history and the impression they make is of bewildering contradictoriness of feeling. There is no incontrovertible internal evidence for dating them. The references to the King in 'The Sun Rising' and 'The Canonization' certainly make it look as if these poems had been written after the accession of James in 1603, but the references to kings in 'Satire II' (l. 70), 'Satire III' (l. 91) and 'Satire IV' (ll. 74–80, 181), written while Elizabeth still reigned, mean that even this evidence cannot be entirely relied on. And not much can be made of a few other crumbs.[59]

Most commentators think that the Elegies were written before Donne's marriage.[60] Helen Gardner thinks that they circulated in manuscript as a book of elegies. There is a strong Ovidian flavour to the collection. All are written in pentameter couplets (apart from 'The Dream'), which would be an English equivalent for Ovid's elegiac couplets. Some, like 'The Autumnal' and 'The Perfume', degenerate for stretches into series of witty points, the sort of thing that Ovidizing couplets easily fell into. In a diffused way, many are inspired by Ovid's *Amores* and translate Roman libertinism to Elizabethan London. Some, like 'Jealousy', 'The Perfume' and 'To his Mistress: Going to Bed' take hints, which they develop in their own way, from situations in the *Amores*. 'Sappho to Philaenis' is modelled on Ovid's heroic epistles. To the extent that the Elegies sound like the work of Jack Donne, the elegant libertine, Donne is Ovidizing.

---

59. Helen Gardner (Donne 1965, p. 193), argues that 'A Valediction: of the Book' must have been written after 1602 because Donne must have got the idea that Homer's poems had been written by a woman from Lipsius's *De Bibliothecis Syntagma* of 1602. But as Empson 1993, pp. 153–54, points out, Donne might have picked up the idea from one of his learned acquaintances, who would have gleaned it from the commentaries of Eustathius of Salonica printed in Rome in 1542–50 and in Basle in 1559–60 (mentioned by Gardner). 'The Expiration' appeared in a song book of 1609 (Donne 1965, p. 159) and 'Break of Day' in one of 1612 (Donne 1965, p. 158) and consequently they must have been written before these books appeared. If Lucy, Countess of Bedford, is the cruel mistress in 'Twickenham Garden', then that poem cannot have been written before 1607 when she moved to Twickenham Park (Donne 1965, p. lx).

60. But see Patterson 1990b, pp. 37–67, for another view.

But two of the Elegies, 'His Picture' and 'On his Mistress', have nothing of Ovid remade by whatever personal inspiration or force of invention. They are as serious about parting as some of the valedictions in Songs and Sonnets, and yet there is no reason to think they were written after the other Elegies. Donne probably wrote 'His Picture' before he departed in 1596 on the Cadiz expedition. 'On his Mistress' in the Bridgewater Manuscript is subtitled, 'His wife would have gone as his Page'. But there is no known occasion, such as the poem envisages, when Ann More could have accompanied Donne in disguise on a journey over the Alps. We cannot then say that the Ann More affair and his marriage to her furnished the sole occasions of Donne's serious love poems. And we cannot make up a simple biographical scheme in which the Elegies represent an Ovidian phase succeeded by a more passionate and vulnerable phase represented by the Songs and Sonnets.

It is not just in their concern with parting that the Elegies and Songs and Sonnets run into each other. The notion of a love religion, so marked a feature of such Songs and Sonnets as 'A Valediction: forbidding Mourning' and 'The Canonization', comes into 'To his Mistress: Going to Bed', and the theme of the reflection of one self in the other that crops up time and again in the Songs and Sonnets receives a curious and elaborate treatment in 'Sappho to Philaenis'. Above all, the flippancy and libertinism of the Elegies appears in many of the Songs and Sonnets as a disturbing background or as the main burden.

In the absence of strong evidence for dating or clear distinctions between the Elegies and Songs and Sonnets, Helen Gardner made an ambitious attempt to order the poems in a roughly developmental scheme. For her, they are not about actual loves but are essays in love, very loosely related to his life. We can find developing attitudes and interests but should not imagine that these have a direct bearing on actual experiences of love. So most of the Elegies and some of the obvious pose poems in Songs and Sonnets, such as 'The Indifferent' or 'Community', were written to explore the literary possibilities of libertine love when Jack Donne was interested in these things, and the idealizing and platonizing Songs and Sonnets were written in a later phase when Donne had had leisure to read the Italian cabbalists and neoplatonists. This is a plausible theory for many of the Elegies. 'The Perfume' is a free adaptation of Ovid. No one could believe that the story it told bore much relation to an actual escapade. If the elegy had the slightest basis in Donne's life, his genius as a writer has all gone into fabricating a dramatic sketch, into caricature and role playing, something to delight his chums at Lincoln's Inn. But the theory that Donne's poems are literary games does not work well for other poems. It would mean that 'A Valediction: forbidding Mourning', for instance, was a fantasy about an

ideal mutual love written, in Dame Helen's scheme, after the disappointment of his marriage. According to her, it could not be written to Ann
Donne because a wife need not be told to conceal her grief at parting; the
distinction made between the laity and the initiated clergy of love would be
inappropriate for a couple married in the eyes of the world; also marriage
with children and an ailing wife would not lend itself to idealistic celebration. These arguments are thin. And whether the poem was writen to Ann
or not, it is unlikely that the 'Valediction' and the other Songs and Sonnets
celebrating love given and returned were written as 'hallucinatory erotic
day dreams'.[61] These poems are extraordinary for the way that Donne puts
his mind to love. They cerebralize but they combine thought with feeling.
It is not so much (as Eliot would have it) that a thought to Donne was
an experience as that the thinking has descended, as Donne says the soul
should, 'To affections and to faculties' ('The Ecstasy', ll. 65–66) and the
whole man comes out in their utterance:[62]

> For love, all love of other thoughts controls,
> And makes one little room, an every where.
> Let sea-discoverers to new worlds have gone,
> Let maps to others, worlds on worlds have shown,
> Let us possess one world, each hath one, and is one.

('The Good Morrow', ll. 10–14)

It is hard to think he could work this sort of thing up from nothing or as an
imaginary alternative to a marriage he found disappointing. It is also hard
to think that a poem of bitter resentment like 'Love's Alchemy' was merely
a literary exercise.

   Though poems such as these seem clearly not to be just dramatic sketches
for a single voice, there is simply not enough evidence to make up a convincing account that would lay down when and how they belong to what
we know about his life. We may reasonably feel sure that 'A Valediction:
forbidding Mourning' was written out of an experience of love, but we
cannot say whether it was written to his wife or another woman. In this
uncertainty there are still some minimal points that can be made. Most of
the Elegies were almost certainly written before Donne's marriage. It is most
unlikely that none of the celebrations of love in the Songs and Sonnets came
out of his love for Ann More. Given the pressures on their relationship

---

61.   Empson 1993, p. 148.
62.   Eliot 1932, p. 288.

before marriage, some of the suspicious or mock flippant poems might have been written out of that love too. And the themes of the world well lost and of the lovers' being a whole world to each other would come very forcibly to mind, as they do for instance in 'The Canonization', after a marriage that was disastrous from a worldly point of view. Further than that it would be foolish to venture, which means that we simply have to accept that the variety of the Songs and Sonnets is confused; no principles can be made out behind the orderings of the 1633 and 1635 editions and no other schemes carry conviction; there is a lot to be said for A. J. Smith's alphabetical ordering in the Penguin edition.

The Elegies

The Elegies take place less inside Donne's head than the Songs and Sonnets do. They are more involved in the social world. The woman in 'On his Mistress' (she must be a girl) has a nurse; the one in 'The Perfume' has an 'immortal mother', who feels her anxiously to see if she is pregnant and tries to trap her into confessing her affair by herself confessing the sins of her own youth's 'rank lustiness' (l. 24). The woman in 'Jealousy' has a husband who, when 'swoll'n, and pampered with great fare, / Sits down, and snorts, caged in his basket chair' (ll. 21–22). The ingenue in 'Nature's lay idiot' is amusingly characterized as knowing no love tricks beyond 'household charms' before the Ovidian cad, who speaks the poem, sophisticated her. A bare reference to parents' grudging in 'The Flea' is the only meagre piece of comparable social context in the Songs and Sonnets. Love there eliminates the world, whereas in the Elegies social ties make us see love from the outside and usually contribute a rank flavour of Jonsonian comedy as well.

In most of Donne's love poems, the speaker performs a dramatic sketch. Since he addresses a lover, not the reader, we have to gather the situation in the course of the speaker's outpouring. In 'The Perfume', for instance, we learn from his tirade that he was sneaking up stairs when a strong perfume he had put on had brought the father out of his room: 'Had it been some bad smell, he would have thought / That his own feet, or breath, that smell had wrought' (ll. 45–46). This makes a far more circumstantial narrative context than anything in the Songs and Sonnets and makes us see the narrator as someone in a play. Donne's relation to the speaker is far more detached than it is with the speaker of 'A Valediction: forbidding Mourning' or 'The Ecstasy' or even 'The Apparition'. The character of the speaker in many of the Elegies is unattractive and the situations in which he is involved are ugly or shameful. In 'The Perfume', he wears a perfume and besides gallantly tells his love that her 'beauty's beauty, and food of our love' is hope of her father's wealth – he's only in it for the money. His parting couplet, 'All my perfumes, I give most willingly / To embalm thy father's corse; What? will he die?' is amusing, but the joke is on the viciousness of the speaker. And he is not only laughably, openly and jeeringly caddish, but, like many of the lovers in the Elegies, chagrined. In writing Ovidian pieces about a licentious lover, Donne obviously took pleasure in offending the decencies of ordinary people. Here he would be fitting in with the taste of the Inns of Court and the class war waged by upper-class youth on London citizens. But he is also playing up to an image of himself as rake. These pieces, written in the first person, are performances for Jack Donne and must have delighted his friends, whether they took them for true or not. The role playing here implies a rather curious attitude to himself, accentuated by the humiliating or shameful postures in which the speaker is frequently caught. It would be socially adroit and at the same time expressive, like the Satires, of an alienated relation to the world. He could not simply be himself but had to play himself in disguise.

With such an ironic attitude to himself, he might find relief in love as an exchange in which he could find himself loved. This is really the great recurrent theme of the Songs and Sonnets. But one notices how 'His Picture' makes a pathetic and charming appeal to his lover to take his image to her heart. First he gives her his picture as he is now, presumably with the dew of his youth still upon him, and then pictures himself as he may return from the wars,

> When weather-beaten I come back; my hand
> Perhaps with rude oars torn, or sun-beams tanned,
> My face and breast of haircloth, and my head
> With care's rash, sudden hoariness o'erspread,
> My body a sack of bones, broken within,
> And powder's blue stains scattered on my skin.

(ll. 5–10)

Donne always imagines disaster will overtake him when he goes abroad, and he is filled with tenderness for himself here. 'My head / With care's rash, sudden hoariness o'erspread' makes the scalp tingle sympathetically with the strangeness and sorrow of his fate. But Donne is able to feel like this about himself because he is thinking of how he will appear to his lover. He can feel accepted in her eyes. Again in 'On his Mistress', he thinks of how his lover may cry out 'with midnight startings' when he has gone abroad,

'Nurse, O my love is slain, I saw him go
O'er the white Alps alone; I saw him, I,
Assailed, fight, taken, stabbed, bleed and die'.

(ll. 52–54)

This terrible yet loving picture of himself in another's mind enables him to say something unusually tender and self-abolishing: 'Augur me better chance, except dread Jove / Think it enough for me to have had thy love' (ll. 55–56).

If one thinks of 'To his Mistress, Going to Bed' as a role-playing poem with an eye to the Inns of Court crowd, then it is possible to read it as swagger at the woman's expense. Jack Donne presents himself with an impatient erection as he lies naked 'In this love's hallowed temple, this soft bed' insolently ordering her to undress and join him in full nakedness. The way in which he notes the expensive clothes and the chiming watch advertises that it is a lady he is with. The poem is a boast and a jeer.[63] But this interpretation runs up against the tone of voice unmistakably heard in

Licence my roving hands, and let them go
Before, behind, between, above, below.
O my America, my new found land,

(ll. 25–27)

or

Full nakedness, all joys are due to thee.
As souls unbodied, bodies uncloth'd must be,
To taste whole joys.

(ll. 33–35)

The accent of these lines is of someone who has been taken out of himself and we are seeing things from the point of view that makes a little room an everywhere – or almost, for the tone is uneven. The indecency and the blasphemy of the poem assert a transvaluation of values. Between the lovers, full nakedness is a necessary condition for pleasures that, half as a joke, half as revelation, they think true mystical transports. In this spirit, 'Cast all, yea, this white linen hence, / Here is no penance, much less innocence'

---

63. Carey 1990, pp. 90–93, is the *locus classicus* for this view.

arrogant / domineering

(ll. 45–46) means, not 'Innocence? Come off it', but 'In the free and libertine world of our pleasure, "husband, wife, lust, modest, chaste or shame, / Are vain and empty words"'.[64] The imperiousness, the swagger, the egotism, are more an expression of sexual urgency than a contemptuous exercise of power. No one would argue that the question and demand, 'Thou hast made me, and shall thy work decay? / Repair me now', mean that Donne is lording it over God. In something of the same spirit in 'To his Mistress', the peremptory tone is a direct and wholehearted expression of desire, though since it is spoken between lovers, fun or play naturally enters in as well.

On this interpretation, 'To his Mistress' is not a role-playing poem, but a self-dramatizing one. Donne is certainly interested in himself, but as lover in the closed world of the lovers, not as a figure in the outer world of the Inns of Court. Like most of his best-known poems, 'To his Mistress' is self-dramatizing in the sense that the 'I' of the poem speaks to someone else in such a way as to create a dramatic present or situation. Donne's poem focuses on the moment of undressing and the whole utterance of the poem is directed towards full nakedness. Yet the naked woman is not described. We are not allowed to wander, as in Ovid's *Amores*, I, 5, over 'Nipples inviting caresses, the flat / Belly outlined beneath that flawless bosom'.[65] The gain in concentration is enormous, but the concentration is on the speaker of the poem and what he is doing in words. If he offers detail, it works like 'Your gown going off, such beauteous state reveals, / As when from flowery meads th'hill's shadow steals' (ll. 13–14), which tells us about the speaker's excitement about nakedness, not what the woman looked like.

This self-centredness does not mean that Donne is narcissistic. He is not in love with his own image. In this he is unlike Sir Philip Sidney, who in his sonnet sequence *Astrophel to Stella* (1591) repeatedly gazes with loving concern at the spectacle of himself in love:

> Then thinke my deare, that you in me do reed
> Of Lover's ruine some sad Tragedie;
> I am not I, pitie the tale of me.[66]

This is narcissism. Stella is there to mirror him to himself as a passionate fellow. The image of himself changed by love into someone in a romance is

---

64. For the first view, see Gardner in Donne 1965, p. 133, for the second, Thomas Carew, 'The Rapture'; cf. Donne's 'The Dream', ll. 26–27: ''Tis not all spirit, pure, and brave, / If mixture it of fear, shame, honour, have'. But perhaps the reading of other manuscripts and of the 1639 edition, 'There is no penance due to inocence', should be accepted.
65. Ovid 1982, p. 92. See also Gill 1972.
66. *Astrophel and Stella*, XLV.

what excites him. What Donne wants, by contrast, is to see himself loved rather than to love himself in love, or in 'To his Mistress' for his nakedness to be met with his lover's. Even Sappho in 'Sappho to Philaenis', though picturing Philaenis as her other self, her reflection in a mirror, or as resembling herself as one eye, or lip or thigh does the other member of the pair, is not exactly admiring herself. Though very different from Donne as he presents himself as a lover (she is a woman; Donne does not deal with the erotics of unrequited desire elsewhere), she still has to pass herself through another to love herself. 'Sappho to Philaenis' was presumably undertaken as a witty exercise on a curious sport of love, like 'Xerxes' strange Lydian love, the platan tree' ('The Autumnal', l. 29). But the conventional Elizabethan attitude gives way to something more imaginatively felt, and the lesbian lovers begin to feature a reflexiveness that Donne himself sought in love, that was indeed the ideal solution to his alienation from the world. The strong treatment of that is the Songs and Sonnets.

'Air and Angels'

To see how Songs and Sonnets work, let us take 'Air and Angels' as a specimen.

> Twice or thrice had I loved thee,
> Before I knew thy face or name;
> So in a voice, so in a shapeless flame,
> Angels affect us oft, and worshipped be;
>   Still when, to where thou wert, I came,
> Some lovely glorious nothing I did see,
>   But since my soul, whose child love is,
> Takes limbs of flesh, and else could nothing do,
>   More subtle than the parent is
> Love must not be, but take a body too, 10
>   And therefore what thou wert, and who
>   I bid love ask, and now
> That it assume thy body, I allow,
> And fix itself in thy lip, eye, and brow.
>
> Whilst thus to ballast love, I thought,
> And so more steadily to have gone,
> With wares which would sink admiration,
> I saw, I had love's pinnace overfraught,
>   Every thy hair for love to work upon
> Is much too much, some fitter must be sought; 20

> For, nor in nothing, nor in things
> Extreme, and scatt'ring bright, can love inhere;
>   Then as an angel, face and wings
> Of air, not pure as it, yet pure doth wear,
>   So thy love may be my love's sphere;
>   Just such disparity
> As is 'twixt air and angels' purity,
> 'Twixt women's love, and men's will ever be.

This is one of Donne's most difficult poems, one of the ones Dryden may have had in mind when he said that Donne 'perplexed the minds of the fair sex with the nice speculations of philosophy'.[67] In an obvious way it is a Metaphysical poem, for it argues about souls and bodies and uses a theory about how angels make themselves bodies of air. In fact the metaphysical ideas are used for conceits and behind the ethereal figures one can make out an unexpectedly substantial sense. But on the surface the poem appears very fine drawn and abstruse.

It is also one of the most volatile of Donne's poems, continually and unpredictably changing shape. Most of Donne's poems, even the Satires up to a point, take the form of dramatic sketches for solo speakers, whose doings in words, expostulating, jeering, lamenting, arguing and so forth, make the poems. At first glance, 'Air and Angels' seems to be more narrative than dramatic. Both the first and second stanzas tell a story in the past. But in both stanzas, the story comes up to a present, the moment where a next step is to be taken and the love made more nearly perfect. The story is told from the point of view of the present and is addressed to a 'thee' so that it is in fact delivered dramatically and we are interested in how the speaker will declare himself. And at the same time the story follows a dialectical progress. Each stanza develops a problem and offers an answer. The problem of the second stanza develops out of the answer in the first. After the second answer, the poem concludes with a twist, a jocular distinction between the purity of men's love and of women's. The argument of the poem towards a new understanding of love also helps to make the poem, even as it looks back, evolve in the dramatic present, the present as it turns to the future, which is characteristic of Donne's most exciting verse. The mind of the speaker is not made up before the poem begins. It is in process, making itself up as it goes along.

According to Samuel Butler, 'Dr *Donne's* writings are like Voluntary or Prelude, in which a man is not tyd to any particular Design of Air, but may

---

67. Dryden, *A Discourse Concerning the Original and Progress of Satire* (1693) in Dryden 1900, II, p. 19.

change his Key of Mood at Pleasure; So his Compositions seem to have been written without any particular Scope'.[68] This calls attention, not only to the freedom and spontaneity of Donne's play of mind, but also to the virtuosity of his writing. Although a poem like 'Air and Angels' gives the process of thinking rather than working up what has already been thought, the thinking is thinking, not associative reverie. Donne moves sequentially from a state of love that is ethereal and insubstantial to one that is overwhelmingly, sensually, variously physical, and from that to a sort of happy mean between these two. And this movement of thought is elaborated with the paraphernalia of logical discourse. 'Still', 'But', 'therefore', 'then', 'so' – these are the conjunctions that mark the steps of an argument.

The poem not only flaunts the way it carries out its agile logical operations, it also runs through an exactingly patterned stanza. The Songs and Sonnets written in stanzas number forty-nine, forty-four of which are written in stanza forms that are not repeated, the stanza of 'Air and Angels' being one of those.[69] This and the intricacy of its stanza are a measure of Donne's metrical inventiveness. The rhyme scheme goes *abbabacdcddeee*, and the sequence of line lengths in iambic measure, allowing for trochaic substitution, goes 44555545454355. The first and fifth lines of the poem are odd. In the first there appear to be only three stresses, and the last syllable on which the rhyme falls is unstressed. A possible, if strained, scansion to give four stresses would be to consider the first foot as lacking the unstressed syllable and the last two as trochaic substitutions: 'Twice | or thrice | had I | loved thee'. As for the fifth line, what I hear at the beginning of 'Still | when, | to where | thou wert, | I came' is two feet lacking unstressed syllables. There is a sufficient pause between 'still' and 'when' for that to work, and, besides, the clause inserted between commas requires that 'when' should be emphasized more than usual, both by stress and pause, so that the syntactical connection may carry over. Otherwise, Donne has taken few of those liberties that make reading his Satires or some of his Holy Sonnets metrically difficult. Carrying off his intricate stanza once might not be hard, but carrying it off twice, and with *sprezzatura*, with an air of negligent grace, as if the turns of rhyme and line length lent themselves to what he had to say and the tone of voice in which he wished to say it, makes a dazzling performance. Of course, to be able to rhyme 'is' with 'is', 'gone' with '[admirati]on', or '[puri]ty' with 'be' would have made things easier. And

---

68. Butler 1759, II, p. 498; cited A. J. Smith 1975, p. 144.
69. Legouis 1928, p. 16. It has been argued that each fourteen-line stanza is an inverted sonnet divided between the first six lines and the second eight instead of the usual octave and sestet. See Wiggins 1982, p. 88.

characteristically Donne inverts syntax so that verbs fall at the end of lines, and in this way he can rhyme 'be' and 'see', 'is' and 'is'.[70] But we feel that as a trick of style, not as a straining after rhyme; it goes with his wiry, riddling manner:

> But since my soul, whose child love is,
> Takes limbs of flesh, and else could nothing do,
> More subtle than the parent is
> Love must not be, but take a body too.

The way that piece of sentence is drawn variously out from line to line is at once unpredictable and firm, involuted and spry. What might look like licence to cope with the inordinate demands of his verse form comes over as the freedom of someone in command of the lucky effects he can strike from them.

What Donne's voluntary or prelude conveys is both exceedingly rarefied and at the same time recognizable as a history of desire. The story that the first stanza tells is that Donne had inklings of what the true object of his love would be in the women he loved before; as in 'The Good Morrow', he is saying, 'If ever any beauty I did see, / Which I desired, and got, 'twas but a dream of thee'. When he meets the real thing at last, he is dazzled, unable to take in what he can only apprehend as 'some lovely glorious nothing'. It takes him some time before he can make up his mind that she is indeed the embodiment of his deepest intuitions about what love might mean for him.

That is an indication of what Donne is saying, sufficiently rough to be recognizable. Donne's way of saying it, however, is not general but extraordinary in the claims it makes to an experience entirely out of the ordinary. Donne is one whom 'angels affect . . . oft' and in whom love first works a sort of etherealizing or rarefaction, so that he has to make an effort to bring it down to earth and fix it in the actual woman. Here, as in 'The Ecstasy', or as in 'A Valediction: forbidding Mourning' where he explains how love 'Like gold to airy thinness beat' will mysteriously connect the lovers when they are apart, Donne imagines metaphysically; that is, he imagines spiritual or supernatural states of being. It is not that Donne wants to be a magus. His concern is with love, not with gaining mysterious powers. He may spiritualize, but he is also talking about life as it is recognizably lived in the body. We could not be interested in his poetry for long if it dealt only in the private exaltations of one 'born to strange sights'. Besides the solemnity, there runs a certain playful sense of his hyperbole: he is telling his love she

---

70. See Austin 1992, p. 29.

is an angel, more or less; for all his egotism, that sets Donne in a world where there are other people to reckon with.

But however recognizable the experience and part of our common world, the effect of rarefaction is unforgettable. The verse, with its irregular movement in line 1 and trochaic substitutions in line 3, wobbles on the edge of taking shape. Again the effect of having the first five words of line 4 begin with vowels ('angels affect us oft and') conveys the softness and indefiniteness with which the angels make their presence felt. The movement of 'So in a voice, so in a shapeless flame' also suggests a tentative unfixed state of being. The repetition of the syntactical pattern and the way that the longer second phrase seems to cancel the first one suggest an angel fading from one shape into an other. Similarly the wandering echoes in the internal rhymes and half-rhymes ('Twice', 'Thrice', 'face', 'voice') suggest the fitfulness of angelic epiphanies in unbodied voices and flakes of fire.

Intimations give way to the glorious full apparition that stands before him when he at last meets the woman to whom the poem is addressed. The apparition asserts itself in a metrical device that Donne uses for emphasis: each of the three successive words, 'lovely, glorious nothing', is trochaic by itself (I am assuming 'glorious' elides to a trochee), but at the same time they fit into the iambic line without inversion, at once conforming and running counter to the measure with a rippling, affirmative surge. The same triumphant effect can be heard in 'But this, all pleasures fancies be' ('The Good-Morrow'), or 'All glory of honours, beauties, wits' ('The Anniversary').

But Donne is not content with the apparitional state of love, however lovely and glorious, and turns to argument to get the vision to take flesh: his soul cannot act without the body it has assumed; love is the child of his soul; so his love, like his soul, should assume a body and take shape in her. He delivers his argument in a remarkably lofty tone: his to command his love as an ambassador to negotiate with the 'lovely, glorious nothing' and his to 'allow' his love to take her shape. He is sharing a joke with her about her being the realization of his dreams while making out he was very lordly and exacting in his choice. And yet however smiling, the argument reminds one of the general drift of 'The Ecstasy' from a vision of love to a choice of love in the flesh. But it leaves the mutuality of 'The Ecstasy' out. It is he that is entranced, not each in the other, and it is of her as the fulfilment of his dreams that he speaks, not of each as 'one another's best'. It is for him that the materializing out of thin air in 'thy eye, lip and brow' has taken place. To some extent this self-centredness will be redeemed in the second stanza.

For Donne is still not satisfied, and the poem slips again into the past tense to arrive at a solution in the present or future that answers to his heart's desire. The trouble with his love having assumed the body of the woman is that he is overwhelmed by its physical richness. He is afraid of drowning in his intent sensual absorption: 'Every thy hair for love to work upon / Is much too much' – the syntactical inversion swells the splendid hyperbole and catches at once his admiration, his desire to take all her beauties in and his feeling that they are too much for him. Although this may hint at anxiety about physical excess, it unresentfully leads to the grand theme of Donne's love poetry, the mutuality of loving and being loved. For it now appears to him that the true object of love is not the disembodied vision or the distracting richness of the body but love that is returned. It is there on second thoughts that Donne wishes his angelic ideal of love to realize itself.

This solution gives a fine turn to the argument of the poem and to its figures of soul and body. And it is also a sound ending to the story. At last the woman is not just an object of contemplation but is asked to join him in love. But at this point Donne seems to throw away his poem and betray its seriousness and, one might add, its high spirits:

> Then as an angel, face and wings
> Of air, not pure as it, yet pure doth wear,
> So thy love may be my love's sphere;
> Just such disparity
> As is 'twixt air and angels' purity,
> 'Twixt women's love, and men's will ever be.

It sounds as if wantonly Donne is moved in the last three lines to slight the woman and the ideal of love given and returned with a jibe that women's love will, of course, always be inferior to men's. That Donne would be capable of such a contemptuous swerve is hard to deny. Suspicion and scorn in general and of women in particular are emotions that he likes to display. And caprice and lightning changeableness go with his art of 'prelude or voluntary'. With the skill of a conjuror, he could twist from the serious discussion of the true object of his love to an accident of his conceit (the disparity between spirit and embodiment) and pull that out until it looked like a leg for the poem to stand on. At the same time that this was clever it would be a way of reducing intensity (a joke) and a way perhaps of expressing insecurity about whether he was loved as much as he loved.

This conclusion of 'Air and Angels' is a poor thing, though. After the exalted questing and sequential search for the true object of his love and his finding it in love given and returned, to say that women's return of love must always be less pure than men's is a face-pulling betrayal of his 'best' to the commonplace opinion about women's inferiority to men, their comparative unspirituality, lustfulness and all the rest of it, in a word, their impurity.

Donne was probably capable of such a betrayal, but there is another interpretation, put forward by Empson, that would give the poem, if not a strong conclusion, at least not a weak or vicious one. According to this interpretation, Donne is making a joke of the relative purity of men's love and women's. He is playing on the banal view of the matter and puffing it and the whole absurd concern away: 'Just such disparity / As is 'twixt air and angels' purity / 'Twixt women's love and men's will ever be'.[71] The 'Just' makes great intellectual play of fixing the disparity between men's and women's love with exactness, only to come up with a difference that must elude the finest observation, the disparity between the purity of air and of angels. What makes this ending possible is to assume that 'it' in line 24 has 'air', not 'angel', for antecedent (could an angel be an 'it'?). The angel takes a body of air by condensing it, so becoming visible but making the air less pure – that is, less transparent (however shining) – than it was before. Similarly Donne's love may incarnate itself as a condensation of the airy substance of his lover's love, less pure than it, though pure; the same sort of relation holds for a shining heavenly body moving in a crystal sphere. Other considerations about spheres and angels might complicate the picture, all in the end to tease the mind in an abstruse way about a difference which is nothing. The poem sets out at a level of extraordinary refinement and ends by joking about refinement and metaphysical apprehensions. In this, the poem is not sabotaging itself but coming to itself, arriving at an idea of love that might be humanly lived.

The force of Empson's arguments, their combination of subtlety, good sense and fun, needs to be savoured in the original. But even as I have given them, they make a better poem than the lurch into misogyny, and a generous criticism would give Donne the benefit of the doubt.

Songs and Sonnets

A comparison with a love poem by Ben Jonson in *Underwoods* will help to bring out the special note of Donne's writing in Songs and Sonnets:

XVIII An Elegy

Can beauty that did prompt me first to write,
Now threaten, with those means she did invite?
Did her perfections call me on to gaze,
Then like, then love; and now they would amaze?
Or was she gracious afar off, but near
A terror? Or is all this but my fear?
That as the water makes things, put in't, straight,

---

71. Empson 1993, pp. 117–18; see also Sykes-Davies 1965.

Crookèd appear; so that doth my conceit:
I can help that with boldness; and love sware,
And fortune once, to assist the spirits that dare.   10
But which shall lead me on? Both these are blind:
Such guides men use not, who their way would find,
Except the way be error to those ends:
And then the best are, still, the blindest friends!
And how a lover may mistake! To think,
Or love, or fortune blind, when they but wink
To see men fear: or else for truth, and state,
Because they would free justice imitate,
Veil their own eyes, and would impartially
Be brought by us to meet our destiny.   20
If it be thus; come love, and fortune go,
I'll lead you on; or if my fate will so,
That I must send one first, my choice assigns,
Love to my heart, and fortune to my lines.

After Donne, the lack of intensity of 'An Elegy' perhaps strikes us first.
Jonson is agitated, but he is solid. The solidity is attractive. Though Donne
always sounds like Donne, it is hard to say what sort of man he is behind
the unmistakable manner. Jonson, by contrast, never evaporates; his 'moun-
tain belly, and [his] rocky face' can always be made out through his words.
The argument of 'An Elegy' is a deliberation whose rapid toing-and-froing
is the movement of a mind hesitating urgently how to act. It shows by contrast how the evolutions of Donne's mind, his famous arguments, are not
really arguments so much as fancies. They may rehearse weighty concerns,
they may even be engaged with how to act, but as arguments they are flimsy
or even sophistical. What Donne is saying in the first stanza is entirely
serious, but his argument by analogy with the relation of child and parent
that love must take a body is, like all arguments from analogy, tenuous, and
besides we have to reckon with what he means by his fancy of love's taking a
body. By contrast Jonson's analogy with the way water distorts appearances
serves to clarify and make vivid what has been said, not to supply premises
from which a conclusion may be drawn. And it also has a pleasing conspicuousness and clarity in a poem otherwise figuratively spare; in comparison,
Donne's conceits are like gold to airy thinness beat. Not that Jonson's
straightforwardness is without subtlety. His self-interrogation about the
conventionally blind love and fortune turns and twists in a constantly fresh
and surprising manner until it finds, in the last lines of the poem, a way that
answers to both desire and reason.

What is admirable about Jonson's poem is its firm presence in the world.
It has its feet on the ground even if the sinewy process of its thought makes

that appear an unexpectedly fine achievement (one notes how limber and responsive to the turns of thought Jonson's handling of conventional iambic pentameter is). The splendour of 'Air and Angels' lies, by contrast, in its way of taking us out of our usual ways of thinking and feeling, and if it turns to entering the world in which our lives are lived, it does so as a thought adventure, in which things have to be worked out analytically in terms of an ideal negotiation between love and object of love and spirit and body. Economically, Donne's circumstances were only relatively straitened between his dismissal from Egerton's service and his entering the Church. But literally, he had difficulty in keeping body and soul together. The parting of the two in rapture or death, whether real or metaphorical, and the joining of the two, as in 'Air and Angels', are almost obsessive motifs in the Songs and Sonnets and indicate his trouble with being firmly present in the world.

As an ideal solution to this trouble, he turns repeatedly to love given and returned as a little world in which he can come together. His ideal that love finds its object in the love of another stands out from what most Renaissance love poets celebrate. Among them, the inaccessible Petrarchan heroine and the broody feelings she excites supply a favourite subject, sometimes with truly memorable results, such as Fulke Greville's *Caelica* XXII and Ben Jonson's 'Celebration of Charis'. Sidney and Drayton are interested in their feelings, Shakespeare in the object of these feelings (but the object is a man and that means that he is seen as a person apart from the poet's feelings). But there are no memorable treatments of mutuality apart from Donne's, though the exchange of hearts or glances was a Petrarchan commonplace,[72] as it indeed remains in some of the Songs and Sonnets, such as 'The Legacy' or 'Witchcraft by a Picture', however novel or amusing the way in which it has been worked up.

Donne is rightly thought to be egotistical. Probably he uses 'I' more assertively than other poets. But his vaunting or caressing use of 'we' and 'us', assumed as a point of view, can hardly be missed in poem after poem. 'We two' in 'A Nocturnal' or 'The Ecstasy' advertises an intimacy closed against that other 'we', the world. The use of the first person plural in 'We owe them thanks, because they thus / Did us, to us, at first convey' suggests how in the 'us' the lovers have encountered a new creature compounded of both. With 'we' and 'us' goes 'thou and I': 'I wonder by my troth, what thou and I / Did, till we loved', 'If our two loves be one, or thou and I / Love so alike, that none do slacken, none can die' ('The Good Morrow'); 'This flea is you and I' ('The Flea'); 'Since thou and I sigh one another's breath, / Whoe'er sighs most, is cruellest, and hastes the other's death' ('A

---

72. E.g. in Sir William Alexander's 'Aurora', sonnet 33.

Valediction: of Weeping'). The last example brings in not only an idea that 'thou and I' have exchanged life and breath, but also another key pro- nominal compound, 'one another'. The lovers are 'They who one another keep' in the 'Song' ('Sweetest love') or 'one another's all' in 'Lovers' Infinite- ness'. 'We two' are 'one another's best' in 'The Ecstasy' or 'one another's hermitage' in 'The Canonization'. They are 'made of one another' in 'The Dissolution' and watch 'one another' with a rapt exchange of gaze in 'The Good Morrow'. Twice in 'The Anniversary', the lovers find themselves in one another; in one case 'When thou and I first one another saw' the 'thou and I' formula is worked in also, as in 'A Valediction: of Weeping'.

Another of Donne's verbal means of featuring mutuality is his extra- ordinary fabrication of words beginning with 'inter'. 'Interview' was current in its modern sense but also in the sense ('interview', 2, *OED*) of an exchange of glances, and that, if not the head meaning, can surely be felt as a subsidiary meaning in 'By our first strange and fatal interview, / By all desires which thereof did ensue' (Elegy 'On his Mistress'). And then there are the glowing intensifications of words to express joining in love: in 'A Valediction: forbidding Mourning' the lovers are 'interassured of the mind'; in 'The Ecstasy' they 'intergraft' their hands and

> When love, with one another so
> Interinanimates two souls,
> That abler soul, which thence doth flow,
> Defects of loneliness controls.

> (ll. 41–44)

In the 'Eclogue, 1613', the benediction on the married pair is that they should 'interbring / Daily new joys' (l. 17). Even Donne's fish in 'Metempsychosis' 'intertouch' as they spawn. And his haters too, tyrants and their subjects, have such intimate feelings that they 'interwish' ('The Curse') each other's destruction.

The theme of mutual exchange makes an early and unlikely appearance in the 'Epithalamion Made at Lincoln's Inn':

> Leave, leave, fair Bride, your solitary bed,
>   No more shall you return to it alone,
> It nurseth sadness, and your body's print,
> Like to a grave, the yielding down doth dint;
>   You and your other you meet there anon;
>   Put forth, put forth that warm, balm-breathing thigh,
> Which when next time you in these sheets will smother
>   There it must meet another,
>   Which never was, but must be, oft, more nigh.

> (ll. 2–10)

Thigh meeting thigh as like to like, we have already met in 'Sappho to Philaenis'. Donne has a battery of other figures for the exchange of selves in love. The most obvious one is the reflection of each in the other's eyes or tears, for in that way the lovers can see themselves contained in the other or something of the other.[73] So most famously: 'My face in thine eye, thine in mine appears' ('The Good Morrow'), where the braiding of the syntax suggests the interchange as well. And there are other examples of mutual eyework in 'The Canonization', where the lovers find an epitome of the whole world in each other's eyes because these eyes reflecting each other contract or concentrate them, who are a whole world to each other, as they find each in the other, or again in 'The Ecstasy', where making images in the eyes is thought of as propagation. Pregnancy in an age before convenient contraception must have been an awkward topic to bring up in poems where love is supposed to be everything, but again it is a figure for mutuality, the joining and mingling of the lovers' bloods in Aristotelian and Renaissance theory of seed.[74] So when Donne thinks of his tears in 'The Valediction: of Weeping' as bearing his lover's reflection, he improves on that image of lover within lover by adding that the tears are 'pregnant with thee', exceptionally allowing something of his to be contaminated with the feminine in order to suggest how completely they are united. Even in 'The Flea', a poetic stunt and yet one that features his ideas of mutual exchange with surprising comprehensiveness, the flea, which has sucked blood from both lovers, 'pampered swells with one blood made of two'. Other flea poets wished that they could find their way to those parts of their lovers' bodies to which the fleas, not they, had access.[75] But for Donne, the flea is there to unite and mingle 'in these living walls of jet' the lovers that parents keep apart.

The 'living walls of jet' belong to the flea metaphorized as a cloister (it has just been a 'marriage bed, and marriage temple'). However flippantly, this brings in the love religion that Donne made of the 'us'. There was an element of jocularity in its early appearance in 'To his Mistress' with the talk of the bed as 'love's hallowed temple' and 'full nakedness' as the condition of mystic transport. The tone is still half joking in 'The Canonization'. But the joke would not be so good if Donne did not at least half mean too what he said figuratively:

73. For a psychoanalytic account of the exchange of looks, see Shullenberger 1993.
74. Gardner in Donne 1965, pp. 174–75.
75. See Gardner's note in Donne 1965, p. 174, for a summary of this Renaissance tradition stemming from the *Carmen de pulice* ascribed to Ovid.

> The phoenix riddle hath more wit
> By us; we two being one, are it.
> So to one neutral thing both sexes fit
> We die and rise the same, and prove
> Mysterious by this love.

(ll. 23–27)

Obviously this is indecent and blasphemous. The Phoenix becomes more packed with riddling significance (or wit) if, as Donne would have it, it is made into an emblem of the union of two lovers who together make the perfectly hermaphroditic creature the Phoenix was supposed to be and rise from death in orgasm as the Phoenix from its ashes. The suggestion is that the Christian mystery of the resurrection is more truly and substantially apprehended in the lovers' acts of love. Riding this high horse, Donne imagines himself triumphing over the world he has lost for love. He puts forward himself and his lover and the love they make together as inspirational types of a new and true religion of love and, like the saints and martyrs who suffered on earth for the old one, they mediate between the heaven of love and its worshippers below. The fire of the poem fluctuates. Before the lines I have quoted, he is joking with a kind of gallows humour about their burning themselves up like moths at candles. In the stanza following he modulates into light banter with his worldly interlocutor about making verses that will serve at once as a memorial and as hymns of their sort of love. And as for the last stanza, it is at once a turning the tables on his worldly critics and a magnificently self-aggrandizing fantasy:

> all shall approve
> Us canonized for love:
>
> And thus invoke us: 'You whom reverend love
>   Made one another's hermitage;
> You, to whom love was peace, that now is rage;
>   Who did the whole world's soul contract, and drove
>   Into the glasses of your eyes
>   (So made such mirrors, and such spies,
> That they did all to you epitomize,)
>   Countries, towns, courts: beg from above
>   A pattern of your love!'

(ll. 35–45)

'Love' is the last word of every stanza, and the way the prayer, running through its parallelisms and surging over its syntactic suspensions, comes to ring a last change on 'love' sounds too splendidly assertive for parody.

68

Under the cavorting, this says that as far as love and its religion go, the lovers are an ideal pattern.

How far Donne actually believed this 'private gospel' is hard to say.[76] More soberly than in 'The Canonization', he talks of the lovers in 'A Valediction: forbidding Mourning' as if they were a priesthood in charge of religious secrets: ''Twere profanation of our joys / To tell the laity our love'. In 'The Ecstasy' the lovers are adepts in an alchemical or neoplatonic mystery rather than a Christian one. A voyeur, who looked on their mutual trance and listened to its rapturous monologue would himself undergo an alchemical spiritualizing and 'part far purer than he came' (l. 28). Donne's analogies between love and spiritual things assert that the exchange of love between the lovers is something to be adored, both by themselves and by the world. Like the comparison of lovers to princes, the love religion is at the very least a hyperbolical way of talking about love as a sovereign thing. Donne may also in his high moments of desire or defiance have entertained the idea that in love he had come at the source of religion. Even in 'The Relic', which sounds like a disclaimer of the love religion in 'The Canonization' because it represents the devout as superstitiously venerating the bones of himself and his lover as those of a Mary Magdalene and a Jesus, a double bluff is being mounted. In some sense he does feel that he and his love are a Christ and a Mary Magdalene, lovers according to one unorthodox whisper.[77] But the sense is visionary and excited. Donne is not setting himself up as love's heresiarch with flat conviction. The love religion is highly unstable because it celebrates a love utopia cut off from the world and maintained in defiance of the world only by the high spirit of the lovers. The spirit comes and goes. Donne seems to have been more subject to depression and exaltation than most, and the Songs and Sonnets rather reflect moods than state positions. That means that Donne does display himself as a 'flibberty-gibbet', to grasp firmly Empson's unpleasant name for the alternative to the Shelleyesque idealist he wants him to be.[78] Donne is an idealist, of course, but a complex and uncertain one, subject to the suggestions of other voices. Still, that is exactly what fascinates most people in Donne's poetry, its flair for unstable and contradictory expression.

---

76. To misappropriate a phrase from 'To the Countess of Bedford at New Year's Tide', l. 65.
77. Even *The Golden Legend* suggests at least an amorous friendship between Christ and Mary: Voragine, 97v.
78. 'I think he was an earnest young man all the time he was working on his love poems instead of being a flibberty-gibbet as T. S. Eliot once said. [T]he more you regard him as serious . . . I mean as having a basis of conviction behind what he says . . . even if talking in a riddle manner, I think that makes the poetry better' (from a transcript of a record of an interview between Frank Kermode and Empson [cited by John Haffenden, Empson 1993, p. 16]).

The love religion with its distinctions between love's mysteries and common knowledge, love's priesthood and the laity, the initiates and the profane, opposes his ideal love to the ordinary world. The opposition places the lovers at the centre and pushes the world to the edge. In other ways too he has means of banishing the world and at the same time claiming for the lovers all that the world has to offer. In 'The Sun Rising', 'She is all states, and all princes, I, / Nothing else is'. Princes may stand by metonymy for their countries and countries for their princes, so both are all and apart from them there is nothing. Again and again the rhetoric of all or nothing places the lovers in a divine centre that takes in everything. 'Love / Makes one little room, an every where' ('The Good Morrow'), it contracts 'the whole world's soul' in the mutual gaze of the lovers ('The Canonization') and, since 'the world's contracted thus', as far as the sun is concerned 'This bed [its] centre is, these walls, [its] sphere' ('The Sun Rising', ll. 26, 30). Again, like the love religion, this is a hyperbole ('We are the whole world to each other'), but again it expresses a troubled relation to the world and an urge to abolish the space limits imposed by life in the body, to escape from the world as it is normally experienced. From the first, being in the world was a problem for Donne, and the problem was brought to a head by his marriage. For someone who experienced the world in this estranged way, love given and returned would be particularly present as the ideal, the utopian, community, hence Donne's particular drive to make a new world of it (with a new religion and new physics) in the world's despite.

An obvious way to escape the world, at once an answer to alienation and a final estrangement, is death. By his own confession, suicide was one of Donne's familiar thoughts.[79] Death comes into the Songs and Sonnets as an even more obsessive theme than the language of love's exchange. Donne imagines himself cut up, disinterred and rising on the last day. The cruelty of a lover or of parting make a ghost of him. A favourite mode of address for him is from outside the body or from beyond the grave. But among the Songs and Sonnets, except perhaps in 'Farewell to Love', Donne does not combine love and death with Jacobean disgust (it is different with the 'Anniversaries'). D. H. Lawrence's idea, taken up by Christopher Ricks, that Donne's association of love and death expresses a syphilis horror does not hit the mark.[80] It is rather that with him death is first of all a dark hyperbole, as the love religion and the love world are shining ones, for extreme feeling. But then, like those other hyperboles, it can carry more. The parting of soul from body, which death involves, is brought about by those ecstasies

---

79. Donne 1648, pp. 17–18.
80. Ricks 1996, p. 41; Lawrence 1936, p. 552.

and infinities that Donne is seized by, and at the same time love draws his soul back to life in the body as a condition of love. Love as an ideal anti-world is like death and is entered on in the spirit's leaving the body behind; love as an ideal state of being in the world brings body and soul back together.

We have already seen how love moves to disembodiment and then to ideal embodiment in 'Air and Angels'. The same dual movement comes out in 'The Ecstasy'. In a superb reversal of the usual idea that the body is the prison of the soul, the joint love-soul that is speaking declares the soul must be empowered by the body, 'Else a great prince in prison lies' (l. 68). One notes also the embryological overtones of soul becoming body in the womb in the account of how the soul is united with the body as if the joint love-soul were imagining the coming back from the disembodiment of ecstasy as a remaking of themselves:

> As our blood labours to beget
> Spirits, as like souls as it can,
> Because such figures need to knit
> That subtle knot, which makes us man:
>
> So must pure lovers' souls descend.

(ll. 61–65)

Donne's specifically metaphysical imagery of soul and body in his love poetry expresses his unusually acute feelings of being only precariously in the world. However playful and intellectualizing, it figures in a rather deep way his love concerns, his being attached to his own life in the body through an exchange of love with someone else. His mathematical and geometrical imagery does the same sort of work. The compasses in 'A Valediction: forbidding Mourning', at once divided and joined and engaged in figures of perfect love, manage to suggest a union of mind and body between the lovers, though, in absence, that is impossible and so very spiritual, unlike 'Dull sublunary lovers' love'. More carnally, the ideal of a disembodied pure love gives way in 'Love's Growth' to 'Gentle love deeds', a delightfully Chaucerian phrase, suggestive of freedom and bounty and breeding:

> Gentle love deeds, as blossoms on a bough,
> From love's awakened root do bud out now.
> If, as in water stirred more circles be
> Produced by one, love such additions take,
> Those like so many spheres, but one heaven make,
> For, they are all concentric unto thee.

(ll. 19–24)

71

Here the geometric analogy of the rings produced by one initial ripple stands through concentricity both for the perfection and therefore the spirituality of his love and for the physical impulses of 'love's awakened root', which are directed toward the woman while radiating from her. This is at once an ingenious solution to the metaphysical question of the one and the many, the ideal and the changing, and a joyfully exuberant figure for Donne's especial concern with bringing soul and body together. One is struck by the exact, analytic observation of the way many ripples start from one. Unlike Jonson's simile of the diffraction of appearances by water, Donne's analogy depends on an observation that is a thought as well as a perception. He has not just seen ripples but seen how they work. This is comparable to the description of waves making 'a rolling trench' in 'The Storm' or an observation in a letter to Sir Henry Goodyer that 'all shadows are of one colour, if you respect the body from which they are cast (for our shadows upon clay will be dirty, and in a garden green and flowery)'.[81] The observation is already an analysis ready to be used (and used, except in the case of the example from 'The Storm') for analysis of something else through analogy.

It is characteristic of much in Songs and Sonnets that the beautiful conceit in 'Love's Growth' is succeeded by a discordant one:

> And though each spring do add to love new heat,
> As princes do in times of action get
> New taxes, and remit them not in peace,
> No winter shall abate the spring's increase.

(ll. 25–28)

Perhaps this does not insinuate that love, like princes, is extortionate, but at least the crooked political analogy lowers the intensity that was generated in the preceding lines. Such lurches of mood are frequent. This brings up a last matter arising from 'Air and Angels': inconstancy. On one interpretation, 'Air and Angels', having argued its way to an ideal of mutuality in love, veers off in the last lines into a jibe at women's love being less pure than men's. There is a lot in Songs and Sonnets to support that interpretation. Even for someone writing in the age of Shakespeare, Donne's jibing at women and his suspicions of betrayal seem excessive. In 'A Valediction: of Weeping', amidst imagery of the exchange of selves (his tears in which his

---

81. Donne 1990, p. 190.

lover is reflected, which have become pregnant with her), he cannot keep himself from the sly jab that they are emblems of more grief: 'When a tear falls, that thou falls which it bore, / So thou and I are nothing then, when on a diverse shore'. That is, she will betray him as soon as he is abroad and the love world and love selves they make together will be annihilated. Even in 'The Good Morrow', perhaps the most triumphant of his celebrations of one-anothering, there is a shadow of a fear of betrayal:

> And now good morrow to our waking souls,
>> Which watch not one another out of fear;
> For love, all love of other sights controls,
>> And makes a little room, an everywhere.

(ll. 8–11)

At first this seems to describe a happiness in which the lovers are open to each other without self-protective anxieties and in which the rule of love makes a whole world of love for them. But more closely examined, the passage turns out to say something less heartening: the two need not keep a jealous eye on one another, for love will keep their affections from straying and supply them with all the world has to offer. Out of the corner of one's eye, one glimpses the grotesque, exploitative world of Jonsonian comedy and of some of Donne's poems, such as 'The Apparition' or 'A Tale of a Citizen and his Wife'.

But it is not just that poems that seem to stake themselves on the mutuality of love are shot with darts of suspicion. The sort of poetry that Donne is writing in Songs and Sonnets is extremely volatile. Their remarkable air of improvisation means that they capture the changeableness of the self at any instant. In their display of inconstancy and inconsequence, they share Montaigne's insight that the self is a being *'ondoyant et divers'* ('fluctuating and various').[82] In some moods we may prefer the declaration of a mind made up as in Shakespeare's sonnet 116, 'Let me not to the marriage of true minds admit impediments'. In others, there is no one like Donne for expressing the mercurial darting of how we think and feel. This may take the form of a sudden flounce as in 'Woman's Constancy', where having exclaimed against a lover's changeableness and the sleights by which she defends it, he ends,

---

82. 'Of Books', Montaigne 1962, p. 392; he is speaking of Seneca as an author but the phrase sums up his ideas of the self he describes in 'Of Repentance'.

Vain lunatique, against these 'scapes I could
Dispute, and conquer, if I would,
Which I abstain to do,
For by tomorrow, I may think so too.

(ll. 9–11)

And sometimes it may take the form of a genuine reflux of the mind or change of attitude as in his Elegy 'The Dream' ('Image of her whom I love'), where having begun by preferring the dream woman to the reality ('For, all our joys are but fantastical. / And so I 'scape the pain, for pain is true'), he ends by choosing the woman he knows in waking, even if that risks hurt ('Filled with her love, may I be rather grown / Mad with much heart, than idiot with none').

Religious verse

Apart from 'Satire III', which was written earlier, most of Donne's religious verse belongs to the years after his marriage before he became a church-man. Most of the Holy Sonnets[83] were probably written between 1609 and 1611 when, depressed about his prospects, often ill and engaged in courting the great and frequently unsavoury, Donne had every reason to be an-guished about his place in the world and the state of his soul. Less desperate but still clamouring for deliverance from the distraction of the world is 'Good Friday, 1613. Riding Westward'. To this period too belong the verse letters to great ladies and the 'Anniversaries' (1611 and 1612), poems in which he salutes certain women as pieces of heaven in a corrupt world. There are also the remarkable 'Obsequies to the Lord Harrington' (1614) and other funerary verses, characterized by the same anatomy of cor-ruption and idealizing and written to court Lucy, Countess of Bedford, by praising her friends or relations. Not all the religious poems of those years are written along the same gloomy world-rejecting lines. Two are exercises in religious wit. 'The Cross' (1604?) is a series of discoveries of the cross in unexpected places. The 'La Corona' sonnet sequence celebrates the para-doxes of Christ's life and death (1607?, 1608–9?). 'A Litany', though written

---

83. I adopt the usual title for these poems, though Smith, in Donne 1971, calls them 'Divine Meditations'.

on his sickbed (1608–9) and a prayer for deliverance, is so full of moral analysis of motive that it turns to the subject of how to live well, where issues of leaving the world and dying well would have been more expected and more in line with Donne's best known sickbed poetry, the 'Hymn to God my God, in my Sickness' and the 'Hymn to God the Father'. Once he entered the Church, Donne spent his literary energies chiefly on his sermons. But to those years belong the Hymns, the verse letter 'To Mr Tilman, after he had taken orders' (1619?) and at least two of the Holy Sonnets, the one on the death of his wife in 1617 ('Since she whom I loved') and the one on the true church ('Show me, dear Christ, thy spouse') of 1620.[84]

The Verse Epistles and Anniversaries

Along with 'Who makes the past, a pattern for next year', written to Sir Henry Goodyer, 'To Mr Tilman, after he had taken orders' is by far the most attractive of Donne's verse letters. The first is written by a man to his friend, the second by a divine to a colleague. In the first, Donne's concern for his friend is felt behind the firm, rather abrupt moralizing. In the second, Donne shares a religious enthusiasm for his calling. Its tone is socially warm and spiritually ardent:

> Or, as we paint angels with wings, because
> They bear God's message, and proclaim his laws,
> Since thou must do the like, and so must move,
> Art thou new feathered with celestial love?
> Dear, tell me where thy purchase lies, and show
> What thy advantage is above, below.
>
> (ll. 19–24)

This is the last of a series of questions expecting the answer 'yes' from Tilman about whether becoming a divine has not touched him with the divine. Donne is perhaps not so much addressing Tilman as glorying within himself at having found a way of being both in and out of the world. Still, he comes in this letter as close as he ever does to an easy epistolary style, a style capable of modulating from a Metaphysical conceit suggesting a mysterious life in things in

---

84. For the dating, see Gardner in Donne 1978, pp. 121–27.

> Dost thou find
> New thoughts and stirrings in thee? and as steel
> Touched with a loadstone, dost new motions feel?

> (ll. 6–8)

to shrewd worldly commentary on the world's contempt for the ministry (see above, p. 24). The poem ought to be more widely admired.

The 'Anniversaries' and verse letters he wrote to great ladies before he took orders lack this happy poise. Ben Jonson flattered great ladies almost as grossly and quite as designingly. But he does not make an unpleasant impression because he puts himself in the social position of a poet seeking a deserving and liberal patron. Donne as gentleman has no such fixed social role. He comes forward as worshipper and mystagogue. He is more than just Petrarchan lover in the style of Elizabeth's courtier poets. As devotee of a religious cult, he is reduced to the self-immolations and self-exaltings of one who declares himself to be nothing in comparison to the object of his adoration, everything as accepted by her. And it is not just that the cult that he makes of the lady is full of inappropriate intensities as well as hyperboles, but that the lady is not unique. The Countess of Bedford, the Countess of Huntingdon and the Countess of Salisbury all received similar worship, and still more extravagantly, Elizabeth Drury. Donne was embarrassed when his 'Anniversaries' about her were published because it showed his patronesses that another woman might stretch his verse as high. Writing to the Countess of Bedford in 1612 from France, where he was travelling at Elizabeth Drury's parents' expense, he attempts an elaborate apology for squandering on others the praises of which she is the true object, but soon finds that he cannot go on. Writing to the Countess of Salisbury in 1614, he explains that his earlier encomiastic verse was called forth by meaner objects, but that, since he had not yet made her acquaintance, he knew no better and what he said was true according to his lights at the time. Shufflings such as these show a willingness to grovel that was no doubt taken in tolerably good part by his patrons.

What if Donne had meant at least some of his adulation? That would show more serious servility than an extravagant playing of a game of expected insincerity in the hope of enjoying some aristocratic bounty, what Milton called 'the trencher fury of a rhyming parasite'. It seems impossible to clear Donne entirely of the charge of sincerity in the case of Lucy, Countess of Bedford, whom he called 'God's masterpiece'.[85] He seems to

---

85. 'To the Countess of Bedford' ('Madam, / Reason is our soul's left hand'), l. 33.

have been charmed by her high station and kindness to poets and fell for her, as men were allowed to fall for an aristocratic woman, as a creature of another sphere, except that Donne's extravagant expressions of admiration lifted the matter out of the usual terms of compliment. In one flight she is God:

> Reason is our soul's left hand, Faith her right,
> By these we reach divinity, that's you.[86]

On a lower flight, she is human but her body is made of almost incorruptible purity:

> This, as an amber drop enwraps a bee,
> Covering, discovers your quick soul; that we
> May in your through-shine front your heart's thoughts see.[87]

Touchingly, Donne is concerned for the fate of this transparent paragon in a corrupt world and repeatedly warns her that virtue is not enough at court. Discretion and even a kind of machiavellianism to good ends are repeatedly enjoined on her:

> [God] will make you speak truths, and credibly,
> And make you doubt, that others do not so;
> He will provide you keys, and locks to spy,
> And 'scape spies, to good ends, and he will show
> What you may acknowledge, what not know.[88]

Sir Henry Wotton, one recalls, recipient of an early verse letter on remaining uncontaminated by the world, had a spy's tool kit as part of his diplomatic equipment.[89] The best that can be said for Donne's letters to the Countess of Bedford is that while flattering her as a creature of unworldly perfection, he is recommending an infusion of worldly wisdom. But a worldliness so free from the world, without companionship, with no check other than the solitary conscience, is hard to distinguish from cynicism.

'Obsequies to the Lord Harrington' develops the theme of virtue in a corrupt world more sustainedly and yet with every appearance of

---

86. Ibid., ll. 1–2.
87. 'To the Countess of Bedford' ('Honour is so sublime perfection'), ll. 35–37.
88. 'To the Countess of Bedford' ('This twilight of two years'), ll. 51–55.
89. Walton 1927, 'Life of Sir Henry Wotton', p. 147, sidenote.

mercenary extravagance. Donne wrote this piece on her brother to gratify the Countess of Bedford, and she was so touched that she promised to pay off his debts. In the event, finding herself in financial difficulties, she came up with a mere thirty pounds. The praise lavished on her brother had not been stinted. Contemplating Harrington's soul at midnight, Donne falls into an ecstasy:

> All the world grows transparent, and I see
> Through all, both church and state, in seeing thee;
> And I discern by favour of this light,
> Myself, the hardest object of the sight.
>
> (ll. 27–30)

Harrington, however, is not God but a telescope to God: his human virtues bring God's perfection nearer to the eye. Countering this transport out of the world, runs a train of reflection about how virtues engage with the world. Harrington is a pattern of virtue; his death has robbed the world of virtue so 'that if a man would have / Good company, his entry is a grave' (ll. 165–66); nevertheless he has died too young to be a truly valuable example. His virtues are all infolded. He has mastered the passions within him and yet his virtues have not unfolded themselves in the course of a mature life in the sort of dealings with the world that concerned Donne himself. Donne makes a pretty show of reproach, in fact flattering Harrington by regretting he was unable to give the practical examples of virtue he was exceptionally fitted to give. Possibly under the show of such indirect praise Donne is avoiding sycophancy over someone whose Puritan politics he could not condone.[90] Above all, though, Donne is rehearsing a moral imagining, if not a moral thought (it is all very general), that mattered to him.

Although Donne's most celebrated poems are dramatic sketches, he could write excellent discursive poems, as 'Satire III: of Religion' shows. The discursive train of thought in the 'Obsequies' is not sustained at the same level of concentration as in the Satire, and, as with the 'Anniversaries' and Sermons, one goes to it rather for its magnificent set pieces than its overall exposition. Once these lapse, as they do after line 176, the poem flags. The set pieces after the description of the midnight trance (ll. 15–40) are analogical conceits. The following will serve as an illustration:

---

90. See Pebworth 1992, pp. 17–42.

As when an angel down from heaven doth fly,
Our quick thought cannot keep him company,
We cannot think, now he is at the sun,
Now through the moon, now he through th'air doth run,
Yet when he's come, we know he did repair
To all 'twixt heaven and earth, sun, moon, and air;
And as this angel in an instant knows,
And yet we know, this sudden knowledge grows
By quick amassing several forms of things,
Which he successively to order brings;
When they, whose slow-paced lame thoughts cannot go
So fast as he, think that he doth not so;
Just as a perfect reader doth not dwell,
On every syllable, nor stay to spell,
Yet without doubt, he doth distinctly see
And lay together every A and B;
So, in short-lived good men, is not understood
Each several virtue, but the compound good;
For, they all virtue's paths in that pace tread,
As angels go, and know, and as men read.

(ll. 81–100)

This double conceit analyses how in a short-lived good man virtue is comprised in an epitome rather than worked out in time in exemplary actions. First there is the analogy of angelic motion through the universe and angelic thought, which are so much quicker than human thought that 'they whose slow-paced lame thoughts cannot go / So fast as [an angel], think that he doth not so' (the hobbling measure of the first line catches the lameness of our thoughts in comparison with an angel's). Then riding on top of this is the analogy of the reader who grasps words, not spelled out but as wholes, almost instantaneously yet humanly. The compound conceit is much more elaborate than required by the idea it conveys, but it exalts the good man hyperbolically by making his human virtue almost spiritual and above all it rehearses Donne's concern with the condition of incorporated minds, his angelical leanings and his attempt to come to terms with human being in the world.

With that pasage, compare a rather similar set piece from 'The Second Anniversary':

But think that death hath now enfranchised thee,
. . .
And think this slow paced soul, which late did cleave

79

To a body, and went but by the body's leave,
Twenty, perchance, or thirty mile a day,
Dispatches in a minute all the way
'Twixt heaven, and earth: she stays not in the air,
To look what meteors there themselves prepare;   190
She carries no desire to know, nor sense,
Whether th'air's middle region be intense;
For th'element of fire, she doth not know,
Whether she passed by such a place or no;
She baits not at the moon nor cares to try
Whether in that new world, men live and die.
Venus retards her not, to inquire, how she
Can, (being one star) Hesper; and Vesper be;
He that charmed Argus' eyes, sweet Mercury,
Works not on her, who now is grown all eye;   200
Who, if she meet the body of the sun,
Goes through, not staying till his course be run;
Who finds in Mars his camp, no corps of guard;
Nor is by Jove, nor by his father barred;
But ere she can consider how she went,
At once is at, and through the firmament.
And as these stars were but so many beads
Strung on one string, speed undistinguished leads
Her through those spheres, as through the beads, a string,
Whose quick succession makes it still one thing: 210
As doth the pith, which, lest our bodies slack,
Strings fast the little bones of neck, and back;
So by the soul doth death string heaven and earth.

(ll. 179–213)

The spiritual movement here is away from the earth, not towards it, and the passage, typically of the 'Anniversaries', celebrates liberation from the human condition through death. Yet even in this apparently unqualified escape from a corrupt world, the life of the body makes a curious return. The passage of the soul is so swift through the heavenly bodies that it 'doth string heaven and earth' as the spinal cord strings the vertebrae and connects brain and body. While following the soul shooting forth from the discarded body, the mind still cleaves to the body from which it tries to launch itself in thought. It has no other frame.

The 'Anniversaries' are poems that reject the world, the First being an anatomy of the world's decay, the Second, a call to spurn this world in favour of the next. It is hardly surprising that, in this rejecting of the world and the body, the world and the body should survive as that which is denied, distorted, or mutilated to set the soul free. But vestigial or defaced survival is not really a sign that for Donne the union of body and spirit and being in the world were after all the main concern. The case is rather that the 'Anniversaries' stand out among Donne's poems by how little qualified the impulse is in them to part the body and the soul and leave the world. The incorporation of soul in body in the womb, the source of so much earlier fascination in Donne, is now the condition of a hermit, 'Which fixed to a pillar, or a grave doth sit / Bedded, and bathed in all his ordures' (ll. 170–71). The inconstancy of lovers, the source of so much pain and liveliness in the Songs and Sonnets, now becomes a disgusted vision of bodily decay:

> So flows her face, and thine eyes, neither now
> That saint, nor pilgrim, which your loving vow
> Concerned, remains; but whilst you think you be
> Constant, you'are hourly in inconstancy.

> (ll. 397–400)

Only in heaven will the soul attain true knowledge, freed of the errors attendant on the limitations of bodily senses; there 'Thou shalt not peep through lattices of eyes, / Nor hear through labyrinths of ears' (ll. 296–97). This captures the mind's impatience with the limits of the body. But the brilliant metaphorical disparagement of the physical in 'lattices' and 'labyrinths' is a crude thing compared to the feeling for embodiment in 'Metempsychosis', that earlier 'Progress of the Soul', or in 'The Ecstasy' or 'Air and Angels'.

In the midst of so much contempt for the body as the prison of the soul and itself in decay, Donne is nevertheless able to imagine an ideal material-izing in the person of Elizabeth Drury:

> from whom
> Did all things' verdure, and their lustre come,
> Whose composition was miraculous,
> Being all colour, all diaphanous,
> (For air, and fire but thick gross bodies were,
> And liveliest stones but drowsy, and pale to her).

> ('The First Anniversary', ll. 363–68)

Like the Countess of Bedford, Elizabeth Drury has a visionary body made of stuff so fine that the soul may inhabit it without enduring the corruption of the material world in its fallen state. Though not as pure as the soul itself, nevertheless her body is so pure that when she blushes 'one might almost say, her body thought' ('The Second Anniversary', l. 246).

Donne goes further than just transferring to a dead girl his imaginings of the union of body and soul. He makes her the pattern or informing principle of the world, the soul animating its matter. It was from her, for instance, that all the colours and the glow of the world took their rise. She was, as Empson puts it, the Logos through which the world was sustained.[91] Now she is dead, Donne has elaborate explanations of how the world keeps up a semblance of life, including the one in the passage we have already examined (pp. 29–30) about motion in corruption, where it makes convulsive movements like a beheaded man. What Donne thought he meant by this 'enormous and disgusting hyperbole' eludes me. His lame explanation that he described 'the idea [or ideal] of a woman' does not help; such a creature would be a monster, however ideal.[92]

Holy Sonnets and Hymns

Though 'full of blasphemies', as Ben Jonson said, the religious cult of Elizabeth Drury does not platonize in the sense of attempting a shamanistic flight out of the world up to an ideal celestial state of being while still on earth.[93] It is only through death that the soul strings heaven and earth. However unorthodox, the private religion of the 'Anniversaries' is on this point compatible with the Christianity of the Holy Sonnets, 'A Litany' and the Hymns.

In the Holy Sonnets, Donne writes in the dramatic mode of most of the Songs and Sonnets, not the discursive one of the Anniversaries and verse letters. Dramatizing is his way of making imaginatively vivid to himself his spiritual predicament and concentrating on the need for repentance before it is too late: 'What if this present were the world's last night?' Most of the sonnets are concerned with death and judgement, when 'my ever-waking part shall see that face, / Whose fear already shakes my every joint' ('This is my play's last scene', ll. 7–8). The sonnets not only express fear of judgement but try to work it up. Like the spiritual exercises of St Ignatius, the founder of the Jesuit order, they aim to harness imagination, emotion and thought to stimulate a devout frame of mind.[94] But we are frequently more

---

91. Empson 1993, p. 85; 1935, pp. 78–84.
92. 'Conversations with Drummond', Jonson 1975, p. 462.
93. 'Conversations with Drummond', Jonson 1975, p. 462.
94. See Martz 1962, esp. pp. 22–33, for a thorough attempt to relate Donne's religious poetry to Catholic meditational strategies of composition of place, premeditation, analysis and colloquy.

conscious of the straining than the devoutness; what strikes us is the desperateness of the attempt to bring home to himself what he must believe. In, for example, 'What if this present were the world's last night?', like a terrified Faustus, Donne tries to persuade himself of Christ's mercy; he does so by arguing that Christ's bloody and broken body is a 'beauteous form' and (as he 'said to all [his] profane mistresses') beauty is a sign that he will have him, whereas ugliness would be a sign he would reject him. The feebleness of the argument, let alone the strain of the analogy between Christ and his mistresses, displays Donne's helplessness to change his heart as he ought. As with the Songs and Sonnets, so with the Holy Sonnets, at least part of the interest lies in their dramatic gift for self-display of conflicting feeling, in Donne's giving himself away. Similarly the flimsy arguments in 'Death be not proud', where Donne triumphs over death in Christian assurance, tell us that Donne is terrified of death.[95] This is not how spiritual exercises are supposed to work, but the betrayal of desperation breathes life into what might have been merely a technique of religious arousal.

Other things come into play, as we can see from a brief examination of one of the best Holy Sonnets:

> Thou hast made me, and shall thy work decay?
> Repair me now, for now my end doth haste,
> I run to death, and death meets me as fast,
> And all my pleasures are like yesterday,
> I dare not move my dim eyes any way,
> Despair behind, and death before doth cast
> Such terror, and my feeble flesh doth waste
> By sin in it, which it towards hell doth weigh;
> Only thou art above, and when towards thee
> By thy leave I can look, I rise again;   10
> But our old foe so tempteth me,
> That not one hour I can myself sustain;
> Thy Grace may wing me to prevent his art,
> And thou like adamant draw mine iron heart.

As with 'Air and Angels', one is struck by the effortless way in which Donne manages his intricate form, including the Italian sonnet's demand for eight rhymes on two sounds in the octave. One notes also the telling enjambment over lines 6–7, which stresses 'Such terror', and the one over lines 9–10, which catches the straining to look upward. And as in 'Air and Angels', the ideas of air and angels, soul and body, are beautifully organized into a

---

95. See Carey 1990, pp. 33, 185.

pattern, so here the horizontal directions before and behind are complemented in the sestet by the vertical directions above and below, and the scheme in which Donne's hopeless position is plotted resolves itself in the final couplet: 'Thy Grace may wing me to prevent his art, / And thou like adamant draw mine iron heart'. The tone of the couplet is, however, unresolved between doubt and hope: God has the power to save but may not put it forth. This final statement comes with the force of a realization because of the way the thought is turned. Glancing back to the opening demand for rescue, it becomes a prayer, but a prayer now qualified with fear and very much lacking in assurance.

Unlike the Songs and Sonnets, the Holy Sonnets do not develop extended conceits. Intellectual exuberance and playfulness would be out of place in their gloomy circumstances. In 'Thou hast made me', everything is concentrated in the last simile. If Donne's heart is iron, God the magnet may still attract it; if he cannot turn of his own volition, God may work a miracle. This is a strikingly Lutheran or Calvinistic note, one frequently heard in the Holy Sonnets. Donne cannot do anything from himself, the source of nothing but crooked desires; only God can bring about a change. God must batter his heart, 'break, blow, burn', make new and finally rape him ('Batter my heart'). Donne cannot even repent by himself: God must 'teach [him] how to repent' ('At the round earth's imagined corners'). All he can do is to raise a cry for a power outside himself to take him over. In this despair of himself, the tone is consistently melancholy, sometimes violent and strained, sometimes, as in 'Thou hast made me', grave and subdued. The turns, such as the final couplet, do not play with ideas or attitudes. If they perform a somersault, it is an attempt at a somersault of faith, by which Donne tries to throw himself on a divine power outside himself. The patterning of verse form and ideas is all concentrated on that.

In the Songs and Sonnets, the world gave way to the private world of the lovers, rarely more than a room with a bed. Here in the Holy Sonnets, the outer world has sunk away and we are left with Donne alone with God and the devil, death and sin and the decay of his body. In this inner world, he may contemplate or summon religious pictures, such as Christ on his cross or the day of judgement. But the outer world in which he has to live a religious life is not present, except perhaps for his 'dim eyes': Donne suffered from eye trouble in his illnesses,[96] but this is brought in more as a sign

---

96. Bald 1970, p. 278, says that as far back as September 1613 Donne had eye trouble; he might have suffered earlier.

of the imminence of death than as something he has to cope with in life. And not only is Donne locked up in an inner world, the plight he imagines is very general, despair behind, death in front, God above, the devil below. These axes make his human condition a religious one, but they reduce its specificity. We know that sin weighs him down, but learn nothing about his sins apart from their being a general contamination.

The Hymns are equally inner-worldly and equally composed in the shadow of death. Even the 'Hymn to Christ, at the Author's Last Going into Germany', though written on the eve of the unhazardous crossing to Hamburg, is a *nunc dimitis*, a making away of all his earthly ties and affections:

> As the tree's sap doth seek the root below
> In winter, in my winter now I go,
> Where none but thee, th'eternal root
> Of true love I may know.

> (ll. 13–16)

'The Hymn to God my God, in my Sickness' and the 'Hymn to God the Father' were probably written during an illness of 1623, when Donne expected to die. But the tone of these poems, unlike the tone of the sonnets, is serene. Even the 'Hymn to God the Father', after expressing Donne's great fear as a lover that he is not loved as he loves, ends in assurance:

> I have a sin of fear, that when I have spun
> My last thread, I shall perish on the shore;
> But swear by thy self, that at thy death thy son
> Shall shine as he shines now, and heretofore;
> And, having done that, thou hast done,
> I fear no more.

The verbs in the last two lines are in the present or present perfect, not the conditional or future perfect. Donne has persuaded himself that indeed God has Donne.

The pun on his name strikes a note of sacred playfulness, which does not, however, disrupt the grave, spectral mood of the poem. For apart from that pun and the one on 'son' ('sun'), the figures of the poem are unusually unintellectual. The spinning of his thread, the shore, the shining of the sun, are mysterious and at the same time drawn from a common stock of imagery. In the 'Hymn to God my God, in my sickness' on the other hand, Donne writes in the highest of intellectual spirits:

85

> Whilst my physicians by their love are grown
>   Cosmographers, and I their map, who lie
> Flat on this bed, that by them may be shown
>   That this is my south-west discovery
> *Per fretum febris*, by these straits to die,
>
> I joy, that in these straits, I see my west;
>   For, though their currents yield return to none,
> What shall my west hurt me? As west and east
>   In all flat maps (and I am one) are one,
>   So death doth touch the resurrection.

(ll. 6–15)

His decaying body, in the Holy Sonnets the focus of his horror and fear, has now become a source of sacred riddling. The course of his disease, plotted by his doctors on the map of his body, becomes a voyage of discovery into an unknown ocean and there follows a splendid turn on the way that the far west (of death and the sun's going down) on a flat map is also the far east (of rising again). Along with the intellectual play, however, the figuration, as in the 'Hymn to God the Father', draws on a common stock (the ocean of death), which deepens and solemnizes the feeling, as does the Latin phrase speaking mysteriously in another language: *per fretum febris*. It is good to find Donne on the point of leaving the world (as he thought) in such fine form, both serious and joyful. He even manages to say a kind, if mocking, word about his doctors (not just one doctor at a fashionable sickbed).

Donne's style lends itself to religious verse; its extravagant expressions and all-or-nothing rhetoric belong also to the language of the Bible and Christian prayer. Its running to paradox goes well with a religion in which the spirit confounds the world and turns its values upside down. So, for example, the crucified criminal is at the same time the power that made and sustains the world: 'Could I behold those hands which span the poles, / And turn all spheres at once, pierced with those holes?' ('Good Friday, 1613. Riding Westward', ll. 21–23). Again in Christianity, the unseen spiritual world discovers parables expressing sacred truths in the material world, and to that purpose Donne's conceits are very apt, as in 'Good Friday, 1613. Riding Westward', where he makes of his riding westward a whole extended conceit for his being turned away from his soul's concern with Christ's crucifixion in the east by the distractions of worldly business. And finally Donne's persistent uneasiness with the world, expressed particularly in his theme of the soul's precarious union with the body, solidifies in the Christian framework of preparing for death and leaving the world.

At the same time, something is lost, as 'solidifies' will perhaps suggest. The play of mind, feeling and attitude is restricted. In the Holy Sonnets, he may express ambivalence but only as fear, not as flippancy or real doubt. 'Contraries meet in one', but that he must represent as sin. Even from a religious point of view, Donne's devotional verse is limited. Its intense inwardness means that we have Donne only as a spiritual man. How Donne the courtier, Donne the amusing companion, Donne the husband and father of an increasing family come in we do not learn, except where he puts some of these things behind him, as in his sonnet on the death of his wife. As with the love poems, so here a comparison with Ben Jonson seems apt. In 'To Heaven', Jonson begins with an outburst against scoffers: 'Good, and great God, can I not think of thee, / But it must, straight, my melancholy be?' His friends, he implies, are saying that his religious motions are brought on by a fit of depression. That social context immediately strengthens and deepens the prayer by making it the utterance of someone placed in the world, whose religion, in consequence, has to come to terms with his life outside his chamber. It also forces him to look within and question his motives. If his prayers arose from 'weariness of life, not love of [God]', they would be worthless. One looks in vain for that sort of self-examination in the Holy Sonnets and Hymns.

Not all of Donne's religious verse is self-dramatizing in the way of the Holy Sonnets, which, for all its intensity and brilliance, becomes monotonous. 'Satire III, of Religion' grapples with issues that lead outside the inturned world of sin and repentance. And 'A Litany', though a prayer and written on a sickbed, employs Donne's intelligence in acute moral analysis such as 'From thinking us all soul, neglecting thus / Our mutual duties, Lord deliver us' (ll. 143–44). That the prayer is the prayer of 'us', not of 'me', helps Donne to turn a critical eye on the religious life and on himself. Considerations such as this do not make 'A Litany' a first-rate poem, though it is certainly the work of an interesting mind; it is a pity that the critical attention to motive it displays in its second half makes so little appearance in his most celebrated and gripping religious verse.

The special character of Donne's inwardness, the simultaneous attraction to the world and estrangement from it, whether expressed in the libertine role playing of the Elegies, the oddly self-reflexive humour of the Satires, or the complexity of feeling about the incorporated mind in love or out of it in the Songs and Sonnets, finally takes a form at once conventional and magnificently bizarre in the religious verse. Out of this last configuration he made a celebrated career as a preacher. It was in that capacity that he wished to be remembered as a literary figure. With his sermons, he took care over publication in his lifetime. Gathering his energies within the framework of orthodox divinity, he was able to make a work of art of his end, not just in his farewell to the world, his sermon 'Death's Duel', but in the picture of himself he had drawn in his winding sheet, later made into an engraving and sculpted in his funerary bust, dead to the world but expecting incorporation in a better one.

John Donne in his winding sheet, from the frontispiece to *Deaths Duell*, 1632. Bodleian Library, University of Oxford.

George Herbert, from a drawing by Robert White (after an earlier painting). By permission of the Houghton Library, Harvard University.

CHAPTER TWO

George Herbert

Life

Izaak Walton's beguiling 'Life' of Herbert is one of a series of lives (the others are of Richard Hooker, Sir Henry Wotton, John Donne and Robert Sanderson) written during the Commonwealth and Restoration to furnish examples of a tradition of high church Anglican piety. His account of Herbert as an ambitious man who was brought round to finding his true vocation in the Church when his hopes of worldly preferment were disappointed is notoriously unreliable. But though misleading in many ways, Walton is right in outline. Herbert was ambitious, and if his spirituality did not spring from the disappointment of his designs, disappointment gave it its fine edge. Not all his frustration had its source in the failure of what Walton calls his 'Court hopes'. Illness and physical and nervous weakness unfitted him for a worldly career. But the thwarting of an eager, energetic and proud spirit from whatever cause is the stuff of those conflicts out of which he made much of his poetry.

George Herbert was born in 1593, the fifth son and seventh child of Richard and Magdalene Herbert. Both parents came of notable families of Welsh border gentry. He was, besides, fourth cousin of William and Philip, third and fourth Earls of Pembroke, both sons of Sir Philip Sidney's sister, Mary. Though he was not born in a castle as Walton would have it (Montgomery Castle had to be made fit for habitation by his brother, Sir Edward, later Lord Herbert of Cherbury), and though as fifth son he did not inherit land or position, still, unlike Donne, placed by his Catholic origins outside the world of power and influence that he chose to join, Herbert belonged, by the circumstances of his birth, to the ruling classes.[1]

---

1. Walton 1927, 'Life of Mr George Herbert', p. 260.

His father died when he was three, but his mother, Donne's friend and patron, saw to it that his education made the most of the advantages of his birth. She moved to Oxford and then London, where Herbert became a pupil at Westminster School, and from there he was admitted in 1609 to Trinity College, Cambridge, as King's Scholar. After taking his BA in 1613, he became a fellow of Trinity and over the years rose to various minor posts in Cambridge until, in 1620, he was made University Orator. He wrote to his step-father:

> The Orator's place . . . is the finest place in the University, though not
> the gainfullest . . . but the commodiousness is beyond the Revenue; for the
> Orator writes all the University Letters, makes all the Orations, be it to
> King, Prince, or whatever comes to the University; to requite these pains,
> he takes place next the Doctors, is at all their Assemblies and Meetings,
> and sits above the Proctors, is Regent or Non-regent at his pleasure, and
> such like Gaynesses, which will please a young man well.[2]

The post was an entry from the University to the world. His two immediate predecessors had gone on to become Secretaries of State.

As University Orator it was his job to flatter James, and he carried out this duty with a will. He may have had contact before with Francis Bacon, the Lord Chancellor, but it was during his spell as Orator that he wrote official letters to him and recommended himself sufficiently for Bacon to secure his assistance in the translation of *The Advancement of Learning* into Latin, this presumably before Bacon's fall in 1622.[3] It is only fair to add that on Bacon's death in 1626, when the University held back from officially celebrating a disgraced man, Herbert seems to have been active in getting together a volume of funerary verse. It may also be that he took a principled stand as Orator. In 1623, Prince Charles returned from Spain, where he had been attempting to win the Catholic Infanta as bride. The match fell through to the delight of the country, and Charles and the Duke of Buckingham pushed the failing James towards war and the confounding of a lifetime's policy of peacemaking. Herbert's oration on the Prince's visit to Cambridge shortly after his return contains a powerful outburst against war, which cannot have recommended him to those now in charge of affairs.[4]

Herbert then seems to have been ambitious to court the great, though not to the point of going against his loyalties or principles. Certain events

---

2. George Herbert 1941, Letter VII, pp. 369–70.
3. *De Augmentis Scientiae* came out in 1623. Herbert's Latin poem that praises Bacon's intellectual project is dated by Hutchinson (George Herbert 1941, p. 597), between January 1621 and May 1622.
4. George Herbert 1941, p. 601.

may have dashed his hopes. According to Walton, they came to an end with the deaths in 1624 and 1625 of those he looked to for support, Ludovick Stuart, Duke of Richmond, James, Marquis of Hamilton, and King James himself.[5] Perhaps also Herbert was disillusioned by what he saw of the workings of government while he sat as MP for Montgomery in the Parliament of 1624. The Crown through the Privy Council had squashed the Virginia Company, a colonial scheme, and the more than one hundred MPs who were also members of the Company were unable to raise the matter before James dissolved Parliament. Herbert's stepfather, Sir John Danvers, and Herbert's friend, Nicholas Ferrar, the future founder of the Little Gidding religious community, were active in the Company's affairs and in the attempts to prevent its suppression. Herbert himself had written in 'The Church Militant' of his hopes for the spread of Christianity in the New World. In his gloomy picture of the history of the Church, Christianity has always been overtaken by the corruption of the world as it advances westward. The only hope for true religion lies in its advancing edge. So, about to leave Europe, 'Religion stands on tip-toe in our land / Readie to passe to the *American* strand' (ll. 235–36).[6] The suppression of the Virginia Company would have made it hard for Herbert to imagine that 'Court hopes' could sit with that sort of missionary and colonialist idealism.[7]

In Walton's account, Herbert, like Donne, decided to enter the Church only on the collapse of his hopes of worldly advancement. There is certainly evidence in his poems that Herbert was ambitious. 'The Church Porch' has excellent advice on how to deal with one's superiors and get on. 'The Pearl' and 'Submission' speak of the thwarting of worldly designs by the demands of religion. And above all, 'Affliction' (I) complains that God has cheated him of his true life:

> Whereas my birth and spirit rather took
> The way that takes the town;
> Thou didst betray me to a lingring book,
> And wrap me in a gown.

> (ll. 37–40)

He feels he is better fitted by class and temperament to cut a figure in society, perhaps like his brother Edward, a courtier and soldier, who became a

---

5. Walton 1927, 'Life of Mr George Herbert', p. 276.
6. All citations of Herbert's poetry are from George Herbert 1941.
7. For the dating of 'The Church Militant', see Hutchinson (George Herbert 1941, p. 476), and Charles 1977, p. 82.

diplomat, than to spend his days in a university. The gown that wraps him, as Helen Vendler points out, carries suggestions of a shroud, and the striking transferred epithet 'lingring', with its suggestions perhaps of lingering disease, certainly of fretfulness about time passing, also speaks of the feeling that his life is wasting in study.[8] The gentleman of spirit in Herbert feels that academic life calls for 'simpring', and he is full of disgust at the unmanly deference and meekness to which he has been reduced.

But Walton improves on life and his version of how Herbert was brought to the Church in spite of himself is a case in point. He seems to suppose that when Herbert complains in 'Affliction' (I) that 'my friends die', he means the deaths of his supporters, the Duke of Richmond, the Marquis of Hamilton and James. It would follow that for him the poem dates from the mid 1620s and that Herbert was still at that time undecided between a religious and a secular career. But as Amy Charles has argued, the poem was probably written in 1617 at the point when he was about to enter on the study of divinity. He had been ill, two of his brothers ('friends' in an obsolete sense of the word) had just died, and already five of his six brothers 'had distinguished themselves in military exploits or otherwise met the demands of active life with physical courage'.[9] This would account for a desolate feeling at twenty-four that his way of life, though in the service of God, was futile.[10] 'Affliction' (I) would then speak less of Herbert's disappointment in at least half-formed secular ambitions, than of bitterness that ill-health forced on him a choice of life that thwarted his high spirit and sense of what it was to be a Herbert.

This does not mean that Herbert did not entertain worldly hopes while he pursued a course in divinity. Reading divinity did not necessarily end in ordination. Churchmen, besides, might serve the Crown, and even when he was ordained, Herbert may not have meant to end his life as a country parson. Probably disappointment and a sense of futility were recurring, a place of defeat and victory that he kept coming to, and some such recurrences might have occasioned 'The Pearl', 'Submission' and even 'The Collar'.[11] But at any rate instead of Walton's story of a sudden and forced renunciation of

---

8. Vendler 1975, p. 42.
9. Charles 1977, p. 86.
10. When Herbert says that he was 'without a fence or friend' (l. 35), he must be exaggerating his griefs in the manner of the Psalms. He was not without friends or family either in 1617 or even in 1627, when in addition to the deaths mentioned above, Bacon, Lancelot Andrewes and Magdalene Herbert had died.
11. 'Submission' and 'The Collar' were probably written later than 'Affliction' (I) since they appear in 'Tanner 307' but not in 'Jones B62' – that is, in the ms that contains revised versions of the poems that appear in the other, as well as additional poems (see below p. 100) and is therefore later – whereas 'Affliction' (I) appears in both the earlier and the later mss.

the world about 1625, we should probably think of a more drawn-out conflict complicated by Herbert's dissatisfaction with himself and the life he had to choose. Certainly the poems do not necessarily tell Walton's story.

Herbert was probably already ordained deacon in 1624, before the deaths of at least two of the men upon whom Walton thought Herbert's secular hopes depended (the Marquis of Hamilton and King James). He need not have already decided to enter the priesthood. His friend Nicholas Ferrar was ordained deacon though he intended not to take full orders.[12] Still, Herbert had at least entered on a course that would naturally lead to a career in the Church. After his ordination as deacon, however, six years elapsed before he was ordained priest. Ill-health may have been one cause of delay, diffidence of his calling perhaps another. In 1626, he was installed as canon at Lincoln Cathedral and as prebend of Leighton Ecclesia. As prebend he undertook to raise funds for the renovation of the church of Leighton Bromswold, a cause in which he enlisted the purses of his family and friends. Charles thinks 'The Crosse' records his frustrations in this task.[13] Neither of his posts required his residence (his preaching duties could be supplied by others for a fee), and he seems to have lived after his ordination as deacon at a succession of houses belonging to family and friends. In 1628, he moved to Dauntsey in Wiltshire to the house of the Earl of Danby, brother of his stepfather. There, Walton says, his health improved.[14] He married Jane Danvers, a cousin of his stepfather, in March 1629, and in 1630 was installed rector of Bemerton in Wiltshire and finally ordained priest able to administer the sacraments. But before three years were out, his health failed and he died in March 1633 not yet forty, of 'a Consumption' according to Walton.

We do not know what lay behind Herbert's accepting an obscure country living. The contrast with Donne, who saw to it that ordination would bring wealth and advancement and no stop to his London life, is striking. Poor health again may have entered into Herbert's decision and also the agreeable proximity of the Earl of Danby and the chance to visit Salisbury Cathedral twice a week and make music with friends. But what he made of his choice was a life of exemplary dedication to the vocation of country parson. *The Country Parson* is indeed the subtitle of his *A Priest to the Temple*, a book of practical advice, some of which must have been won from his experience as rector of Bemerton. It shows a will to apply himself to his duties as minister in a narrow sphere. One of the charms of the poems is their miniaturizing. Herbert may, for example, take a rose as a figure for

---

12. Maycock 1938, pp. 119–20.
13. Charles 1977, pp. 127–29.
14. Walton 1927, 'Life of Mr George Herbert', p. 285.

pleasure. *The Country Parson* shows the same habit of bringing his mind to bear on a limited thing. It also shows his love of order and of the set forms of the Church of England. Distinctly, he takes a gentleman's view from above, however unassuming. *The Country Parson* is a pastoral work in both senses. There may have been an element of Christian gallantry in his burying himself in a country charge, but at the same time Bemerton gave scope to his peculiar bent.

Two further questions arise about Herbert's life: his church politics and the dating of his poems.

The question about churchmanship that bears on Herbert's poetry is Arminianism.[15] This is first of all a theological matter. Arminians took issue with Calvinists over the question of predestination. A Calvinist believed that God had predestined everyone either to salvation or damnation, and that in these matters no human effort counted. An Arminian believed that while human efforts could not save, one could reject God's grace, which for a Calvinist was irresistible. Herbert's poetry is intensely occupied with the surrender of his human will to God's, and in poem after poem his own human efforts are shown to be self-deluding. He courts with all the resources of his wit the sense that God is working in him or that in confounding him God has mysteriously taken him over. On the face of it this looks like a Calvinist preoccupation with entire dependence on God. But does this concern really make Herbert a Calvinist rather than an Arminian?[16] Arminians, like Calvinists, believed that God was the source of all truly spiritual impulses. In a later period, Milton, a Puritan Arminian, shows his heroes Samson and Adam and Eve dependent on divine motions within them. God's working in them is necessary (though not sufficient) for them to move beyond their collapsed selves. On the specific issue of predestination Herbert's poetry is equivocal. 'The Watercourse' sounds at first as if everything lies in God's predestinating will, for he 'gives to man as he sees fit $\left\{\begin{array}{l}\text{Salvation}\\\text{Damnation}\end{array}\right\}$'. Yet it

---

15. On Arminianism, see Danielson 1982, pp. 58–91; also, Tyacke 1993, pp. 51–70, and with more theological refinement, Julian Davies 1992. See also Guibbory 1998, pp. 46–71, for Herbert's combination of Arminian and Puritan strains, and Clarke 1997, esp. pp. 182–89.
16. Summers 1954 puts the case forcibly for Herbert's Calvinism. But none of his evidence is cast-iron. Nor do I feel that the arguments, though backed up by much exact interpretation of poems, of those who have followed him here are irresistible, see e.g. Lewalski 1979, p. 286, and Strier 1983, though he makes Luther's doctrine of justification by faith the key to understanding Herbert's poetry rather than the specific formulations of Luther's follower, Calvin. This does not mean that they and commentators such as Fish 1972, pp. 156–223, and Nuttall 1980 and, in a less straightforward way, Harman 1982 are not right to point out that Herbert in *The Temple* tries to abolish himself in the face of God to put on a divine self.

might simply be that Herbert was thinking of God as sovereign judge of human lives at the Last Day. Again, though he says the human effort of repentance 'can purchase heaven' in 'Vanitie' and in this sounds Arminian,[17] the truth is that the Calvinist position was so paradoxical that good Calvinists might sometimes speak in the ordinary way as if one could do something for oneself with God. But it is not just that it is impossible to decide from the poetry whether Herbert was Calvinist or Arminian; an answer would not really bear on what is remarkable about his treatment of the self and God. His conflicts with himself and God pare him down to the quick. The demand for submission to God's will brings out in both his resistance and his acceptance a vivid sense of his life, his quickness. This is connected with what I should call, with hesitation, his gift for suffering – it is not meant cheaply. Settling the question of whether Herbert was Calvinist or Arminian would not unfold that central interest of his poetry. Raising the question can, at best, bring us roughly to where that central interest lies.

The question of Arminianism involves also matters of church order and parties within the Church. The Calvinist doctrine of predestination meant that a Calvinist's spiritual life was not accountable to any earthly institution. Only God could dispose to good or ill in matters of religion. An Arminian, who admitted the use of some human effort, might admit the use of human helps to the human will. Ceremony, music, the enlisting of the emotions in public worship might all dispose the believer to spiritual good. Arminians were in consequence in Herbert's time high churchmen, where Calvinists were usually Low Churchmen or Puritans. The stress on good order in *The Country Parson* as well as in Herbert's poems suggests high church leanings. He was a friend of Lancelot Andrewes, one of the leaders of high church or Arminian opinion in the Jacobean Church, and they certainly shared some ecclesiastical views. They shared, for instance, a belief, as anti-Puritan as it was anti-Catholic, that the English Church should be a *via media* between a grotesquely ornamental Rome and an indecently naked Geneva.[18] Herbert's idea of the Eucharist (again anti-Puritan in tendency), not just as communion in the spirit but also as a physical cordial that helped to prepare and subdue the body for the operation of the spirit, has much in common with Andrewes' views and with his stress on the efficacy of ritual in the life of the Church.[19] And the same anti-Puritan tendency is to be seen in Herbert's love of church music, insistence on kneeling in time of prayer and care for the physical fabric of churches. But the poetry that Herbert makes of the Church

---

17. But see Strier 1979.
18. See 'The British Church'. In this belief, Andrewes was self-consciously the disciple of Hooker.
19. See 'The Banquet' and for Andrewes, Lake 1991, pp. 125–29; see also Ellrodt 1960, I, pp. 324ff.

and its sacred stories always spiritualizes. When, for example, he calls to mind the crucifixion in 'The Agonie', his concluding couplet does not dwell so much on the image of Christ on the cross as on a theological meaning to it:

> Love is that liquor sweet and most divine,
> Which my God feels as bloude; but I, as wine.

Even the unobtrusively astonishing word 'feels' is charged with thought as well as feeling. Crashaw, on the other hand, a member of the extreme high church party in the 1630s, sensualizes when he dwells on the wounds of Christ:

> O these wakefull wounds of thine!
> Are they Mouthes? or are they eyes?

('On the Wounds of Our Lord')

The sensuality is strange and disturbing, and it is that that fills the mind to arouse devotional feeling. If Herbert was Calvinist, his Calvinism had a strong infusion of the beauty of holiness called for by the high church party. If he was an Arminian, his poetry never materializes the fabric, ceremonies or mysteries of the Church but always plays between figure and idea in such a way as to focus on how the divine works on the human. He fits into stereotypical pictures of neither side, and when divisions of the Church hardened after his death, he might be taken up by either Laudians such as Walton and Joseph Beaumont or Puritans such as Richard Baxter and Robert Leighton.[20]

When Herbert wrote, these divisions were not clearly drawn. The Jacobean Church was theologically without distinct leadership. Andrewes never led a politically effective high church party. And while James in his last years encouraged some anti-Calvinist measures, such as the articles forbidding the discussion of predestination in sermons by anyone less than a dean or university doctor, either his wisdom or his slackness prevented matters from coming to a head. All that was changed with the accession of Charles I. William Laud, a zealous proponent of high church views, gained the ear

---

20. Richard Baxter's views on predestination, however, distinctly seem to have been modified in an Arminian direction (see Keeble 1982, p. 72); Robert Leighton, at the time of writing his *Commentary on Peter*, was still some sort of Covenanter and certainly Calvinistic enough for Coleridge to praise him in *Aids to Reflection* for maintaining unmerited grace in the face of what he calls the Erasmian Grotian tendency of English theology in the seventeenth and (far more) eighteenth centuries. Edward Taylor, the poet and New England divine, is another example of a Puritan deeply impressed by Herbert. Compare, in any case, Herbert's attack on inappropriate theological precision in 'Divinitie' with Donne's position in 'Satire III, of Religion'.

of the King, who began to make church appointments and enforce church discipline of a distinctly Arminian and anti-Calvinist sort. Laud did not become Primate till 1633, after Herbert's death, but from 1628, when he was made Bishop of London, and earlier, he was a power in the land. The Parliamentary opposition had no doubt where the new men and the new measures were tending. By the Three Resolutions of March 1629, the last Parliament before Charles resorted to Personal Rule linked Arminianism with Popery and denounced it along with other innovations as a threat to English liberty. This certainly points to fears about the direction of Church policy that would later drive Parliament to the execution of Laud and war against the King. But in spite of the Three Resolutions, differences in the Church had not been pressed in Herbert's time to the point where he might feel required to take a stand.

Walton tries to make Herbert into a Laudian, but even Herbert's connections as a churchman do not support that story. Herbert was appointed deacon at Lincoln by Bishop Williams, an opponent of Laud. And he owed his rectorship at Bemerton to the patronage of the third and fourth Earls of Pembroke, who were no friends either to the Duke of Buckingham, Laud's patron, or to Laud himself. As for his friendship with Nicholas Ferrar, it was only after Herbert's death that Laud recognized that Little Gidding might be drawn into an Anglo-Catholic design.[21] But if there are no grounds for thinking that Laud found Herbert a congenial spirit and encouraged his career, neither are there sufficient grounds for arguing that Herbert belonged to an anti-court, anti-Laudian movement in the Church of England.

In short, is not possible to reduce Herbert's religion to an expression of a moment or movement in the English Church. This is partly because the evidence is inconclusive and conflicting but also partly because until after Herbert's death, the work of Charles and Laud had not gone so far as to force conformity or nonconformity to a Laudian policy. Although Herbert's spirituality is of a severe, high-flying cast, more characteristic of Charles's reign than of his father's, its inwardness, unlike say Crashaw's, is not clearly shaped by political party.[22]

As for the dating of Herbert's poems, here also few definite conclusions can be reached. *The Temple* was published in 1633 from a manuscript committed by Herbert on his deathbed to Nicholas Ferrar with the instruction that the poems should be published only if he thought they might '*turn to the advantage of any dejected poor Soul*'.[23] Until this posthumous publication, Herbert had not been known as a poet in English. Two sonnets written to his mother as a New Year's present in 1609, when he was still sixteen, survive in the

---

21. On Ferrar and Laud, see Hodgkins 1993, p. 157.
22. See Peter White 1993 for the background to Herbert's churchmanship.
23. Walton 1927, 'Life of Mr George Herbert', p. 314.

letter to her preserved in Walton's life. They show that he was already an accomplished poet and already scornful of poetry written to women, not to God. If he ever wrote secular love poems, they have not survived.

The Temple must have been some time in the making, if only because MS Tanner 307, which was the copy used for the 1633 printing, revises poems that appear in the only other surviving manuscript (Jones B 62). Some poems have been deleted and many added. It is supposed that the additional poems in Tanner 307 were written later, though there could be other explanations and it is not easy to see any change of direction or of art in the supposed new poems. Even if the additional poems were written later, it remains undetermined when they were written. It is often assumed that Herbert wrote many of his poems at Bemerton, but, as Charles points out, his duties as rector would have taken up most of his time; more likely he composed the bulk of them during his residence at Dauntsey, before he was ordained.[24] Specifically, she suggests that 'The Priesthood' was written at Dauntsey in a mood of diffidence about ordination. At the other end of his career, she suggests that 'Affliction' (I) may have been written in 1617.[25] Otherwise it is difficult to attach poems in 'The Church' very definitely to the known events of Herbert's life. As for 'The Church Porch', Charles, noting correspondences with a letter of advice written in 1614 to his brother, Henry, on how to conduct himself, thinks that parts of the poem may have been written about the same time,[26] but a good deal of it is surely the work of a maturer moralist. 'The Church Militant' seems to be early work. The favourable comments on Spain, despite the overall hostility to Rome, might indicate that the poem was written before the failure of the Spanish match. The possible traces of the evangelizing plans of the Virginia Company would imply that it was written before the Company was deprived of its patent in 1624.[27]

The plan of *The Temple*

Omitting the printer's note and the dedication, *The Temple* is divided into three parts. The first consists of a long poem of moral advice on how to live a good life as a Christian gentleman ('The Church Porch'), followed by a short one inviting the reader to enter the second part, 'The Church'. Although

---

24. Summers 1954, p. 35, supposes that he 'revised many of his earlier poems and composed over half' of his poems at Bemerton; Charles 1977, p. 138.
25. Charles 1977, pp. 140–41.
26. Charles 1977, p. 78.
27. Hutchinson in George Herbert 1941, p. 543.

the 162 poems in this, the longest and most interesting section, include a long monologue by Christ on the cross ('The Sacrifice') and a long reflection on the chain of being ('Providence'), the majority of the poems treat the intercourse between God and the Christian believer. The third section consists of a long apocalyptic history of the Church ('The Church Militant') and an envoi. The first section of *The Temple* treats the moral life of a Christian living in the world, the second his spiritual life, and the third the history of the religious society of which he is a member up to the Day of Judgement.

The difficulty of the design lies in the arrangement of the poems in 'The Church'. It is to this part that Herbert's description of *The Temple* in Walton's account would apply: '*a picture of the many spiritual Conflicts that have past betwixt God and my Soul, before I could subject mine to the will of* Jesus my Master'.[28] This does not mean that the poems make up a spiritual autobiography. Only 'Affliction' (I) could be called an autobiographical poem. The other poems picture spiritual conflict in other modes such as psalms *de profundis* or colloquies with God in suffering or prayers or allegorical narratives. And some are impersonal musings, self-counsellings, hymns of praise, or fancies. Nevertheless there is a master theme running through 'The Church': Herbert's difficulty in bringing himself into accord with the divine. The poems in this section in all their variety of form and also of feeling, now anguished, now joyful, now blending these feelings, carry on a troubled conversation with God, or with himself about his conversation with God. They begin with poems on Christ's sacrifice and on accepting that sacrifice, whether by allowing his heart to be made an altar for it or by recollecting baptism, the sacrament that is the original figurative making over of the believer to the terms of Christ's sacrifice. For Herbert, the divine sacrifice is the point of entry into a spiritual life. After 'H. Baptisme' (I) and (II), the plan becomes less obvious. Herbert took care over the arranging of his poems; the later manuscript not only adds and deletes but changes the order of poems in the earlier one. He avoids obvious groupings such as placing all the Affliction poems together. Rather he seems to have put together a likeness of the vicissitudes of the inner life, the unpredictable and self-dispossessing succession of despair, inkling, joy, assurance, doubt, 'fallings from us, vanishings', that for him must have made up the many-stranded twist of experience that drew him to God. If there are 'constellations of [his] storie', it is because, as he said of the Bible, 'This verse marks that, and both do make a motion / Unto a third, that ten leaves off doth lie' ('The H. Scriptures' II). 'The Church' ends appropriately with last things, 'Death', 'Dooms-day', 'Judgement', and, in 'Love' (III), an anticipation of feasting in heaven. These last poems are deeply meditated

---

28.   Walton 1927, 'Life of Mr George Herbert', p. 314.

lookings forward to future events from the point of view of someone who in the middle of his life is trying to bring the life of his spirit to mind. Even 'Love' (III), which unlike the others is written in the narrative past, as if the future were already accomplished fact, still imagines his final acceptance in heaven of Christ's sacrifice in terms of his earthly trouble with it. He goes over in an unearthly mode the struggle for mastery between himself and God in order to bring his acceptance home to himself now on earth.

The medley of poems that make up 'The Church' does not display a mercurial temperament or a brilliantly inconsistent and fragmentary experience of things as Donne's Songs and Sonnets does. It displays, rather, the mixed experience of the inner life that makes the believer ready to die and weans him from earth and himself to heaven and God. In that way it is exemplary. It is not that Herbert presents himself as an adept, but rather that he goes through a representative experience of Christian life with unusual wit and intensity of spirit. He has various methods of generalizing his experience, such as allegorizing or casting it into biblical types; one method that concerns us here where we are still considering the plan of the book is his titles. Most, such as 'Affliction', 'Confession', 'H. Scriptures' and so on, are general topics of Christian interest, the sort of thing one might find in an index. Unlike Donne's 'Good Friday, 1613. Riding Westward' or 'A Hymn Made at the Author's Last Going into Germany', Herbert's titles point away from personal experience to the commonplaces of Christian life.[29] Besides, the title, 'The Church', for a collection of poems about the spiritual life, directs the reader to think of the experience they treat as a general one: such, it seems to say, is the devotional interior one enters as a Christian and therefore a member of the Church. This generalizing of Herbert's experience does not stop 'The Church' from expressing a strong individuality, and not just in manner, sensibility or ruling themes, but as an interest in himself. But his interest in himself comes out typically in the process of self-correction or self-effacement, of giving himself to the universal turns of a Christian life.

Interiority is imposed on Herbert by the subject of 'The Church': the devotional life. More specifically, Herbert's interiority turns on his trouble with the self-cancelling demands made by his religion. He is too honest or too rooted in the world for that to be easy. He cannot evaporate into the divine like Crashaw, or Vaughan, or Traherne. And unlike Donne, he was not born into alienation from the world. For Herbert the spiritual life consorts with suffering: at worst he is 'a wonder tortured in the space / Betwixt this world and that of grace' ('Affliction' [IV]); at best he is surprised by joy, but almost always as in 'Church-Musick' or 'The Flower' as temporary remission

---

29. See Ferry 1993.

from pain or grief. Oddly, Herbert's verse, whose entire scope is bounded by religion and whose dominant note is grief, gives as much pleasure as any Metaphysical's, as much perhaps as Donne's.

Johnson on devotional poetry

Let no pious ear be offended if I advance, in opposition to many authorities, that poetical devotion cannot often please . . . Of sentiments purely religious, it will be found that the most simple expression is the most sublime. Poetry loses its lustre and its power, because it is applied to the decoration of something more excellent than itself. All that pious verse can do is to help the memory, and delight the ear, and for these purposes it may be very useful; but it supplies nothing to the mind. The ideas of Christian Theology are too simple for eloquence, too sacred for fiction, and too majestick for ornament; to recommend them by tropes and figures, is to magnify by a concave mirror the sidereal hemisphere.[30]

It is curious that Waller, not Herbert (or Donne, or Crashaw, for that matter), should be the occasion for so sweeping a pronouncement on devotional poetry. But Herbert would not have occasioned a different judgement. Johnson asked for a certain philosophical generality of approach. What pleases in Herbert is a surprising particularity in the turning of his thoughts, which makes the subject his and so ours. This would not have pleased Johnson since it would have afforded only another instance of how the Metaphysicals 'broke every image into fragments'.[31]

In 'Affliction' (IV), for example, Herbert broaches no new theological idea. God's withdrawal from those he loves and his anger towards them are familiar topics from the Psalms, and complaint to God is a familiar way of coping with suffering. Both idea and type of utterance are conventional. But the utterance itself is extraordinary:

> My thoughts are all a case of knives,
>   Wounding my heart
>   With scatter'd smart,
> As watring pots give flowers their lives.
>   Nothing their furie can controll,
>   While they do wound and pink my soul.

(ll. 7–12)

---

30. Johnson 1952, I, pp. 202–4.
31. Johnson 1952, I, p. 15.

No one was better fitted to understand religious melancholia than Johnson, but his critical principles would have had it that the novelty of the expression here has trivialized the subject and emptied it of the grandeur of human generality. But clearly the low and cruel metaphor of the case of knives catches exactly the way one's thoughts turn on one in distress. It impressed Philip Larkin enough for him to borrow it for the thoughts of a raped woman in the 'The Less Deceived'. Herbert goes on to compare the heart stabbed by its thoughts to plants prickled by jets of water from watering-cans and perhaps at the same instant, with the inconsistency of thought pictures, to a watering-can itself as, punctured by knives, it sprinkles blood.[32] The incongruity and inconsequence of the simile goes with the splintered state of mind Herbert is describing. At the same time with dream vividness it expresses a wild, momentary grasping at a way of turning or transcending his suffering; his wounding will somehow make him live spiritually. The 'watring pots' are a transformation figure, tucked away like the thorn in 'The Collar'. 'Have I no harvest but a thorn?' (l. 7), the speaker asks there in anger, thinking of the sterility of his life, and a religious answer is buried in the question: his grief might be made a way of sharing Christ's crown of thorns. The language of Christianity is made up of such transformative or transvaluing figures that turn grief to joy and Herbert makes liberal use of them. But his watering-cans do not belong to the Christian repertoire. Like his case of knives, they seem to have been immediately struck out of an experience at once psychological and physical, out of his body-soul, with considerable violence. The pleasure (and it is pleasure) that one takes in this sort of poetry has partly to do with exactness. Though Herbert is writing in the hyperbolical manner of Christian affliction, he is writing truthfully about what his suffering feels like. He does so by particularizing the feelings of fragmentation and of the uncontrollable and furious going on of his wounding thoughts. That is a source of intellectual pleasure; we recognize that what he is saying is so. But we also take an aesthetic pleasure in the exactness and tautness of Herbert's art. His figures are not vast and illimitable but small and definite: a case of knives, even if possessed with displaced malevolence, and 'watring pots'. When Donne compares lovers to a pair of compasses, its

---

32. Watering cans with roses are pictured from the early seventeenth century in emblems, e.g. van Veen 1608, pp. 78–79 and Emblem LXI, 'Nil Tamen Haeret', in Zincgref 1619. More primitive pots pierced with holes for sprinkling were in use from the fifteenth century (see Palliser 1870, p. 188), as the device of Valentine, Duchess of Orleans, illustrates. A remarkable example in Pona 1645, p. 57, shows one such shaped like a heart with the explanation in prose that the flowers of the spirit are irrigated by the tears of the heart. I owe this information to Dr Brent Elliott of the Library of the Royal Horticultural Society and Dr Michael Bath of the University of Strathclyde. The emblems I have seen persuade me that Herbert was not working from an emblematic repertoire in this case.

circles expand to suggest a field of spiritual force uniting distant lovers. Even Donne's flea grows large enough to be the lovers' marriage temple. But Herbert's case of knives contracts, rather than expands, his pain. It is an example of his miniaturizing. If Johnson had complained about how Herbert's figures rendered large ideas in small things, he would have been missing the energy and vividness Herbert gains by compression.

Herbert on devotional poetry

Some of the ideas that Herbert expresses on poetry and devotion are surprisingly close to Johnson's view that, where it treats religion, the art of poetry is at best inessential, at worst a distraction. 'Jordan' (II), 'The Forerunners' and 'A true Hymne' in different ways say that the essential thing about devotional expression is its heartfelt utterance. The first two of these banish or renounce poetry and in doing so betray Herbert's own gift for it. It is only in the third that Herbert manages both one of his finest expressions of religious love and a miracle of art without the one betraying the other.

In 'The Forerunners', Herbert, noticing grey hairs on his head, addresses the lively wit and fancy that had enabled him to turn poetry from the 'stews and brothels' of human love to its true object, 'true beautie', which 'dwells on high':

> take your way:
> For, *Thou art still my God*, is all that ye
> Perhaps with more embellishment can say.
> Go birds of spring: let winter have his fee;
> Let a bleak palenesse chalk the doore,
> So all within be livelier then before.

> (ll. 31–36)

There is something wrong with both Herbert's turning from human love as the theme of poetry and his resignation to losing his power to write devotional poetry. His severity with both is mistaken. He dismisses love poetry: 'Let foolish lovers, if they will love dung, / With canvas, not with arras, clothe their shame'. This is still the zeal of the boy who wrote in 'Sonnet' 2, sent to his mother,

> Open the bones, and you shall nothing find
> In the best *face* but *filth*, when, Lord, in thee
> The *beauty* lies, in the *discovery*.

Herbert is repudiating the body and earthly love with an asceticism that he could not maintain in life (at least one hopes not) since he took a wife.[33] His account in 'The Forerunners' of how he baptized the language of erotic poetry in the tears of Christian repentance equally misrepresents him. His phrases for the poetic charms he took over for religion, 'Lovely enchanting language, sugar-cane, / Hony of roses', simply do not describe the language of his baptized love poetry accurately. It is true that Herbert's sensuality was drawn to sweetness, and among sweet things he found particular solace in sweet smells. 'Sweet' is a word that he works very hard. The sweetness of his language, however, is not the sweetness of the love sonneteers but a sweetness that goes with cleanness of phrase, neatness and the release of a surprising flavour in plain and quiet speech. In the last line of 'Prayer' (I), 'The land of spices; something understood', the first phrase for prayer might, unusually for Herbert, just qualify as 'sugar-cane, / Hony of roses'. But it is the pregnantly understated second phrase that is the truly Herbertian enchantment, and it cannot be worked up into a contrast with the wintry essentialness of '*Thou art still my God*', as the sweetly ornamental 'hony of roses' can. What Herbert is resigning himself to lose with age in 'The Forerunners' is not the real triumph of his art – the subtle simplicity of something understood. He has applied severe, but conventional, distinctions between divine and earthly love, between heartfelt simplicity and ornamental eloquence, that do not fit his case.

The same sort of misplaced self-correction and confused renunciation take place in 'Jordan' (II). I assume the poetry he is criticizing is his early work, which he did not admit to *The Temple*, where many of the poems are delightfully bizarre and inventive, but none is extravagant enough to answer the description he gives in stanza 1:

> When first my lines of heav'nly joyes made mention,
> Such was their lustre, they did so excell,
> That I sought out quaint words, and trim invention;
> My thoughts began to burnish, sprout, and swell,
> Curling with metaphors a plain intention,
> Decking the sense, as if it were to sell.[34]

Yet if he is mocking early work, what he mocks as vain elaboration must have been involved with his mature creative pleasure in words: 'I often

---

33. *The Country Parson*, ch. IX (George Herbert 1941, p. 231), probably written after his marriage, observes that celibacy is best for the clergy.
34. He is imitating Sidney's 'Astrophil and Stella', I and VI, and perhaps fitting the story of his life as a poet into a conventional view of the poet as one tempted by ornament and fiction rather than speaking the truth. It is this conventional view that seems to me unapt.

blotted what I had begunne; / This was not quick enough, and that was dead'. Like 'sweet', 'quick' is a hard-worked word in *The Temple* and one that is associated with his idea of himself as sharp, witty, vivid, sensitive, 'quick' then in both senses. And there is nothing absurd about blotting one's lines, in selecting the live and nimble phrase and pruning the dead ones.

The same misdirected animus comes out in stanza 3, where he condemns his vanity in writing poetry, his self-interested designing, in such a way as to throw out at the same time his concentration of himself in his matter through his way with words:

> As flames do work and winde, when they ascend,
> So did I weave myself into the sense.
> But while I bustled, I might heare a friend
> Whisper, *How wide is all this long pretence!*

Winding or twisting is an important motif in Herbert. As in *Paradise Lost*, the motif may tend to good or evil. On the one hand, winding may suggest vain contrivance as in the 'winding stair' of 'Jordan' (I) or the 'curling with metaphors' that he is scornful about in 'Jordan' (II). More sinisterly, perhaps prompted by the rheumatic pains from which he suffered, 'sorrow did twist and grow' in him like a tree ('Affliction' I), 'No scrue, no piercer can / Into a piece of timber work and winde, / As Gods afflictions into man' ('Confession'), and sin, 'working and winding' like the roots of a sycamore, prises open the joints of the world's masonry ('The World'). But winding and twisting are also the motion of divinely inspired joy and also of the divine working in the world in intricate, oblique and elusive ways. Herbert, the viol player, would not be insensible to the complex braiding of the church music he loved. As a lutanist in 'Easter' his fashion of adoration is that there should 'Consort both heart and lute, and twist a song'. Similar happy convolutions come into 'The Starre', where he wishes to become a beam of Christ's heavenly countenance,

> That so among the rest I may
> Glitter, and curle, and winde as they:
> That winding is their fashion
> Of adoration.

God takes the winding path, and not just when, as in 'Confession', he 'a torture hath design'd'. In 'Providence', winding motion suggests the complex and hidden way he runs things:

> How finely dost thou times and seasons spin,
> And make a twist checker'd with night and day!
> Which as it lengthens windes, and windes us in,
> As bouls go on, but turning all the way.

(ll. 57–60)

In 'The Pearl', after three stanzas marvellously appreciative in renunciation of the ins and outs and complications of knowledge, glory and pleasure, Herbert turns to the divine twisting thread that has led him out of these mazes:

> Yet through these labyrinths, not my grovelling wit,
> But thy silk twist let down from heav'n to me,
> Did both conduct and teach me, how by it
> To climbe to thee.

Winding or twisting, spinning or weaving, may take a good or a bad turn, but the weaving of himself into the sense 'As flames do work and winde, when they ascend' in 'Jordan' (II) sounds as if it ought to be good and draws imaginatively on Herbert's feeling for both the spiralling upward of adoration and the way God makes the world go round. It is only by a sort of trick that 'So did I weave myself into the sense' does not mean that in writing Herbert brought himself to a sort of impersonality that at the same time involved him wholly in saying 'what one should say', but means instead that all his efforts only succeeded in making himself the object of devotion, the cardinal sin of Augustinian and Protestant theology, as if like a weaver he had intended to damask a figure of Christ but somehow it turned out to be an image of himself. Here Herbert has confused vain elaboration with his own creativity as a religious poet. He was, no doubt, led into this confusion by a high and severe ideal of true devotion, like Johnson's, and notions of sacrifice and religious renunciation must have played their part too. The whisper of the friend in the last lines, *'There is in love a sweetnesse readie penn'd: / Copie out onely that, and save expense'*, reproaches him in love and conscience with the sweetness of God's love, sweetness implying to someone with Herbert's appetite for sweet things, irresistibleness and strength, but also simplicity and directness, qualities associated with God's sweetness in accommodating himself to human weakness. But Herbert is moved to sacrifice too much: weaving himself into the sense was a way in which he could genuinely attain the strong sweetness enjoined on him by his mysterious friend. It is all very well to pluck out your eye if it offends you, but not the wrong one.

I do not think that, far from being mistakenly ascetic, Herbert is in fact being subtly severe. If he meant that not just his immature writing, but his best, slyly aggrandized himself, even in divesting himself of himself, then 'Jordan' (II) would fall under its own condemnation. In condemning itself, the poem would render itself self-referentially incoherent, and in abolishing his best efforts Herbert would leave himself nothing as poet except an empty or unattainably pure ideal of copying love. Herbert is not a subtly intro-spective poet in the manner of the Eliot of 'Ash Wednesday', whose art is a turning on turning on himself. He is, rather, in a muddle, the sort of muddle that a great gift for religion as well as for poetry might easily fall into.[35]

Herbert speaks more accurately about the relation of his poetry to his devotion where it is untroubled. 'The Flower' describes his 'quickning' when God returns after a period of desertion or anger: 'I once more smell the dew and rain, / And relish versing'. Versing goes with the revival of his sense of smell, the most lively of his senses, here keenly taking in the smell of rain, something less conventionally delightful than flowers or spices. There may be a musical reference in 'relish'. A relish was a grace note or trill.[36] To 'relish versing', then, may imply not just enjoyment but a winding and curling one. At any rate it is clear that for Herbert making verse, his craftsmanship, his feeling for words, went with a pleasurable sense of his life. In writing he was in touch with himself and also in touch with God. A verse, he says in 'The Quidditie', 'is not a crown',

> It is no office, art, or news,
> Nor the Exchange, or busie Hall;
> But it is that which while I use
> I am with thee, and *most take all.*

'*Most take all*' is the winning trick at cards. When he makes verses, the world is well lost; it is a way of being with God.

But it is in 'A true Hymne' that Herbert works out best how he might be at once with himself and with God in making verse:

---

35. Tuve 1952, pp. 188–90, 93, maintains that 'Jordan' (II) is directed against his early sonnets to his mother. These might perhaps be blamed for embellishing a plain intention and they both mention flames, though not working and winding ones. They speak, however, about writing about the beauty of God instead of a profane object of love and so cannot be said to be the adoration itself that is implied by 'Nothing could seem too rich to clothe the sunne'. Besides if Herbert heard his 'friend' remonstrate, why did he not reject his poems instead of sending them to his mother? See also Fish 1972, pp. 193–202; Strier 1983.

36. When Herbert writes in 'The Pearl' of his knowledge of pleasure, 'the sweet strains, / The lullings and the relishes of it', he is consistently using the language of music to unfold sensual complications (Summers 1954, pp. 158–59).

My joy, my life, my crown!
My heart was meaning all the day,
Somewhat it fain would say:
And still it runneth mutt'ring up and down
With onely this, *My joy, my life, my crown.*

Yet slight not these few words:
If truly said, they may take part
Among the best in art.
The finenesse which a hymne or psalme affords,
Is, when the soul unto the lines accords.

He who craves all the minde,
And all the soul, and strength, and time,
If the words onely ryme,
Justly complains, that somewhat is behinde
To make his verse, or write a hymne in kinde.

Whereas if th' heart be moved,
Although the verse be somewhat scant,
God doth supplie the want.
As when th' heart sayes (sighing to be approved)
O, could I love! and stops: God writeth, *Loved.*

Again there is an apparent opposition between poetry and devotion and again an apparent self-contradiction in writing an exquisite poem about the sufficiency of broken expression as long as it comes from the heart. But in fact that is not how the poem works.

The poem opens with an observation of himself. Herbert has been haunted by a phrase all day. The pause, the waiting for something after the short line, 'Somewhat it fain would say', is met with a comical inability to bring out anything as the heart runs up and down still muttering, '*My joy, my life, my crown*'. He is in love with God. Herbert has not just taken over for religion part of the repertoire of the love poem, even if the Sidneyan lover frequently delights in noting the foolishness to which love has reduced him; the self-observation is a particular triumph of Herbert's way of being in touch with his own life in his poetry.

In the rest of the poem, Herbert makes a characteristic return upon himself, pointing out that his absurdity is not to be despised. In religion, heart counts for more than art. This is not to dismiss the art of poetry, but to remind himself and us that devotion is devotion: 'The finenesse which a hymne or psalme affords / Is, when the soul unto the lines accords'. He is thinking here of singing, and there will be a quibble on 'chord' and 'accord'. Devotionally speaking, the splendour of a psalm or hymn is when it is sung in such a way that the soul of the singer puts itself into the words. If he had been thinking first and foremost of his own writing, Herbert would have written, 'when the lines unto the soul accord'. But what he has in mind is the use others make of what has been written, of their putting their life into the words.

But the accord of soul and verse is also a matter of composition, a subject he turns to in the third and fourth stanzas. 'If the words onely ryme' in a poem, if there is no accord between soul and words, then the art is empty. Here though he is speaking of art's insufficiency, his own art is particularly fine. The sentence drawn over the long line, with its repetition of 'all' and 'and', strains to meet the idea of God's inexorable demand for wholehearted worship, only to go slack with the inadequate offering of the short third line, with its interrupting deferred conditional clause:

> He who craves *all* the minde,
> *And all* the soul, *and* strength, *and* time,
> If the words onely ryme,
> Justly complains . . .

There is a touch of dry humour in the picture of God as creditor or perhaps employer of a craftsman in the last two lines of the stanza. It is after all with the verse of Herbert's absolute God that 'somewhat is behinde', and the missing 'somewhat' (the inexpressible 'somewhat' of the first stanza) is required for 'a hymne in kinde', primarily, that is, for a true hymn, but perhaps also for making a return in kind. The blame is ironically mild.

Having considered the case of art wanting soul, Herbert turns in the last stanza to consider the converse: the 'somewhat' that 'is behinde' is the soul's being 'somewhat scant' of art. The third line says that God graciously allows for any scantness in that respect if the utterance is heartfelt. But the comparison in the last two lines, by a kind of innocent trick, involves God more deeply in the matter: 'As when th' heart sayes (sighing to be approved) / *O could I love!* and stops: God writeth, *Loved*' (the parenthesis and the colon beautifully suggest the breaking of the sigh and the heart's incapacity to come out with what it is full of). Though Herbert puts forward this account of the motions of the heart only as a comparison with what happens with heartfelt verse whose art is wanting, making heartfelt verse is really an instance of the way of the heart with God. In verse-making it is not just that the deficiencies of expression are made good by God but that the heart that is diffident of its ability to love is empowered to love by God's having first loved it. That is what the heart needed. Sighing to be approved, it was sighing to be loved so that it could love. This takes us back to Herbert's Calvinism, if that is what it is, his insistence that truly spiritual motions come from God. But it also shows how this doctrine comes alive in his

111

poetry. It does so in the personification of the sighing heart.[37] And strikingly it comes alive in Herbert's making of verse. It is true that the point of 'God writeth, *Loved*' is first of all general: God has written his promises of love in the Bible, and by a bold appropriation the heart that would love may feel that, in its realization of the scriptural promise, God recapitulates the writing of the promise to it in the present. But the writing of Herbert's poem also is involved. It is his heart, after all, that has been running up and down muttering. It also must sigh to be approved and stop and make its discovery, and Herbert finds that, as he writes of this, it turns out that his poem has been 'supplied' by God. With '*Loved*', God has supplied the point of the poem, its divine reversal, and simultaneously the concluding rhyme.

It is often hard to know whether a poet is having a vision or just speaking figuratively. But surely Herbert is not implying that God completed his poem by a miracle. And on the other hand, surely he did not think up the end of his poem as a pious wheeze. The witty turn would come to him with the force of a discovery that would make him feel that in his versing 'I am with thee'. And while he would not feel that God literally wrote the last word of his poem for him, he still might feel that in a figurative or spiritual sense he had been taken over by God, an assurance he courts or intimates in different ways in poem after poem. Both as pastor and poet, then, Herbert is saying to himself and any other Christian that God makes good the utterance of religious love. In so far as Herbert has his poem specifically in mind, he is not saying with repellent false modesty that it is a lame perform- ance in need of God's amending, but that both its art and heart depend on the action of God's love in him, as his poem exemplifies. If his art, as well as heart, manages to discover this divine action, then that will be a variation on the relish he found in versing when he felt his life divinely renewed.

In 'A true Hymne', anyway, Herbert has managed to avoid an opposing of poetry to devotion that would have meant the undoing of his own poem. And in the art of versing he has managed to bring God in without render- ing himself null and void.

Herbert's relation to himself and to God

'A true Hymne' brings Herbert's self into accord with the divine more easily than most of his poems, and he is not often writing about writing. We should turn now to the troubled matter of Herbert's relation to himself and to God.

---

37. For diffidence, cf. 'Dullnesse'.

Herbert clearly had a vivid inner life and seems to have been pleased to observe its motions. We have seen how that is so in the opening of 'A true Hymne', with its amused observation of his being unable for a whole day to get a phrase out of his head, how he renders the particularity of his suffering in 'Affliction' (IV), and how in 'The Flower' he connects his pleasure in writing verse with the return of the current of his life:

> And now in age I bud again,
> After so many deaths I live and write;
> I once more smell the dew and rain,
> And relish versing: O my onely light,
> It cannot be
> That I am he
> On whom thy tempests fell all night.

(st. 6)

Admittedly in 'The Flower' the return of his life makes him feel strange to himself. After the suffering and privation with which God has punished him, he hardly knows himself, and the rather terrible point of the poem is that the return to himself can only be a moment in a recurring series of being killed and quickened by God so that he will transplant his life from earth to heaven. But if the poem teaches surrender of one's life, it expresses at least in this stanza a joyful return to one's life from depression.

One of the ways in which Herbert makes us feel he is in touch with himself is the boldness with which he lets dream distortion run through his poetry. Herbert attended to his dreams. In 'The Size', urging himself to curb his natural appetite for joy and expect little of it on earth, he concludes by referring to a dream with an abruptness that shows that he is communing with himself:

> Call to minde thy dream,
> An earthly globe,
> On whose meridian was engraven,
> *These seas are tears, and heav'n the haven.*

The dream was clearly talismanic for Herbert. He has been trying to persuade himself not to hope for much joy on earth and turns to his inner spiritual store to find comfort, the memory of a dream that transformed disappointment into a voyage toward heaven. If he actually saw the terrestrial globe in his dream, that would be an unusual cosmic expansion for a Herbert poem, suggesting that elated grief had already transported him beyond the world. But more likely, given Herbert's fondness for the small, the manageable, the enclosed, he saw the earth mapped on a globe and supported by a brass ring round the equator.[38] It would make the same point without the spatial transport, but either way would show how Herbert paid attention to the signs of his inner life.

Metaphysical bizarreness in Herbert frequently suggests dream, where in Donne it expresses the violence of a mind subduing the world to its own designs. Particularly in Herbert's allegories, oddity suggests the distortion of narrative by thought in dreams. In 'The Bag', an extraordinary recasting of the Christian story of redemption, in which the wound in Christ's side makes a receptacle for prayers close to his heart, Christ descends to earth, dies, addresses his brethren and then starts returning to whence he came. With dream inconsequence his death has no more effect on his life than a sneeze because the thought is that Christ rose from the dead and is immortal. Equally strange and showing the compression of thought in dream pictures is the end of 'Redemption', a fable about how acceptance of Christ's sacrifice puts the believer's relation to God on a new footing. Most of the poem is taken up with the narrator's search for Christ as landlord in order to change the terms of his lease, where the legal figure stands for the idea of a covenant between God and the believer. In the end he is granted a new lease, a new dispensation according to which all payment is made by God himself with his sacrificial death.[39] This is how the new lease is granted:

> At length I heard a ragged noise and mirth
>> Of theeves and murderers: there I him espied,
>> Who straight, *Your suit is granted*, said, & died.

The strangeness here is almost inexhaustible, but perhaps the strangest thing is that the landlord knows what the narrator wants before he has said a word and immediately dies. The thought is conventional but the incident it makes is entirely disruptive of what one expects should happen in a story. The landlord's company is odd too. It suggests those who crucified Christ; it also suggests the two thieves who were crucified with him, one of whom was told that he would feast with Christ in Paradise. And besides, given that the narrator has been looking for his landlord in the places of the great and powerful, the mirth that he finds him amidst suggests Christ's fondness for low company. His crucifixion becomes a sinners' party, which after all is what the Eucharist is.

Christian iconography and the Renaissance emblem delight in paradoxical and surrealistic riddle pictures. Herbert sometimes works in these traditions. In 'The Agonie', for instance, he uses the traditional figure of Christ in the

---

38. Hutchinson, George Herbert 1941, p. 525, citing *OED*.
39. On the Covenant of Works and Herbert's hostility to Covenant theology, see Strier 1983, p. 87.

winepress and does so in a way that shows that he can release vivid oneiric distortion of the natural from traditional thought pictures.[40] But he does not owe 'The Bag' or 'The Redemption' to traditional sources. Whether recalling or inventing, Herbert had a gift for dreamwork.

What we have been looking at so far are indirect expressions of self-presence. But Herbert also has considered ideas of self. These are very evident in 'The Church Porch', a poem of prudential moral advice addressed to one 'whose sweet youth and early hopes inhance / Thy rate and price, and mark thee for a treasure' (ll. 1–2). As moralist, Herbert appeals to a self-regarding sense of oneself as a treasure and enjoins an ethic of self-command and mastery of one's passions:

> Envie not greatnesse: for thou mak'st thereby
> Thy self the worse, and so the distance greater.
> Be not thine own worm: yet such jealousie,
> As hurts not others, but may make thee better,
>   Is a good spurre.

(ll. 259–63)

Herbert gives admirable advice about doing justice to oneself, on dressing as an index of character, or on how to maintain a reputation as wit in a competitive social world. He ties this social self-regard to the imagined regard of the king, socially speaking the eye of eyes: 'Doe all things like a man, not sneakingly: / Think the king sees thee still; for his King does' (ll. 121–22). But as 'treasure' perhaps also suggests, the ethic of self-command goes with holding back, of turning in on oneself as a kingdom or possession. The self is like spring in 'Vertue', 'A box where sweets compacted lie':

> Man is a shop of rules, a well truss'd pack,
> Whose every parcell under-writes a law.
>   Lose not thy self, nor give thy humours way:
>   God gave them to thee under lock and key.
>
> By all means use sometimes to be alone.
> Salute thy self: see what thy soul doth wear.
> Dare to look in thy chest, for 'tis thine own:
> And tumble up and down what thou find'st there.

('The Church Porch', ll. 141–48)[41]

---

40. See Tuve 1952, pp. 112, 118–19, 127–28. Her comments on 'The Bag' fail to make any real connection with the mass of lore she expects Herbert to call on.

41. For the same idea of a treasury within, see 'Content', ll. 35–36: 'He that by seeking hath himself once found, / Hath ever found a happie fortune'.

The wealth of the inner man lies in order, in the tying of himself into parcels. The enjoyment one is supposed to take in tumbling one's soul's clothes out of the chest where they are kept will not undo that good order but rather be an inspection of the goods the soul keeps closed in its boxes.

'The Church Porch' deals with the self-direction and duties of the social man. 'The Church', on the other hand, deals with the relation between self and God; there a sense of one's inner riches may be fatal. In 'The Flower', those 'Swelling through store, / Forfeit their Paradise by their pride'. The ethic of temperance and self-regard, which in 'The Church Porch' Herbert teaches should rule one's social relations, comes under question where God is concerned. In the world of the spirit, the sense of self, on which Herbert's social morality is grounded, has to be given up. In 'The Flower', self-treasuring arouses God's anger until, after repeated killings and quickenings, Herbert comes to what he believes is the salutariness of being left with nothing. In 'Confession', keeping things within boxes within boxes provokes God's cruelty. Herbert tells us that

> within my heart I made
> Closets; and in them many a chest;
> And, like a master in my trade,
> In those chests, boxes; in each box, a till:
> Yet grief knows all, and enters when he will.

The beautiful carpentry recalls the shop in 'The Church Porch', where the self is neatly parcelled under the rule of temperance and its humours placed under lock and key. But here self-containment is the cause of horrible suffering rather than pleasure. God's tortures for the self-enclosed,

> Like moles within us, heave, and cast about:
> And till they foot and clutch their prey,
> They never cool, much lesse give out.
> No smith can make such locks but they have keyes:
> Closets are halls to them; hearts, high-wayes.

> Onely an open breast
> Doth shut them out.

Admittedly Herbert is talking about sinful secrets. But in the terribly exacting world of his devotion, ordinary sins would not go unacknowledged. He cannot just be suffering the pangs of guilt. The sins must be hidden from himself. They must be something like the self under the rule of temperance now discovered in affliction to be a warren of pride. The moles of grief, like

116

the thoughts that are like a case of knives in 'Affliction' (IV), have an extraordinary vividness, at once physical and psychological. According to Walton, Herbert said that he had ' "a Wit, like a Pen-knife in too narrow a sheath, too sharp for his body" '.[42] It sounds as if the workings of his mind made him ill, or at least that he associated physical pain with mental anguish. The sweet interiority of his temperate self turns to the self-enclosure of pain and of a mind that feels with intense self-reproach separated from God.

Or the sweet self of 'The Church Porch' may turn in affliction to disorder. Instead of the tidy parcels and compartments of the temperate self, Herbert speaks of his being broken in pieces, of being all at sixes and sevens. He is not speaking of intemperance, of unleashed passions, but of a state of nervous collapse, brought on by the intensity of his attempt to reach God in prayer. His diagnosis, both in 'Deniall' and 'Affliction' (IV), is that his longing for God has been met with 'soul-desertion'.[43]

Deniall

When my devotions could not pierce
Thy silent eares;
Then was my heart broken, as was my verse:
My breast was full of fears
And disorder:

My bent thoughts, like a brittle bow,
Did flie asunder:
Each took his way; some would to pleasures go,
Some to the warres and thunder
Of alarms.

As good go any where, they say,
As to benumme
Both knees and heart, in crying night and day,
Come, come, my God, O come,
But no hearing.

O that thou shouldst give dust a tongue
To crie to thee,
And then not heare it crying! all day long
My heart was in my knee,
But no hearing.

---

42. Walton 1927, 'Life of Mr George Herbert', p. 275.
43. A phrase I have borrowed from Rutherford 1727, whose whole treatment of the subject (pp. 46–68) deserves to be better known.

Therefore my soul lay out of sight,
       Untun'd, unstrung:
My feeble spirit, unable to look right,
       Like a nipt blossome, hung
               Discontented.

O cheer and tune my heartlesse breast,
       Deferre no time;
That so thy favours granting my request,
       They and my minde may chime,
               And mend my ryme.

There is no better example of Herbert's art of imitative form. One is moved to speak of the ingenuity of its contrivance, but of an ingenuity that is all resonant with a jarring mind. As usual in Herbert, the phrasing is worked inside the verse form so that the play of long and short lines, of runover and pause, brings out the weight of his words. So his thoughts in the first line of the second stanza are held tensed by the phrase between commas comparing them to a brittle bow, only for them to snap in the succeeding dimeter line. Again, the enjambment in the last two lines of the fifth stanza ends dully on the single word line, 'Discontented', to convey the shrivelled state of his soul. Where form is brought to so fine a point, a small adjustment is telling. The exceptional repetition of the 'But no hearing' of the third stanza as the last line of the fourth makes a bitter, general muttering his own and so conveys without more words the blankness of God's silence and his own desperation. And more obviously, the withholding of rhyme in the last lines of all the stanzas, except the last one, deftly suggests his jangled state, until the rhyme finally proffered brings in the harmoniousness that Herbert would enjoy if God restored him to favour. The verse form here not only imitates the sense but intimates a correspondence between his versing and the way God works in him. Unlike Donne, who frequently achieves his effects by wrenching his form, Herbert achieves his by working with his form. Nor is it only the expressive turning of his verse form that conveys fragmentation, but also his figures of speech, his striking use of grotesque metonymic displacements. The transferred epithet 'silent' (a sort of metonymy) in 'When my devotions could not pierce / Thy silent eares' refers to God's mouth; his ears are deaf and he makes no response. The silence displaced to the ears suggests both a wilful deafness and a serene distance untroubled by human cries. And it also works as a figure of disorder like the surrealistic misjoinings in the fourth stanza: 'O that thou shouldst give dust a tongue'; 'My heart was in my knee'. There is also the 'heartlesse breast' of the last stanza, not a misjoining but a metonymic amputation equally figurative of a state of physical derangement.

In addition to these indirect expressions of anguish, there is the direct expressive force of Herbert's writing, particularly in stanzas 3 and 4, with their indignation for himself at the 'silent eares' that give (rather than have) 'no hearing'. Even the formulaic last stanza, patterned after the collects, which make a petition and follow it with a clause of purpose ('that so . . .'), is tellingly formulaic. In his state of separation and denial, he cannot realize a state of harmony between himself and God, only put it as a formal prayer. To do so, he moves from narrative past to present entreaty. How the one is connected to the other is not entirely clear. It sounds as if, unlike Donne, who concentrates his faculties by dramatizing in the present, Herbert cannot bear to speak in 'Deniall' from the moment of separation and distress but puts the narrative into the past tense so that we may imagine with the switch into the present, if not respite, at least sufficient discontinuity for a new prayer to gather.

Herbert's feeling for his own quick of life, whether expressed as a sweet or as a tormented interiority, often goes with a self-conscious distancing of himself from himself. This has something to do with the being in charge of oneself enjoined by his ethic of self-command, and something also to do with the habit of vigilant self-correction, evident in the unfolding of many of his poems. The 'I' is frequently distanced by the narrative past or by various ironic and generalizing forms. The character he gives himself or the persona he adopts is often naive or indignant on his own behalf. He is often surprised, and surprised unpleasantly.

There is, for instance, the much put-upon, foolish and wonderfully compliant allegorized self in 'Love Unknown', subject to monstrous caprice from the lord of the manor. This allegorized self tells the tale of his sufferings to a 'Deare Friend', on whose love he presumes. He took, for example, 'a sacrifice out of my fold', a formulation that makes us think of a lamb but allows us to think of some offering from his heart in the fold of his robe:

> But as my heart did tender it, the man,
> Who was to take it from me, slipt his hand,
> And threw my heart into the scalding pan;
> My heart, that brought it (do you understand?)
> The offerers heart. *Your heart was hard, I fear.*
> Indeed it's true. I found a callous matter
> Began to spread and to expatiate there.

(ll. 33–39)

This is comedy of a cruel sort. It is not just that this is the second time that the narrator has had his heart plucked out by a ready servant of his landlord, not just that his dear friend responds to the indignation with which he recounts his injuries with considerable coolness, but that he so readily comes round to an understanding that takes sides against himself. The narrator is a self-parodic version of the spiritual self in 'The Church', and Herbert clearly stands apart from him, using his narrator's blindness and amenableness to make us see that affliction quickens.[44]

Looking down on the self works well while the allegorical narrative runs through conventionalized turns of Christian life. The conventionalized affliction in 'Love Unknown' lends itself to fresh and strange figurative invention. But in 'The Collar', the rebellion against a service that seems to give nothing in return for discipline and devotion bursts out of the conventionalizing frame and escapes the ironically distanced self who is speaking. At first all is well. The complaint of the angry self, with his flowers and 'garlands gay', characterizes him as petulant. Herbert is able to patronize himself, even in recounting this anger, so that the voice he hears at the end calling him 'Child' is already implied in the narrative. Yet in the midst of self-diminishing, of a certain self-caricature, Herbert utters rebellious counsels to himself that are not foolish:

> leave thy cold dispute
> Of what is fit, and not. Forsake thy cage,
> Thy rope of sands,
> Which pettie thoughts have made, and made to thee
> Good cable, to enforce and draw,
> And be thy law,
> While thou didst wink and wouldst not see.

Here, he is not just kicking over the traces. He thinks now of the discipline he lives by as what Blake called 'mind-forged manacles'. He is bound by ropes of sand, which are nevertheless good cable to him. The energetic, angry wit conveys his disgust at himself for what he now sees as wilful self-deception. There is real insight here into the self-punishing, autosadistic and self-defeating way we may use the discipline to which we submit ourselves. But alongside this real criticism of the discipline he has lived by, Herbert spurns any moral restraint, as when he counsels himself to 'leave thy cold dispute / Of what is fit, and not'. That does warrant his retrospective dismissal of his rebellion as a tantrum:

> But as I rav'd and grew more fierce and wilde
> At every word,
> Me thoughts I heard one calling, *Child!*
> And I reply'd, *My Lord.*

---

44. See Vendler's discussion of the allegorized self (1975, p. 92).

And yet it is not good enough to dismiss the real criticisms as if they were the same thing as the wild outbursts that assume a libertine freedom of spirit not his to choose, though he can pretend it is as long as he shouts loud enough. But that is what these last lines do, and as with his scorning his own creativity in 'Jordan' (II), he has trivialized something that he should have taken seriously.

'Affliction' (I), on the other hand, does not sell Herbert short. Distancing from himself, rebellion and capitulation are all involved. But the ending has the strength of his pain. Herbert is not brought round from anger with God. He is crushed. 'Affliction' (I) begins by playing on Herbert's love of sweet things, his love of fine houses and flowers, to suggest his naive intoxication with God's service when he was first enticed into it: 'My dayes were straw'd with flowr's and happinesse; / There was no moneth but May'. After that one knows that he will come to grief, though one hardly expects the tormenting that follows. But here Herbert takes himself seriously, for all his play with the figure he cuts. Even if he smiles at his youthful bliss, he is obviously respectful of the fiery soul that was ambitious for a place with no one less than the ruler of the universe: 'my sudden soul caught at the place, / And made her youth and fiercenesse seek thy face'. Moreover, the account of his suffering at God's hands is autobiographical and specific where in other poems the self-representation is generalized. He even brings in his body subject to agues: 'Thinne and lean without a fence or friend, / I was blown through with ev'ry storm and winde'. At the same time, he runs his lack of social protectors together with the unprotectedness of his body so that the one becomes a metaphor for the other. Yet while Herbert is playing on his appearance here, he is not playing on it in a spirit of devotional self-deprecation. And the specificity of the trouble resists a religious interpretation that would dismiss it, for instance as divine punishment for pride, the interpretation he gives to the generalized 'killing' that he is subjected to in 'The Flower'. When he reaches the present in his story of God's subjecting him to such thwarting that he has lost all sense of the direction of his life, he seems entirely at one with the man who complains:

> Now I am here, what thou wilt do with me
> > None of my books will show:
> I reade, and sigh, and wish I were a tree;
> > For sure then I should grow
> To fruit or shade: at least some bird would trust
> Her houshold to me, and I should be just.

> (ll. 55–60)

It is understandable that Herbert should be weary of his life and touching that in his weariness of life he should wish to do another creature good. But his famous capitulation in the next stanza is hard to understand and seems to undo the seriousness of his complaint. It makes one wonder if he has made this show purposely, humanly speaking, though religiously he might be attempting a *salto mortale*:

> Well, I will change the service, and go seek
> > Some other master out.
> Ah my deare God! though I am cleane forgot,
> Let me not love thee, if I love thee not.

> (ll. 63–66)

Helen Vendler suggests that the 'other master' in the circumstances must be the devil and that Herbert is frightened by what he has brought himself to say into realizing that he cannot live apart from the habit of loving God.[45] Even if God has forgotten him, he will go on loving God – 'Damn me if I don't' (not to love God would be damnation for Herbert).[46] Vendler's suggestion gets rid of the unpleasant suspicions that Herbert might be coquetting with God or making a theatrically self-immolating gesture. But then what has happened is dreadful. Herbert has been broken. The paradoxical form of the last line suggests the baffling self-contradiction to which Herbert has been reduced. It would be wrong to think of this collapse as a mature realizing that his life cannot run through only the eager sweetness of his youth but must take in frustration and pain.[47] What Herbert represents is rather the distressing surrender of someone who has received nothing but harm from God yet finds he has nowhere else to turn. Doubtless we are meant to suppose that there is something spiritually salutary about this breaking of the self. The title 'Affliction' will be meant to point us towards thinking of Herbert's story as one of trial and divine tempering. But otherwise there is little pointing, and what we are shown is simply the abrupt cancelling of Herbert's self by religion.[48] We do not receive the impression that a wiser and spiritually matured Herbert has taken over from a wayward one and that the wiser Herbert is in charge of the poem's proceedings. He speaks out of helplessness and devastation. It makes a strong but desolate poem.

---

45. Vendler 1975, p. 45.
46. One of the interpretations proposed by Empson 1953, p. 184.
47. Knights 1951, pp. 124–29, talks of 'Affliction' (I) as about the 'achievement of maturity'.
48. Harman 1982, p. 101, cites Coverdale's translation of Psalm 31, v. 12: 'I am cleane forgotten as a dead man', which would be an oblique pointing since the psalm is both a complaint and a declaration of trust.

No other poem of trouble between himself and God ends with so distressing a crushing of himself. He probably (and quite rightly) could not bring himself to visit that self-defeat so unconsolingly again. The accounts of being out of joint or broken in pieces in 'Deniall' or 'Affliction' (IV) end with his imagining what it would be to be restored by God to harmony and sweetness in himself. But whether crushed or restored (at least in hope), the sense of his own life comes out strongly in conflict with God or desertion by him.

At the same time that bringing himself into accord with God meant grief, Herbert's inklings of a life in God brought joy. He has both a strong sense of his own vital current and a strong impulse to graft himself on another centre of being than his own. That is at work even in poems that do not directly concern his relation to God. In 'Church-Musick', for example, he speaks of dissolving into a new life in music:

> Now I in you without a bodie move,
>   Rising and falling with your wings:
> We both together sweetly live and love,
>   Yet say sometimes, *God help poore Kings.*

Usually Herbert's divine imaginings are very much from his life in the body, but pain has made him seek comfort here in disembodiment. He is not simply dissolved in ecstasies, however, like the young Milton or Crashaw, but living in another. A similar, though sinister, making over of the self (he is speaking generally, not particularly of himself) comes up in 'Avarice', where he gives a rather remarkable picture of how money alienates human life:

> Nay, thou [i.e. money] hast got the face of man; for we
> Have with our stamp and seal transferr'd our right:
> Thou art the man, and man but drosse to thee.

But where above all being adopted by another centre of self comes into play is in Herbert's relation to God. It is a theme to which he keeps returning, like Donne harping on the exchange of selves in his love poetry, and it is often the point of those turns of his verse that most stir with a strange life. We have already examined both the theme and one of those turns in 'A true Hymne'.

'The Odour' is another delightful example. It begins like 'A true Hymne', observing his pleasure in repeating a title of Christ:

> How sweetly doth *My Master* sound! *My Master!*
>   As Amber-greese leaves a rich sent
>   Unto the taster:
>   So do these words a sweet content,
> An orientall fragrancie, *My Master.*

> With these all day do I perfume my minde,
>   My minde ev'n thrust into them both:
>   That I might finde
>   What cordials make this curious broth,
> This broth of smells, that feeds and fats my minde.

Here Herbert is able to indulge grossly through metaphor and analogy the one sensual appetite he allows himself to gratify, though notably it is his mind that he thrusts into the broth of smells and his mind that he feeds and fats. In the midst of his enjoyment, the typical Herbertian counter-movement occurs and he wishes that '*My servant*' might 'creep & grow / To some degree of spicinesse to thee!' From that point on, Herbert works out how there might be an exchange between himself and the divine:

> For when *My Master*, which alone is sweet,
>   And ev'n in my unworthinesse pleasing,
>   Shall call and meet,
>   *My servant*, as thee not displeasing,
> That call is but the breathing of the sweet.
>
> This breathing would with gains by sweetning me
>   (As sweet things traffick when they meet)
>   Return to thee.

At first sight it looks as if there were a mutual exchange and interpenetration between '*My Master*' and '*My servant*', for that is what is suggested by the way the perfume breathes and traffics with another sweet scent. But what Herbert in fact describes is a circulation flowing from God, its source, and returning to him. '*My Master*' alone is sweet, but by going forth and sweetening '*My servant*' will meet with a return of sweetness. The idea figured here is that, having nothing worthy of God in himself, Herbert may in some sense take Christ as himself by accepting Christ's sacrifice and start returning a good smell to its source. Though this is not a mutual exchange, there is still a merging of one in the other suggested in the play on name and thing. The sweetness of '*My Master*' is both the sweetness of Christ and the sweetness of uttering the words. In uttering them, Herbert is already breathing sweetness and in one sense he, and in another sense Christ, are calling to each other in them. As for '*My servant*', it would be graciously sweet of Christ to address these words to Herbert, and the grace or acceptance implied in them and their echoing in his mind would make Herbert sweetly exhale upwards in a life of praise and thanksgiving to '*My Master*'. This is different from the exchange of self sought by Donne. With Donne, exchange is mutual and love is given and returned by each of the lovers. With Herbert, God is the sole authentic centre of self, the sole giver, which has the consequence that God is also the receiver, Herbert having given up himself to put on a divine self through which God reflects himself to himself.

Complete absorption in God is possible only in heaven. Herbert's poetry is about a Christian life on earth, where there are only intimations of what it would be to live in God. 'The Church' is full of such intimations in figures, turns of phrase, half hidden paradoxes. In 'A true Hymne', God's 'supplying' of Herbert's poem is both discovery and invention of the secret working of God. In 'Deniall', the return of God Herbert prays for will set his being in tune. Even God's absence seems to show in strange effects that he is Herbert's life principle. It is a consequence of the inability of Herbert's devotions to pierce God's 'silent ears' that his thoughts, bent to loose the arrow of prayer, snap and fly apart. This reverses the ordinary train of cause and effect because for Herbert, as for Donne, God is both ear and cry, both the receiver and the inspirer of true petitions. Again because God does not look at him, he is unable to look up to God:

> Therefore my soul lay out of sight,
>   Untun'd, unstrung:
> My feeble spirit, unable to look right,
>   Like a nipt blossom hung.

Herbert's preoccupation and inventiveness are such that one could pursue this theme endlessly. I shall have to limit myself to two striking ways in which he represents himself as sharing the life of God. The first is through suffering. 'The Crosse' tells a story, like 'Affliction' (I), of God's thwarting him. Even when Herbert's wish to serve is gratified, God turns 'th'edge of all things on me still', poisons his joy and makes him feel 'ev'n in Paradise to be a weed':

> Ah my deare Father, ease my smart!
> These contrarieties crush me: these crosse actions
> Doe winde a rope about, and cut my heart:
>   And yet since these thy contradictions
> Are properly a crosse felt by thy Sonne,
> With but foure words, my words, *Thy will be done.*

In the midst of God's cruelty, Herbert manages to feel that he has been touched by divinity. He identifies himself with Christ on the cross: he too is God's son and he makes Christ's words of submission his words. In 'Affliction' (III), Herbert's arguments for God's being in his grief are positively sophistical, like some of Donne's love talk: 'My heart did heave, and there came forth, *O God!* / By that I knew that thou wast in the grief'. What is more, God gave him breath, and if sighs use up breath and shorten our lives, God in Herbert's affliction is in fact producing 'A gale to bring me sooner to my blisse'. Besides,

> Thy life on earth was grief, and thou art still
> Constant unto it, making it to be
> A point of honour, now to grieve in me,
>   And in thy members suffer ill.
>   They who lament one crosse,
> Thou dying dayly, praise thee to thy losse.

It is hard to be quite sure of Herbert's tone, but probably he is striking a note of Christian chivalry, which expresses itself in high-spirited absurdity. Certainly his argument for giving praise for one's sufferings is absurd. But for Herbert it is all gold because, like the rest of the sophistical tissue of the poem, it rehearses the sovereign truth that God is in him.[49]

The second way in which he imagines his life is God's is the operation of Christ's blood in him. In 'The Banquet', he speaks of the Eucharist as magic food and drink, which enters and takes him over:

> Welcome sweet and sacred cheer,
>   Welcome deare;
> With me, in me, live and dwell:
> . . .
>
> O what sweetnesse from the bowl
>   Fills my soul,
> Such as is, and makes divine!
> Is some starre (fled from the sphere)
>   Melted there,
> As we sugar melt in wine?[50]

Herbert has avoided grossly cannibalistic figures. The phrasing of 'sacred cheer' allows us to pass without embarrassment from the idea of food to a spiritual notion of rejoicing. And it is the 'sweetnesse from the bowl' that makes divine, a formulation that allows for a spiritual interpretation. But at the same time, the ideas of eating and drinking allow him to think of God as becoming part of him.[51] Again in 'The Agonie', Herbert brings in Christ's

---

49. Compare the way in which his grief becomes Christ's and Christ's his in 'Affliction' (II).
50. Cf. 'H. Communion' and Herbert's position on Communion discussed in the section treating his *Life*.
51. Cf. 'Love' (III), where the veiling of the notion that the host serves himself up as meat for the guest at once allows us to read the matter spiritually and yet discern a solemn and dreadful weight in the words; contrast Schoenfeldt 1991, pp. 258ff.

blood in such a way as to allow a spiritual interpretation and yet to suggest with extraordinary physical intimacy the sharing of God's life: 'Love is that liquor sweet and most divine, / Which my God feels as bloud; but I, as wine'. The operative word is 'feels'. It is not just that Christ felt his blood in the agony in the garden and again, by metonymy, in his suffering on the cross, but that a feeling of blood in the veins is a primitive feeling of one's life itself. That Herbert should *feel* this as wine conveys his elation when Christ's life passes into his bloodstream.

Herbert puts on Christ (as the Pauline formulation has it) or adopts God as the principle of his life in order to bring about a transformation in himself. He gets a new self on terms of surrendering the old. And nothing can come from himself. In the realm of the spirit, he cannot even make a true confession of his sins except as God moves him ('The Holdfast'). But on earth, he can be changed only in part. The life of God in him means a constant conflict between his old self and God. That is why he is 'A wonder tortur'd in the space / Betwixt this world and that of grace'. Even his apparently pious desire to make some return to God must be thwarted and corrected. In many poems he tries to enter into a sort of competition with God, but the upshot of these competitions is always a realization of total indebtedness. In 'Love' (III), the apparent sweetness of the colloquy masks a dire struggle in which God inexorably demands that the speaker should accept everything from him. The speaker's attempts to evade this demand (through expressing shame about his sinful condition and a wish to serve) are shoved aside in what, under the ply of courtesy, is actually a taut wit contest, where the narrator has to capitulate: 'You must sit down, sayes love, and taste my meat: / So I did sit and eat'. The love relation in Herbert is not an equal one. Though in 'Love' (III) the anguish has diminished, what is required of Herbert is a surrender of himself that leaves no room for self-acceptance in the ordinary sense. In contrast with the colloquy with God that Milton invents for Adam in *Paradise Lost*, Book 8, about his need for a fellow human being, Herbert's colloquies with God move to submission. It is true that Adam's creative exercise of choice in asking for Eve is the motion of God's free spirit within him, as God does not fail to point out. Theologically there may be little difference between Milton's position and Herbert's. And yet the whole spirit in which Adam speaks with God is free, however deferential, however much the conversation exhausts him. Herbert would never allow himself to stand up for what he thought humanly right in the face of God's seeming dismissal of it as Adam does. He may rage or complain about God's ways, but only to give himself over. It would be unhelpful, though, to use Milton as a stick to beat Herbert. What the comparison may usefully do is bring out the severity with which Herbert drove himself to give himself over. The more he can surrender himself, the more he can be assured that the new self, which is God in him, is really new and not just a continuation of his old self.

In many of Herbert's poems the demand for the surrender of self goes with a distressing cruelty in God. One of the impressive things about 'Love' (III) is that, although the demand for surrender of self is relentless, Love is not imagined as cruel. In a way, it makes sense after all to talk of self-acceptance. The hard thing for the narrator is to accept that he is accepted by Love. Love having welcomed him as a guest 'worthy to be here', the speaker retorts,

> I the unkinde, ungratefull? Ah my deare,
>> I cannot looke on thee.
> Love took my hand, and smiling did reply,
>> Who made the eyes but I?
>
> Truth Lord, but I have marr'd them: let my shame
>> Go where it doth deserve.
> And know you not, sayes Love, who bore the blame?
>> My deare, then I will serve.

What Love urges the speaker towards is taking another point of view on himself: the look he cannot return to Love in his shame, he should think of as having been given in the first place by Love. 'Who made the eyes but I?' equivocates on 'eye' and 'I' to suggest a way of seeing himself from outside the perspective of his shame-centred 'I', which would choose the hell it feels it deserves. So that when finally the narrator sits and eats and accepts that his blame is borne not by himself but by Love, it might be said that his new self is the self that accepts itself on terms of total indebtedness to the acceptance of Love. The spiritual transaction that 'Love' (III) imagines cannot, I think, be translated into Helen Vendler's terms of the self making peace with a higher self.[52] There is something finally intractable to translation in Herbert's Christian terms of absolute indebtedness to a God of love. All the same, it is surely right to feel with her that this, the last poem in 'The Church', is the song of a man who has come through.

Life and death

It would be wrong to think that all of Herbert is taken up with Hopkinsian intensities between God and himself. In 'Life', for instance:

---

52. Vendler 1975, p. 275.

I made a posie, while the day ran by:
Here will I smell my remnant out, and tie
                    My life within this band.
But time did becken to the flowers, and they
By noon most cunningly did steal away,
                    And wither'd in my hand.

My hand was next to them, and then my heart:
I took, without more thinking, in good part
                    Times gentle admonition:
Who did so sweetly deaths sad taste convey,
Making my minde to smell my fatall day;
                    Yet sugring the suspicion.

Farewell deare flowers, sweetly your time ye spent,
Fit, while ye liv'd, for smell or ornament,
                    And after death for cures.
I follow straight without complaints or grief,
Since if my sent be good, I care not if
                    It be as short as yours.

Part of Herbert's strong sense of his own life is a feeling for life tending to death. That is clear in 'The Pilgrimage', an allegory of human life, where he would have liked to dally in 'Fansies medow', 'But I was quicken'd by my houre'. The wording concentrates his feeling about the temporality of life, 'quicken'd' meaning at once 'made alive' and 'hastened on' by an hour that is at once his time of life and a time (such are the religious connotations of 'hour') that is in God's hands. In 'Mortification', the idea that in the midst of life we are in death receives macabre development, every stage of life affording figures of the grave; even infants' swaddling clothes are metaphorized as a winding sheet. What enlivens this strained series of conceits is Herbert's tender feeling for the fragility of the life that breath gives. Infants' 'young breath / Scarce knows the way'. 'When boyes go first to bed, / . . . onely their breath / Makes them not dead'. And so on to the phlegmy suffocation of old age. 'Life' contracts a feeling for the transience of life into a posy that withers. 'The day ran by' while he picks the flowers, perhaps like a brook, but at any rate pleasantly and carelessly. But then time is figured as a mysterious beckoner to death, whose gestures the flowers obey. Although Herbert calls this a 'gentle admonition', the gentle shock advancing towards his life-centre in 'My hand was next them, and then my heart' is nevertheless unsettling.

'Life' is a good example of Herbert's miniaturizing. He winds and works all his sweetness into a bunch of flowers, tied with a band. It sometimes seems as if, in his preference for tight forms, images of small, particularly enclosed, things, Herbert is cramming himself into an ornamental bottle. And sometimes the result is twee. But here the sweetness is firm and taut with meaning. The wish to 'smell his remnant out' and tie his life within the band of a posy figures an intense wish to give himself up to his delight in flowers and sweet smells, almost the same impulse, less extravagantly expressed, to which Marvell surrenders himself in 'The Garden'. One recalls also the intense sensuality of the nose that comes into 'The Odour' and how Herbert thrusts his *mind* into the sweet perfume there. Here, once the pretty fancy of smelling his remnant out is untied and unfolded by Time's admonition so that the mortality implied in the wish is clear, Herbert's mind without more thinking takes in the idea of death with the immediacy of a smell: Time makes his mind, not nose, smell his 'fatall day'.[53] The final stanza unravels the figure of his life as a posy of flowers in a gracefully resigned analogy, neatly turned in the last two lines. In 'if my sent be good, I care not if / It be as short as yours', Herbert has allowed his analogy to dilate. Instead of writing, 'If my sent be good, I care not if / My *life* be short as yours', he has talked of his scent, not just as the goodness of his life and its good example to others, but as his life itself in its fleetingness. Although this is a metaphor, in which vehicle and tenor, scent and life, are related only figuratively, it still touches in conclusion the poem's beginning, where the posy was not so much an emblem for Herbert's life as an enclosure he wished to enter, a sweetness he wished to become.

Nothing could be more conventional than a bunch of flowers as a figure for mortality. Nothing could be more personal and alive with the peculiar way that Herbert weaves himself into the sense of what he has to say.

Herbert as Metaphysical

If the Metaphysicals are characterized by interiority, then the inwardness of Herbert, his concern with the self and its surrender to God, has been sufficiently discussed. Apart from interiority, Herbert's verse shares little with Donne's. It lacks most of the paraphernalia of metaphysical ideas, particularly noticeable in Donne's Songs and Sonnets. If Herbert is interested in souls, it is not in an alchemical or platonizing way, in which he might escape the time limits and space limits imposed by life in the body, but in the Christian and evangelical way of Donne's Holy Sonnets, in which the soul is an inwardness to be given over to God. 'The Temper'

---

53. On the mind smelling, see Stein 1968, p. 173.

(I) ends: 'Thy power and love, my love and trust / Make one place ev'rywhere'. This does for once recall Donne's metaphysical vein in Songs and Sonnets: 'For love, all love of other sights controls, / And makes a little room, an everywhere' ('The Good Morrow'). But where Donne wants his love to expand to a whole universe, Herbert, who has been complaining about the universal height and depth to which God stretches him, concludes that, for him, love contracts to hold him in the place of his creaturely existence, wherever that should be. 'The Temper' (I) takes an unusual cosmic flight for Herbert, but he flies through space to arrive at where he is. If this should recall the return to life in the body in 'The Ecstacy' or 'Air and Angels', I should add that, unlike Donne, Herbert has no inclinations towards rarefied spiritual states to overcome. If in 'The Temper' (I) he should sometimes rise above forty heavens and sometimes sink to hell, the cosmic flight is only a figure for emotional states in the devotional life of a Christian on earth. Even in their poems of religious anguish, Donne and Herbert bear little resemblance to each other, either in expressive form or in subject. Here and there one may detect an echo but not enough to justify talking of a school of Donne.[54] The most one can say is that Herbert shares with Donne, perhaps caught from him, a flair for using the bizarre, the paradoxical, the counter-to-nature, as a way of exploring the looking-glass world of religious inwardness. But one points to that common ground only to draw distinctions.

It is a weakness of Donne's religious poetry that it is on the whole the poetry simply of a man talking to God. The social man was excluded and Donne was left to use his intensity not entirely profitably against himself. 'The Church' is as innerworldly as the Holy Sonnets and yet it is not liable to the same objection. This is partly because a rather densely imagined social world is present in Herbert's devotion, sometimes allegorized, usually given a spiritual meaning, but still implying a context of life lived among other people. The personifications of the temptations in 'The Quip', for example, show a gift for tart social observation equal to Donne's, which Donne almost entirely left out of his devotional life. For Donne the social world falls away partly because fear of death and judgement blot out all relations except the self-enclosed one between himself and God. Herbert, by contrast, in 'Dooms-day' much less desperately speaks of 'we' rather than 'I' and imagines a comic, if grotesque good fellowship of dust at the last trumpet: 'While this member jogs the other, / Each one whispring, *Live*

---

54. See, for instance, in addition to the correspondence noted in 'The Temper' (I), the recollection of Donne's 'Valediction: of Weeping' in the play on life as breath in 'Affliction' (III) (discussed pp. 125–6 above).

you, brother?' Donne's relation to God is *sui generis* but Herbert is always finding social analogies for his, for example in 'Redemption' and 'Love Unknown', the relation of landlord and tenant. And while there is no social nuance in Donne's devotions, Herbert's conversation with God frequently suggests social relations in which the rules of courtesy are outraged. So in 'Affliction' (I), God has grossly abused the position of social superior and master. In 'Love' (III), on the other hand, the strangeness of the host's insistence is masked in what is at least at first a courteous exchange. The materiality of the social world is also present. Herbert's is a world where fine building, good furniture and above all elegant dress and cloth are prized.[55] He speaks in 'Gratefulnesse' of 'Tears sullying [God's] transparent rooms'. 'Transparent', a deliberately lavish word, calls up a room, not just well windowed, but so set in order as to delight socially as well as aesthetically with an impression of clarity. That the tears sully it suggests the social disgrace of unfitting behaviour in so gracious a space, while allowing us also to think of the bright room as an inner space dimmed by tears.

Donne's poems are typically performances. His sense of self is made by the performance and he knows how to impress others with that self. Herbert knows how he strikes others and he may play on his character, but his poetry is not a form of self-assertion. The virtuoso character of Donne's verse is lacking. Although Herbert's poems are usually highly organized and sometimes very ingenious, they do not impose an argument on their materials, let alone an argument that flaunts its sophistry. And while a poem by Herbert typically returns upon itself, as for instance in time's admonition to Herbert's wish to tie himself up in a bunch of flowers, that turning is not a mercurial veering for self-expressive *éclat*, but a characteristic move of self-correction. This is true even of the surprise ending of 'Affliction' (I), 'Let me not love thee, if I love thee not', though that tends more than usual in the direction of self-dramatizing.

Donne characteristically argues by analogy, and his conceits give scope to his ingenuity and to his urge to impose his designs on the world. Even in his more sprightly sallies, Herbert's mind is more passive to the way things are, more a discoverer than a contriver. Even in those poems that imitate the shape of their topic, 'The Altar' and 'Easter Wings', Herbert seems to be finding a way to make his words say what he wants rather than twisting 'iron pokers into true-love-knots'. This is partly because of Herbert's modest, or at least quiet, persona and partly because the ingenuity of the forms is equalled by a skilful tact in fitting his phrasing inside the form he has chosen, something that contrasts sharply with Donne's *maniera*, his stylish

---

55.   On the transposing of court to heaven see Singleton 1987, esp. pp. 164–95.

and masterful treatment of his forms. The titles 'Jordan', 'The Pulley' and 'The Collar' make their poems into do-it-yourself conceits or riddles. We have to guess the correspondence between them and the stories the poems tell without any mention of the Jordan, or pulleys, or collars. That Herbert leaves the invention of the conceits to his readers is a way of making the wit a matter of discovery more than contrivance, something shared more than displayed. When Herbert does run to an extended conceit, as in 'Life' or 'The Odour', much of the meaning is subtly implied, where Donne in his *tours de force*, such as 'Good Friday, 1613. Riding Westward' or 'Hymn to God my God, in my Sickness', explains how he brings his heterogeneous ideas together, how he is like a deflected planet or a flat map. The pleasure in Herbert arises from the subtlety of implication; in Donne it arises from the force and ingenuity of his explanation.

Herbert can strike off far-fetched comparisons. Consider, for example, from 'Giddinesse',

> O what a sight were Man, if his attires
> Did alter with his minde;
> And like a Dolphin's skinne, his clothes combin'd
> With his desires!

The dorado, a kind of mackerel, with an iridescent skin, was popularly known as a dolphin.[56] Usually Herbert draws his figures from familiar, not to say homely, regions, whereas Donne loves to bring in references to curious or highly intellectualized learning. With Herbert a dolphin, let alone an iridescent one, makes an unusually exotic simile. Yet however striking, this comparison only serves to lend charm to an already amusing fancy. The simile is brief and it does not carry a burden of argument. Herbert's mind simply does not run, as Donne's does, to speculative and intellectual subtlety. Herbert's subtlety is, rather, emotional and moral. In consequence, this stanza from 'The Discharge' is probably less speculative, less meta-physical, than it looks:

> For death each houre environs and surrounds.
> He that would know
> And care for future chances, cannot go
> Unto those grounds,
> But through a Church-yard which them bounds.

> (ll. 36–40)

---

56. See Hutchinson's note, in George Herbert 1941, p. 522.

If Donne had written this, he would have meant that we can know the future only from the perspective of eternity and he would have worked the contrast of eternal and temporal knowledge perhaps into several conceits. If that is what Herbert means, it is an uncharacteristic speculative flight. He probably means only that at any moment we may die, that that thought should bend our minds to living well in the present, and that by association the future belongs to death, so that by metonymy our future is the grave.

As in this example, some of the most imaginatively enlarging turns of Herbert's wit are metonymic, whereas with Donne they are almost always analogical. We have already noted the strange metonymic derangements in 'Deniall'. Other examples crowd to memory: 'Light without winde is glasse' ('Providence'); 'heav'n lies flat in thee [i.e. the opened Bible], / Subject to ev'ry mounters bended knee' ('The H. Scriptures' [1]); urging himself to sing his grief to his lute in 'Ephes. 4.30: Grieve not the Holy Spirit', he remarks, 'Marbles can weep; and surely strings / More bowels have, then such hard things'; he tells Death, the skeleton, 'our Saviours death did put some bloud / Into thy face' ('Death'). 'God gave thy soul brave wings' from 'The Church Porch' contains the metaphor 'wings', but the development of the counsel against sloth is metonymic, and it is the development that is witty: 'put not these feathers / Into bed, to sleep out all ill weathers'.[57]

In all these examples, metonymy enlarges by compressing. It transfers complex real connections to simple and surreal connections between things. A whole theology of redemption is compressed, for instance, in the way death's skull begins to take on a fresh complexion. It is a useful figure for a poet like Herbert, who tends to miniaturize and in doing so charge his small, bounded images with intellectual and emotional life. The strings of the lute, being made of gut, express the bowels of his compassion and the complicated skill required to play a lute feelingly is transferred to the parts of the instrument. The transference or displacement of the player to his lute, of agent to instrument, may suggest why the figure should be cultivated by a poet who is preoccupied with other transferences of self, whether it is music, wine, money or Christ that takes over. The last lines of 'Agonie', 'Love is that liquor sweet and most divine / Which my God feels as bloud; but I, as wine', are too complex to be reduced to simple metonymic substitution; much depends on the word 'feels', as we have already seen. Nevertheless the metonymizing of love as a liquor, which is at once blood and wine, helps to bring about the extraordinary sensation of living in God that Herbert produces here.

---

57. Cf. Donne's 'To Mr Tilman after he had taken orders', ll. 19–22.

The compression, or at least terseness, of Herbert's style owes something also to a kind of metaphor more common in him than the sort instanced in the dolphin's skin. Urging himself to take no thought of future grief, he says, 'God chains the dog till night' ('The Discharge'). Complaining of how God took away his sense of fun, he says, 'My mirth and edge was lost; a blunted knife / Was of more use then I' ('Affliction' [I]). These metaphors perhaps do not abbreviate what he wants to say. They put what he has already said in a pithy way with an air of folk saying. The blunted knife is a homely image and fills out the metaphor lying unobtrusively in the phrase 'my . . . edge was lost'.

Metaphors such as this come out of the vigour of Herbert's plainer style. He made a collection of 'Outlandish [i.e. foreign] Proverbs'. He had a patriotic as well as writer's feeling for his native tongue: 'I like our language, as our men and coast: / Who cannot dress it well, want wit, not words' ('The Sonne'). He was attuned, as Donne was not, to the expressive potential of ordinary speech:

> I know the wayes of Honour, what maintains
> The quick returns of courtesie and wit:
> In vies of favours whether partie gains,
> When glorie swells the heart, and moldeth it
> To all expressions both of hand and eye,
> Which on the world a true-love-knot may tie,
> And bear the bundle, wheresoe're it goes:
> How many drammes of spirit there must be
> To sell my life unto my friends or foes:
> > Yet I love thee.

> ('The Pearl')

The man who wrote that had clearly renounced a vocation as courtier with difficulty. The first seven lines are instinct with the social sense of one whose body and spirit vibrate to the romance of power. But the whole wonderfully knowing account is conveyed, except for a subdued play of metonymy, in the plainest language until it turns to the stock (and yet, as Herbert uses them, superbly dry) metaphors of the true-love-knot and the bundle. This is followed by the satirically reductive comment on the expense of spirit required by the man of spirit, with its passing metaphorical glint on 'spirit' as a drug calculated with great exactness by those who know what social competition involves. Here Herbert's wit draws on the resources that lie to hand in spoken English rather than on those personal discoveries of paradox and conceit that we associate with Metaphysical wit. And even when his wit takes a more acrobatic Metaphysical form, a subdued wit in the sensitivity to the words and phrasing of ordinary speech is also present.

Though it is easy to contrast Donne's flamboyant self-centredness with Herbert's more social self, something they both have in common is perhaps more important, for it sets them apart from Herbert's followers, Crashaw and Vaughan, and also from Traherne. Donne, for all his angelical leanings, and Herbert, for all his life in God, are firmly set in their earthly life. Their spirituality is the spirituality of those who have to contend with the world and the flesh and see only through a glass darkly. Herbert's poems in their variety and sometimes within their own individual compass convey a feeling for the mixed condition of human life, even when it is lived in intense prayer, for the vicissitude of pleasure and pain, quickness and dullness. Donne, more focused on the dramatic instant of utterance, conveys what it is to be torn between bodily and spiritual existence. And both in their flashes of wit apprehend the supernatural through distortions of the earthly world in which they live. Crashaw, Vaughan and Traherne have, by contrast, little earthly substance and in consequence the relation between the earthly and the spiritual in them is not anguished, though it may be wistful. They melt into the divine in a way that Donne and Herbert never do, and that, if we have Donne and Herbert in mind for comparison, diminishes the vigour of their poetry and its hold on us.

CHAPTER THREE

Richard Crashaw

Life

Richard Crashaw was born some time between late 1612 and early 1613. His father, William Crashaw, was a clergyman, preacher at Bridlington in Yorkshire, afterward at the Temple Church in London until 1613, when he took up a living in Yorkshire again, and then from 1618 rector of St Mary Mapleton in Whitechapel. He was a learned controversialist against Rome. The contrast between the anti-Roman father and the son who became a Roman convert is striking but less significant than might appear. For one thing, William Crashaw died in 1626 when Richard was fourteen. For another, Richard became an Anglo-Catholic or Laudian before he converted to Rome and the relation between his father's polemical work and Laudianism cannot be forced into a simple opposition. The Laudian reform of the Church did not get under way till the 1630s. William, a friend of James Ussher, later Archbishop of Armagh, may have been a Calvinist and vehement anti-papalist, but he was firmly enfolded in the Jacobean Church and in no sense a Puritan malcontent. As controversialist, he argued that the teaching of the medieval Church had been largely that of the reformed Church of England, but that the Jesuits and the Council of Trent had distorted it. Accordingly he brought out the continuities between the medieval and the reformed English Church. After his death, the Laudians would develop the idea of continuity in an Anglo-Catholic direction.[1] That direction was not imagined by the father, but the son in adopting it ardently cannot exactly be said to have reacted against his father's views.

---

1. Healy 1986, pp. 14–32; I am generally indebted to Healy for details of Crashaw's life.

The other important events of Crashaw's childhood were the death of his mother (when is not known), his father's remarriage in 1619 and the death of his stepmother in 1620. Ussher, preaching the stepmother's funeral sermon, remarked on her 'singular motherly affection to the child of her predecessor'. It is hard to resist connecting Crashaw's early losses of mothers with his way of attaching himself to powerful women throughout his life and his celebrating the Virgin and various women saints.[2]

In 1629, fatherless as well as motherless, he was admitted to Charterhouse school and from there entered Pembroke College, Cambridge, in 1631. He was an outstanding product of his classical training. In 1634, the year of his graduation, he published a collection of sacred epigrams, *Epigrammatum sacrorum liber*. He had also made a name for himself as a poet in English: he wrote, among other pieces, verses for the 1632 edition of Lancelot Andrewes' sermons, and proficient, if not remarkable, poems on such occasions as a college poet might be expected to commemorate. But he had probably also written extraordinary poems, '*Bulla*' and 'Musicks Duell', if, as seems plausible, most of his secular poetry was written before he went to Peterhouse.[3]

In 1635, Crashaw was elected fellow of Peterhouse and, continuing in that capacity, took orders and was appointed in 1639 curate of Little St Mary's, a parish church, though it was attached to his college. During his years at Pembroke he had adopted high church views. The Master, Benjamin Laney, had succeeded Samuel Harsnett, himself the successor of Launcelot Andrewes, all men of an Anglo-Catholic stamp. At Peterhouse, Crashaw was at the centre of Anglo-Catholicism in Cambridge. John Cosin, its Master, was a leading spirit in the Laudian ceremonial reforms. He enriched the decoration of the college chapel with a crucifix and stained glass and the ritual of its services with incense and bowing at the name of Jesus so that it became a focus of high church devotion and of Puritan hostility. Crashaw himself, according to one account, seems to have preached with a baroque eloquence in keeping with the Laudian stress on the part played by the emotions in worship: his sermons 'ravished more like Poems . . . scattering not so much Sentences [as] Extasies'.[4] At Peterhouse, he made a close friend of Joseph Beaumont, another Laudian and poet, scholar and divine. The two of them discovered in Teresa, the inspirational saint of the Counter-Reformation, a model for their own spirituality, ardent, erotic and seeking self-loss in God. Crashaw, writing from exile, probably to Beaumont, described Peterhouse as a 'little contenfull [*sic*] kingdom'.[5] Within the fractious

---

2. Williams in Crashaw 1970, p. xviii.
3. Martin in Crashaw 1957, p. lxxxix.
4. Crashaw 1957, p. 416.
5. Crashaw 1957, p. xxix.

kingdom of England, Peterhouse felt like a secure inner kingdom, a nest, to use one of his favourite words, where his own devotional work could flourish. Its extravagance, its intensity, and its aesthetic sophistication were all nurtured in this Anglo-Catholic milieu.

Besides Peterhouse, there was the devotional community of Little Gidding, which had been taken up by the Laudians in the 1630s. Crashaw tutored Ferrar Collett, nephew of the founder, Nicholas Ferrar, and was a regular visitor. He attached himself particularly to Ferrar Collett's sister, Mary, who, like himself, had vowed herself to celibacy. He speaks of her in his letter to Beaumont from Leyden as 'my gratious mother', 'to whome I had so holy and happy adherence'.[6] She was thirteen years his senior and had been 'Mother' of the Little Gidding Community. But he takes denial of access to her by her uncles in Leyden more as the loss of a close friend or of a lover than as the loss of a mother; he has a delicately honourable concern that the severance should not be taken to reflect badly on her and wishes to make some return for her kindness by ensuring that her brother Ferrar should succeed to his Fellowship at Peterhouse.

One should see his relation to her and indeed his religious life as well in a wider context of friendship. Crashaw clearly gave himself to close ties with others. His poem 'On Mr. G. Herberts booke . . . sent to a Gentlewoman', the odes 'On a prayer booke sent to Mrs M. R.' and 'To the Same Party Councel concerning her choise', and 'A Letter . . . To the Countess of Denbigh' assume an easy, affectionate yet respectful spiritual intimacy. Beaumont and Thomas Car, a Roman Catholic with whom Crashaw became acquainted in Paris, speak of their friendship with him as an exchange of selves in the manner learned from Cicero's *De Amicitia*. With these men and women, friendship was at least in part an overflowing of religious ardour. But his friendships were not limited to an Anglo-Catholic, or later Roman Catholic, community of spirit. He made friends with Abraham Cowley at Cambridge on the strength of poetry rather than religion, for though Cowley sided with the King in the Civil War, his churchmanship was probably anti-Laudian.[7] When the third edition of *Poetical Blossomes* came out in 1637, Crashaw sent him a charming complimentary poem 'Vpon two greene Apricockes', which turned on the extraordinary precocity of Cowley's talents ('apricot' comes from the Latin *praecox*). Later finding Crashaw in Paris, himself also an exile, Cowley probably helped him to an introduction to the Queen. On Crashaw's death, Cowley wrote one of his finest poems,

---

6. Crashaw 1957, p. xxx. For Beaumont as recipient, see Duncan-Jones 1990, pp. 174–79.
7. See his poem congratulating Bishop Williams on his release from prison to which he had been condemned after Laud had brought a successful case for libel against him.

celebrating rather a friendship that respected difference of religion and poetic inspiration than the sort of union of soul Beaumont and Car speak of.

We have run ahead of events. Crashaw's sheltered life at Peterhouse involved him in the political conflicts that came to a head in the Civil War. The ritualistic Christianity in which he expanded as a poet aroused widespread fear that the King, encouraged by his Roman Catholic Queen and by the triumphant Laudian party, would overturn the English Protestant settlement and take the country back to Rome. With this went other fears, in particular that Charles in advancing the Laudian party was investing the monarchy with divine sanctions that implied despotic rule. Laudianism was sacerdotalist, setting the priesthood apart from the laity. As Supreme Governor of the Church of England, Charles took on sacred powers, priestly as well as kingly. And apart from matters of mystique and image-making, Charles involved the Church in political power by appointing bishops to positions that the landowning classes thought should be theirs.

Trouble with the Laudian Church first broke out in Scotland, where Charles's attempt to impose a Prayer Book after the English model inflamed the resentment, national and ecclesiastical, of that irritable nation and afforded its nobility an opportunity to lead a popular revolt against the rule of bishops. The two short Bishops' Wars that followed in 1638 and 1640 as a result of Charles's inability to negotiate forced him to turn to the English Parliament for money, first for an army, then to pay off the victorious Scots. Opposition to the King in Parliament was focused on the bishops. It began with the debate on the Root and Branch Petition for their abolition. Episcopacy was not in fact abolished by Parliament until 1643 after war had broken out, and the Court of High Commission, the body through which the bishops exercised coercive power, was only one of the props of Charles's personal rule to be removed in the earlier proceedings of the Long Parliament. Nevertheless, the bishops rather than royal despotism were the target of Parliamentary opposition, and a target that at first united many against Charles who later would take his side.[8]

Following the Irish Rebellion of late 1641, which brought to a head every sort of fear of a Catholic absolutism, it became obvious that the issues between both sides could only be settled by war. Fighting began in 1642. In 1643, Cromwell occupied Cambridge for Parliament and the rooting out of Anglo-Catholicism began. Parliamentary Commissioners went about the work of desecrating Peterhouse and Little St Mary's in December. Crashaw had already fled in January 1642. By February 1644, he was in Leyden, excluded there from the society of Mary Collett, perhaps because her uncles

---

8. Morrill 1993, pp. 295–96; see also Marvell 1971b, pp. 133–35.

suspected him of turning to Rome. His letter to Beaumont speaks with extraordinary obscurity of the need for 'fixing', which may refer to the possibility of converting.[9] Perhaps later in 1644 he drifted to Oxford, then held by the King. But no certain information of his whereabouts exists before a letter of September 1646 from the Queen in Paris, which, in the course of recommending him to the Pope as a convert, says that he has been close to her for a year. It is unlikely he had not gone over to Rome by the time he had joined her in 1645. He may, of course, have converted earlier.

We can only conjecture what his reasons for conversion were. The Peterhouse of Cosin and Beaumont was staunchly Church of England. The apparently Roman Catholic cast of Crashaw's religion, its asceticism, its sensuality, its ritualism, its celebration of the Virgin and of the saints, in fact went with Anglo-Catholicism. Even his 'Letter to the Countess of Denbigh', persuading her 'against Irresolution and Delay in matters of Religion' to fix on Rome, argues simply for commitment and the surrender of self to God, not for any distinct Roman position. Perhaps he thought that Anglo-Catholicism was beyond restitution. It was clear after the Battle of Naseby in June 1645 that the King had lost the war; Laud had already been executed in January. Crashaw may have decided that the only place left for religion as he understood it was in the Roman Church.

The Queen's recommendation did not secure Crashaw papal employment. A second letter eventually got him a place in the retinue of Cardinal Palotto in Rome; but after he complained about the immorality of the Cardinal's servants, he was transferred for his own safety to Loreto, where he obtained a living in return for singing the offices. He died within a few months in August 1649. The cathedral of Loreto, a celebrated pilgrim centre, is built around the Santa Casa, supposedly the house of the Virgin transported by angels from Palestine to Italy. One feels that Crashaw would have imagined for his end such a place and such an occupation.

It is not easy to say what sort of man Crashaw was. For Cowley, he was '*Poet* and *Saint*' ('On the Death of Mr Crashaw). His Catholic friend Thomas Car, who knew him in Paris, certainly represents him as otherworldly:

> What he might eate or weare he tooke no thought.
> His needfull foode, he rather found then sought.
> He seekes no downes, no sheetes, his bed's still made.
> If he can find a chaire or stoole, he's layd,
> When day peepes in, he quitts his restlesse rest.
> And still, poore soule, before he's vp he's drest.[10]

---

9. Crashaw 1957, p. xxxi.
10. 'Crashawe the Anagramme, He was Car', ll. 29–34 (Crashaw 1957, p. 233).

Anthony à Wood puts it that he was a 'meer Scholar, and very shiftless'.[11] He seems to have been lost outside the secluded devotional circles of Peterhouse and Little Gidding; perhaps he found a replacement in Loreto. He was ascetic, a voluptuary only in poetry and, once he entered Peterhouse, only on sacred themes. He is one of the happiest poets in English, but his happiness is of one for whom the world is well lost. Still, that is in poetry, and how his poetry, supremely artificial and precious, links up with his life, or life in general, is not easily made out. In comparison with representatives of nineteenth- and twentieth-century waves of Anglo-Catholicism, Crashaw seems intellectually and emotionally uncomplicated. Again, in comparison with the Aesthetes and Decadents like Swinburne, with whom he has been compared, he seems curiously innocent and free from melancholy in his defiance of nature.[12] He is not in the least a fallen angel. He had, of course, enormous institutional backing for his eccentricity. His extravagance has a quality of high-spirited, if dotty, self-sacrifice that would be hard to carry off in another period but goes with Cavalier disdain of mediocrity.[13] And even if he belonged to an Anglo-Catholic clique, he drew on fairly universal traditions of Christian thought and feeling.

Apart from the *Epigrammatum sacrocum liber* of 1634, he published nothing. It was probably Joseph Beaumont who brought out the two-volume edition of his sacred and secular verse in 1646 entitled *Steps to the Temple* and *Delights of the Muses* while Crashaw was in Rome, and then a second edition with revisions and additions in 1648. Thomas Car was responsible for the 1652 posthumous Paris edition of the religious poems, *Carmen deo nostro*, again with revisions, perhaps in a Roman Catholic direction and incorporating the previously unpublished 'Letter to the Countess of Denbigh'. The 'Letter' was published in England in 1653.

Crashaw's poetry

Crashaw's exotic talent is often said to be unEnglish. It was, nevertheless, nurtured in an academic environment intensely involved in English religious politics. Only if we judge Anglo-Catholicism unEnglish would it follow that Crashaw's religion was imported from the continental Counter-Reformation. Besides, eroticized piety had already appeared in Giles

---

11. *Athenae Oxonienses* (1691), 2, vol. II, col. 688, quoted by Martin in Crashaw 1957, p. 417.
12. Praz 1958, p. 247.
13. Cf. Beaumont, *Psyche*, canto xxi, sts 3–7; Benlowes, *Theophila*, II, liv: 'Anathema to lukewarm souls'.

Fletcher's *Christ's Victory and Triumph* of 1610. It was given epical treatment in Joseph Beaumont's *Psyche* (1648) and very curiously taken up in the *Theophila* (1652) of Beaumont's admirer Edward Benlowes. Beaumont and Benlowes were high churchmen, but Fletcher was not. And so far from being limited to those whose religion was of a ritualistic and so, it might be argued, at least crypto-Roman cast, extravagant expressions of religious love might be found among spiritually high-flying Puritans of the Civil War period. Francis Rous, Walter Craddock and above all the Scots Covenanter Samuel Rutherford write in styles that draw heavily on the love talk of the Song of Solomon. Rutherford's writing is a splendid site for the botanist of the visionary and grotesque forms that sacred love may take: Jesus as lover, Jesus as mother and even Jesus as Capuchin ('For that the Gospel tongue of the Physician Christ should lick the rotten Blood of the Soul's Wound, speaketh more than imaginable Free-love').[14] Along with those eminently respectable figures, whose raptures, however wild, were at least contained within socially, if not politically, conservative frameworks, we might place the Ranters, whose dissolving of boundaries between high and low, spiritual and carnal, was lived out in radical style.[15] At least one context then for Crashaw's poetry is British dithyrambic writing of the 1630s and 1640s.

At the same time that Crashaw's mystical piety was solidly embedded in the Laudian movement, it obviously took inspiration from abroad. His teachers of heavenly love were the saints of the Counter-Reformation, such as Teresa and François de Sales.[16] And his art also looked to European models. When he wrote sacred Latin epigrams as academic exercises at Pembroke, the masters of this form, with its turns and conceits, were the Jesuits.[17] He developed the scope of this pointed style in English by imitating the Latin *'Bellum musicum'* of the Jesuit Strada in his 'Musicks Duell' and translating the first book of Marino's *La Strage de gli innocenti*, *'Sospetto d'Herode'*. In the first, he astonishingly overgoes his original; in the second, he improves the wit of the acknowledged Italian master of the conceit. In his more ambitious sacred poems he may have learned from the Spanish masters as well.[18] But his relation to European *concettismo* is not servile: he writes as a master, using what he picked up for his own purposes. In contrast to Drummond of Hawthornden, an equally literary artist, equally in touch with European poets of late Petrarchism, Crashaw does not borrow phrases

---

14. Rutherford 1727, p. 38.
15. See Nigel Smith 1983.
16. Allison 1948.
17. Warren 1939, pp. 78ff.
18. Praz 1958, pp. 233–45; Young 1982. See also Schwenger 1976, for Crashaw's connections with Italian theories of wit.

or diffuse effects but develops and concentrates the tricks of the style for his own ends. Perhaps it is not so much his debt to Italian or Spanish writers as his aesthetic sophistication that makes him seem foreign. After all Petrarchism, if not in its latest, most evolved forms, had long passed into English poetic currency.

The artifice and skill of Crashaw's poetry can be seen on a small scale in an epigram:

> Her eyes flood lickes his feets faire staine,
> Her haires flame lickes up that againe.
> This flame thus quench't hath brighter beames:
> This flood thus stained fairer streames.[19]

Crashaw is working with the story of the repentant prostitute, by tradition identified with Mary Magdalene, who *'began to wash his feet with teares and wipe them with the haires of her head* (Luc. 7)'.[20] Typically, he at once reduces and elaborates his given to the play of two sets of contraries, water and fire, stain and beauty (which will include shining and purity), to produce two paradoxes, fire that is the brighter for being extinguished, water that is the purer for being stained. Unlike Donne's paradoxes, Crashaw's rarely have an intellectual point. When Donne writes that Christ is 'Zenith to us, and to'our antipodes', he is grasping at an idea of divine transcendence of space. When Crashaw transforms the behaviour of water and flame, he aims at an artificial reversal of the laws of nature, which in this case suggests fantastically the presence of the divine.

The playful surprise of art is made possible by the Petrarchan conventionalizing and stylizing of the elements of the narrative. Tears are made floods and streams so that they may pass into the curling as well as the shining of the hair, and the shining and curling of hair and water pass into flame.[21] And both flood and flame may be said to 'lick'. 'Lick' also carries suggestions of loving greed, a wish to absorb the thing it loves frequently suggested in Crashaw's language of drinking and being drunk (in both senses), bathing in what one drinks. That infuses the transposition of contrary terms, which might be the last frigidity of art, with a warm erotic impulse. The oxymoronic transformation of the dirt on Christ's feet into 'his feets faire staine' and the way the stain cleanses the water that washes it away plays on a Petrarchan fancy of the beloved bathing and 'washing the

---

19. Crashaw 1957, p. 97; all citations of Crashaw are to this edition.
20. This, prefixed by 'She', is the title of Crashaw's epigram.
21. Etymologically 'torrent' and the Scots word 'burn' are metaphors drawn from the swirling of fire. Magdalene's hair was sometimes pictured as red.

waters with her beauties white'.[22] In doing so it suggests not just Christ's divinity, or even that tears of repentance in washing sin away are heavenly; it suggests an adoration and self-abasement that make stains fair.

These feelings are not so much Mary Magdalene's as feelings aroused aesthetically, drawn by art from the idea of her. Crashaw's art is in some ways about nothing. It plays with conventionalized literary counters. The artifice concentrates sensations and combines them expertly to arouse feeling in an enclosed world or 'cabinet of sweets', in Herbert's phrase. The effect is enhanced by the patterning of word and sound. There is assonance on 'a' and alliteration on 'f', 'fl', 'b' and 'st'. One notes also the collocations of strongly stressed monosyllables in the first couplet, which help to make the sounds glow richly. The repeated syntax of the first and second lines is varied as if with a pleasing quaver since, while the flood licks, the flame licks up; and again in the second couplet, the absence of 'hath' in the last line allows us to wobble between the pattern of the third line ('The flood thus stained [hath] fairer streames') and dropping it and thinking of 'streames' as a verb. The epigram is cut off from any imagining of what it might have been to be Mary Magdalene or even of what it is to repent. Its patterning of sound and sense concentrates not on making the biblical story come to life, but on the aesthetic possibilities of tears, feet and hair. It is curious that so precious a concoction works on the emotions so powerfully.

It is not surprising that Crashaw wrote a masterpiece on art, and on the art of music at that, whose abstract patterns work immediately on the emotions. 'Musicks Duell' is not really a poem about anything; it is a fantasia that explores in words the art emotions aroused by music. The narrative is charmingly inane. A lutanist, playing at midday under an oak, stirs up a nightingale to rival him in song. He opens with a sweet '*Præludium*' and the nightingale responds in kind. Twice they return to the contest, each straining higher, and twice she outdoes him. Shamed, he outdoes himself; in vain she struggles to bring out a single note in answer and dies, 'Falling upon his Lute; ô fit to have / (That liv'd so sweetly) dead, so sweet a Grave' (ll. 167–68). This preposterous tale was translated from the Latin into Italian and embellished by Marino and widely imitated in English.[23] Like the lutanist and nightingale, Crashaw is entering a competition and seeking to outdo his predecessors by force of art.

His art shows itself in an astonishing display of onomatopoeia in which he catches in verse the different sounds of lute and nightingale:

---

22. Greville, *Caelica*, XXII.
23. Warren 1939, p. 107.

His nimble hands instinct then taught each string
A capring cheerefullnesse; and made them sing
To their own dance; now negligently rash
Hee throwes his Arme, and with a long drawne dash
Blends all together; then distinctly tripps
From this to that; then quick returning skipps
And snatches this againe, and pauses there.
Shee measures every measure, every where
Meets art with art; sometimes as if in doubt
Not perfect yet, and fearing to bee out
Trayles her playne Ditty in one long-spun note,
Through the sleeke passage of her open throat:
A cleare unwrinckled song, then doth she point it
With tender accents, and severely joynt it
By short diminutives, that being rear'd
In controverting warbles evenly shar'd,
With her sweet selfe she wrangles.

(ll. 27–43)

The combination of 't's and short 'i's in 'His nimble hands instinct then taught each string' or 'then distinctly tripps / From this to that; then quick returning skipps / And snatches this againe' imitates the plucked chirping of the lute, and the pauses and enjambments skilfully suggest the runs and rests of virtuoso lute playing with a *sprezzatura* that seems 'negligently rash' yet picks out the notes with the distinctness of great accomplishment. As for the lines devoted to the nightingale, they will delight and astonish, with their rendering of liquid trills and flutings, anyone who has heard that bird. A churring harshness in the sweetness comes out in the play on 'r': 'Shee measures every measure, every where / Meets art with art'; 'With her sweet selfe shee wrangles'. Setting off that, she 'Trayles her playne Ditty in one long-spun note, / Through the sleeke passage of her open throat: / A cleare unwrinckled song'. The punctuation here cannot disguise the sustained unornamented sound carried on from line to line. Long vowels and again Crashaw's trick of running together series of strongly stressed monosyllables help to spin out the note.

As well as matching sound and sense by onomatopoeia, Crashaw awakens sounds in the mind's ear by synaesthesia. 'The sleeke passage of her open throat' makes us feel the vocalizing with delicious smoothness. Similarly the smoothness of 'a cleare unwrinckled song' is seen or felt, though a steadily held note is meant, which can only be heard.

By a kind of paradox the single note is said in its fullness to constitute a song in itself, without the changings or wrinklings that make a melody.

146

That points to another aspect of Crashaw's art, his appreciation of the art of music. So when the nightingale first hears 'the soft report' of the lute, she 'mold[s] the same / In her owne murmures' (ll. 12–13). This means she quietly accompanies the lute, but the synaesthetic word 'mold' brings in tactile and visual arts of shaping to suggest how the nightingale feels her way as an artist of the voice into another's music. Crashaw delights in her after all more as a soprano than as a bird. He is a connoisseur of how she 'Carves out her dainty voyce' (l. 22) as he is of every 'delicious stroake' (l. 131) of the lutanist. He searches out with an exact analytic sensuality how music is made to fall on the ear. So, to illustrate at greater length, the lutanist, after being magnificently carried away by a sort of heroic fury, plays softer

> and anon
> Creeps on the soft touch of a tender tone:
> Whose trembling murmurs melting in wild aires
> Runs to and fro, complaining his sweet cares
> Because those pretious mysteryes that dwell,
> In musick's ravish't soule hee dare not tell,
> But whisper to the world.

> (ll. 139–45)[24]

Crashaw will have some definite musical effect in mind when he writes of 'trembling murmurs melting in wild aires'; though I have not been able to find what that is, the way slow, quiet music may tremble on the edge of eddying rapture ('wild' carries the sense of 'ecstatic' in 'Musicks Duell') should be familiar enough, and of course the strings of a lute tremble in sounding.

At this point, Crashaw's combining of opposites, soft and wild, explores not so much the art of music as the soul of music, the effect on the listener rather than the way of playing, and, in describing the effect, seeks to reproduce it in words. The effect he is after is ecstatic. Here the 'sweet cares' of which the lutanist complains are not love pains but the delicious pains his music gives him. One notes, all the same, the eroticizing of musical sensation: trembling melts into wildness; the soul of music is 'ravish't'. Erotic suggestions lend a warm glow to the analysis and also suggest a momentum and a melting of one thing into another that must find its end in rapture. So it is that the lutanist's 'blest soule' is 'snatcht out at his Eares / By a strong Extasy' and seated 'In th' *Empyraeum* of pure Harmony' (ll. 147–50). More

---

24. The Tanner MS has 'murmure' (l. 141), which makes grammatical sense (Crashaw 1957, p. 153).

secretly, if music's soul is ravished, it can only be by music itself, just as the lutanist is carried away by his own playing. Where the music becomes overwhelmingly present to itself, it is self-ravished into a platonic ecstasy. Earlier the nightingale's song has transported her:

> Her little soule is ravisht: and so pour'd
> Into loose extasies, that she is plac't
> Above her selfe, Musicks *Enthusiast*.

> (ll. 102–4)

An enthusiast is someone inspired by a god; the nightingale is ravished by the godhead of music present in her own singing. The erotic motif is carried a stage further in the death of the nightingale possessed by the ambition of a song too huge for her to utter. She dies of a desire for the illimitable, and if her death is not a love-death exactly, still in the same way as Crashaw's equivocation on death and orgasm in his religious poetry eroticizes the extinction of self, so the anguish of the nightingale's death is sweetened by its association with music and absorbed into musical feeling.

Crashaw's art has been called in a gaudy but apt phrase an art of ecstasy.[25] An ecstasy is a withdrawal from the world we share with others. Crashaw's exceedingly unreal tale of the lutanist and the nightingale gives him a start in taking leave of the world His embellishment of the tale transforms its mimetic emptiness or freedom from real content into a self-conscious display of art, a performance like the performances it describes. 'Musicks Duell' is not a self-referential poem exactly, about itself. But although I have spoken about Crashaw's exploring and analysing the effect of music and of his describing performances, it would be better to say that he exuberantly descants on the performances and that in doing so his art aspires to the condition of music and indeed almost dissolves the boundaries between the poem and its subject:

> From this to that, from that to this hee flyes
> Feeles Musicks pulse in all her Arteryes,
> Caught in a net which there *Appollo* spreads,
> His fingers struggle with the vocall threads,
> Following those little rills, hee sinkes into
> A Sea of *Helicon*.

> (ll. 119–24)

---

25. Petersson 1970.

Does this passage strive to imitate lute-playing by a remarkable derangement of the senses or does it take memories of lute-playing and mix them with other sensations to create an effect reminiscent of the delights aroused by lute music without being tied to imitation of it? Whatever the case, it is clear that the point of Crashaw's ornamentation or encrustation of lute-playing is to awaken an impulse toward ecstasy, an art ecstasy in which the ordinary terms of life are suspended.

The same combination of artifice and rapture can be found in the Neolatin poem on a bubble, '*Bulla*'. Even more flauntingly than in 'Musicks Duell', the subject of Crashaw's fantasia on a bubble is almost nothing, and, like 'Musicks Duell', '*Bulla*' ends in extinction. 'O sum (scilicet O nihil)', exclaims the bubble with abandon ('I am O, not anything'), meaning not just that it is round like O but has burst. Around nothing, Crashaw stretches a shimmering phantasmagoria, inspired perhaps by the iridescent crawling of the bubble's film and the glancing, wobbling reflections on it:

> Over your changing skin
> Drunk with a thousand dyes,
> The Rainbow, analine,
> Shining, slippery, flies
> With a rout of wandering
> Shapes in colourful dance,
> Goddess! wantoning
> In whirling insouciance,
> Treacherous giddiness,
> Chasing herself. She falters
> Beautifully, then flows,
> So delusive, alters
> Continually and goes
> All possible winding ways
> Of coming back. A vein
> Stains the wandering maze
> And spills a drunken train.[26]

'Bulla' takes off from its ostensible subject even further than 'Musicks Duell'. The pulse it moves to is not so much erotic as a wild dance in which everything mingles and this allows Crashaw as extravagant and licentious a synaesthetic play as in 'Musicks Duell'. Moreover the whirling rout involves the whole universe:

---

26. *Cujus per varium latus, / Cujus per teretem globum / Iris lubrica cursitans / Centum per species vagas, / Et picti facies chori / Circum regnat, & undique / Et se Diva volatilis / Jucundo levis impetu / Et vertigine perfidâ / Lascivâ sequitur fugâ / Et pulchrè dubitat; fluit / Tam fallax toties novis, / Tot se per reducas vias, / Errorésque reciprocos / Spargit vena Coloribus; / Et pompâ natat ebriâ* (ll. 19–34).

The lovely lascivious reel
Here blushes green and there
Greens red. The teetering wheel
Traced by its starry tail
Revolves in a higher sphere.
Complexity in heaven!
Spheres run into each other.[27]

Everything is reduced to what Crashaw calls 'lovely Chaos' (l. 42).

In '*Bulla*', unlike 'Musicks Duell', there is no definite centre of consciousness to be extinguished by the riot of sense or to go into raptures. The nearest is the bubble itself, personified as a giddy woman, who at the end declares her not being. In an amusing way, this will correspond to the self-loss of the nightingale and the lutanist and the self-loss to which Crashaw aspires religiously. Strikingly, Crashaw's art exercises itself as much about the empty case as about those that must have mattered more to him, and strikingly, if we accept the conjectural dating of these masterpieces to his earlier Pembroke years and not to his religiously devoted Peterhouse ones, secular even more than religious subjects were those on which he first developed his art of ecstasy.

Crashaw's art of ecstasy is most famously at work in his St Teresa poems, above all in 'The Flaming Heart'. There, one is tempted to say, his talent for poetic rapture found its true vocation. But aesthetic refinement and even playfulness are at work even in that ardent prayer for self-immolation. A rapture for Crashaw is not the occasion for the art of a solemn, if magnificent, spontaneous overflow of recalled visionary transport of the sort one comes across in Wordsworth.

'The Flaming Heart' treats St Teresa's 'Transverberation'.[28] In that, the most famous of her mystical experiences, a beautiful angel appeared to her holding a golden burning dart, which he plunged into her vitals causing her pain and pleasure beyond expression. Crashaw's treatment begins in a vein of precious gallantry, probably on the model of Carew's 'To a Painter'. He takes to task the artist who drew this incident to illustrate her *Life*, maintaining gaily that Teresa should have been represented as the angel burning with heavenly love and the angel (overcome with shame at being outdone as heavenly lover) as a veiled nun. Or, he continues, if convention must overrule and the angel appear with the attributes that should by rights be hers,

---

27. *Illîc cum viridi rubet, / Hîc & cum rutilo viret / Lascivi facies chori. / Et quicquid rota lubrica / Caudæ stelligeræ notat, / Pulchrum perdit ambitum. / Hîc coeli implicitus labor, / Orbes orbibus obvii* (ll. 88–95).
28. See St Teresa 1957, ch. 20.

Leaue HER alone THE FLAMING HEART.
  Leaue her that; & thou shalt leaue her
Not one loose shaft but loue's whole quiuer.
For in loue's feild was neuer found
A nobler weapon then a WOVND.
Loue's passiues are his actiu'st part.
The wounded is the wounding heart.
O HEART! the æquall poise of loue's both parts
Bigge alike with wounds & darts.
Liue in these conquering leaues: liue all the same;
And walk through all tongues one triumphant FLAME
Liue here great HEART; & Loue and dy & kill;
And bleed & wound; and yeild & conquer still.
  . . .

O thou vndaunted daughter of desires!
By all thy dowr of LIGHTS & FIRES;
By all the eagle in thee, all the doue;
By all thy liues & deaths of loue;
By thy larg draughts of intellectuall day,
And by thy thirsts of loue more large then they;
By all thy brim-fill'd Bowles of feirce desire
By thy last Morning's draught of liquid fire;
By the full kingdome of that finall kisse
That seiz'd thy parting Soul, & seal'd thee his;
By all the heau'ns thou hast in him
(Fair sister of the SERAPHIM!
By all of HIM we haue in THEE;
Leaue nothing of my SELF in me.
Let me so read thy life, that I
Vnto all life of mine may dy.

(ll. 68–80; 93–108)

As in '*Bulla*' and 'Musicks Duell' there is a giddy synaesthetic play, here especially with drinking. Teresa swallows light, she drinks 'liquid fire' from 'brim-fill'd Bowles of feirce desire'; there may be an equivocation on 'bowls' and 'bowels'; in any event the 'liquid fire' she drinks is desire itself and so illimitable, a desire that is both hers and divine. Her final kiss is a 'full kingdome'. One thing passes into another with a rapid, diffuse excitement and the effect is made the more overwhelming by the repeated liturgical strokes at the beginnings of lines of 'By all' (anaphora). Allied with synaesthesia in the confounding of sense is the startling combination of opposites. That is already there in the liquid fire. But above all it comes out in the splendid topsy-turvydom of 'in loue's whole feild was never

151

found / A nobler weapon than a WOUND'. Not only does this produce a miraculous inversion of wound and weapon, it also overturns the rule of Petrarchan love that the wounds caused by the beloved's beauty only increase her coldness and cruelty. In the realm of sacred love to be wounded with the desire for God is to draw a response from an unfailing divine lover and also to wound others with the same passion. There are other suspensions of the natural order in the playful or wilful forcing of conceits. It is not enough that the flaming heart should live in the leaves of her book or that things as slight as leaves should be conquering; the heart walks, and walks in a flame through all tongues. Possibly there is a pun on leaves; almost certainly the double sense of tongues is exploited for incongruous and unnatural effect as well as for doubling of meaning – Teresa's book will be translated into all languages and her story will be in everyone's mouth; and there will be an allusion to the tongues of Pentecostal fire: 'And there appeared unto them cloven tongues like as of fire, and it sat upon each of them. And they were all filled with the holy Ghost, and began to speak with other tongues, each of them' (Acts, 2). It is hard to say where preciosity, a conscious play with the absurdity of figurative expression, ends and visionary grotesqueness begins.

In addition to artificiality, 'The Flaming Heart' shares with 'Musicks Duell' and '*Bulla*' a drive to extinction. Crashaw invokes the ardour of St Teresa to induce in himself a mystic death of self:

> Leaue nothing of my SELF in me.
> Let me so read they life, that I
> Vnto all life of mine may dy.

Self is sin, what separates one from God; ecstatic self-loss is dying into the divine. As is frequently said, Crashaw's is a ritual art, seeking to abolish by incantatory repetition and patterning a sober sense of self and world. Unlike Herbert or Donne, he does not struggle with himself at prayer; he joins in hymns and re-enactments of the feasts of the Church. The last sixteen self-immolating lines of 'The Flaming Heart' echo the liturgy of the Book of Common Prayer.[29] But equally important in the reduction of self is the play Crashaw makes of St Teresa's book.

'The Flaming Heart' starts by cavilling at an edition of St Teresa's *Life* and celebrates the way the book works on him. By metonymic reduction, St Teresa becomes a heart on fire and the sphere of her activity is similarly compressed into the incongruous and punning figures of leaves and tongues

---

29. Warren, p. 142.

involving books that we have already examined. Or consider this delightful converting of her book into sunlight coming through trees:

> Let all thy scatter'd shafts of light, that play
> Among the leaues of thy larg Books of day
> Combin'd against this Brest at once break in.

(ll. 87–89)

His prayer is that he may 'so read [her] life that I / Vnto all life of mine may dy'. Crashaw contracts Teresa's life and inspiration of him into a frame of reading and perhaps writing about reading rather as the maker of a Byzantine icon might reduce spatial relations to a two-dimensional flatness and boundedness the better to absorb and deepen concentration, to produce a sacred space in which devotional operations might be imagined. Crashaw's rapture can then take place on the page.

In other poems involving books, Crashaw comes in as an intermediary rather than as the person to be worked on, the passive to be made active by love. But again the working of divine love is contracted into the agencies of book and reader. So in 'On Mr G. Herberts booke intituled the Temple ... sent to a Gentlewoman', Crashaw manages to suggest a Herbertian love sacrifice in a Petrarchan love exchange between God and the book's recipient all in terms of the eye and the page:

> Know you faire, on what you looke;
> Divinest love lyes in this booke:
> Expecting fire from your eyes,
> To kindle this his sacrifice.

(ll. 1–4)

The agency of the book, Crashaw then personifies as an angel miraculously present and sporting in the breathing of the prayer and spiriting it upward:

> When your hands unty these strings,
> Thinke you have an Angell by th' wings.
> One that gladly will bee nigh,
> To wait upon each morning sigh,
> To flutter in the balmy aire,
> Of your well perfumed prayer.

(ll. 5–10)

'Wings' is another of Crashaw's puns that spiritualizes the book: it means the book bindings as well as the angel's wings. The strings are the ribbons that tie the wings shut.

Crashaw eroticizes the relation of reader and book. He does so not just in terms of the Petrarchan eye but of another confined space, the lady's chamber, to which he has a privileged entry as giver of the book. One is reminded of Belinda's boudoir in *The Rape of the Lock* and the extraordinary play of erotic fancy around her, except that Pope is teasing and debunking about the spiritual agencies surrounding his heroine, where Crashaw takes the part of devotional go-between, of courtier for God, playfully but innocently, or at least with fond intentions. He salutes the gentlewoman as 'faire' and compliments her balmy breath to awaken a sense of her desirability and to transfer that to religious longing. All the gentlewoman's sweetness is to be rolled up into religious desire, which will make her prayer well perfumed in God's nostrils like an acceptable sacrifice. In this mixing of sacred and profane desire, it is hard to know who is the desired and who the desiring. Is it that the woman is moved to religious desire by being wakened to consciousness that she is desirable? Is it that Crashaw is moved to religious desire by imagining himself close to the woman aroused to prayer by his love talk? As the book he proffers on the altar of her white hand is an intermediary agent between the woman and God, so the inflamed and inflaming woman is the intermediary agent in his own devotional feeling. His whole art is bent not to distinguish himself and her, but to blend them together in a flame of desire, not (of course) for each other but for the divine beyond themselves. And consequently, where Pope takes a sly revenge on Belinda as love-creature, Crashaw's delight is to enter a woman's

> Amorous languishments; luminous trances;
> SIGHTS which are not seen with eyes;
> Spirituall & soul-peircing glances
> Whose pure & subtil lightning flyes
> Home to the heart, & setts the house on fire
> And melts it downe in sweet desire
>   Yet does not stay
> To aske the windows leaue to passe that way.

(ll. 69–77)[30]

This transposition of the amorous moodiness of an upper-class woman into a religious key comes from another of Crashaw's book poems, 'An

---

30. Crashaw 1977, p. 330.

Ode, which was Praefixed to a little Prayer-book giuen to a young Gentle-woman'. One thinks of the diffuse languishings of Olivia in *Twelfth Night* or perhaps of Susanna in Wallace Stevens's 'Peter Quince at the Clavier'. It is probably to the point to add that these are all men's imaginings of women's love impulses. How does Crashaw know about the young gentle-woman's 'sweet desires'? Still his enthusiasm in these matters is likeable. But it must be added that his enthusiasm is ascetic. Like Pope's Ariel, Crashaw is jealous lest there should be 'an earthly lover lurking at [his gentlewoman's] heart'. Human loves belong to 'the god of flyes' (l. 51), Beelzebub. Only where the appetite is for God can love be given free rein. Just how free is startling. As in 'The Flaming Heart', Crashaw borrows from Carew, this time from his pornographic 'Rapture'.[31] In Crashaw's invitation that his gentlewoman should in her 'sweet ecstasy expire', Carew's imaginings become

> O let the blissfull heart hold fast
> Her heauenly arm-full, she shall tast
> At once ten thousand paradises;
>   She shall haue power
>   To rifle & deflour
> The rich & roseall spring of those rare sweets
> Which with a swelling bosome there she meets
> . . .
>
>   What joy, what blisse,
> How many Heau'ns at once it is
> To haue her GOD become her LOVER.

(ll. 111–17; 122–24)

Like St Teresa, the woman will take the active part as lover; her ardour will take heaven by storm.

Like Herbert, only more boldly, Crashaw wondered why the devil should have the best tunes. The task of converting the language of carnal love to religious ends was made easier by Carew's having already perfumed his invitation to sexual enjoyment in Petrarchan language and the fiction of a love Elysium. Before ever Crashaw got to work on on it, human desire had been transported to paradise and only through metaphor and insinuation did it come to earth. Crashaw had only to reverse the charge of the metaphor, transposing its tenor from earth to heaven, and to drop the insinuation,

---

31. See Allison 1947.

for the paradisal fiction to bear a religious sense. In redirecting Petrarchan eroticism, he was taking a risk of falling into what Burns called 'Spiritualized bawdry'.[32] And perhaps there is a distasteful suggestion of devotional pimping about the 'Ode'. But the eroticism of the poem and of 'The Flaming Heart' and 'On Mr G. Herberts Booke' is surely too diffuse to deserve Yvor Winters's stricture that Crashaw confused orgasm with mystical union with God.[33] The libertinism of Crashaw's own time, like the naturalism of the century of Pope and Burns or of our own century, would have been quick to make that reductive interpretation. Crashaw must have been aware of the danger. His art of making strange compounds makes any decoding in physical terms forced. It attenuates and etherealizes the erotic impulses it awakens. Crashaw may even have welcomed the risk of low-minded misreading in a vein of high-spirited defiance of the world, happy to lose in human, earthly feeling what he gained in angelic eroticism. That does not mean that he is free from faults of taste, as perhaps in the 'Ode', where enlarging on the delights of divine love in his ardent way, he allows himself to appear too much in the role of God's procurer. In spite of all his art, Crashaw has trouble in grounding the human sense of poems so set on heaven.

'A Letter to the Countess of Denbigh', on the other hand, is a wholly pleasing adaptation of erotic poetry to religious ends. In it, Crashaw does not write about the closed world of the chamber or the book or about the ecstasies of prayer, but adopts some of the arguments and manners of the seduction poem to persuade the vacillating Countess to convert to Rome. He does not use the prospect of heavenly rapture as a persuasion. His arguments are more witty and paradoxical. The fun lies partly in the reversal of conventional values in the religious sphere. To yield to a man is something to which a virtuous woman must offer resistance. But as Crashaw puts it, to yield to God is a duty as well as a pleasure. The earthly seducer must deploy every art of sophistry to overcome the arguments of religion, morality and modesty. As heavenly seducer, Crashaw has rather to invent ways of representing the Countess's reluctance as chastity at the same time as he argues for its unreasonableness. The game is amusing and tactful. It makes out that the Countess's delay is honourable, while allowing Crashaw to remonstrate with ardour. And by reducing the issues between Protestantism and Rome to resistance and yielding, he can also suggest, in seducer mode, that the hesitating will must have a delicious inclination to what it resists:

---

32. Prefatory note to 'Holy Willie's Prayer', Burns 1969, p. 56.
33. Winters 1967, pp. 91–93.

What Heav'n-besieged Heart is this
Stands Trembling at the Gate of Blisse:
Holds fast the Door, yet dares not venture
Fairly to open and to enter?

(ll. 1–4)

This could be read as an indignant rebuke to religious withholding.[34] But it is softened and made affectionate by the game of seduction, where the 'Trembling at the Gate of Blisse' becomes not so much the Countess's devotional pusillanimity as a perverse inability to give herself to joy. Crashaw's preciosity insinuates self-contradiction. The gate of bliss is the gate to heaven, but heaven must besiege its own gate because the Countess's heart holds it shut. Similarly the Countess may hold fast the door both in resistance and clinging. In this sparkling poem anyway, Crashaw manages to combine the erotic and divine with assurance. The gallant and risqué playfulness gives Crashaw's soul-concerns a light, but also human, warmth and friendly assumption of intimacy with the Countess in her notorious dithering.

It is more difficult to do justice to Crashaw's eroticizing of wounds. 'On the Wounds of Our Lord' is a particularly daunting instance. As one of his sacred epigrams it flaunts its preciosity and artfulness. As one of his Magdalene poems, it uses the amorousness of a woman saint as an intermediary between himself and Christ. We have seen these things before in 'The Flaming Heart', but here, even more grotesquely than in that prayer for love-death, Crashaw blends the horrifying and the erotic with an aesthetic effect that is recognizably strong and yet, whether disturbing or simply repellent, beyond most people's emotional range:

O these wakefull wounds of thine!
  Are they Mouthes? or are they eyes?
Be they Mouthes, or be they eyne,
  Each bleeding part some one supplies.

Lo! a mouth, whose full-bloom'd lips
  At too deare a rate are roses.
Lo! a blood-shot eye! that weepes
  And many a cruell teare discloses.

O thou that on this foot hast laid
  Many a kisse, and many a Teare,
Now thou shal't have all repaid,
  Whatsoe're thy charges were.

---

34. See Strier 1969.

This foot hath got a Mouth and lippes,
  To pay the sweet summe of thy kisses:
To pay thy Teares, an Eye that weeps
  In stead of Teares such Gems as this is.

The difference onely this appeares,
  (Nor can the change offend)
The debt is paid in *Ruby*-Teares
  Which thou in Pearles did'st lend.

Even if it is hard to share the delights of the Magdalene, one can see what Crashaw is trying to do – to effect an aesthetic transformation of the gruesome into Petrarchan beauties. The poem begins by combining beauty and horror in metaphor. In the first stanza, wounds are mouths and eyes, in the second (focusing on one wound), a mouth with rosy lips or an eye weeping tears of blood. The lips are roses 'at too deare a rate' because they are bleeding: feelings of love and grief awakened by the wounds are fixed in this strange aesthetic bloom. In the fourth stanza, the perverse unions return to bring about a miraculous transformation of blood into jewels. It is in this stanza that metaphorical incongruity brings about the most grotesque effect of bodily distortion – the foot has a mouth that is also an eye. What is alarming about these metaphors – the effect is hallucinatory – is not just that a wound is made into Petrarchan beauties but that these Petrarchan beauties are displaced from the face to the foot. One is drawn into adoration so intense that the wound on the foot can take over from the normal expressive indices of the person, the mouth and the eye in the face. And at the same time, this displacement develops a conventional paradox of the Magdalene epigram: in her humility Mary lavished on Christ's feet while he was alive the tears and kisses an ordinary lover would have spent on his face. The most disturbing discords of the poem are at the same time refinements of preciosity, a combination of artifice and expressive violence that we have seen already in Crashaw's ecstatic verse.

The transformation of the wound on the foot into loved parts of the face and of gouts of blood into rubies is effected through a number of steps. It is not by any means that Crashaw just harps on wounds, eyes, mouths, blood and tears until they run riot.[35] Only '*Bulla*' approaches that Swinburnian delirium. Here, there is a method behind the derangement of sense. The wounds are first metaphorized as mouths, that metaphor is developed through 'full-bloom'd lips' into roses, and only then is the mouth transferred to the foot. At each graduation there is an effect of wit, a joining of

---

35. Praz 1958, pp. 247–49.

the physical incongruity with a point appropriate to Magdalenian devotion. At the same time the sound of the verse changes from solemn to gay as the transformation occurs. In the first three lines of the first two stanzas, a heavy trochaic movement rocks across the iambic tetrameter (the opening syllable has been cut). The heaviness is accentuated by alliteration and the movement slowed down by collocations of heavily stressed monosyllables and the prevalence of long vowels. The sound is particularly rich and magnificent in the second stanza. In the fourth stanza, trochees have disappeared. The varied syntactic position of the clauses beginning 'to pay', together with the repetition of 'teares' in 'In stead of Teares', positively skips with the neatness of the substitution. And the agility goes with the devout frivolousness or absurdity into which the poem has modulated. The last stanza in fourteeners ends the poem with a sprightly tinkle.[36] After all, the wounds of Christ are supposed to make a Christian happy.

Whether Crashaw brings off his miraculous transformation of wounds to sources of rubies, of grief to rejoicing, lies beyond my powers of judgement to decide. His wonderfully artificial effects here may convey an angelic gaiety, but the gaiety is inhuman. Talk of the Baroque or of the Christian mystical tradition, both of which may distort the human frame to suggest the breaking in of infinity upon the creaturely and limited, will not resolve the difficulty, though it might help us to accept it. By contrast, 'The Nativity Hymn' does manage to reconcile the unearthly and the warmly human without recourse to difficult feelings.

As so frequently, Crashaw uses the precious to suggest a miraculous suspension of the way of the world. The 'Hymn' is written for two shepherd voices and chorus; it belongs to that most artificial of genres, the amoebean or responsive pastoral. Crashaw's shepherds, Tityrus and Thyrsis, are obviously not country people but exquisites fit to perform the steps of pastoral response. The pair recall the choices of what would make the best bed for the infant with agreeable garrulity. Tityrus rejected snow because, though its 'fleece is white', it 'is too cold'. Thyrsis, on the other hand,

> saw the obsequious SERAPHIMS
> Their rosy fleece of fire bestow.
> For well they now can spare their wings
> Since HEAVN itself lyes here below.
> Well done, said I: but are you sure
> Your down so warm, will passe for pure?

> (ll. 58–63)

---

36. On this effect and others in Crashaw's verse, see Schleiner 1979.

Tityrus then can come in with the ideal solution uniting the warmth of the Seraphim and the white purity of the snow:

> No, no. your KING's not yet to seeke
>   Where to repose his Royall HEAD
> See see, how soon his new-bloom'd CHEEK
>   Twixt's mother's brests is gone to bed.
> Sweet choise, said we! no way but so
> Not to ly cold, yet sleep in snow.

(ll. 65–70)

It is possible that for Crashaw, whose ardour was sensual and yet severely ascetic, the opposition between cold and warm expressed a real conflict, here happily resolved. But it is the artificiality of the way he works up the opposition that will strike most readers, that and the aesthetic blending of qualities. So, for instance, the feathers of the Seraphim, which burn with heavenly love, are described as a 'rosy fleece'. Fleeces are white, and though it is the flocculence and warmth of fleeces that are brought out in the metaphor, 'fleece' nevertheless catches at a thought of whiteness, active because of the equally fleecy snow in the previous stanza. The union of contraries deliciously etherealizes the sensations of warmth. The same combining of contrary qualities and etherealizing of sensuality is at work in the picturing of the Virgin's breasts as warm snow. And at this point the rosiness of the angels' fleeces of fire has been transferred to the new bloomed cheeks of the child. We have seen this sort of mixing of sensations in the dithyrambic couplets of 'The Flaming Heart', but although the mixing here also moves to devout adoration and, in the final chorus, to the characteristic Crashavian prayer for extinction of self, the movement in the Hymn is restrained by the lilting rhythm and more intricate evolution of its stanza.

This exchange is preceded in the 1648 and 1652 versions by a couple of stanzas that are generally considered the finest things in the Hymn:

> *Tity.* Poor WORLD (said I.) what wilt thou doe
>   To entertain this starry STRANGER?
> Is this the best thou canst bestow?
>   A cold, and not too cleanly, manger?
> Contend, ye powres of heau'n & earth.
> To fitt a bed for this huge birthe.
>
>   *Cho.* Contend ye powers
>
> *Thyr.* Proud world, said I; cease your contest
>   And let the MIGHTY BABE alone.

The Phænix builds the Phænix' nest.
   Love's architecture is his own.
The BABE whose birth embraues this morn,
Made his own bed e're he was born.

(ll. 37–56)

These stanzas prepare us both for the contest between heaven and earth over which is to provide the bed for the infant, and for the outcome, which is that both heaven and earth provide the ideal bed between the Virgin's breasts. In them, the aesthetic mixing of contraries is replaced by a more intellectual uniting of heaven and earth. The starry stranger is 'The BABE whose birth embraues this morn'. As God of love, he created the mother who is his own best bed – the grand word 'architecture' hints at a palace in the eye of love. And dying to his heavenly being to be born on earth, like the phoenix, he made the nest that gave him birth and nurture. In this beautiful rehearsal of Christian paradoxes, the 'Great little one' is the place where contraries meet. On him another characteristic turn of Crashaw's style is lavished. He is the point of the universe where the self possesses itself, where those self-reflexive expressions of which Crashaw is so fond rest in themselves. The shepherds saw him 'by [his] own sweet light'. His 'architecture is his own'. For other creatures, such self-embracing is not possible. Their fulfilment is extinction in him, as with the shepherds who pray that 'burnt at last in fire of [his] fair eyes, / Our selues become our own best SACRIFICE' (ll. 107–8). But one notes also that the infant, the self-complete one into whom all others die, is himself the type of self-immolation, a phoenix dying to himself, here in the incarnation as later in the crucifixion.[37]

In Crashaw to an extraordinary degree stylistic mannerism expresses the unfoldings and infoldings of the devotional mind. The self-reflexive flourish, for instance, in the Hymn asserts the triumphant being in itself of the divine. As for the glow with which he invests the mother and child, again the intensity of his art goes with a curious intensity of devotional feeling. The child's eyes do all that a Petrarchan lady's should. The breasts of the Virgin are as desirable and as unattainable as those of the most idealized mistress. The kindling of a heavenly eros by these means lies open to psychoanalytical interpretations, some of which seem apt.[38] It is surely a

---

37. On Crashaw's love of self-reflexive formulations, see Ellrodt 1960, I, p. 379, n. 8; Freer 1979, pp. 78–101.
38. Two psychoanalytical interpretations are Camden 1983 and Fischer 1983.

strength of Crashaw's art that he can waken resonances of the Freudian pre-Oedipal stage or the polymorphous perverse. The infantile explorings of Vaughan and Traherne do not trawl at such a depth.

It is also a strength that at least in the case of the Virgin or women saints he can take pleasure in the female body. His enthusiasm for bosoms, breasts, milk and nests is notorious. Even the name of Jesus when it comes forth in procession has a 'Bosom big with Loues' ('To the Name above Every Name', l. 160), and also a womb with conceptions and a birth. It is difficult to imagine a name with these things, but for Crashaw its adorable divinity is a sort of romantic chasm into which he can heap in metaphor the feminine attributes he adores. Ann More bore a child to Donne almost every year of their marriage until she died. But his poetry does not celebrate mother-hood, or infancy, or the powers of the female body to give birth. If he has a sympathetic feeling for women's bodies it is expressed with a curious indirectness through mathematical, anatomical or metallic figures.[39] In contrast to his exaggeratedly masculine spirit, Crashaw's celibate and highly conventionalized fancy luxuriates amidst female softness, amorousness and motherliness. In 'The Weeper', he dwells on the Magdalene's miraculous tearfulness for thirty-one stanzas. The seventh goes:

> The dew no more will weepe,
> The Primroses pale cheeke to decke,
> The deaw no more will sleepe,
> Nuzzel'd in the Lillies necke.
> Much rather would it tremble heere,
> And leave them both to bee thy Teare.

The art of displacement at work here through metaphorical personification plays on the different meanings of 'trembling' when done by someone or by a drop of water to transfer human feeling to the dewdrop. The concentration of emotion in the drop and its artificial extraction from any human context somehow release feeling as pure quality. The metaphor 'Nuzzel'd' for the clinging of the dewdrop evokes the drawing of childish comfort from a maternal body with startling physicality. No suggestion could be more incongruous for cold dew and chaste lily. The incongruity 'Warmes in the one, cooles in the other' ('Nativity Hymn', l. 90), an effect much sought after in the strange compounds of Crashaw's art. But besides tempering feeling, the incongruity introduces an intentional element of absurdity that

---

39. Carey 1990, ch. 5, 'Bodies', esp. p. 125; but see the salutes to the Virgin in 'La Corona', 2, l. 14 and 'A Litany', l. 41.

takes care of what might otherwise have been an embarrassing indulgence in unmotivated sentiment. It goes with the absurdity cultivated throughout 'The Weeper' as a happy suspension of rationality and natural law in the presence of the divine and feminine.

Conventionally worship is attended by fear. The chariot of paternal deity in which Milton's Son comes forth grasping ten thousand thunders is adorable because dreadful. Donne imagines a terrifying God in the Holy Sonnets to force a change of heart in himself. Herbert, on the other hand, writes sometimes of a lovable God, but with moving spareness; as we have seen he veils literal expressions of the grotesque forms heavenly love may take. Crashaw veils nothing, and he always writes smilingly and never in dread. He treats the more than Keatsian embarrassments of his religious love themes playfully and meltingly. His imagery, unlike Donne's or Herbert's, is drawn from a literary and highly conventionalized stock – no princes lying in prison or cases of knives with him. All is sweet and soft and suppled by having been worked over by previous poets.

Since Crashaw's imagery is so highly conventionalized and takes in so little of the awkward and difficult edges of things, it need answer only to his own designs, and his design is usually impelled by a desire for extinction or self-loss in the divine. That enormously simple and radical scheme gives an intellectual cast to his loosest and most sensual or precious wanderings. So, for example, in 'The Nativity Hymn' Thyrsis recounts how

> Winter chidde aloud; & sent
>   The angry North to wage his warres.
> The North forgott his feirce Intent;
>   And left perfumes in stead of scarres.
> By those sweet eyes' persuasiue powrs
> Where he mean't frost, he scatter'd flowrs.

(ll. 24–29)

Here the eyes of the infant bring about the enantiodromia of one thing into its opposite routinely attributed to the eyes of the Petrarchan mistress. The absurd fiction here suggests both the suspension of the natural in the presence of the divine and the adorableness of the divinity in the child. Feelings of love and worship are aroused and also ideas of things dying into their opposites that will naturally find their term in the shepherds' final plea for self-extinction. Crashaw's method here is quite different from T. S. Eliot's in the famous spring in midwinter ecstasy with which 'Little Gidding' opens:

> Now the hedgerow
> Is blanched for an hour with transitory blossom
> Of snow, a bloom more sudden
> Than that of summer, neither budding nor fading,
> Not in the scheme of generation.
> Where is summer, the unimaginable
> Zero summer?[40]

While Crashaw's raptures are all emanations or resonances of the body, Eliot's inhuman ecstasy freezes the body and its senses to suggest something beyond 'the scheme of generation'. He is working with paradoxes of absence and nothingness that can take in a fairly detailed experience of the English countryside, where Crashaw's winter is simply a literary idea that lends itself to lilting celebration of the divine child. Crashaw is all ardour and affirmation; Eliot all suspension of affirmation. The contrast shows that there is a lot to be said for Crashaw's warmth. At any rate the dangers of Eliot's renunciation of desire are surely as great as Crashaw's enlargement of it.

Crashaw as Metaphysical

Crashaw owes almost nothing to Donne and very little to Herbert. It is not easy to find echoes of either poet, certainly nothing to match the borrowings from Carew or even Shakespeare.[41] True, the title *Steps to the Temple* curtseys in Herbert's direction. But neither Crashaw's art nor his matter are Herbertian. Typically, Donne, as religious poet, and Herbert write self-centredly from a place of divided will. Their poems express their struggle to make themselves over to God. In Crashaw there is no struggle; he is all ardent longing for the extinction of self. And he is present in the first person only at the margins of his poems, the energy of his devotion having gone into imagining strong examples of consuming love, such as Mary Magdalene or Teresa. In consequence, the form and rhetoric of his poems take different shapes from what one finds in Donne and Herbert.

Crashaw's devotion is not personal, like Donne's or Herbert's, nor in the least introspective. He writes to inflame religious love without examining or

---

40. Eliot 1963.
41. 'Med'cinable Teares', 'The Weeper', st. 12, is borrowed from *Othello*, V, 2; see Warren, pp. 98–101, for echoes of Donne; Allison 1947, p. 36, notes Crashaw's borrowing of 'sugred Lyes' ('An Ode . . . Praefixed to a little Prayer-book', l. 56) from Herbert's 'The Rose'.

reproaching the life it has to spring from. This means that his poetry deals with the ideal, unlimited by experience, and in consequence lacks what one might call human interest. But, though impersonal, it nevertheless has in full measure Metaphysical interiority. Crashaw's appropriation of conventional erotic poetry for religious purposes has an expressive strangeness equal to Donne's or Herbert's. He has a battery of tricks of style that subjects whatever he touches to a strong inner direction: the persistent topsy-turvydom of his effects and his play with synaesthesia and self-reflexive turns ('thee with thyself' replacing Donne's 'one another') 'pursue conclusions infinite / Of easy ways to die', run everything, that is, toward self-immolation, evaporation, melting like a lump of incense. And whether we wish to interpret this direction psychoanalytically or in terms of the phenomenology of religious desire, it clearly turns inward toward its own vortex away from the public world. It transposes gallantry and preciosity to a religious key and in doing so converts their social currency into play with private intensities. Whatever we make of that play, it is clear that it is concerned with a strong pull out of the world we think we know into a world ruled by compulsions or spiritual operations dear to Crashaw's heart.

On the whole Crashaw does not argue like Donne, though his 'Letter to the Countess of Denbigh', being a persuasion, does so, and by analogies. And it is rare, outside the epigrams, to find the tight patterning that is typical of Herbert's work, though the exchange between the shepherds in 'The Nativity Hymn' affords an instance. Typically Crashaw's structures are much looser and more repetitive; what is developed is not so much an argument or design as an emotional trajectory. With Cowley, he may be credited with the development of the ode in English, and perhaps his surging, rapturous manner is more suited to it than Cowley's good sense.[42] His syntax is on the whole not complex. Generally it fits into his lines neatly without suspensions and qualifications that go with enjambment and heavy midline punctuation. Compared to Donne's, or even some of Herbert's, his versification is not intricate; nor does it seek ingenious closure, except in his epigrams. Most frequently, he writes in couplets and generally his rhythms accentuate his metre, except as we have noticed where he gets a rich sound by placing together heavily stressed monosyllables, often with long vowels. He aims at musicality rather than speech uttering thought.

Typically a poem by Crashaw will invent an extravagant fiction with some sort of emblematic or allegorical import. Mary Magdalene's tears fall upward and float as cream on the milky rivers of heaven:

---

42. Wallerstein 1959, p. 39, distinguishes Crashaw's irregular form from Cowley's pindarics.

Every morne from hence,
A briske Cherub something sips
Whose soft influence
Adds sweetnesse to his sweetest lips.
Then to his Musicke, and his song
Tastes of this breakefast all day long.

('The Weeper', st. 5)

The spiritual sense of this amusing nonsense would be that the repentance of Mary is heavenly and that it all turns to magnifying the glory of God. In a poem like 'A Valediction: of Weeping', Donne's tissue of conceits, ostensibly an argument by analogy, makes up a fiction that suggests, for all its extravagance, an emotional history of love-trouble. Herbert also may make use of a fiction, as in 'Life'. His fictions almost always go with a confounding of the self or at least a surprise upon it. Donne's fictions are not necesarily self-confounding, but typically their extravagance conveys anxiety or a sense of disaster. In Crashaw, by contrast, extravagance is always celebratory, usually a sacrifice of common sense to the divine. Even in his 'Epiphany Hymn', worked out on Pseudo-Dionysian ideas that in God there is a deep and dazzling darkness, the intellectual or theological paradoxes (rather than his more usual emotional or sensory ones) are still overwhelmingly affirmative. He wishes to put out the light of reason with the infinitely greater illumination of divinity. That points us yet again, however, to Crashaw's master impulse as a devotional poet, the desire for self-extinction in God. Celebratory and affirmative as his fictions are and, by contrast with Donne's and Herbert's, without emotional ambivalence or discovery of fault, still they tend to a self-contradiction, only the self-contradiction is Crashaw's happy ending, the sacrifice of oneself and dying into God.

CHAPTER FOUR

Henry Vaughan

Life

Henry Vaughan and his twin brother, Thomas, were born at Newton-upon-Usk in Breconshire in 1621, sons of a litigious small landowner descended from a powerful local family.[1] Place and descent make their mark on Vaughan's writing. Most of his books, from *Olor Iscanus* (The Swan of Usk) on, give the author as 'Henry Vaughan, Silurist', the Silures being a tribe inhabiting South Wales according to Tacitus.[2] Evidently Vaughan's sense of himself as writer, prose man and verse man, attached itself to Welsh origins. Much has been made of the influence of his native landscape on his poetry.[3] The country he grew up in was beautiful, green, well-wooded, abounding in streams, primrosed in spring, frequently misty and in sight of the Brecon Beacons; there was a small lake nearby and standing stones with mysterious carvings.[4]

The twins received a good classical grounding from Matthew Herbert, rector of Llangatock. Both later saluted him in poetry; he appears as Amphion in Henry's pastoral elegy 'Daphnis' (ll. 55–62). After this schooling, both went to Oxford in 1638, Thomas to study for the Church, Henry to study without taking a degree, prior to going on, probably in 1640, to legal

---

1. On the pathology of twinship and its mark in Vaughan's poetry, see Stevie Davies 1995, pp. 32ff.
2. Hutchinson 1947, p. 78. I am indebted to Hutchinson throughout this account of Vaughan's life.
3. E.g. Hutchinson 1947, pp. 21–24; and Trickett 1981.
4. Hutchinson 1947, p. 24.

studies in London.[5] A general knowledge of the law was thought useful for country gentlemen, and Henry, the elder twin, presumably picked this up in two years before being called back by his father to Wales. There he took up a post as secretary to Sir Marmaduke Lloyd, Chief Justice of the Brecon circuit, a job that would have come to an end with Lloyd's capture and imprisonment by the Parliamentarians after the siege of Hereford in 1645. He published *Poems with the Tenth Satire of Juvenal Englished* in 1646, the same year that he married Catherine Wise. By the next year, he had already prepared *Olor Iscanus* for the press according to the date of the Dedication, 17 December 1647. But the volume did not come out until 1651 after the publication in 1650 of the first edition of *Silex Scintillans*. By that time, according to the preface to the second edition of *Silex Scintillans*, he would have been made a convert by the 'holy life and verse' of 'the blessed man, Mr *George Herbert*', and repented his earlier 'idle' verse. When it did come out, therefore, *Olor Iscanus* had undergone revision: the volume contains a considerable number of poems written after 1647, some of the more 'idle' pieces may have been suppressed, as also some of the more dangerously Royalist ones, and the volume is said to have been 'published by a Friend', a sign that the author of *Silex Scintillans* did not wish to be seen to bring out secular poems, however innocent, now that he had taken to religious verse. The second edition of *Silex Scintillans*, with its second part containing fifty-five new poems, came out in 1655.

By that time Vaughan had published two devotional works in prose, *The Mount of Olives* (1652) and *Flores Solitudinis* (1654). The latter consists entirely of translations; the former ends with a short piece, *Man in Glory*, translated from Anselm. Both books deal with retreat to a life of solitary devotion. In 1655, he published a translation of Heinrich Nolle's *Hermetical Physic* and in 1657 a translation of Nolle's *Chymist's Key*. He may himself have begun to practise as a doctor already in the 1650s, though there is no record of his taking a medical degree then or indeed at any time. Whether he practised at this time or not, these treatises show that he sided with alchemical or Paracelsan medicine against the established tradition deriving from Aristotle and the second-century medical writer, Galen. In this he would be encouraged by his brother, Thomas, who, probably even before his eviction by the Commonwealth authorities from his parish of Llansantffraed in 1650, had gone to London to make a living as an alchemist and proponent of alchemical thought, and who, after the Restoration, collaborated in alchemical experiments with Sir Robert Moray, one of the leading spirits behind the founding of the Royal Society. In the middle of this decade of literary

5. Hutchinson 1947, p. 30.

activity, Henry Vaughan married his deceased wife's sister, Elizabeth, in 1655, though the canon law of his church forbade it. When Catherine Vaughan died is not known.

After the Restoration, Vaughan published only a third volume of poems, *Thalia Rediviva* (1678), which also contains some poems by Thomas, who had died in 1666. Some of Henry's poems were clearly written earlier, some perhaps having been excised from the original *Olor Iscanus* for one reason or another. But others, including 'Daphnis', a pastoral elegy for Thomas Vaughan, must have been written after the Restoration.[6] Otherwise Vaughan's literary activity ceased. It is certain that he was practising medicine after 1677 and involved in litigation with two of his children in the early 1690s. He died in April 1695.

Vaughan's politics

I have left out Vaughan's involvement in the Civil War because this is a topic that deserves uninterrupted discussion. He was in London studying law between 1640 and 1642 during the last stage of the contention between Charles I and Parliament before the outbreak of war. For a decade Charles had ruled without Parliament. That came to an end with the Bishops' Wars with the Scots. He dissolved the Short Parliament in haste in 1640 when it seemed that it would not vote him the supplies he required. With the Long Parliament, a considerably more intransigent body, Charles was forced to make concessions while Parliament under the leadership of Pym started to dismantle the means by which he had succeeded in ruling without it. The Earl of Strafford, Charles's able and ruthless chief counsellor, was imprisoned in November 1640 and executed the following May. Vaughan was in London while these things were happening. The demolition of the institutions of personal rule was not accomplished without dissension in Parliament between Lords and Commons, moderate and radical, nor without inept attempts to suppress Parliamentary opposition by the King and rowdy libertarian mob demonstrations in London, probably encouraged at critical junctures by a resolute faction of Parliamentarians. Two matters in particular combined to split Parliament. The Irish Rebellion and massacre of Protestants seemed to Parliamentarians under Pym a Royalist plot and they

---

6. Watson 1986 makes a vigorous case for thinking that many of the poems in this collection were written during the Restoration, arguing that Vaughan was able to write again because dislike of Restoration profligacy gave even an Anglican like himself an opportunity to deplore the times and retreat to the same position of prophetic isolation and waiting for the end of the world that he had taken up under the Commonwealth.

would not entrust an army for the suppression of Ireland to the King's command in case it should be used against them. This and their Grand Remonstrance, a recital of wrongs perpetrated by Charles's government, could not be accepted by him or by those owing loyalty to monarchical government who so far had joined in the resistance to what they saw as Charles's unconstitutional measures. In this state of affairs, Charles's bungled attempt to arrest five Parliamentarian leaders in the House of Commons made it clear to both sides that the issue between them could only be settled by war. Early in 1642, Charles withdrew to York, Parliament was left in possession of London and both sides began to raise armies.

About the beginning of the Civil War, Vaughan returned from London to his father's house in Wales. His first volume of poems has nothing to say about the war, but its poems of 'mistressing and compliment'[7] imitate the small beer of Cavalier versing and there are at least two poems that may express Royalist views of political events that took place while he was in London. The account of the fall of Sejanus in the translation of Juvenal's Tenth Satire may be a veiled treatment of the fall of Strafford. Speaking of the translation, the prefatory address makes a very general comparison between the 'infirmities of [the Roman] state' and 'the distractions of our owne'.[8] But it is hard to see any particular glancing at the times, except perhaps the implied advice to retire from a world in which ambition is vain. More specifically Royalist is 'A Rhapsodie'. Like 'To My Ingenuous Friend, R. W.', 'A Rhapsodie' is a convivial poem celebrating drink and companionship. That, during Vaughan's years in London, might have been enough to strike a Cavalier attitude. And the toasts he proposes to Caligula, Caesar and Sulla, all Romans who defied or overrode the Senate, are clear enough signs where his loyalties lay in the 1640s.[9] It must be said that the political involvement of 'A Rhapsodie' is not thoughtful. It is a poem of cheerful partisan solidarity and it is uncomplicated by religious feeling. But then in 1646, when the *Poems* came out, Vaughan could have given only covert and restricted expression to Royalist thoughts: the first Civil War had ended in the defeat of the King and South Wales had been reduced to submission by the Parliamentary forces.

The poems in *Olor Iscanus* that treat events of the Civil War are even less troubled by the great constitutional issues at stake, though again proposed publication in 1647 and actual publication in 1651 would have imposed restrictions and even excisions of indiscreetly partisan pieces. After the crucial

---

7. Donne, 'To Mr Tilman', l. 30.
8. Vaughan 1963, p. 2; Hutchinson 1947, pp. 42–43.
9. Hutchinson 1947, pp. 43–44.

defeat at Naseby in June 1645, Charles visited South Wales, a region so far untouched by war, to recruit, and then, if not before, Vaughan seems to have enlisted in the Royalist forces. Two elegies, 'An Elegie on the Death of Mr *R. W.* slain . . . at *Routon* Heath, neer Chester 1645' and 'An Elegie on the Death of Mr *R. Hall*, slain at *Pontefract* 1648', together with a humorous piece, 'Upon a Cloke lent him by Mr *J. Ridsey*', suggest that Vaughan was involved with the Royalist side in 'the late unfortunate differences'. A poem 'Upon Mr *Fletcher's* Playes, published, 1647' attempts some satire against the Puritans, but passes it off as directed against 'Scottish zeal', a safe target. A convivial poem, 'To his retired friend, an Invitation to *Brecknock*', takes up the Royalist causes of wit and wine but in a context of Horatian cosiness and retreat from 'the time's ridiculous misery'.

The political cast of *Silex Scintillans* is more interesting. The defeat of Charles in the First Civil War by early 1646 and again in the Second Civil War of 1648, followed by his execution in January 1649 and the rule of Cromwell, was attended by a series of repressive measures against the former Church of England. Episcopacy had been abolished in 1643. Laud was executed in 1645 and the use of the Prayer Book forbidden in 1646. Incumbents of parishes who were of known Royalist persuasion were evicted from their livings. Thomas Vaughan was evicted from his in 1650 by the Act for Propagating the Gospel. At some time after 1647, when he had his original version of *Olor Iscanus* ready for the press, Henry Vaughan turned to an intense devotional life, and the persecuted church of Laud became the focus of his political loyalty. In adopting Herbert as his model, he assumed, like Walton, that the spirituality of *The Temple* was of a Laudian sort. He enlarges a hint from poems of Herbert's such as 'Church-rents and Schismes' to deplore the destruction of the Church by Puritan saints. In 'The Constellation', for example, having contrasted the order of the heavens with the disorder in the human scene, he expands on human disorder to take in the evils of the Rule of the Saints in a piece of vigorous, if unpolished, invective:

> But here Commision'd by a black self-wil
>   The sons the father kil,
> The Children Chase the mother, and would heal
>   The wounds they give, by crying, zeale.
>
> Then Cast her bloud, and tears upon thy book
>   Where they for fashion look,
> And like that Lamb which had the Dragons voice
>   Seem mild, but are known by their noise.[10]

---

10.   All citations of Vaughan's poetry are to Vaughan 1963.

'Self-wil' is a cant phrase used to disparage their opponents by the sort of people who sat on Commonwealth commissions and wished to claim a regenerate will for their actions – here turned against them. The sons who kill the father will be the parricidal killers of Charles; the children chasing their mother will be the persecutors of the episcopal mother church, who find their warrant in God's book, the Bible, and speak the language of peace, like the terrifying lamb-antichrist in the Apocalypse.[11] After that, Vaughan ends with a prayer that apostate Britain may become 'an humble, holy nation' and the Church may be restored to 'her perfect, and pure dress, / *Beauty* and *holiness*', the 'beauty of holiness' being a Laudian slogan.[12] There are many such murmurings and prayers that the evil of the time should pass in *Silex Scintillans*. The Commonwealth authorities must have been remarkably lax about what was published.[13]

Curiously, Vaughan's Episcopalianism sounds Puritanical. His concern with regeneration at least seems to divide the elect from those whom God has not chosen to enlighten. It is possible that there are other interpretations of the pebbles that dance through the pool in 'Regeneration' as against the dark stones that remain fixed to the centre (ll. 53–60), and of the flowers that open to the sun as opposed to those that remain shut (ll. 65–68); possible again that those who work the way of the world in 'The World' and according to a mysterious voice are not among those whom Christ will take to himself may simply be evil doers rather than the eternally repro-bate.[14] But the natural interpretation of these poems is that Vaughan believes in double predestination and feels himself to be unaccountably yet surely among the chosen. There were, however, Calvinist Episcopalians, such as Strafford himself, in spite of Laud's Arminian campaign, and Herbert may have furnished Vaughan with what seemed a precedent in this matter. More unusual for an Episcopalian is Vaughan's apocalyptic streak. Like the sectaries, he lived in expectation of the Second Coming.

It is in the second part of *Silex Scintillans* that this waiting for the end becomes political. In the first part, Vaughan looks forward to the Second Coming as personal deliverance from exile on earth in the same way that he longs for the presence of Christ or for death, or he uses the thought of the end of things to jolt himself out of carelessness.[15] But in the second part,

---

11. Or if not the Antichrist, at least its prophet: Revelations, 13.11–18.
12. Cf. 'Dressing' for kneeling at communion and 'Christs Nativity' for celebration of church feasts.
13. But see the openly Royalist poems in Herrick's *Hesperides* (1648).
14. Chambers 1968, pp. 146–49. But see Lewalski 1979, pp. 320–21, for an account of the poem in terms of grace and reprobation.
15. E.g. 'The Dawning'.

he takes a more prophetic line. In his reading of the times in the light of the Bible, particularly of the Canticles and the Apocalypse, the Church has fled to the wilderness to escape those who persecute and despoil her and dwells in isolation in the cells of the hearts of the devout.[16]

In the faith that divine intervention is at hand, he turns to quietism. 'Jesus Weeping', ostensibly about Christ's grief over Jerusalem, clearly points at the Commonwealth that will not repent its evil ways and alludes to the last days when the wicked, it is prophesied, shall drink blood.[17] 'The Men of War' contrasts the Saints of the time, who conquer by arms, with the true Christian martyrs, who, with 'A sweet, revengless, quiet minde', await the judgement that will vindicate them; it is among those that Vaughan prays to be numbered. Meek, human revengelessness in Vaughan always trembles on the edge of prayer for supernatural vengeance. 'Abel's Blood', starting from Abel's murder, which cries to heaven for vengeance, turns to the sea of blood of the martyrs in the Civil War, 'Whose urgent *sound* like unto that / *Of many waters*, beateth at / The everlasting doors above'. But at this point, Vaughan turns to Christ as martyr, who prayed that his enemies might be forgiven, and prays that the blood of the Royalist dead may be heard for peace. This is revengelessness with a hint of imprecation behind it. In 'The Day of Judgement' the meekness unravels and the man who has renounced violence turns to call for more than human violence to be visited on his enemies and God's, particularly on those who wrest Scripture to their own purpose:

> O God! though mercy be in thee
> The greatest attribute we see,
> And the most needful for our sins;
> Yet, when thy mercy nothing wins
> But meer disdain, let not man say
> *Thy arm doth sleep*; but write this day
> Thy judging one: Descend, descend!
> Make all things new! and without end!

(ll. 39–46)

In this passage, the desire for eternity and deliverance from the world, Vaughan's 'mystical' longing, is gathered up in his prophetic bodings about his political grievances. With Vaughan, perhaps more than any other Metaphysical, interiority is shaped by the pressures of his age.

---

16. See 'The British Church' and 'Jacob's Pillow and Pillar'; also Revelations, 12.6, and Hebrews, 11.38.
17. Revelations, 16.5–6.

In turning to a life of devotion, Vaughan renounced his former, mildly roystering cavalier self. He prays to be free of the temptations of friendship in 'Day of Judgement' (ll. 37–38) and repents in 'Misery' that 'Excesse of friends, of words, and wine / Take up my day' (ll. 25–26). What is not Puritan but entirely of Vaughan is the turn he gives this renunciation of fun towards solitude and the life of a hermit. In his 'Man in Darkness, or, A Discourse of Death', in *The Mount of Olives*, he quotes Jerome on the hermits of the Thebaid.[18] He adopted this eremitical existence for his own spiritual life, which, in its unsociability, is neither Episcopalian nor Puritan, though it goes with his quietism. In 'Misery', an admirable passage describes how after rebellion he returns to his 'cell' (ll. 35, 38) and sits 'with thee by this new light, / And for that hour th'art my delight' (ll. 53–54), only to become understandably fidgety:

> 'The Age, the present times are not
> 'To snudge in, and embrace a Cot,
> 'Action and bloud now get the game,
> 'Disdein treads on the peaceful name,
> 'Who sits at home too bears a loade
> 'Greater than those that gad abroad'.

(ll. 65–70)

The temptation to distraction speaks the language of Royalist swashbuckling. Vaughan imitates the passionate flinging off to a life that is 'free as the rode, / Loose as the winde' in Herbert's 'The Collar', with an interestingly ambiguous note in the final lines. Vaughan's rebellious voice would slight those who bear their loads pacifically at home, but at the same time might whisper in Vaughan's regenerate ear that sitting at home is the truly heroic task. The references to war are admittedly very general, and, as is not the case in many of Vaughan's poems, the times come in as at most passing allusions; the times have been made into a metaphor, or, better, examples among others of unspirituality, rather than its apocalyptic manifestation. Nevetherless, here, as elsewhere more explicitly, the experience of defeat and repression shapes his spirituality toward retreat.[19]

Vaughan's retreat into himself or to the green peace of rural solitude may run to remarkable expressions of hermetically sealed self-enclosure. In 'Joy', which reverses the usual value of happiness or unhappiness assigned to joy and grief, he adjures himself,

---

18. Vaughan 1963, p. 182.
19. On retreat as the Cavalier response to defeat in poetry, see Røstvig, 1, p. 121; Miner 1971, p. 179; also Loxley's attempt (1997) to qualify this picture, pp. 201–32.

174

> As leafs in Bowers
> Whisper their hours,
> And Hermit-wells
> Drop in their Cells:
> So in sighs and unseen tears
> Pass thy solitary years,
> And going hence, leave written on some Tree,
> *Sighs make joy sure, and shaking fastens thee.*

(ll. 23–30)

The self-enclosed bowers seem to be leading a hermit's existence as the sound of their leaves carries metaphorical suggestions of whispering the hours of a breviary and the unseen dripping of water in the self-enclosed wells suggests the tears of the hermit's life of repentance. The melancholy is fanciful and self-pleasing and at the same time rather disturbingly inturned from human life. Chris Fitter has argued that Vaughan's transports in the morning, as in 'The Morning-watch', interrupt with a transposition of Cavalier violence to the celestial sphere the unearthly calm and silence that Vaughan so values in his serene and blessed moods.[20] I cannot myself easily discern this motif, though it would certainly make an entertaining example of the return of the repressed soldier and drinker. It seems to me rather that if we are to look for the impress of politics on Vaughan's soul, we shall find it, not in a recrudescence of the Civil War in the heavens and the divine workings of the universe, but in his absences or withdrawals into the cell of the self, often expressed in figures startlingly charged with psychic life.

Vaughan as poet of retreat

In 'A Rhapsodie', Vaughan displays a surprising talent for convivial poetry, and if he is frequently described as a Wordsworth out of phase, the following passage may suggest Fergusson, the eighteenth-century Edinburgh poet, in its excited reporting of sights and sounds of city night-life:

> Now when each narrow lane, each nooke & Cave,
> Signe-posts, & shop-doors, pimp for ev'ry knave,
> When riotous sinfull plush, and tell-tale spurs
> Walk Fleet street, & the Strand, when the soft stirs

---

20. Fitter 1992, pp. 123–47.

Of bawdy, ruffled Silks, turne night to day;
And the lowd whip, and Coach scolds all the way;
When lust of all sorts, and each itchie bloud
From the Tower-wharfe to Cymbelyne, and Lud,
Hunts for a Mate, and the tyr'd footman reeles
'Twixt chaire-men, torches, & the hackny wheels:
    Come, take the other dish.

(ll. 37–47)

Someone who responded so eagerly to London might have found the life and conversation of a Welsh country gentleman dull, even if he had a few intelligent and educated friends among the local clergy. In any event, when he turned to a life of rural seclusion Vaughan redirected a talent as well as a way of life. Night-life in *Silex Scintillans* still arouses some of Vaughan's keenest poetry, but both the conviviality and the excitement have been transformed.

The experience of defeat in the Civil War shaped Vaughan's spirituality, but other things entered into it. Probably he had some mystical experience of regeneration. The poem titled 'Regeneration', though allegorical and general rather than autobiographically particular, seems to speak of an experience of spiritual awakening that leaves him impatient for a fuller gust of the Holy Spirit to blow on him. 'Ascension Day' begins with a rapture brought on by meditating on Christ's Ascension until he shares in it and feels himself at once soaring upwards into the clouds and wandering in the past through the scenes of the biblical events preceding the Ascension. While he does so, he brings in a present experience of sunrise:

I see that morning in thy Converts tears,
Fresh as the dew, which but this dawning wears?
I smell her spices, and her ointment yields,
As rich a scent as the now Primros'd-fields.

(ll. 19–22)

Behind the imagined morning of the Resurrection lies 'this dawning' in Wales, one of those creation mornings that Vaughan returns to with the same details repeatedly. The dew of the one calls up the dew of the other and both are called up by the tears of Mary Magdalene. Similarly her ointment somehow clinging to her from an earlier evening summons up the scents of both dawns. After that comes a vision of the Apostles transfigured and shining in the light of the morning sun, which is also the Son, and here again Vaughan works the Bible story into his own favourite imagery of dawn and light, and, while imagining Christ's last days on earth, anchors his imagining sufficiently to his own experience to suggest a supernatural visitation:

> What stirs, what posting intercourse and mirth
> Of Saints and Angels glorifie the earth?
> What sighs, what whispers, busie stops and stays;
> Private and holy talk fill all the ways?
> They pass as at the last great day, and run
> In their white robes to seek the risen Sun.

(ll. 25–30)

Four poems further on, the talk of diabolic infestation in 'The Proffer' sounds like the imagining to which those who came out of highly strung spiritual communings were notoriously prey.[21] It is impossible to say with any certainty that Vaughan actually underwent conversion experiences or was subject to visionary spells, but his poetry, unlike Donne's and Herbert's, strikes a visionary note, and when it does so it modulates into something mysterious and beautiful, quite outside the compass of his usual less than arresting pieties.

His spirituality was also shaped by his discovery of Herbert. He had already grafted an adaptation of some lines of Herbert's 'Discharge' on Horace's Ode, I, ix, to make a convivial poem, 'To My Worthy Friend Mr T. Lewes', about taking no thought for the morrow. But Herbert is only one of the many poets he quarries in his earlier collections, whereas, in *Silex Scintillans*, Herbert has become the paramount literary source and inspiration apart from the Bible, to such an extent that some of Vaughan's weak poems, such as 'Idle Verse', are a collage of quotations from 'The Church', and even some of his best, such as the remarkable 'The Night', contain at least reminiscences of Herbert's phrasing, though changed into something entirely his own. Here we have a case of exclusive and uncritical absorption in another author.

In 'Obedience', Herbert wishes that 'some kinde man would thrust his heart / Into these lines' and, in doing so, share in his making himself over to God. In 'The Match', Vaughan responds to this wish:

---

21. See Yeoman 1995, p. 93. At the same time one can accept the political interpretation that Vaughan had been made an offer that he felt would compromise his loyalties.

> Dear friend! whose holy, ever-living lines
> Have done much good
> To many, and have checkt my blood,
> My fierce, wild blood that still heaves, and inclines,
> But is still tam'd
> By those bright fires which thee inflam'd;
>
> Here I joyn hands.

(ll. 1–7)

Vaughan's weakness in the sort of intimate address in which Herbert excels comes out clearly. The protestation of 'fierce, wild blood' sounds preposterous, like Duke Orsino's talk of his passion in *Twelfth Night*, and while perhaps Vaughan intends some oxymoronic play, the flames that tame by inflaming are confused rather than witty.[22]

In subject matter too, Vaughan has imitated Herbert in such a way that he flattens and conventionalizes the central concern of Herbert's devotion, the making over of himself in his entirety to the divine will. Vaughan wants his earthly passions, which distract him from his spiritual self, to be tamed or shut out. His is the prayer of the neoplatonist who wants something to be subtracted so that he may be holy. Herbert's is the prayer of the Protestant who wants to be taken over as he is, guided and refashioned. With the flattening and conventionalizing of Herbert's struggle with himself and God goes a diffuseness in Vaughan's sense of sin. Typically sin is a mist between himself and God, or a dispersal of attention, rather than a contrary will. The sense of himself he conveys in his verse is vague, as is also his sense of God as a person other than himself, and in consequence the debate between himself and God, the taut spring of so much of Herbert's best verse, is slack. Another consequence is that his confessional self-analysis is uninteresting. Though he may protest that he is 'the worst of men' ('Misery', l. 90), his confessions of stain or pollution are generally unconvincing.

An exception occurs in 'Misery', where after confessing to becoming bored with solitary contemplation and breaking out with the Cavalier impatience we have already looked at, he comments, 'Thus do I make thy gifts giv'n me / The only quarrellers with thee' (ll. 71–72). This return upon himself is certainly Herbertian in spirit, but the sharp observation of how he turns God's gifts of 'Calm and silence' (l. 59) against him is not borrowed. Still, this is an exception; in imitating Herbert's poetry of conflict with God, Vaughan was generally working a vein that did not suit him.

---

22. See Bird 1984, p. 11, for a hostile account of Vaughan's self-cancelling.

What Vaughan could appropriate with profit was more general. *The Temple* was a serious call to a devout life that represented the spirituality of Vaughan's now persecuted church at its finest. It meant that for Vaughan, as Royalist and poet, devotion might be the cell in which he concentrated himself and his energies. In addition 'The Church' furnished Vaughan with a model of a collection of poems that were in some sense a record of a life of prayer, as a sonnet sequence, with its exclamations, exaltations, depressions, reflections and whims, might be said to be a record of a love affair. In this sense, *Silex Scintillans*, like 'The Church', is the record of a love affair with God, but a record that even less than 'The Church' tells a clear story. It is natural to begin the collection with a dedication of its poems to Christ as their only begetter and to follow that with an admonition to profane wits to mend their eyes. But after that, until the concluding 'L'Envoy', there appears to be no design behind the arrangement of the poems beyond what one takes to be events in Vaughan's emotional history and certain short runs of poems linked by theme. Perhaps he deliberately attempted to let the returns and departures of God or his own ebbings and flowings shape the sequence or at least give an impression of the unaccountable course of a life of prayer.[23] With that absence of plan as his plan, he could enter upon a devotional interiority that sometimes allowed him to write as a visionary: 'So some strange thoughts transcend our wonted theams, / And into glory peep' ('They are all gone into the world of light!', ll. 27–28).

As a visionary, Vaughan is a poet of death. Here many strands of Vaughan's interiority come together. We might begin by considering another external influence (like the Civil War and his reading of *The Temple*): the death of his brother William and perhaps also the death of his first wife. Some of the untitled poems are elegies, but more than that, repeatedly in the collection there is strange talk of being in touch with a world of spirits and at the same time of exile from it, which might well come partly out of an experience of death in the family.[24] Of course, most seventeenth-century Christians thought that life on earth meant separation from God, apart from intermittent visits and glimpses; only after death would the regenerate soul live continuously in his presence. Death, then, might stand in a devout life as almost interchangeable with the Second Coming or with a strong mystical persuasion of God's presence in an experience of regeneration. Both Donne and Herbert brought themselves to look forward to death as

---

23. But see Lewalski 1979, pp. 319–23, for an account of the two parts as stages in Vaughan's religious development.
24. See Stevie Davies 1995, pp. 89ff. for an interesting discussion of Vaughan's clinging to mourning and melancholia.

heaven. But Vaughan arrives at this state without anguish, and for him life and death mysteriously interpenetrate. Lines such as his salute to the night as 'The souls dumb watch, / When Spirits their fair kindred catch' ('The Night', ll. 35–36) describe a communication with blessed spirits that sounds more like Rosicrucianism or nineteenth-century Spiritualism than conventional Christian belief. Vaughan is haunted by the dead and himself haunts the grave.

How that is so emerges clearly in 'They are all gone into the world of light!':

> They are all gone into the world of light!
>   And I alone sit lingring here;
> Their very memory is fair and bright,
>   And my sad thoughts doth clear.
>
> It glows and glitters in my cloudy brest
>   Like stars upon some gloomy grove,
> Or those faint beams in which this hill is drest,
>   After the Sun's remove.
>
> I see them walking in an Air of glory,
>   Whose light doth trample on my days:
> My days, which are at best but dull and hoary,
>   Meer glimering and decays.
>
> O holy hope! and high humility,
>   High as the Heavens above!
> These are your walks, and you have shew'd them me
>   To kindle my cold love,
>
> Dear, beauteous death! the Jewel of the Just,
>   Shining nowhere, but in the dark;
> What mysteries do lie beyond thy dust;
>   Could man outlook that mark!
>
> He that hath found some fledg'd birds nest may know
>   At first sight, if the bird be flown;
> But what fair Well, or Grove he sings in now,
>   That is to him unknown.
>
> And yet, as Angels in some brighter dreams
>   Call to the soul, when man doth sleep:
> So some strange thoughts transcend our wonted theams,
>   And into glory peep.
>
> If a star were confin'd into a Tomb
>   Her captive flames must needs burn there;

But when the hand that lockt her up, gives room,
   She'l shine through all the sphaere.

O Father of eternal life, and all
   Created glories under thee!
Resume thy spirit from this world of thrall
   Into true liberty.

Either disperse these mists, which blot and fill
   My perspective (still) as they pass,
Or else remove me hence unto that hill,
   Where I shall need no glass.

The arresting first line imitates some of Donne's and Herbert's abrupt openings, but its mysteriousness (who are 'They'?) is all Vaughan's. The poem begins as a memory of a vision, which, in the intensity of loss, becomes a present vision ('I see them walking'). It may be that in the first three stanzas Vaughan is recalling the bright apparitions of 'Ascension Day', which occurs two poems previously. But the 'Ascension Hymn', which comes between the two, turns Vaughan's mind to death and resurrection: the ascended Christ alone can

      Bring bone to bone
      And rebuild man,
   And by his all subduing might
  Make clay ascend more quick then light.

          (ll. 39–42)

Although apparently discussing the resurrection on the last day, that the 'clay' ascends 'more quick than light' might equally allow one to think by metonymy of the immediate translation of the soul redeemed on death from clay to heaven. Vaughan happily appropriates Herbert's word 'quick' to convey a life disembodied in light rather than physically reconstituted, an alchemical sublimation rather than a renewal of the flesh. This suggests that 'they' in 'They are all gone into the world of light!' might be Vaughan's dead relatives translated to another world. Besides, its general reflections on death, which the opening vision gives way to after the third stanza, would obviously go with his having communicated with the spirits of his own dead. That would make a stronger poem than a visionary imagining of the apostles and Christ ascending, followed by a general turning to heaven and the spirit world. But whichever interpretation we pick, whether the shining ones are from his family or out of the Bible, the spirits of the dead and ascended are present to Vaughan in his life and leave him with a longing to join them in their spirit existence.

The mysterious vagueness of Vaughan's spirituality comes out in a beautiful reminiscence of Herbert's 'Death', where the bones of the dead are called 'the shells of fledge souls', which at the Resurrection 'shall wear their new aray, / And all [Death's] bones with beautie shall be clad'. Conspicuously, Vaughan is not interested in this orthodox Christian miracle of reincorporation at Doomsday. He takes up Herbert's figure of the bird hatched from the egg, leaves its metaphorical connections with the soul suggestively floating and develops a wonder concerning the whereabouts of the flown nestling to invest the bird-soul with wistful hints of the unknown and the beyond. Herbert's focus on his concrete figures and his definite theological idea dissolve in Vaughan's transcendental suggestions.

For Vaughan, the spirit seems to be an attenuation of physical life. Light is the least bodily of physical existences and Vaughan is eminently the poet of light. He strives toward light as a sort of incorporeal existence, and the spirits who have left their bodies appear to him as lights. Noticeably, he has an intense sensibility for effects of light in darkness. The memory of the blessed spirits 'glows and glitters' like starlight or again shines like the afterglow on a hillside when the lower world has been left in darkness. He himself on earth, separated from God by the mist of earthly existence, leads a life amidst 'glimmers'. This is picked out in 'hoary', which suggests not just dullness or greyness but a faint light such as the reflection of moonlight. Vaughan plays on selected sensations in a way that is quite foreign to the art of Donne or Herbert. It is not that he is an aesthete like Crashaw. For him, light is the divine stuff of the universe and his pleasure in its effects is a form of illumination.

In 'They are all gone into the world of light!', his feeling for light is not, as in 'Ascension Day' or the first two stanzas of 'The Morning-watch', for sheer white light, but, as in the most magical of his poems, 'The Night', for *chiaroscuro*, light in darkness, and even for a transformation of light and dark. So death is a jewel that shines 'nowhere, but in the dark'. This reflects the memory of the blessed spirits; but it also suggests the darkness of death has a peculiar light about it that daylight does not have. A similar transformation of night and day, death and life, occurs in stanza 8, another of Vaughan's mysteriously floating metaphorical figures, but this time of a bold, bizarre, emblematic sort. The star in the tomb will be a figure for the soul in the living body: life is death and privation of light. When the star is released from the tomb, it will shine in the night sky as the soul escaped from the body will be glorified in death: death is life and light.

Vaughan celebrates both light and darkness, both sunrise and night, both celestial quickness and death. Deep explanations are usually banal, and probably to say simply that Vaughan delighted in both morning radiance and evening glimmerings would turn one most profitably to the poetry. Nevertheless I cannot help repeating that in Vaughan light is an attenuation of physical existence, a purity attained by withdrawal from human life to a 'white celestial thought', and then drawing the connection to darkness and death as the privation of colours and qualities of life. Both light and darkness signify the spirit in Vaughan because he makes both retreats from the life we live with other people in the world and both, for him, signify death, the final abstraction from life.

Vaughan uses the words 'shade' and 'shadow' with a range of meaning or suggestion that takes in the ambiguity of light and dark in his poetry. Sometimes 'shade' means simply darkness, obscurity, gloom, as for example in 'The Lampe', where the candle light and the stars, like glow worms, shine in a night in which 'Horrour doth creepe / And move on with the shades'. This sort of shade hides and is hidden from the light of God: so Vaughan would 'lay [his] trespasse in the shade' ('Misery', l. 22).[25] But elsewhere 'shade' is benign, not to say divine. God is 'The Rock of ages! in whose shade / They live unseen, when here they fade' ('The Book', ll. 3–4).[26] In this case, shade is associated with death and a translation of light and darkness follows. We are more or less at the place where in 'The Night' darkness is the effulgence of God's holiness and Vaughan wishes to escape the profane light of life and live in God 'invisible and dim', an extraordinarily naked expression of recessive desire in the hermit seer.

But mediating between the extremes of light and dark, 'shadow' sometimes means 'shade' but also often means 'reflection'.[27] So in 'The Retreate', his infant soul, gazing on some '*gilded Cloud, or flowre*', might 'in those weaker glories spy / Some shadows of eternity' (ll. 11, 13–14). The creation reflects the glory of the creator or shines with a divine infusion of the Father of lights, who pours himself into it. Again in 'I walkt the other day', he prays to the Holy Spirit, who 'by a sacred incubation / Fed with life this frame [the Universe]' (ll. 45–46),

> That in these Masques and shadows I may see
> Thy sacred way,
> And by those hid ascents climb to that day
> Which breaks from thee
> Who art in all things, though invisibly.

> (ll. 50–54)

---

25. See also 'Repentance', ll. 51–52, 'The Tempest', l. 41.
26. Note the remarkable inversion in 'Thou art the faithful, pearly rock, / The Hive of beamy, living lights' ('The Agreement', ll. 31–32).
27. For 'shadow' as obscuring divine light see 'The World', where the 'great *Ring* of pure and endless light' of Eternity is accompanied by the shadow of Time and its various shady indwellers; also 'Cock-crowing' (l. 40).

The shadows in this case are created things, which, like the bulb that he has just dug up, bear a secret sign of divinity, a reflection that may be traced by the devout mind back to its source in God. The idea of nature as a reflection of divine light, open to the reflection of the enlightened mind, is platonic, passed through neoplatonism and hermeticism into alchemical thought. Vaughan's use of the idea in his poetry is not particularly esoteric, but he invests it with the charm of mystery through his play with light and dark and his language of tracing and tracking elusive glimmerings and reflections. Even in broad day in the grove of 'Regeneration', where 'The unthrift Sunne shot vitall gold / A thousand peeces' (ll. 41–42), the light will be broken by the leaves into flashes and dazzling spots. At the same time, Vaughan gives out an alchemical glint in 'vitall gold'; if in neoplatonic thought God proceeds into his creation through the reflection of light, sunlight infusing itself into the earth grows a metallic reflection of itself in gold. What excites Vaughan's mind and eye is the hinting and glinting of light in darkness, and this dependence of the one on the other is perhaps written on the two sides of the word 'shadow', as he uses the word.

As for 'shade', it too bears an intermediate sense between darkness and the blinding or invisible light of God. Repeatedly Vaughan uses 'shade' as a metonymy for foliage. He speaks of a 'green shade' in 'Corruption' with an implication of immateriality: before the Fall, '*Paradise* lay / In some green shade' (ll. 23–24). Like Marvell, Vaughan contracts the whole garden momentarily to a tree, and if he does not annihilate all that's made to a green thought, still his tree as a green shade enjoys an ideal incorporeal existence as a function of light. That is why it is paradisal for him.

And yet Vaughan has a feeling for vegetable growth. In 'The Book', the 'green shade' he speaks of carries no suggestion of ideality. It is there to allow him to make a 'point' about the cover of the tree that has been turned into the wooden boards that cover the book. But in passing he mentions that 'it flourish'd, grew and spread, / As if it never should be dead' (ll. 13–14). He responds sympathetically to the life of green stuff and not just in trees but in herbs and flowers, as he does not to human physical life. Usually he uses the upward growth of plants toward the sun and their increase in bulk as a figure for spiritual movement. So in 'The Starre', it is natural for him to pass from the 'restless, pure desire' that makes the starlight 'wind and curle, and wink and smile' to the desire of the heart for God and so to compare that with the spirit of vegetable growth.[28] Whoever turns the desire of his heart to God 'shall feel / That God is true, as herbs unseen / Put on their youth and green' (ll. 31–33). 'Feel', perhaps an

---

28. Vaughan has appropriated the curlings of Herbert's 'The Starre'.

inspired memory of Herbert's use of the word in 'The Agonie' ('Love is that liquor sweet and most divine / Which my God feels as bloud; but I, as wine'), manages to transfer a sense of vegetable burgeoning to the secret life of the soul in God. There are similar treatments of 'Dear, secret *Greenness*' in 'The Seed growing secretly', and a startling running together of the ideas of vegetation and spirituality with death in 'As time one day by me did pass'. There Vaughan salutes death's bright beauty, 'For whose dry dust green branches bud' (l. 35). He does not mean that plants are born to die, but that they shoot towards the light of death. That they should flourish for 'dry dust' is one of the places where Vaughan's play with *discordia concors* comes off oddly well, here to suggest that vegetation has attained the spiritual state of being amphibious between life and death.

It is true that Vaughan prays frequently for death or the Second Coming, for an end, but most memorably he is the poet of intermediate states, of an existence persisting in withdrawal from life. Hence his feeling for plants, for glimmers rather than the full extinguishing blaze of God, for timber that retains a 'strange resentment after death' of storms ('The Timber', l. 19). And hence also his interest in hermetic sympathies in herbs and stones. Outside the human volitional and affective world they carry on a mysterious, ideal transposition of human life where:

> his own living works did my Lord hold
> And lodge alone;
> Where *trees* and *herbs* did watch and peep
> And wonder, while the *Jews* did sleep;

> ('The Night', ll. 21–24)

> So hills and valleys into singing break,
> And though poor stones have neither speech nor tongue,
> While active winds and streams both run and speak,
> Yet stones are deep in admiration.

> ('The Bird', ll. 13–16)

It is not surprising that in reducing life to the vegetable and inanimate, Vaughan should suffer from lethargy and melancholy, though he tries to give both a spiritual turn;[29] it is unsurprising too that in turning down his quite boisterous flame of life so low he should be prey above all to the temptations of distraction. But the crumbling into particles that he fears in

---

29. See 'Misery' and 'Fair and yong light!'

'The Resolve' and 'Distraction', or the running 'To ev'ry myre' that he reproaches himself with in 'The Night', perhaps undergo a transformation in the spiritual wandering to which he is given:

> 'Tis now cleare day: I see a Rose
> Bud in the bright East, and disclose
> The Pilgrim-Sunne; all night have I
> Spent in a roving Extasie
> To find my Saviour.

('The Search', ll. 1–5)

In an imaginative trance, he has spent the night wandering the Holy Land. There is a sort of answering flash in the sun, which is also a pilgrim, and even the clear sky (not the night of imagination) suggests the birth of another sun or son from the rose in the east (a figure combining, by the way, light and plant). Pilgrimage or wandering, like tracking God in his traces, crops up frequently in Vaughan's verse. In 'The Search', he reproaches himself for such 'gadding', such dwelling on 'The skinne, and shell of things' as 'got / By meer Despair / of wings' (ll. 81, 85–7). The same reproach is expressed with greater brilliance in 'Vanity of Spirit'. But these are unusual severities. More often he strays among hints of the divine, content with intimation. And while he usually brings his poems to quite vigorous, sometimes astonishing conclusions, the progress to the conclusion is often rambling and repetitive. In 'Regeneration', the walk leads through two sunny spring scenes and through two allegorical figures for the regenerate and the unregenerate. Two repetitions do not amount to the interminable series of dissolving vistas in the tradition of poetic reverie descending from 'Il Penseroso', but a tendency toward reverie is all the same both a strength and weakness in Vaughan's poetry, and a predilection for the intermediate, the not yet resolved, goes with his roving and passing from one thing to another.

I have derived my description of Vaughan's spirituality as amphibious between life and death from Marvell's 'amphibium of life and death', a phrase he uses in 'The unfortunate Lover'. It was taken over by Jonathan Wordsworth for William Wordsworth's writing about liminal states.[30] It is in fact here that the frequently claimed kinship between Vaughan and Wordsworth is to be found. Wordsworth's odd feeling for a life in rocks and stones and trees, his absent-minded attention to his leech gatherer, who

---

30. Wordsworth 1982, p. 5.

seemed neither alive nor dead, the refusal of the little girl in 'We are Seven' to see that the dead are no longer part of her family – these and any number of further examples bring up states of mind that, like Vaughan's visions and intimations, have slipped outside the ordinary bounds of life. If Wordsworth matters more to us than Vaughan, it is not that Wordsworth had behind him the Enlightenment's exploration of the life of the mind; Vaughan is extraordinarily bold in expressing strange impulses ('strange' is a favourite word of his) and has Metaphysical and esoteric traditions of paradox to support him. It is rather that, where Vaughan's amphibiousness is solitary, Wordsworth was challenged by traditions of Revolutionary thought and Romantic sociability to work his visionary states into sympathies with other people and notions of human culture. It is curious that Vaughan was not moved by Christianity in the same direction, but the tradition of spirituality to which he belonged turned away from the world to the soul's intercourse with God. Vaughan's withdrawal from the world and his poetic persona as hermit and seer simply accentuate the unsociability of orthodox devotional life. The Christian alternative, enthusiastic participation in a sanctified community, appalled him. Such was the life of the Saints he denounced in his prophetic or apocalyptic moments.

In comparison with the shared feeling for states between life and death, the concerns with childhood and the natural scene, frequently taken as instances of an affinity between Vaughan and Wordsworth, show only super-ficial resemblances. In 'The Retreate', Vaughan takes an idea from Plato about the pre-existence of the soul[31] and a hint from Herbert's 'H. Baptisme' (II) ('the growth of flesh is but a blister; / Childhood is health'), and boldly reverses the direction of growth and maturing: the true spiritual direction is a diminishing toward becoming not only as a little child but even the disembodied spirit one was before life:

> Some men a forward motion love,
> But I by backward steps would move,
> And when this dust falls to the urn
> In that state I came return.

('The Retreate', ll. 29–32)

---

31. *Phaedo*, 70c–77a (Plato 1993); 'But (ah!) my soul with too much stay / Is drunk, and staggers in the way', seems to owe something to Plato's account of the condition of the soul contaminated by the senses with material things: 'it wanders about itself, and is confused and dizzy, as if drunk by, by virtue of contact with things of a similar kind' (79c); I owe this reference to Joanne Hall.

Or as he puts it in 'Distraction', 'I find my selfe the lesse, the more I grow' (l. 10). 'Angel infancy' for Vaughan features the impulse to attenuation of life that peculiarly makes up his interiority.[32] It has nothing to do with real childhood. 'The white celestial thought' he attributes to infancy in 'The Retreate' or 'Those white designs which children drive' he speaks of in 'Childe-hood' (l. 4) are simply radiant absences of anything. Conceivably Wordsworth's 'Ode on Intimations of Immortality' may borrow from Vaughan, but even in that poem, Wordsworth resigns himself to growing up and usually his interest in childhood, far from imagining innocence, attends quite robustly to the sensual bond between mother and child and child and world. Wordsworth's going back into his past turns up material that might inform a psychological study of childhood, but Vaughan's simply expresses with a flair for psychological resonance the recessive turn of his spirituality.

Vaughan as nature poet

As for nature, undoubtedly *Silex Scintillans* is set in rural retirement.[33] Unlike the city, which is man-made, the countryside might be supposed to be closer to the world God made: 'If *Eden* be on Earth at all, / 'Tis that, which we the *Country* call' ('Retirement', *Thalia Rediviva*). So 'The Morning-watch' celebrates the waking world adoring its creator in '*Hymning Circulations*' reminiscent of the rising of creation in praise in the great morning hymn in *Paradise Lost* (5, ll. 144–208). Vaughan's countryside, like Milton's Paradise, is a landscape of the imagination. It possibly contains more resemblance to Breconshire than Drummond of Hawthornden's Arcadian landscape does to Midlothian. But topographically it is unlocalized. There are no prospects such as had begun to appear in Denham's 'Cooper's Hill' or even such glimpses as appear in Marvell's 'Upon Appleton House'. His favourite pastoral countryside is the Bible's because in both Old and New Testaments men conversed with God and other spiritual beings by trees and wells and on hillsides. But usually the country or nature is present, not as a landscape, but as a reservoir of images on which he draws for his religious reflections. He finds parables and religious signs in rainbows, stars, plants, waterfalls,

---

32. For attenuation as spirituality, see 'The Tempest', ll. 42–44, where he laments the earthbound grossness of man, 'though all / He sees (like *Pyramids*,) shoot from this ball / And less'ning still grow up invisibly'.
33. On Vaughan as a nature poet see Trickett 1981, Christopher 1973 and Fitter 1992.

rather than in buildings, boxes, watering pots and pulleys. Actual country life and any social relations are absent. He is as alone with his soul concerns as Drummond in his Arcadian landscape with his love melancholy. If there are other rational beings to talk to, or at least address, they are dead, or angels, or figures from the Bible, or God. He can, of course, talk to a bird, timber, a shower and so forth as well. Such indefinite surroundings take on the colour of his mind without resistance, as a world shared with other people would not.

In this vaguely realized world, Vaughan is acutely sensitive to general impressions of light. We have noticed his feeling for light in darkness. The lines in 'They are all gone into the world of light!' comparing the memory of the departed spirits to 'those faint beams in which this hill is drest, / After the Sun's remove' have been praised, not just for their exact observation of a natural phenomenon, but for their tying a personal observation down to a specific time and place in the observer's life ('*this* hill').[34] At least we may agree that there seems to be some running together, as in 'Ascension Day', of an implied real scene 'out there' and a visionary seeing, such as he turns to in the immediately following lines: 'I see them walking in an Air of glory, / Whose light doth trample on my days'. If Vaughan is really attempting a kind of placing himself in a landscape, as Wordsworth places himself near Tintern Abbey, then it must be said that the attempt is fleeting in the poem and hard to match in his *oeuvre*. Nevertheless the observation of the effect of light is striking.

There are other places where he works in what he has seen for himself:

> The Pious soul by night
> Is like a clouded starre, whose beames though sed
> To shed their light
> Under some Cloud
> Yet are above,
> And shine, and move
> Beyond that mistie shrowd.

('The Morning-watch', ll. 25–26)

That takes its rise from a curious idiom ('under a cloud') but expands with a splendid violation of earthbound perspective to a universal and heavenly view of the stars. Vaughan's observation in 'The Morning-watch' is visionary. Unlike Donne's sharp, analytic observation of waves or ripples, Vaughan's

---

34.   Summers 1970, p. 128.

observation of the star gives direct access to a spiritual illumination. In Donne a sally of wit connects ripples and the impulse of love. In Vaughan the true state of starlight is a physical version of the process of divine light that illumines 'the pious soul'. The two things are at root the same; their likeness is a hidden identity, not just a resemblance struck off by the mind.[35]

Frequently the triumphs of Vaughan's art depend on vagueness and sensory blurring:

> O Joyes! Infinite sweetnes! with what flowres,
> And shoots of glory, my soul breakes, and buds!
> > All the long houres
> > Of night, and Rest
> > Through the still shrouds
> > Of sleep, and Clouds,
> > This Dew fell on my Breast;
> > O how it *Blouds*,
> And *Spirits* all my Earth!

('The Morning-watch', ll. 1–9)

The rapturous feeling of the return of life, which is also of the spirit, recalls Herbert's 'The Flower'. But Vaughan runs a description of the morning into a description of his waking with a felicitous impressionism ruled out by Herbert's precise ways of writing. I take it that 'shoots of glory', with Vaughan's usual combination of light and vegetation, means both green sprouts and rays of light such as might sparkle from dew. This in itself runs two things together, as does 'breaks and buds', day breaking and plants budding. But it is the soul of the beholder that breaks and buds with these things, God's joy and infinite sweetness dissolving self and world into praising. Again, the dew turns out to be a sacred influence shed through shrouds, not just of clouds (is it pedantic to complain that dew is not shed from clouds, let alone through them?[36]) but of sleep and on Vaughan's breast as well as on the world. So that the earth that is refreshed and inspirited is more Vaughan's corporeal existence than the world out of doors. '*Blouds*' is one of Vaughan's bold uses of noun as verb, like 'mountained', 'primrosed', 'arted', and by a grammatical wrench suggests a life force that may run through the earth as well as his own body and take the form of spirit, or at least beget vital spirits. Here, then, Vaughan's fluid style goes with his alchemical and neoplatonic

---

35. Cf. Ellrodt 1960, II, pp. 250–51, and for Donne, Beier 1994.
36. Vaughan may have had the well-known Vulgate translation of Isaiah, 45.8, in mind: *rorate coeli desuper* ('Let the dew come down from heaven above').

beliefs in the divine current in nature, and a vagueness about natural appearances conveys a religious feeling of unity with things.

One poem, however, stands out in Vaughan's work for its unusually exact eye for the appearances of the world:

The Water-fall

With what deep murmurs through times silent stealth
Doth thy transparent, cool and watry wealth
     Here flowing fall,
     And chide, and call,
As if his liquid, loose Retinue staid
Lingring, and were of this steep place afraid,
     The common pass
     Where, clear as glass,
     All must descend
     Not to an end: 10
But quickned by this deep and rocky grave,
Rise to a longer course more bright and brave.

  Dear stream! dear bank, where often I
  Have sate, and pleas'd my pensive eye,
  Why, since each drop of thy quick store
  Runs thither, whence it flow'd before,
  Should poor souls fear a shade or night,
  Who came (sure) from a sea of light?
  Or since those drops are all sent back
  So sure to thee, that none doth lack,   20
  Why should frail flesh doubt any more
  That what God takes, hee'l not restore?
  O useful Element and clear!
  My sacred wash and cleanser here,
  My first consigner unto those
  Fountains of life, where the Lamb goes?
  What sublime truths, and wholesome themes,
  Lodge in thy mystical, deep streams!
  Such as dull man can never finde
  Unless that Spirit lead his minde,   30
  Which first upon thy face did move,
  And hatch'd all with his quickning love.
  As this loud brooks incessant fall
  In streaming rings restagnates all,
  Which reach by course the bank, and then
  Are no more seen, just so pass men.
  O my invisible estate,
  My glorious liberty, still late!

> Thou art the Channel my soul seeks,
> Not this with Cataracts and Creeks.   40

The first twelve lines are description, the rest reflection, a not uncommon pattern in Vaughan, distinct in gross outline from the blurring method that we have looked at in 'Ascension Day' and 'The Morning-watch'. It is distinct also from Donne's argumentatively driven sensory analogies or Herbert's weaving of his train of thought into his emblematic figures such as the posy in 'Life'. Vaughan is more leisurely and expansive, and his figure is more striking than his thought. The play of long and short lines works to suggest the liquid lapse of the fall, a sort of felicity not always apparent in his versification. The same can be said of the enjambment between lines 5 and 6 with the pause after 'lingring' and the delightful wordplay on 'loose Retinue', so that time's watery train of retainers are what time retains or momentarily holds back as the water seems to hesitate before it plunges. But at the same time that Vaughan is sharply pictur- ing water movement, he is also insinuating a moral. Time's 'liquid, loose Retinue' means mortals; 'the common pass' means dying; that this is as 'clear as glass' fits the conspicuousness of the fact of death as well as the trans- parency of the waterfall for a few inches anyway before it turns to white and broken turbulence; the gorge below the fall is a 'rocky grave'; the 'longer course more bright and brave' suggests life after death as well as the stream emerged from the gorge. Vaughan's natural description takes in only those natural details of which he can make emblems. If he had stopped at line 12, there would not be so much difference between the thought-picturing in his description and Herbert's in his narrative in 'Life', except that Vaughan's occupies itself with a less conventional object.

But for twenty-eight further lines Vaughan continues to extract 'sublime truths, and wholesome themes'. The first of these themes has a way of blotting out the metaphorizing of the stream in line 12. There the stream emerging from the gorge glances at immortality, but in lines 15–22 Vaughan comes up with another figure for immortality, the return of the water in all its drops to the sea from which it came. The thought of water leads him on to baptism and that to the thought that thoughts, such as he has been having, may be found in 'mystical, deep streams' only at the prompting of the Holy Spirit, who brooded upon the waters of the deep to bring forth the world. There follows a third figure for death: the circular ripples of the fall in the pool below disappear into the bank: 'just so pass men'. This occasions an apostrophe to death, 'my invisible estate, / My glorious liberty', as the true channel of his spirit, and with that he dismisses the stream.

As rather often with Vaughan, the poem goes on longer than its con- centrated writing. Still, the rambling is not without interest. For one thing,

Vaughan suggests that the book in the running brook that he has discovered is not just an invention of his wit but somehow both written in the 'mystical, deep streams' themselves and inspired in him by the Holy Spirit, with an implication that his watery thoughts like the waters of the deep have been incubated on by the Holy Spirit. As with light, Vaughan's ideas are not just ideas but illuminations, and if in the final lines he dismisses the stream, it is because the stream has almost more than metaphorically become the channel of his spirit.

Vaughan as Metaphysical

It should be clear by now that the Metaphysical quality of Vaughan's verse lies apart from Donne's or Herbert's, in spite of his self-proclaimed inspiration by the latter. His interiority is not just devotional, but political, solipsistic, recessive, visionary. His spirituality tends to states of mind, if not trances, outside the usual boundaries of human life. And his wit – his use of analogical figures and his play with the coincidence or exchange of opposites – is not so much wit, with its strong attachment to social life, to the mind that acknowledges its incorporated condition with other minds even while it tries to grasp the paradoxes of religion, as a shift into a mode of illumination. For Vaughan, the correspondences between light and spirit, the circulation of water and the return of the spirit are substantial and written in the secret life of the universe.[37]

Vaughan was not steadily attuned to his strengths as a poet, and much of *Silex Scintillans* is simply sub-Herbertian piety. He lacked the intellectual training or keenness of Donne or Herbert so that he frequently turns his thoughts lamely. But it would be a mistake to go on to say that the vagueness of suggestion associated with Vaughan's most triumphant effects is simply another expression of the inexactness of his mind and dismiss his vagueness as the decadence of the Metaphysical style. The indefinite allowed Vaughan to convey what he felt moved to say religiously. Besides, given that Shakespeare and Milton are also masters of indeterminate reference, it would be curious to reproach Vaughan for falling away from a seventeenth-century standard of definite thought and sense.[38] There was no such standard, though the Eliot tradition tried to invent one. Vaughan's blurrings, so far from spoiling something Herbertian in him, are the places where he manages to make something new of Metaphysical inwardness.

37. See Ellrodt 1960, II, pp. 250–51.
38. See Empson 1953, ch. V, esp. pp. 174–75.

Andrew Marvell, from a painting in the National Portrait Gallery. By courtesy of the National Portrait Gallery, London.

CHAPTER FIVE

Andrew Marvell

Life

Marvell was more directly involved in the political history of his time than other Metaphysical poets. He held office under Cromwell's Council of State and sat as MP during the undoing of the Cromwellian regime and the Restoration. The political revolutions of the time, the execution of Charles I and the Restoration of Charles II, involved him in difficult and rather obscure adjustments. He changed from Royalist sympathizer to Cromwellian and from Cromwellian to anti-Court politician. He was not a time-server like the poet Edmund Waller, or Cromwell's press agent, the twice-turned Marchamont Nedham. But neither did he pursue a course of grand, if not simple, consistency like the republican Milton. It is not easy to make out what his principles were, yet his indefiniteness or reserve allowed him as a pamphleteer to make effective protest against the oppressions of the Restoration episcopacy and what he took to be the advance of a design to subject the country to a Catholic tyranny. In the eighteenth and nineteenth centuries he was seen, along with his friends Milton and James Harrington, as a champion of republican liberties. It is no longer certain that he held republican views, but he was able to do more than either of his friends for the practical resistance to the anti-Cromwellian reaction of the Restoration and its abuses of power.[1]

Impetuousness was at least part of his makeup. He probably had a brief fling with Catholicism as a student. He assaulted a fellow MP and drew a

---

1. The most recent discussion of Marvell's republicanism is to be found in Norbrook 1999; he is forced to a considerable amount of nuance and qualification of the term.

pistol on a troublesome coachman as he was returning through Germany from an embassy to Russia, Sweden and Denmark. Perhaps experience of his natural eruptiveness made him unnaturally withdrawn. According to Aubrey, 'He kept bottles of wine at his lodgeing, and many times would drinke liberally by himself to refresh his spirits and exalt his muse', but 'though he loved wine he would never drinke hard in company, and was wont to say that, *he would not play the good-fellow in any man's company in whose hands he would not trust his life*'.[2] Caution was necessary for a politician during the Restoration, particularly for one associated with Cromwell. Marvell could be indiscreet and drolly self-mocking in writing to his nephew, William Popple, but his official letters to his constituents in Hull never deviate from dry reportage and such expression of opinions as would be acceptable to the authorities if his letters were opened.[3] His reserve, though, must have gone deeper than political caution. His lyrical and meditative poetry is characterized by ironic self-presentation and its secretness is part of its spell. Not that Marvell was morose. His diplomatic work indicates that he must have learned polish and social address. He was accused of frenchified manners, which presumably means that he was more civil and witty in his conversation than his enemies were.[4]

The political changes in which Marvell was involved, his own changes of allegiance, the uncertainties and perhaps ambiguities in his political position, together with his reserve, imply a mind accustomed to living with uncertainty and divided between public appearance and private intention. That would also go with the ironic view of himself he takes in his poetry and the self-division that is the characteristic note of his interiority.

He was born on 31 March 1621, at Winestead-in-Holderness, the only son to survive of Andrew Marvell and Anne Pease. Marvell's father, a clergyman, moved to Hull in 1624 when the town appointed him lecturer at Holy Trinity and master of the Charterhouse. He was a respected local figure as preacher and pastor, 'facetious, and yet Calvinistical'.[5] Two of his daughters married into prosperous Hull merchant families. In spite of his Calvinism and ties to a town that later twice stood siege for Parliament in the Civil War, he was, according to his son, 'a Conformist to the Rites of the Church of *England*, though I confess none of the most over-running or eager of them'.[6]

---

2. Aubrey 1949, p. 73.
3. See Keeble 1990, pp. 111–34.
4. See Bradbrook and Lloyd-Thomas 1940, p. 10, citing Richard Leigh, *The Transproser Rehears'd*; also Larkin 1983, p. 252.
5. Anthony à Wood, *Athenae Oxoniensis* (1691), 4, cols 230–32.
6. *The Rehearsal Transpros'd*, Marvell 1971b, p. 204.

From Hull Grammar School, Marvell went up to Trinity College, Cambridge, in 1633. He graduated with a BA in 1639. He contributed two poems congratulating Charles on the birth of Princess Anne in 1637, one in Greek, the other a Horatian Ode in Latin, to a Cambridge volume in which Crashaw also appeared. Otherwise little is known of his Cambridge years. Trinity was a middle-of-the-road place in religion, neither Puritan, nor, like Crashaw's Pembroke and Peterhouse, Anglo-Catholic. A family story has it that Marvell was converted by Jesuits and ran away from Cambridge to London, where his father retrieved him in a bookshop. He did not stay on at Cambridge to take an MA but left in 1641, probably to travel on the Continent, although in what capacity, whether on a Grand Tour or as tutor to someone who could afford it or as agent for his brothers-in-law at a time when their business was disrupted by the Civil War, is not known.[7] Some time, at any rate, between 1642 and 1649 Marvell visited Holland, France, Italy and Spain, and some time between 1645 and 1647 he was in Rome, where he met Richard Flecknoe, an English poet and Catholic priest, at the sign of the Sad Pelican and satirized him for his hunger and religion.

At this time, he formed attachments that are politically at odds not just with his Hull background but with his later service under the Commonwealth. His elegies on Lord Francis Villiers (died 1648)[8] and on Lord Hastings (1649), and his poem commending Richard Lovelace's *Lucasta* (written 1648; published 1649), not only celebrate Royalists but express anti-Parliamentarian sentiments. He had been abroad during the serious fighting but was presumably back in England when he wrote these pieces and published two of them; the Royalist cause had then clearly been lost.

Some time between May and June 1650 he wrote 'An Horatian Ode', a poem whose political engagement is much more puzzling. The background to its uncertainties is as follows. At Naseby (1645), the Parliamentary forces under Fairfax and Cromwell won a decisive victory. Charles fled to the Scots Covenanting army, which, finding him an impossible person to make terms with, handed him over to the English Parliament. In the hands of Parliament and then the Army, Charles brought on a Second Civil War, disastrous to himself, by his inept scheming. But he had rightly appreciated the division between Parliament, predominantly Presbyterian and naturally jealous of its authority, and the Army, predominantly Independent and Sectarian and conscious of having the real power to sway events, though uncertain how to employ it. Exasperated by the intrigues between King and

---

7. Empson 1984, pp. 4–5.
8. A contested attribution, though I should accept it.

Parliament, the victorious Army purged the Commons, and the so-called Rump then abolished the House of Lords. The way was open for the trial and execution of the King in January 1649.

That iconoclastic act caused an enormous revulsion, naturally among Charles's party, but also among the more moderate Parliamentarians, usually Presbyterians, who had fought against their King only to protect what they took to be their liberties under monarchical rule. But even radicals, inside and outside the Army, were now ranged against the Army grandees, who would not permit free elections and, faced with what appeared to them imminent collapse into anarchy, quashed political and social levelling movements. At the same time, the Scots had crowned Charles II and seemed to be meditating war on the new republic. And Ireland outside Dublin and Londonderry, Protestant as well as Catholic, was united in Royalist opposition to republican rule. When Marvell wrote 'An Horatian Ode upon Cromwell's Return from Ireland', prospects for the Republic had cleared to the extent that Cromwell had ruthlessly subdued Ireland. Invasion from Scotland still threatened, but Cromwell returned in May 1650 and his by now extraordinary standing as a soldier might give confidence to Englishmen that the danger would be met with success, as indeed it was when he invaded and routed the Scots at Dunbar (September 1650) and crushed their invasion of England at Worcester. But Charles, the uncrowned King of England, escaped, and however successful in arms, Cromwell and the Army did not know how to manage the government of the country.

'An Horatian Ode', written when the Royalist cause was lost but the future government of England looked uncertain, is a deeply unsettled poem, reflecting the perplexity of one who was emotionally attached to the Stuarts but who recognized in Cromwell a force with which the English polity must come to terms. If the poem marks a change of allegiance, or at least a hope that Cromwell might save England from anarchy and lead it to victory over the Scots and perhaps even over Catholic powers on the Continent, the submission to his force is profoundly troubled in a way that might appeal to Royalists.[9] It makes a Royalist icon of Charles's death: he 'bow'd his comely Head / Down as upon a Bed' (ll. 63–64). But the poem's Royalist sympathies are very different from the note of heroic intransigence to be heard in 'Tom May's Death', written shortly after. Tom May died in November 1650. He had gone over to the Parliamentary side in the 1640s. In Marvell's poem he is magnificently excoriated by his old master, Ben Jonson, for betraying the office of a poet:

---

9. Brooks 1969, p. 190, points out that the Royalist poet Robert Wild echoed the part of Marvell's poem that deals with Charles.

When the Sword glitters ore the Judges head,
And fear has Coward Churchmen silenced,
Then is the Poets time, 'tis then he drawes,
And single fights forsaken Vertues cause.
He, when the wheel of Empire, whirleth back,
And though the World's disjointed Axel crack,
Sings still of ancient Rights, and better Times,
Seeks wretched good, arraigns successful Crimes.

(ll. 63–70)[10]

It is hard to think that the poet of 'An Horatian Ode' could have written these lines without painful reflections or without acute inner conflict.[11]

But meanwhile an opportunity of employment arose that allowed him to brood honourably and advance his career without for the moment committing himself to England's new rulers. Thomas, Lord Fairfax, to whose generalship the Parliamentary armies owed almost as much as to Cromwell's, had withdrawn from the proceedings of the Commission that sentenced Charles to death and resigned from his command rather than invade Scotland. He retired to his Yorkshire estates. There he was thought (wrongly) to be sufficiently in sympathy with the Royalists for the Commonwealth government to set a spy on him, and there Marvell was employed, probably from early 1650 to July 1652, as tutor to the Fairfaxes' one surviving child, the twelve-year-old Mary. During that time, he wrote the complimentary poems to Fairfax, 'Upon the Hill and Grove at Bill-borow' and its Latin version, 'Upon Appleton House' and 'Musicks Empire' (if it is addressed to him).[12] During that time too, he may have written 'The Gallery' since verbal resemblances make it look as if it drew on William Cartwright's *Comedies, Tragi-Comedies with Other Poems* of 1651 and so might have been written soon after the appearance of the collection.[13] It is often assumed that the bulk of his other lyric pieces were written then. But there is no solider ground for thinking so than that the Fairfax household, whose head applied himself to poetry along with gardening, horsebreeding and designs for his daughter's

---

10. All quotations of Marvell's poetry are from Marvell 1971a.
11. Those who do not like to think that Marvell vacillated at this time should consult the suggestions for a more consistent course, Wallace 1968, pp. 103–4; Chernaik 1983, pp. 83–84, and Patterson 1990a, pp. 201–3. See also Loxley 1995, pp. 31–62, for a highly qualified account of Marvell's Royalist leanings. The easy way out is to question the attribution of 'Tom May's Death' to Marvell. For May, consult Norbrook 1999, index under May.
12. But see Hodge 1973–74, for the view that 'On the Hill and Grove at Bill-borow' and its Latin version were written later.
13. Wilcher 1992, pp. 462–63.

marriage, sounds as if it would have been a leisurely, encouraging place for writing them. 'The Garden', often assumed to have been written at this time, may in fact have been written after the Restoration while Marvell was busy as an MP.[14]

During his time as tutor, Marvell must have decided to make a career in the service of Cromwell's government. Already in 1651 he had written a very flattering poem to Oliver St John, one of the Commonwealth leaders, on his embassy to Holland. Presumably also with an eye to recommending himself to the Commonwealth, which was engaged in a naval war with the Dutch, he wrote a lively squib, 'The Character of Holland'. This was probably written in early 1653, and though not published until 1655 and then anonymously, might still have been shown to people who counted. In 1653 also he applied for the post of Assistant Latin Secretary, what would be now a Foreign Office job, where someone skilled in Latin, the international language of diplomacy and propaganda, was needed. For this, he was splendidly recommended by Milton, who found that, with failing eyesight, he could not continue as Latin Secretary unaided. The application failed, but Marvell secured instead the tutorship of William Dutton, a protégé of Cromwell's, later his ward. With him, he stayed in the house of St John's brother-in-law, John Oxenbridge, a Puritan clergyman, who had returned to England from the Bermudas on the news of the revolution in England. It is generally assumed that Marvell wrote his charming but fanciful poem 'Bermudas', with its suggestion of Protestant incursion on the Spanish Empire, during his time there. A more direct sign of his being attuned to the new order was his complimentary Latin poems for Dr Ingelo, who accompanied an embassy to Christiana, Queen of Sweden, in 1653–54. Two of these went with a picture of Cromwell. The first, 'In Effigiem *Oliveri Cromwell*', probably expresses Marvell's considered grounds for admiring Cromwell:

> *Haec est quae toties* Inimicos *Umbra fugavit*
> *At sub qua* Cives *Otia lenta terunt*
> (This is an image which put his enemies to flight,
> But under which citizens enjoy quiet leisure).[15]

Another complimentary poem, written at the end of 1654, 'The First Anniversary of the Government Under His Highness the Lord Protector', with the usual extravagance of such verse, also praises Cromwell for the peace and order he has established in the face of foes without, and Fifth Monarchists,

---

14. See Pritchard 1983, and Duncan-Jones 1975, p. 275.
15. Translated William A. McQueen and Kiffin A. Rockwell in Marvell 1964, p. 64.

Ranters and Quakers within, the Commonwealth. He compares Cromwell to Gideon: 'by the Conquest of two Kings grown great, / He on the Peace extends a Warlike power' (ll. 250–51) – so to glance at Cromwell's overcoming the forces of both Charles Stuarts and then using his military power to settle the country. The warning note on which the Horatian Ode ends ('The same *Arts* that did *gain* / A *Pow'r* must it *maintain*') has turned to celebration of the warrior who maintains peace. In all this, Marvell puts, as a congratulatory poem requires, a very flattering gloss on Cromwell's Protectorship. Cromwell was as incapable of dealing with freely elected parliaments as Charles had been. He had dissolved the Rump, and its successor, the nominated Barebones Parliament, dissolved itself in 1653 after sitting for only a few months. The next Parliament elected under a new constitution, the Instrument of Government, proved refractory and had to be dissolved also. Admittedly, Marvell wrote before Cromwell dissolved that Parliament in 1655, but at the same time he never showed himself troubled by Cromwell's suppressing popular agitation. For him, Cromwell is the Amphion who magically compels an architecture of state out of warring and resistant people (ll. 49–86), the sailor who seizes the helm from the unskilful steersman and rescues the ship of state from the rocks (ll. 265–78).[16] Even when one has made allowances for panegyric and noted the praise for Cromwell's refusing the kingship (like Gideon) and preserving liberty, one still feels that Marvell's republicanism means, like Milton's (though with a much less powerful impulse to liberty), the dictatorship of the good. He also entertains the idea that Cromwell has been divinely appointed to lead God's Englishmen to bring about the Millennium (ll. 131–44).

Marvell's literary efforts on behalf of Cromwell were rewarded. After visiting Saumur in France and its famous Protestant Academy with William Dutton in 1656, he was finally appointed Latin Secretary to the Council of State in 1657. His duties seem to have been mainly diplomatic. For the marriage of Cromwell's daughter, Mary, he wrote two pastoral songs, in one of which the suitor, Lord Fauconberg, plays Endymion, the shepherd who cried for the moon, the goddess above his sphere, and got her, an ingratiating way of representing the new relations between the old aristocracy and the plebeian, if now princely, Cromwells. But he did not continue Cromwell's servant long. Cromwell died in September 1658, an event Marvell commemorated in 'A Poem upon the Death of O. C.'. The poem is poor but it suggests that Marvell's attachment to Cromwell had become

16.   A welcome consequence of accepting E. E. Duncan-Jones's arguments (1995) that 'On the Victory Obtained by Blake' is not Marvell's would be that he would not have written that poem's urging the crown upon Cromwell (ll. 39–44).

heartfelt. He continued in his Secretaryship and at the same time got himself elected as MP for Hull in the Parliament of 1659. The Army forced Richard Cromwell to dissolve that Parliament, but finding itself incapable of ruling the country, it crumbled and let General Monck call a freely elected Parliament early in 1660. In it, Marvell again represented Hull.

From this point on Marvell's course becomes particularly hard to make out. The puzzles about where he stood have perhaps less to do with uncertainty or inconsistency in him than with the complexities of Restoration politics and his adroitness or deviousness in managing their situations. It is not just distance in time that makes his politics puzzling. In the attacks on him succeeding *The Rehearsal Transpros'd*, it was hinted that he was homosexual or impotent or both. We have no means of knowing whether there was any truth behind what was said. But the lampooning of him for sexual amphibiousness was also a metaphor for political indeterminacy. Even his contemporaries found it hard to make out whose side he was on.[17]

The Convention Parliament of 1660, expressing a national revulsion against Cromwellian rule, restored the rule of King and Parliament and called back Charles II. Scapegoats had to be offered and lists were drawn up of those who should be punished for their association with regicide. Marvell, who had hopefully saluted Richard Cromwell as a worthy successor of his father, accepted Charles II willingly enough as a guarantor of order, but he stood apart sufficiently from the rout to protect Milton from punishment.[18]

The reaction went much further in the Cavalier Parliament. In its first four years (1661–65), it re-established the Church of England as an episcopacy and passed laws that punished Nonconformity. These laws, the so-called Clarendon Code, were engineered by Charles's Chancellor, Edmund Hyde, Lord Clarendon, who, along with the Cavalier majority, had come to see Protestantism without bishops as a politically and socially subversive force. The return of the bishops did not mean a return to the ways of Charles I. Then the rule of bishops had been a branch of royal policy. Charles II, the least zealous of men and a secret Catholic, had no interest in heading a Laudian Church intolerant of dissent. But Parliament, made up of the same class, and in some cases of the same men, as had opposed Charles I's bishops, settled on Charles II a persecuting episcopacy. That Marvell was opposed in some ways to the new order is certain. What is not so clear is how he expressed his opposition as an MP and politician. He was a poor speaker and might for tactical reasons disguise or finesse his aims. Besides, political alignment under Charles II was eddying and confused. But as a writer,

---

17. Paul Hammond 1998, pp. 182–83.
18. Legouis 1968, p. 118.

Marvell comes out consistently against men or institutions of the new regime and, in general direction, expresses views that fit an old Cromwellian. Against the humiliation of the English navy by the Dutch, a reversal of the glorious aggression of the Commonwealth, he wrote 'Last Instructions to a Painter' to lampoon the venality and incompetence of Clarendon's administration. When Clarendon fell in 1667, the persecution of the Nonconformists, the Puritans who would not accept the episcopal settlement of the Church, continued with proposals for harsher coercion. If Marvell was a Nonconformist, he was certainly discreet about it, but his opposition to a persecuting religious establishment was consistent. He laughed at least one proponent of episcopal vigour and rigour into silence with *The Rehearsal Transpros'd* (1672–73). In both these sallies, he avoided attacking the King, perhaps out of respect. Nevertheless, he came round in *An Account of the Growth of Popery* (1677) to attacking (with every pretence that Charles was not his object) what he and an increasing popular opinion took to be Charles's real aims, the reduction of the country to Catholic absolutism on the French model. The *Account* was sufficiently offensive to the government for a price to be offered for the discovery of its author, but Marvell's authorship was not discovered till after he died (poisoned, it was rumoured, by Jesuits) on 16 August 1678.[19]

Marvell did not publish or prepare for publication an edition of his poems. The poems on affairs of state that he did publish were frequently anonymous. In consequence attributions are still contested. His housekeeper, Mary Palmer, brought out an edition in 1681, from which the Cromwellian pieces were excised and the Restoration satires omitted. Marvell's authorship of some poems even in that volume ('Thyrsis and Dorinda', 'Tom May's Death', 'On a Victory Obtained by Blake') has been queried. The other source, a manuscript that originally belonged to William Popple, Marvell's 'beloved nephew', supplies the Cromwellian poems and eighteen Restoration satires, but only some of these seem to be Marvell's.

A final and odd note on a shadowy and seemingly devious (though not unstaunch or feeble) life has to do with his housekeeper. She claimed that Marvell had married her secretly in 1667. This was disputed in a complicated legal wrangle after Marvell's death but accepted by the judges who examined the case.[20]

---

19. In this last period of his life, he was still sniping at bishops in *Mr Smirk or the Divine in Mode* (1676) and more indirectly according to Lamont 1990, pp. 135–36, in *A Short Historical Essay Concerning General Councils, Creeds, and Imposition in Religion* (1676). He also engaged on the Arminian side in Nonconformist controversy over free-will in *Remarks Upon a Late Disingenuous Discourse Writ by TD* (1678), whose political significance is elucidated by Lamont.
20. Empson 1984, pp. 43–95, and Duncan-Jones 1995, p. 121, have advanced robust arguments for not thinking Mary Palmer's story a fabrication.

Marvell's poetry

Though his poetic *oeuvre* is small, Marvell has a greater range than any Metaphysical apart from Donne. He wrote devotional and love poems, pastorals, elegies, complimentary verse and satires and did so in strikingly various literary manners. Marvell is always Marvell but not in the obvious way that Donne is always Donne. The pastoral poet of 'The Mower to Gloworms' has a different voice from the satirist of 'Fleckno, an English Priest at Rome'.

I shall be concerned with Marvell's poetry of self-division. That is determined by the focus of this book on Metaphysical interiority. As it happens, I think his poetry of self-division includes his most interesting work. In any case, I shall not be discussing his political poetry, apart from 'An Horatian Ode', nor his commendatory poems such as the excellent one 'On Mr. Milton's Paradise lost'.

'An Horatian Ode'

After T. S. Eliot's essay, 'poise' and 'urbanity' entered the way people thought about Marvell, especially about 'An Horatian Ode'.[21] That poem has been praised for civilized detachment from the passions of its time. Equally, it has been blamed for a balance that is really political inconsequence or a mask for resignation to the rule of force and willingness to accept as ruler whoever could impose order.[22] The poem does, in fact, show an exceptional freedom from the 'party-colour'd Mind' (l. 106) of the Civil War, making both Cromwell and Charles ideal figures that enlarge the issues of their time. And it does also simplify and reduce matters to questions of the safety of the state, to order rather than justice. But in doing so, it speaks not with poise but uneasiness, out of the anxiety that a thoughtful, patriotic Englishman might feel at the time. When he wrote *Absalom and Achitophel* in the crisis of the Charles II's reign, Dryden spoke for public order against

---

21. Eliot 1932, 'Andrew Marvell', pp. 294, 296, 303; 'poise' and 'urbanity' are Leavis's renderings of Eliot's ideas, 1936, pp. 26, 28.
22. The classical analysis of detachment is Brooks's, which, however, leads to the conclusion (1969, p. 198) that Marvell's detachment went with Royalist sympathies; for the other view see Wilding 1987, pp. 114–37, who argues that 'An Horatian Ode' is a Cromwellian piece that suppresses the political protest that Cromwell's advance crushed. For another Cromwellian interpretation see Norbrook 1990a, and 1999, pp. 243–71, who argues that the discordance of the poem belongs to the style of Lucan, a heroic Republican mode at the time. I find Brooks's account of tone in the details more convincing than interpretations that try to replace it with a less ambivalent one.

anarchy and held up Charles as the power that moderates the passions of
the state. Dryden's tempered rhetoric, judgements and concessions imitate
the moderating power of the authority he celebrates. As poet, he assumes
a magisterial authority. Marvell never writes as an Augustan orator. In his
satires, his utterance lacks imperious rhetorical design and *gravitas*. And in
'An Horatian Ode', it is his misgiving, not assurance, that is the great thing
and what would have spoken to his time if his poem was circulated.[23]

His verse form is uneasy. Its unit, a tetrameter couplet followed by a
trimeter one, misses a beat. And while locally the effect of the trimeter
couplet may be of increased rapidity and energy or of terse, decisive comment, overall the effect is unsettled, so that for example the final lines, in
which Cromwell is hailed as the hope of England, come over as a warning
as much as a salute:

> But thou the Wars and Fortunes Son
> March indefatigably on;
> > And for the last effect
> > Still keep thy Sword erect:
> Besides the force it has to fright
> The Spirits of the shady Night,
> > The same *Arts* that did *gain*
> > A *Pow'r* must it *maintain*.

The 'last effect' will be the defeat of the Scots, looked forward to in the
preceding verses, but the phrase has a way of escaping into disturbing
overtones (what will the last effect of necessary violence be now the rule of
law has been overturned?). Cromwell's sword, held erect like Odysseus's
or Aeneas's in the underworld, will keep the spirits at bay, but with what
haunting shadows his heroic progress is compassed about, not least by the
ghost of Charles, whose death has been so unforgettably recorded earlier.
After that, the final couplet sounds at once, in its summary curtness, resolved
and unhappy. In spite of its neatness, the epigram runs over the line with an
effect of hesitation, and '*Arts*' remind us of the political arts that Cromwell
is earlier supposed to have used to trap Charles. If, as some think, Marvell
was impressed by the ideas about political power of Machiavelli or Hobbes,
he does not write as an 'easy Philosopher'.[24]

The classicizing of the Ode is itself uneasy, as far as possible from the
Augustans' sense that in following the ancients they were in touch with

---

23. Dryden had been a colleague of Milton and Marvell under Cromwell. Certain lines in
    Absalom and Achitophel suggest he knew 'The Horatian Ode'. See Paul Hammond 1988.
24. Vickers 1989 argues for Marvell's being a student of Machiavelli; see also Worden 1981
    and Worden 1987, pp. 158–63.

something sure and well-founded. Seventeenth-century writers, educated in the classics, turned to Roman history for pictures of what was going on in their own time. In Roman history, they found power struggles free from the pieties and mystifications that troubled their own political involvements. Particularly in the Roman Civil War of the first century BC, Englishmen might see the issues of their own Civil War, republican liberty against imperial power, established right against force, rehearsed in a way that might suggest thought about the state not limited to the repertoire of English constitutional ideas. One effect of the classical colouring of the Ode is to open up English history, with a disturbing defamiliarizing, to a possible view of its events as governed by force or necessity. But Roman and English Civil Wars were in fact very unlike. 'An Horatian Ode' calls on Roman analogies in a very confusing way, and, whether that was Marvell's intention or not, suggests an extraordinarily discordant state of affairs.[25]

The poet Horace had begun as a republican but was won over by the victorious Octavian, later the Emperor Augustus Caesar, to write on his side. In writing a Horatian Ode, Marvell is suggesting a change of loyalty on his own part and a submission to the new order. But this is a very general likeness, and in fact the various Odes in which Horace treats Caesar as the bringer of peace and victory to Rome offer straightforward congratulation quite different from Marvell's qualified tribute. Inside the framework of Horatian Ode, the classical analogies are askew. Instead of a Republic defeated, there is a Republic insurgent. And there are two Caesars, not one, and neither can be like Augustus. One is Charles, head of the old order, not founder of the new, whom Cromwell's lightning has blasted. The other is Cromwell, who, with Protestant jingoism corresponding to Horace's Roman imperialism, Marvell hopes will carry war from Britain to France and further:

> A *Caesar* he ere long to *Gaul*,
> To *Italy* an *Hannibal*,
>   And to all States not free
>   Shall *Clymacterick* be.

(ll. 101–4)

The Caesar who conquered Gaul was Julius Caesar, assassinated by Brutus and Cassius for his assumption of dictatorial powers. Can one keep that assassination (or Hannibal's final ruin) out of one's thoughts? Other classical material is more recondite, perhaps not so much allusion as expression of mental conflict. Marvell compares Charles's head to the one discovered

---

25. For discussions of classical allusions, see Norbrook 1990a and 1999, pp. 243–71, Coolidge 1965–66, and Sowerby 1994, pp. 168ff.

in digging the foundations of the temple of Jupiter Capitolinum, which was taken as an omen of the future greatness of Rome. He makes this weird comparison even more jarring by inventing the details that the head was bloody and that the architects were terrified (Charles's head was of course bloody and the courage of the regicides had been dampened by the reaction to the execution).[26] Again Marvell drew details from Lucan's *Civil War* for his picture of Cromwell. Is it significant that in Lucan, Caesar, the victorious general who returned to his country, destroyed the Republic and that Lucan execrated him? Or is it rather the case with this and all the classical material that has gone into his poem that Marvell was trying to make something of stuff that was deeply unresolved in his own mind?

The poem opens by characterizing the times in which Cromwell has appeared so momentously with a glance at 'the forward Youth'. Marvell is thinking of the ambitious young men of his generation, who would have to turn from love poetry and pastorals and the agreeable recreations of peace to action and war, in which Cromwell had made himself the heroic but disturbing contemporary example. He does not necessarily have in mind anything so specific as joining Cromwell on his Scottish campaign or on a Protestant crusade against Papists or even taking up arms for Charles Stuart.[27] But if he includes himself among the clear spirits, he will be recognizing that writing the kind of poetry he is most famous for, apart from 'An Horatian Ode', is not a course for one who who is ambitious to make 'impression upon Time'. Ambition is a theme that recurs in Marvell's poetry with surprising insistence.[28] He imagines striving to mount beyond change to a sphere that is above time because immortal glory may be found there or because it is a sovereign realm from which one can regulate the affairs of time and politics, like Cromwell in 'The First Anniversary'. In the 'Horatian Ode', Cromwell fascinates Marvell's imagination because he is a figure of towering ambition. But here Marvell is deeply ambivalent toward what has such a hold on him. Cromwell is one who

> Could by industrious Valour climbe
> To ruine the great Work of Time,
>   And cast the Kingdome old
>   Into another Mold.

(ll. 33–36)

---

26. Livy, I, lv, and Worden 1987, p. 152.
27. Newton 1972b.
28. On Marvell's ambition see Newton 1972b, p. 139, and Shrapnel 1971, p. 155. On ambition mounting above the world to 'make impression upon Time', see 'The unfortunate Lover', 'To his Noble Friend Mr. Lovelace, upon his Poems' (ll. 47–50), and 'The First Anniversary of the Government under O. C.' (ll. 45–48).

Cromwell has indeed made 'impression upon Time'; he has destroyed the English polity, 'the great Work of Time', a phrase that suggests a reverence for the constitution in its gradual perfection, of the kind that Clarendon would give voice to in his *History of the Great Rebellion*. Marvell would later write of Cromwell with affection as well as respect, but at this point the motive he has magnified in him arouses dismay as well as admiration. Perhaps it is significant that after imagining ambition in so disturbing a shape, he should turn in the poems he wrote in praise of Fairfax to a greatness marked by its retreat from ambition.

Until the poem modulates to patriotic congratulation and hope as it turns to enemies abroad, the drawing of Cromwell praises him only to arouse anxiety:

> So restless *Cromwel* could not cease
> In the inglorious Arts of Peace,
> But through adventrous War
> Urged his active Star.

(ll. 9–12)

Cromwell is more than humanly energetic; he urges the star that rules his fate as if it were a horse.[29] Marvell calls him 'restless', which more than hesitates over the beneficence of his energies, and surely there is something rueful in yielding to Cromwell, the captain of an iron time, the tribute that he has made the arts of peace 'inglorious'.[30] Cromwell is praised as an inhuman force, a portentous agent of angry heaven like lightning, that has struck the kingdom. That may exalt him in a way, but it makes him into an act of God, unaccountable and destructive. Even when he fashions Cromwell in his earlier career in the image of a Roman patrician dwelling in rural retirement until the necessity of the time called him forth, Marvell shoots his picture through with hesitations. He begins, 'if we would speak true, / Much to the Man is due', but what reservations lie in 'To give the man his due . . .'. He goes on to speak of Cromwell's innocent employment in his gardens, 'As if his highest plot / To plant the Bergamot', and yet the craft required to rear Bergamot or royal pears in English soil hints at the plots by which, some lines ahead, Marvell supposes Cromwell to have beguiled Charles into fleeing from Hampton Court only to hand himself over at

---

29. Brooks 1969, p. 190.
30. Cf., by another askew allusion, Virgil, Georgic, IV, ll. 563–64: '*Illo Vergilium me tempore dulcis alebat / Parthenope studiis florentem ignobilis oti*', where Virgil speaks of being engaged in pursuits of ignoble ease (making pastoral poetry) while Augustus urges his active star.

Carisbrooke Castle (ll. 47–52) and perhaps hints also at further designs on the throne (wrongly, Cromwell was thought an arch-schemer).

The poem as a whole is concerned with Cromwell's rise, but an intensely vivid account of the beheading of Charles occupies the moment 'which first assur'd the forced Pow'r' and blights the triumph. Marvell makes of Charles on the scaffold an image of true majesty:

> *He* nothing common did or mean
> Upon that memorable Scene:
>   But with his keener Eye
>   The Axes edge did try.
>
>   (ll. 57–60)

The Stuarts knew how to die. Yet qualifying even this moving picture are suggestions that royalty for Charles was a matter of gesture and image. It requires some sort of greatness to carry off such an act. And yet the phrasing of 'That thence the *Royal* Actor born [i.e. borne] / The *Tragick Scaffold* might adorn' suggests that for Charles, kingship is a matter of show and theatre, and found wanting in the face of the solid facts of Cromwell's power and political craft.[31]

The particular excellence of the Horatian Ode is to allow a divided mind to speak, as it does at least in the first seventy-two lines (before the alarming Cromwell is deflected upon the Irish, the Scots and the Continent) and in the last eight. But Marvell's is not just an art of dubitating. He has a knack of compressing his thought into sharply rendered details such as the rusty armour in the hall that calls up the long peace in England now at an end or Charles's sharp glance at the axe that suggests the eye of majesty in command of death. In comparison, Milton's sonnet 'To the Lord General' makes a poor showing:

> Cromwell, our chief of men, who through a cloud
> Not of war only, but detractions rude,
> Guided by faith and matchless Fortitude,
> To peace and truth thy glorious way hast ploughed.

This is a salute that might well have pleased Cromwell, but his ploughing through a cloud cannot please the imagination. Marvell's Cromwell by contrast,

---

31. I do not accept the implication in the note in Marvell 1971a that the very general use of theatrical imagery in the seventeenth century without any suggestion of theatricality applies here; see also Loxley 1995, pp. 40–41.

> like the three-fork'd Lightning, first
> Breaking the Clouds where it was nurst,
> Did thorough his own Side
> His fiery way divide.

(ll. 13–16)

That does compel the imagination and, even though it is not certain to what events Marvell's lightning metaphor refers, the baleful image of self-division takes the mind by force.[32]

Marvell felt the divisions of the Civil War with peculiar keenness, as if a personal wound. The Civil War has a way of irrupting in odd contexts, as for example into the pastoral recreations of 'Upon Appleton House', where a garden becomes a floral camp or a new-mown meadow suggests a battle-field heaped with corpses, or even more incongruously in 'The unfortunate Lover', where the lover is born from a '*Caesarian Section*' when his mother (floating on the waves after a shipwreck) splits on the rocks – an obscure figure, I take it, for the cutting off of Caesar-Charles's head and the wild conditions that love must contend with in an age of strife, the age of Lovelace's *Lucasta*.[33] These incongruities suggest that the public divisions deeply invaded Marvell's privacy.

The quality of green

Marvell had a flair for other divided states. A number of his poems are dialogues; two treat the arch-division in our civilization, the division between body and mind. In the early seventeenth century, conventional wisdom split a higher from a lower nature, an immortal part of divine origin from an animal part, physical and decaying, and sided overwhelmingly with the spirit. That is the side Marvell takes in his 'Dialogue between the Resolved Soul and Created Pleasure'. There was a line of protest against the perversity of bruising the body to pleasure the soul, descended perhaps from Montaigne and heard not very loud or clear in the libertine poems of Carew and Lovelace. What is remarkable about Marvell's 'Dialogue between the Soul and Body' is that he does not turn the conventional hierarchy of Soul and Body upside down and take the part of the lower against the higher.

---

32. Two of the examples of imaginative force that I have cited owe something to Lucan's *Pharsalia*, Bk I. See Shrapnel 1971, p. 165, for a sharply critical view of the vagueness of reference of Marvell's striking figures.
33. A suggestion floated in Newton 1972b.

Although Marvell's Body has the last word and more words than the Soul, the Body has not defeated the Soul and their debate is without conclusion. It may be that Marvell intended to add something and so decide matters one way or the other, but the distinguished thing about the poem as it stands is that he left the division unresolved. The whole fantastic art of the poem is to exaggerate the conflict and to give expression with sudden jocularity to the view that life is intolerable.[34]

The Soul speaks for the impatience of the mind with the limits imposed on it by life in the body:

> O who shall, from this Dungeon, raise
> A Soul inslav'd so many wayes?
> With bolts of Bones, that fetter'd stands
> In Feet; and manacled in Hands.
> Here blinded with an Eye; and there
> Deaf with the drumming of an Ear.
> A Soul hung up, as 'twere, in Chains
> Of Nerves, and Arteries, and Veins.
> Tortur'd, besides each other part,
> In a vain Head, and double Heart.

Taking the stock metaphor of the Body as the prison of the Soul, Marvell develops the Body's parts as tortures: the ear, for instance, as drummer employed to keep the prisoner from sleep. Both the cruelty of the metaphor and the witty violence of the paradox that the ear drum itself deafens convey the Soul's exasperation. It is not just that the Soul is distracted from spiritual things by the senses, though that conventional idea will be hovering around. More focusedly, the paradox suggests the inadequacy of the senses to take things in as they really are. The thought is like Donne's when he considers how in heaven, released from our earthly bodies, we shall have immediate intuition of things: 'Thou shalt not peep through lattices of eyes, / Nor hear through labyrinths of ears' ('The Second Anniversary', ll. 296–97). Marvell makes a similar point about blinding by an eye and, through lucky etymological chance, about being bound by hand and foot. The hand is manacled by its own freedom to touch or feel ('manacle' is derived from the Latin *manus* = 'hand'), and similarly the foot is fettered by its own free motions ('fetter' deriving from 'foot').

Against this, the Body comes out with the complaint of Caliban against Prospero:

---

34.   Newton 1972a, p. 41; see also Leavis 1968.

> O who shall me deliver whole,
> From bonds of this Tyrannic Soul?
> Which, stretcht upright, impales me so,
> That mine own Precipice I go.

The Body utters the same sort of paradox as the Soul did. To the Soul, the Body's foot is a fetter; to the Body, the Soul has inflicted on it a vertiginous posture so that it is its own precipice ('Precipice', deriving ultimately from *prae caput*, conveying the idea of headlong). Behind this complaint lies the notion that humans walk upright because their souls draw them heavenward and human eyes are therefore better able to gaze upward. One would have thought the snail or the flounder better equipped to gaze at heaven, but such is the theory, already a commonplace when Plato wrote the *Timaeus*. Marvell has turned the implications of this fable topsy-turvy and arrived at an astonished sense of the absurdity of creaturely existence, at once playful and in touch with what must be one of our earliest experiences of the awkwardness of life in the body when we first tried to walk.

Levity and topsy-turvydom are ways in which Marvell can be serious, in which he can entertain things that he might have found difficult to think straightforwardly. The last lines of the poem, however, are not particularly playful but do express the serious complaint of the Body against the Soul:

> What but a Soul could have the wit
> To build me up for Sin so fit?
> So Architects do square and hew,
> Green Trees that in the Forest grew.

Sin is a grief of the higher consciousness troubling the Body, and the Body's resentment at the designs of the Soul imposed upon its natural flourishing comes out particularly in the word 'green'. Decidedly green is Marvell's favourite colour and he brings it in wherever he can. When he compares Cromwell to a falcon, he cannot resist describing the bough on which he perches as green ('An Horatian Ode', l. 94). The dewdrop in 'On a Drop of Dew' 'Shuns the . . . blossoms green', a wilfully mismatching word-choice, even if Marvell meant simply to convey the flourishing of a flower he has already described as purple. A thought is green in 'The Garden'. There is a green night in 'Bermudas'. Altogether 'green' occurs twenty-five times in the 1681 volume,[35] and that leaves out derivatives like 'greenness' and

---

35. Margoliouth, in Marvell 1971a, p. 244. Vaughan has a feeling for green (see above, pp. 184–5) and Herrick at least has a subtle eye to discern it in primroses ('How Primroses Came Green'), but neither is haunted by the colour like Marvell.

synonyms like 'verdant'. Marvell's affinity for green corresponds with his feeling for vegetation, a feeling like Vaughan's, except that Marvell gives it more sustained and critical attention, particularly in 'The Garden' and 'Upon Appleton House'. In the 'Dialogue', the comparison of the Body's life to green trees signals that the Body speaks for something that preoccupied him, an impulse to a unity of being, luxuriating or simply vegetating, such as one might imagine enjoyed by trees undisturbed by civilization and its discontents, or, along with these, by the dividedness of Body and Soul and by feelings of not being oneself but one's own dungeon or precipice. Yet the green world the Body hankers after is no more a reasonable choice for a human being than the death of the Body desired by the Soul, and Marvell does not make it. Rather he develops the contradiction between the two sides of the one being to express, with every appearance of levity and control, an unbearable state of discord.

In 'The Garden' and 'Upon Appleton House', he treated the recessive impulse to the green world at greater length. In 'Upon Appleton House', the countryside is a retreat from the rendings of the Civil War, and in 'The Garden', if not from these, at any rate from the strife associated with worldly ambition and sexual passion.

The wit in 'The Garden' does not turn on cruelty but extols peace and innocence. It nevertheless makes way for these agreeable garden qualities by a sort of violence. Marvell's iambic tetrameter, together with the spare neatness of his formulations, has a clipped force. What he says is almost always a jocular assault on ordinary ways of looking at things. And at the centre of the poem is the antic figure of Marvell himself, self-mockingly presented as engaged in vegetable love.

I

How vainly men themselves amaze
To win the Palm, the Oke, or Bayes;
And their uncessant Labours see
Crown'd from some single Herb or Tree.
Whose short and narrow verged Shade
Does prudently their Toyles upbraid;
While all Flow'rs and all Trees do close
To weave the Garlands of repose.

II

Fair quiet, have I found thee here,
And Innocence thy Sister dear!   10
Mistaken long, I sought you then
In busie Companies of Men.
Your sacred Plants, if here below,

Only among the Plants will grow.
Society is all but rude,
To this delicious Solitude.

III

No white nor red was ever seen
So am'rous as this lovely green.
Fond Lovers, cruel as their Flame,
Cut in these Trees their Mistress name.   20
Little, Alas, they know, or heed,
How far these Beauties Hers exceed!
Fair Trees! where s'eer your barkes I wound,
No Name shall but your own be found.

IV

When we have run our Passions heat,
Love hither makes his best retreat.
The *Gods*, that mortal Beauty chase,
Still in a Tree did end their race.
Apollo hunted *Daphne* so,
Only that She might Laurel grow.   30
And *Pan* did after *Syrinx* speed,
Not as a Nymph, but for a Reed.

V

What wond'rous Life in this I lead!
Ripe Apples drop about my head;
The luscious clusters of the Vine
Upon my Mouth do crush their Wine;
The Nectaren and curious Peach,
Into my hands themselves do reach;
Stumbling on Melons, as I pass,
Insnar'd with Flow'rs, I fall on Grass.   40

VI

Mean while the Mind, from pleasure less,
Withdraws into its happiness:
The Mind, that Ocean where each kind
Does streight its own resemblance find;
Yet it creates, transcending these,
Far other Worlds, and other Seas;
Annihilating all that's made
To a green Thought in a green Shade.

VII

Here at the Fountains sliding foot,
Or at some Fruit-trees mossy root,   50
Casting the Bodies Vest aside,

My Soul into the boughs does glide:
There like a Bird it sits, and sings,
Then whets, and combs its silver Wings;
And, till prepar'd for longer flight,
Waves in its Plumes the various Light.

VIII
Such was that happy Garden-state,
While Man there walk'd without a Mate:
After a place so pure, and sweet,
What other Help could yet be meet!   60
But 'twas beyond a Mortal's share
To wander solitary there:
Two Paradises 'twere in one
To live in Paradise alone.

IX
How well the skilful Gardner drew
Of flow'rs and herbes this Dial new;
Where from above the milder Sun
Does through a fragrant Zodiack run;
And, as it works, th'industrious Bee
Computes its time as well as we.   70
How could such sweet and wholsome Hours
Be reckon'd but with herbs and flow'rs!

The poem begins in its first two stanzas mildly enough with jokes that establish garden retreat as the truly successful and civilized life. The trees themselves wear crowns of oak, bay and palm, which were given to victors in the ancient world. The joke is not just a poetic triumph over successful men of the world. It plays on the notion that the end of action is rest, that even those who disturb peace with their 'industrious valour' do so to be at peace at last. There are perhaps gentle hints of death in the 'short and narrow verged Shade', and an unusual rocking movement against the iambic measure in 'While all Flow'rs and all Trees do close' helps to win everything to quiet.

Stanzas III–VII more extravagantly turn the way of the world into the ways of the garden, for there Marvell makes out that his real passion is for plants not women and invents a mock love theology, a parody of platonic love, to support his unsociable tastes. The classic Renaissance statement of platonic love theory, derived from the *Phaedrus*, but christianized and hetero-sexualized, is the one that Castiglione puts in the mouth of Bembo in *The Courtier* (1528). In his version, sensual love, excusable, if deplorable, in the young, ought to be sublimated in the mature, and physical attraction to the beauty of a woman should give way through a process of abstraction to love of the idea of beauty:

This degree of love, though it is very noble and such that few attain thereto, can still not be called perfect; for since the imagination is a corporeal faculty, and has no knowledge if not through those principles that are furnished it by the senses, it is not wholly purged by material darkness. . . . Wherefore, those who attain this love are like little birds beginning to put on feathers, that, although with their weak wings they can lift themselves a little in flight, yet dare not go far from the nest.[36]

And so, dissatisfied with this partial illumination, the platonic lover takes to 'longer flight', seeking union with the beauty of beauty or God himself. Whether Marvell had Bembo's discourse specifically in mind or not, he makes up a tree-lover's version of the platonic ladder of love.

The first stage is sensual love. Lovers of women adore a lovely complexion – 'red and white' were current shorthand for what a man was smitten by.[37] The lovely complexion for Marvell is green. Ordinary lovers cut their sweet-hearts' names in the bark of the trees Marvell loves, but he will cut only the names of the trees themselves. Marvell rather lets slip the pretence of dendrophilia at the beginning of stanza IV, saying that the garden is a retreat for wearied lovers of women. But he is showing what he wants to say behind his game: the green world is a solace after the disturbance of sexual passion. In that sense it is the true object of love, as his vegetarian accounts of the loves of the gods bear out. The gods come in with a couple of enchanting double entendres:

> *Apollo* hunted *Daphne* so,
> Only that She might Laurel grow.
> And *Pan* did after *Syrinx* speed,
> Not as a Nymph, but for a Reed.

Marvell is fond of puns. They are one of his devices of compression. But double senses also make a point slyly and here convey, as it were to the initiate, the true, occult meaning of the classical myths. There is other less deliberate word-play in this stanza. To 'run our Passions heat' suggests both running through an exhausting course of passion and running a heat in a race. That the gods 'Still in a Tree did end their race' suggests that their pursuit had reached its goal when the nymphs turned into a laurel or a reed and also that the love of plants prevented the gods from reproducing themselves – a curiously resonant suggestion of the deflection of sexual impulse. And then in the seventh stanza, Marvell enters upon an erotically

---

36. Castiglione 1959, pp. 352–53.
37. See Spenser 1910, 'An Hymne in Honour of Beavtie', l. 92, and Suckling 1953, 'Sonnet II'.

rampant garden, where fruit-bearing plants make love to him and in their taste, touch and entanglings imitate sexual play. This is much more abandoned than the kiss that Bembo allows his spiritual lover as a starter or the caresses that Plato allows his, but Marvell would consider the embraces of unmating things more innocent.

The second stage of Marvell's spiritual love of the plants comes with the retreat from the pleasures of physical love ('pleasures less') to an ideal love of plants' beauty. Abstracting the essence of vegetable loveliness by 'annihilating' all particulars, Marvell arrives at the idea of what moves him so, 'a Green thought in a green Shade', and then in a minor ecstasy slips out of his body into the tree above like one of Bembo's birds, though not at this point sufficiently fired for the final stage of ascent, the 'longer flight' to the thought of the green thought or God.

Marvell works into this sprightly parody of spiritual ascent perhaps even more psychological resonance than he did into the sensual stage. He manages at once to be playful and to suggest an intense longing for retreat into untroubled vegetating where he can be blissfully at one with himself, all that is summed up for him in the word 'green'. The anomalous rhythm of the line, again rocking against the iambic measure – 'To a green Thought in a green Shade' – conveys a profound impulse of withdrawal to repose.[38] The poetry gives itself to the impulse in other ways. Though Marvell possibly means that he is having his idea of green in the shadow of a green tree, there are suggestions of the one being lost in the other like the fawn in 'The Nymph Complaining', which is so white it disappears when resting on a bank of lilies (ll. 81–82). If Marvell thought of the ocean and seas as green, it would make more apt the comparison between them and the mind that has taken on the colour green, in its oceanic feeling at once transcending all things and being at one with them. And there are sweeping gestures reducing the whole world to one secluded spot of green. The mind expands to an ocean because, just as some imagined that every earthly thing had a correspondence in the sea (the sea horse, the sea cucumber, the sea mouse), so it was thought that everything had a corresponding idea in the mind. Yet the mind expands further in producing its own abstracted ideal otherworlds, a creation that is at the same time an annihilation reducing everything to the desired essential oneness.

In the eighth stanza, Marvell descends from his transport to make a misogynistic joke about the superiority of the paradisal love of plants to the love of women, a joke that at once passes the matter off lightly and points to the heart of the matter – that his feeling for the garden is a refuge from sexual

---

38. Eliot 1932, p. 298, remarks on Marvell's striking use of caesura in the central position of his tetrameters.

love. Strikingly, sexual love is a source of disturbance in his poetry. It breaks the pastoral harmony of man and nature in his Mower poems. Sexual consummation in 'The Definition of Love' would mean that the earth would be torn with some new convulsion or 'cramp'd into a *Planisphere*' – the violence compressed into 'cramp'd' is extraordinary. And in 'To his Coy Mistress', the union he urges would be a violence against the lovers themselves, involving cosmic disruption. In this connection one recalls that he seems to be more at ease talking love to very young girls or to dwell with more sensory delight on the almost sexless nymph in his 'Nymph Complaining' than on sexually mature women – the exception is Chlora in 'The Gallery' (her Greek name means 'green'). His dewdrop stands with comical unease on a rose petal, which must be a bed of crimson joy, languishing for heaven. And when he presents temptations to himself or others, their appeal is to a sensibility notably refined. In 'A Dialogue between the Resolved Soul and Created Pleasure' sexual pleasure is very remotely figured, and taste is tempted by 'the Souls of fruits and flow'rs', perhaps a way of talking about the exhalations of food apprehended as tastes, but suggesting also that the pleasures the Soul so effortlessly rejects are curiously disembodied. Equally one is struck in 'Upon Appleton House' by the purity of the elements that the nun uses in tempting the virgin Thwaites to leave the world, though Marvell tells us that the nuns' vices are unspeakable. Of course, the nun has to make the vices appear attractive, yet the real temptation seems to be sexlessness not lesbianism:

> 'Each Night among us to your side
> 'Appoint a fresh and Virgin Bride;
> 'Whom if *our Lord* at midnight find,
> 'Yet Neither should be left behind.
> 'Where ye may lye as chast in Bed,
> 'As Pearls together billeted.
> 'All Night embracing Arm in Arm,
> 'Like Chrystal pure with Cotton warm'.

(st. XXIV)

A feeling for innocence, troubled by a consciousness of its limitations, does not keep Marvell from writing coarse and quite amusing satire on Dutch women in 'The Character of Holland' or on some of the promiscuous great ladies of the Restoration in 'Last Instructions to a Painter'. Possibly the jeers about homosexuality made by Marvell's political enemies may point to the source of his feelings about women and love.[39] Whatever the case,

---

39. E.g. Schwenger 1974, p. 370, and Paul Hammond 1998; see also Empson 1984, pp. 14–15, 86–87.

Marvell connected the impulse that drew him to the green world with a wish to escape sexual love and made a deep joke of it.

'The Garden' ends by declaring that its amusements have been innocent: 'How could such sweet and wholesome Hours / Be reckon'd but with herbs and flow'rs!' This is rather blander than the case deserves, but even in this quiet coda there are turns of wit: a sundial in which the dial is drawn by lines and beds of flowers is metaphorized into a zodiac for the sun to run through, and the bee in visiting the flowers may be said to compute its time (or at least thyme). In both these turns, Marvell runs to a sort of figure of compression not uncommon in his poetry, the imagining of little worlds: the dial is a miniature cosmos; the insects have concerns like humans. Another example in 'The Garden' is the ideal otherworlds and other seas the mind creates in platonic abstraction. In 'On a Drop of Dew', the dewdrop encloses the heavens in reflection. Chlora's tears in 'Mourning' are oceans deeper than the real ones, which divers never get to the bottom of. And 'Upon Appleton House' contains a whole series of miniature worlds, including the pastoral scenes, which are in themselves a sort of art of miniaturizing the concerns of the great world and treating the complex in the simple.[40] The play with little worlds is another example of Marvell's tendency to compress, to fold things in upon themselves until they start doubling and mirroring. But in 'The Garden' the effect is more of graceful closure than of curious suggestion: in the garden, world and time are reduced to herbal innocence.

Marvell's playfulness in 'The Garden' is self-mocking and self-aware. Unlike Keats, who is not critical of his wish to fly away with his nightingale into the forest dim, Marvell in his joke about his desire for trees is so extravagant that on the one hand one feels that it is not just a joke and on the other the fact that it is a joke keeps the recessive impulse toward a green shade in its place as a not fully human compulsion, a curiosity or at most a recreation outside the life he has to lead with other people. The particular excellence of Marvell's wit in this poem is at once to give the peculiar impulse expression and to control it. This is not so much poise as a good use of self-division.

'Upon Appleton House' treats divided feelings about retirement at great length, running through an extraordinary series of Marvellesque caprices and freaks of mind. It rambles, though not without design, from Appleton House to its garden, its meadows, grove and river and finally returns to the house. The walk around the estate takes up the theme of retreat first in its opening complimentary salute to Fairfax and his retiring

40. Empson 1935, p. 22.

ways; then in the episode treating the nunnery, which in true Marvellesque fashion tries to enclose the world by walling it out; in the garden, which excludes the Civil War and yet is drawn up in regiments of flowers; in the grove, where Marvell turns to green shade again; and finally by the river, where he vacantly angles. The whole loose expatiation is pulled together by the appearance of Mary Fairfax, who reminds him of his duty as tutor and brings the concerns of the Fairfax estate round to the question of dynastic marriage and relations to the great world outside. 'Upon Appleton House' is generally classified as a country house poem, a poem on the model of Jonson's 'To Penshurst', of a kind that became very popular in the Civil War period, when country houses were the only centres left where Royalists might imagine that the feudal order held. But Fairfax was not a Royalist, the relations of landowner and tenants do not come in, and, in letting the theme of retirement run into various excrescences, the poem takes on a very singular shape for its genre, combining reverie with celebration of a great house in apparently free form in a way that looks forward to Thomson's *Seasons*.[41]

I have space to make only a few points about this, the oddest of Marvell's poems. The disturbing factor in this poem is the Civil War rather than love. In particular, it irrupts into the occupations of the mowers and, with images of carnage, recalls the strife, which Marvell's delight in their activities in the 'Abyss' of grass retreats from. And it crops up elsewhere to suggest a jarring context for Fairfax's abdication from public affairs and Marvell's own burial in the country.

The episode in the grove brings up the motif of entry into the green world that we have seen in 'The Garden' and with the same mixture of acrobatic wit and entranced absorption. He comes to the grove from the meadows that have been flooded after mowing. From this deluge he imagines how he '[him]self imbark[s] / In this yet green, yet growing Ark' (st. LXI), and by the pun on 'bark' has already taken on sylvan being. There follows a passage, whose point is not entirely clear to me but may turn on a submerged Latin pun on *silva*, at once wood and material: the sylvan bulk is a vision of some mass of original stuff before the creation of light, which a new quintessence is to emerge from, no doubt green:[42]

---

41. On the oddity of 'Upon Appleton House' as a country house poem, see McClung 1977, pp. 147ff.
42. The Greek *hyle* is even more to the point, since in addition to 'wood' in both senses and so 'material', it meant 'matter'. Cf. 'The ancients called that kind of body *Sylva* or *Hule*, in which there were works of diverse nature, and matter congested' (Jonson 1975, 'To the Reader', *Underwoods*, p. 122).

LXIII

When first the Eye this Forrest sees
It seems indeed as *Wood* not *Trees*:
As if their Neighbourhood so old
To one great Trunk them all did mold.
There the huge Bulk takes place, as ment
To thrust up a *Fifth Element*;
And stretches still so closely wedg'd
As if the Night within were hedg'd.

The succeeding stanza puts beautifully what it is like to enter dense timber
and find it opening out, not squared and hewed, but its own architecture:

> Dark all without it knits; within
> It opens passable and thin;
> And in as loose an order grows,
> As the *Corinthean Porticoes*.

The wood is full of birds, whose behaviour Marvell interprets more or less
fancifully. He toys with notions that he is almost a bird or a tree, that he has
learned the language of birds and even more strangely that he can spell out
the book of nature in the trees:

> No Leaf does tremble in the Wind
> Which I returning cannot find.

LXXIII

Out of these scatter'd *Sybils* Leaves
Strange *Prophecies* my Phancy weaves:
And in one History consumes,
Like *Mexique Paintings*, all the *Plumes*.
What *Rome, Greece, Palestine*, ere said
I in this light *Mosaick* read.
Thrice happy he who, not mistook,
Hath read in *Natures mystick Book*.

Anyone who has looked up into an oak tree, marked a leaf, shifted his gaze
and then tried to find the same leaf in the 'light *Mosaick*' will realize that
Marvell must indeed be deep in trance, though 'the bright, hard precision of the comparisons'[43] – the Caribbean picture-histories made out of
hummingbird feathers, the mosaic – suggests a mind greatly awake at the

---

43. Eliot 1932, p. 299.

same time. And again, as in 'The Garden', self-mockery combines with self-exaltation, a self-mockery that takes broader forms in stanza LXXXIV, where he imagines himself covered with falling leaves and caterpillars. He has become an oak-being but appears like a fantastic bishop, perhaps druidical, in a cope. In stanzas LXXXVI–LXXXVIII, Marvellesque drolling continues, first in self-congratulation that he is safe in the grove from the disturbances of love and the world (martial imagery bringing in the Civil War), and then in wild but vain prayers to an animated wood to bind him with its honeysuckle, vines[44] and briars and even to stake him down 'That I may never leave this Place'. His impulse to retirement is not reprehensible, as he makes out the nuns' to be, or admirable, as he seems to think Fairfax's, though not without regret, but he clearly wants to say he knows the desire to become a green man is absurd, even while the extravagance of his fancies exposes its strength.

Not all the fancies in 'Upon Appleton House' mean so much to Marvell. Some, perhaps inspired by Cleveland, are exhausting. There is little more in the way the nightingale in squatted thorns sings high music that draws down the highest oak and makes the Jew's ear fungus on the elders prick up its ears than an elaborate play on low and high (st. LXV). Some of the fancies, though, with all their elaborateness, capture an experience. So, for example, when the kingfisher appears 'Flying betwixt the Day and Night', 'The viscous Air, wheres'ere She fly, / Follows and sucks her Azure dry' (LXXXV). The notion of the air being drawn by admiration to cling to the wonderful bird, catches the way a flying kingfisher may seem a '*Saphir-winged* Mist', and the astonished delight such an appearance causes is brought out in a far-fetched way by the stunned clarity that succeeds:

> The gellying Stream compacts below,
> If it might fix her shadow so;
> The stupid Fishes hang, as plain
> As *Flies* in *Chrystal* overt'ane.

> (st. LXXXV)

And some of the wit compresses great energy into its neatness, as for instance into the metonymic reductions of 'What need of all this Marble Crust / T'impark the wanton Mote of Dust?' (st. III). Although Marvell's exaggerations, praising by contrast the modest architecture of Appleton House, are making a standard point about just human proportion, they moralize lightly.

---

44. Vines in Yorkshire?

They are imaginatively enlarging and Marvell seems amused by the impudence of the wanton mote rather than offended by human pretension, as Swift or Pope might be.

The wit and fancy in 'Upon Appleton House' particularly run to picturing little or other worlds, or to turning the world we live in upside down or outside in. The garden is not only a model military camp but also a model of England, 'the Garden of the world' before the Civil War (st. XLI), with five forts instead of '*Cinque Ports*' (st. XLIV); the world was once formed in the image of heaven, but now the Appleton house estate is '*Paradice's only Map*' (st. LXXXXVI). Inside the estate, the river Denton becomes a mirror:

> Where all things gaze themselves, and doubt
> If they be in it or without.
> And for his shade which therein shines,
> *Narcissus* like, the *Sun* too pines.

(st. LXXX)

The grove as a 'growing Ark', 'where all Creatures might have shares', is also an epitome of the world. Inside this field of mirrorings are the cynosures, the nightingale and the kingfisher, that draw things to them, and above all there is Mary Fairfax, Marvell's pupil, who is compared to the kingfisher. More than these birds, she draws her surroundings magically to attention. She is the local goddess (as Elizabeth Drury was the soul of the world to Donne) 'that to these Gardens gave / That wondrous Beauty which they have'. The world around her is a reflection of her:

> *She* streightness on the Woods bestows;
> To Her the Meadow sweetness owes;
> Nothing could make the River be
> So Chrystal-pure but only *She*.

(st. LXXXVII)

Of course Marvell is laying it on thick for the heiress of the house, but one likes to think that amidst the hyperbole about a child who was the object of her parents' dynastic ambitions, he might be sharing a joke with her, for instance about the way he, as tutor, is on his best behaviour with his twelve-year-old pupil (st. LXXXII) or about how she has dedicated herself to making herself speak all languages as well as she does English (st. LXXXIX).

In theory, mirroring should go with some sort of division. In Spenser it belongs to wandering play with seeming and being. In Drummond of

Hawthornden, on the other hand, it goes with a self-absorption in which God is the '*Narcissus* of himselfe', and perhaps that peculiar redundant formulation suggests that for Drummond only in God does Narcissism unite with itself.[45] In 'Upon Appleton House', by contrast, self-absorption is uneasy, and Marvell, particularly in his self-presentation, makes retreat into a private life, a life by oneself, problematic, an issue of doubt or divided mind.

Two love poems

'Upon Appleton House' is decidedly a poem for the Marvell aficionado, for in spite of splendid passages, some of its 'pleasant scenes' are such curious pleasantries that one is forced to make an effort to appreciate their point. With two of his love poems, by contrast, 'The Definition of Love' and 'To his Coy Mistress', the content has taken a shape that makes Marvell's point forcefully, and though they both express ambivalent feelings, they do so strongly.

'The Definition of Love' defines love by the ideal type. Marvell opens with a soaring account of its pedigree:

> My love is of a birth as rare
> As 'tis for object strange and high:
> It was begotten by despair
> Upon Impossibility.

The ideal is a love that cannot be consummated. It cannot find a place in the world because it is too good for the world; its consummation would mean the end of the world in a 'new Convulsion'. If it is true that Marvell's poetry expresses a fear of sexual passion, then, in the form of exalting himself and his love, he should be congratulating himself on an escape. And certainly the imagery of universal disaster for union bears out that interpretation. Yet at the same time the exaltation carries an air of rueful self-mockery, of vaunting to his own chagrin. The self-mockery in Donne's 'Canonization' goes with ruefulness – he has lost the world. But Donne's self-mockery is a defence, and in the end one feels that he really does want to make extravagant claims for his love. Marvell's ruefulness comes through more strongly. The exceeding neatness of the poem seems to have tied him in a knot, and, though he makes his knot his boast, one cannot believe that he is satisfied with so paradoxical a bliss.

---

45. 'Teares upon the Death of Moeliades', ll. 183–84, Drummond 1913. See also Kelly 1990.

The neatness of the poem and its cool, ironic analysis of 'Two perfect Loves' does not mean that this is a pallid treatment of frustration. The neat formulation is extraordinarily muscular:

> And yet I quickly might arrive
> Where my extended Soul is fixt,
> But Fate does Iron wedges drive,
> And alwaies crouds it self betwixt.

The notion of a lover's soul joining him to the object of his love may be borrowed from Donne's 'Valediction: forbidding Mourning', but Marvell's formulation catches how longing is already where it would be, and how the abstract cause of its frustration, Fate with its wedges and crowding between, gets in the way with an effect of physical thwarting. It is hard to think that Marvell is just playing with ideas. Similarly, the geometrical and astronomical figures that analyse the lovers' situation and the turns that Marvell gives them exalt unhappiness with a fierce coolness: so Fate's

> Decrees of Steel
> Us as the distant Poles have plac'd,
> (Though Loves whole World on us doth wheel)
> Not by themselves to be embrac'd.

The lovers are poles apart and by a sudden glorying in his mind Marvell may imagine (prompted by the turning of the world on its poles) that they give a pattern of perfect love to the world; and yet the parentheses in which he places the thick rotundity of the world of love come between them and their embracing.[46] I can think of no other imitation of Donne's mathematical manner that speaks with such force or such independence of its master.

Marvell's relation to his lovers is distant. His love object is 'strange and high', or his coy mistress is addressed as 'Lady'. He writes out of deprivation of contact, where Donne assumes a history of intimacy and a distinct love predicament and situation of utterance. Where or when could 'To his Coy Mistress' be spoken, or how? Marvell's coy mistress, though, is not more vaguely represented than Donne's mistresses, or almost any Cavalier poet's. She is beautiful, a lady and difficult to get into bed. Marvell's love poem is certainly not unusual in ignoring the fact that she has every reason to be coy in an age before reliable contraception. We are also told that in spite of her coyness she is really as eager as he is:

---

46. A point not made by Lennard 1991, pp. 59–60.

> Now therefore, while the youthful glue
> Sits on thy skin like morning dew,
> And while thy willing Soul transpires
> At every pore with instant Fires,
> Now let us sport us while we may;
> And now. . . .

(ll. 33–38)

This is a hopeful reading of the signs, which are, I take it, her youth and vitality. The curious 'glue' presumably means balm, a mysterious life substance that, according to Donne, keeps bodies 'fresh and new', and the glow of the woman's body, the 'instant Fires' sustained from moment to moment, is an expression of the animating soul that turns to life and love.[47] Or so Marvell says, one feels compelled to add, for he could not have imagined that his love talk was in the least inviting or arousing; he could not really be imagining an exchange between lovers at all, only expressing a piercing sense that 'Youth's a stuff will not endure', hence the repetition of 'now' and 'while' and the dwelling on the skin and the pores that are still fresh and young and alive. This *carpe diem* poem is not really about a love relation, nor even about Marvell's lust, but about his feeling for his life in time.

In the first section, he entertains the counterfactual hypothesis that his life, luxuriating grossly in vegetable love, might expand to fill most of the world and its history, like Ygdrasil or Jack's bean-stalk. The movement of Marvell's verse engages with this fantasy, drawing out the sense over the lines and slowing it down in groupings of increasingly stressed monosyllables:

> We would sit down, and think which way
> To walk, and pass our long Love's Day.
> . . .
> My vegetable Love should grow
> Vaster then Empires, and more slow.

In the second section, his lifetime and all its agreeable imaginings shrink to a handful of dust in the prospect of death and deserts of vast eternity. And in the last, he imagines that copulation will somehow break out of the time limits of life by violence when, perhaps like a cannonball, he and his love tear their 'Pleasures with rough strife, / Thorough the Iron grates of Life'.[48]

---

47. Reading 'glue' with Donno, in Marvell 1972, p. 234; cf. Donne's use of 'balm' in 'The Ecstasy' and 'A Nocturnal upon St Lucy's Day' and *OED*'s citation of *Religio Medici*: 'the radical balsome or vital sulphur of the parts' (Browne 1964, p. 41). But see Paul Hammond 1998, p. 198, for a defence of 'hew'.
48. For 'grates', see Donno 1978, pp. 235–36; also Randall 1992.

The movement of the verse over the lines is again instinct with the sense, here the straining of the lovers: 'Let us roll all our Strength, and all / Our sweetness, up into one Ball'. But theirs is an ironic transcending of life since it will hasten their deaths: they will seize control of their lives, (or metonymically of their sun), but they will speed them up, not arrest them in their courses.

The poem works better as an anxious, almost hallucinatorily vivid fantasy about life in time than as a seduction poem. The tone in which the woman is addressed is unpleasant. The contrast between her finding rubies by the Ganges and Marvell's complaint by his native Humber (a Larkinesque river even then) jeers at the fanciful notions of the coy woman, as does the whole imagined ceremony of adoring her while the world lasts until her heart, that inscrutable mystery, is finally revealed, supposing she has one. The prospect of her virginity being taken by worms is an indecent revenge for her refusal of him, with an added sneer about its being 'long-preserv'd'. And the violent love-making he proposes has no fondness behind it, only fear of the grave. The woman is not loved or wooed. She is a shadowy figure (like the 'you' in 'Prufrock'), whom Marvell can bounce his anxieties off. And she, instead of himself, can be the object of his irony, until the final self-defeating twist directs the irony against himself as well as his designs as a lover.

If this is to make the poem an expression of neurotic ambivalence, it is at least to rescue it from being read as a cool and poised piece of insolence. It may aspire to that, but it has a psychological strength arising from self-division that one will not find in the poems of the assured gentlemen whom Marvell may have wished to imitate. It is also more memorable, with the driving syllogistic arrangement of its argument and the strange dilations and contractions of its imagery, than other love poems of his such as 'The Gallery', where ambivalence is more lightly and self-mockingly expressed. In the nineteenth century, Matthew Arnold found self-division a matter to lament in himself and his culture. For him it was a sickness of an age of strife infecting all individual and social projects. He sounds rather solemn now. There is a lot to be said for Marvell's unassuming way of drawing fun and depth out of the melancholy interiority of self-division. For one thing he makes better poetry of it, more succinct, intense, surprising.

Marvell as Metaphysical

What one might call the Metaphysical urge to transcend the time limits and space limits of life in the body is certainly present in Marvell, but, except in 'A Dialogue between the Resolved Soul and Created Pleasure' and perhaps 'On a Drop of Dew', always rendered ironically, so that it comes over as a psychological extravagance rather than a metaphysical passion. The platonic tree-lover's ecstasy in 'The Garden' is a joke, though a serious one. And it is only in 'The Definition of Love' that Marvell appropriates Donne's apparatus of souls and mystical mathematics, and even there with a self-mockery that rules out Donne's transcendental impulses. What Marvell took from Donne, he turned to an elegant and witty art that masked his trouble with himself.

Like the poems in Donne's Songs and Sonnets and Herbert's *Temple* and unlike Vaughan's, Traherne's and most of Crashaw's, Marvell's shorter poems are tightly wrought. But where Donne aims at an effect of extemporized elegance and Herbert at both ingenuity and effects of felicitous inadvertency, Marvell aims at deliberate neatness. His most argued poem, 'To His Coy Mistress', may be sophistical, but its syllogistic structure is sturdy and premeditated compared to Donne's unpredictable moves in, say, 'The Flea'. Deliberateness is part of the effect he intends: he means us, for instance, to think that the last stanza of 'The Gallery' comes last in a series by design and that his preference for the picture of his love there as innocent shepherdess, after her pictures as witch and Venus, might be a complicated one.[49]

The effect of deliberateness comes partly from his bias toward short lines, above all iambic tetrameter, and the lapidary way he works his phrasing into verse. Where Donne's and Herbert's phrasing is typically asymmetrical and slants over the lines and where Crashaw's manages to pour with sweet variety even in tetrameter couplets, Marvell's tends to cast his ideas in end-stopped couplets. The result is sometimes rhythmically dull in the long 'Upon Appleton House', and two faults noted by Leishman, the filling up of the verse with forms of the auxilliary 'do' and a heavy reliance on inversion to secure rhyme, become wearying.[50] Marvell could come up with finely attuned tetrameter effects in 'The Garden' and 'To His Coy Mistress', but for all the deliberateness of his art he could still pass a line like 'Yet thus She you resembles much' ('Upon Appleton House', st. XVI). Still, inversions, expletive 'dids' and all, no one would quarrel with couplets such as these:

> Within this sober Frame expect
> Work of no Forrain *Architect*;
> That unto Caves the Quarries drew,
> And Forrests did to Pastures hew;
> Who of his great Design in pain
> Did for a Model vault his Brain,
> Whose Columnes should so high be rais'd
> To arch the Brows that on them gaz'd.

> (st. I)

---

49. See Nowottny 1969, pp. 314–16.
50. Leishman 1966, pp. 147–51, 163–65.

The effect of polish comes chiefly from the compression of double sense in 'vault' and 'arch'. Such lucky accidents give Marvell's frolics an air of rightness. His 'short but admirable Lines' and the way his sense falls into lines and couplets also help to make us feel that something has been said exactly.

A rather narrow range of sensibility lends an aesthetic finish to his poems (to his lyrics, that is, not his satires). His poetry brings in a world of upperclass Caroline culture, of gardens and statues, picture galleries, the theatre and masque, the court painter Lely, architecture, domestic and foreign, mosaics, marble tombs and a knowledge of the bull-ring such as a Grand Tour would supply.[51] A classical education is in evidence, but not pedantically, and a gentleman's knowledge of the countryside. He has a discerning feeling for music. His acquaintance with the microscope and mathematics is not inelegant. Though his cultural accomplishments are finer than, say, Lovelace's or Carew's, he does not obtrude them on the world of the great as Donne did his, but is content to convert its fashions to his own unconvivial ends.

Some of Marvell's effects are aesthetically refined in a Caroline way, though at the same time entirely the work of his own sensibility. 'A green thought in a green shade' manages to suggest at once a fashionably delicate study in green and an utterly strange awakening of thought in sense. In 'A Nymph Complaining of the Death of her Fawn', a poem in which he manages to avoid even the idea of green, Marvell works up a play of white on white. When the nymph orders her tomb and her pet's,

> First my unhappy Statue shall
> Be cut in Marble; and withal,
> Let it be weeping too: but there
> Th' Engraver sure his Art may spare;
> For I so truly thee bemoane,
> That I shall weep though I be Stone:
> Until my Tears, still dropping, wear
> My breast, themselves engraving there.
> There at my feet shalt thou be laid,
> Of purest Alabaster made:
>   For I would have thine Image be
> White as I can, though not as Thee.

(ll. 111–22)

The nymph lives in the marble but in such white purity that her life is only expressed in tears, a fancy that equals in refinement the study in white of

---

51. Cf. Everett 1979, p. 66.

marble, alabaster and fawn. Marvell may have learned from Crashaw, but the sensations Crashaw mixes are physically generous and grotesque, while with Marvell the sensations are cool and chaste and his effects fine, however paradoxical.

Marvell adapts other Caroline exquisitenesses to his own ends, for instance what Christopher Ricks has called self-involved comparisons: Marvell's dewdrop is 'like its own Tear'; 'stretch'd upright' by the Soul, his Body complains that 'mine own Precipice I go'.[52] Crashaw is again a possible inspiration for such self-reflexive formulations: his Countess of Denbigh lies in 'labour of [her] selfe' until she converts; on the piercing of Christ's side, he exclaims, 'Thee with thy selfe they have too richly clad, / Opening the purple wardrobe of thy side'.[53] These self-reflexive formulations are related to personification in that they claim that an idea has been realized in somebody. Marvell's Body is all tumbling, his dewdrop all tear. The self Crashaw's Countess labours to bring forth is her ideal self; the self Christ runs with is his essential saving nature. Ricks argues that Marvell uses the figure to suggest a division in the self. Marvell's Body is condemned to stand against itself; his dewdrop's grief is about itself. Similarly Crashaw's Countess is at war with herself until she shall yield to Rome, and his purple Christ exploits the shock we feel when we realize the blood running from us is also ourselves. Crashaw's use of this figure is theological and has to do with self-loss and self-recovery in God. Marvell's cannot be reduced so systematically, but at least it lends itself to subtle expressions of the self-division that runs through his most intense work.

Although Marvell achieves very extravagant effects and enjoys turning the world upside-down as much as Donne, he does not generally do so by means of far-fetched comparisons. It is true that he can turn out an analogical set piece such as the comparison of Mary Fairfax to the kingfisher or of Cromwell to Amphion. But these are occasional and encomiastic. His more usual conceits, even in a satire like 'Fleckno', take the form of exaggerating things maliciously or delightedly so that they become fantastic versions of themselves. So in the passage from 'Upon Appleton House', the brain that is vaulted by the architect is not really being compared to architecture. It is true that there is a flash of comparison between the inside of the skull and a vault, but more important is the suggestion that the grandiose project has taken the architect out of his skull by another sort of vault. Far from joining heterogeneous things together, Marvell is distorting with a

---

52. Ricks 1978. Cf. Carey 1978.
53. Crashaw, 'Letter to the Countess of Denbigh'; 'On our Crucified Lord, Naked and bloody'. See discussion above, pp. 161, 165; self-reflexive formulations were generally fashionable, as the poetry of Cleveland and Paman shows.

pun and a little metaphorical wiring two things already connected, the architect's brain and its plan, to bring out the human monstrosity of both. His tree-lover's parody of platonic love might seem to work like Donne's surprising comparisons. But where Donne's compasses and lovers remain heterogeneous, linked only by resourceful comparison, Marvell's tree-love, with some exaggerating fancy, is related to platonic love in a deep and unsettling way. Swift's fictions with their distorting reductions have more in common with his practice than Donne's comparisons.[54]

In order to make things strange, Marvell has two other analytic devices. The first is the fantastic hypothesis, which allows him to suppose absurdities that reflect on things he is considering. 'Had we but World enough and Time' allows him those dilations by which he can stand outside and arrive at the shortness of life. If the two perfect loves in 'The Definition of Love' were united, the world would be 'cramp'd into a *Planisphere*', a convulsion that allows him to stand apart from the convulsions of physical love and idealize his own version. The other device is mathematical description. In 'The Definition of Love' and 'Eyes and Tears', the geometry is genuinely analogical. Like Donne's compasses, the squint and parallel lines in 'The Definition of Love' are similes not descriptions ('As Lines so Loves *oblique* may well / Themselves in every Angle greet'). On the other hand, the geometrical descriptions of the curved hill at Bill-borow or of the tears in 'Mourning' or above all in 'On a Drop of Dew' work, not by comparing them to something other than themselves, but by producing a mathematically reduced and exaggerated version of themselves, out of which he then draws moral properties like humility in 'Upon the Hill and Grove at Bill-borow' or heavenly-mindedness in 'On a Drop of Dew'.

Self-division is not all there is to Marvell, but it is connected with the anxieties and ironies that make his slender *oeuvre* hold our attention and not merely charm and amuse it for a bit like the work of Carew or Suckling. He is able to bring the aesthetic sophistication and elaborate turns of contemporary wit to a fine point of self-reflection. It is a measure of the quality of his best work that Vaughan's quite bulky *oeuvre* in comparison, with its uncomplicated party-feeling and retreat into green solitude, seems to speak of an insufficiently examined life. One notes also that while Vaughan's use of the preciosities of the Cavalier style often disperses his special intensities, Marvell's use of them concentrates.

---

54. Cf. Leishman 1966, pp. 215, 250.

CHAPTER SIX

Thomas Traherne

Life

Thomas Traherne was born in 1637, the son of a cobbler in Hereford. Probably he and his younger brother, Philip, were orphaned young and taken care of by a kinsman, Philip Traherne, an innkeeper in Hereford and twice Mayor of the town. At any rate, Thomas received sufficient schooling to matriculate from Brasenose College, Oxford, in 1653. He graduated with a BA in 1656 and in 1657 was appointed rector of Credenhill near Hereford by the Commissioners for the Approbation of Public Preachers. In spite of having found nothing objectionable in entering the Church under the Commonwealth, he not only had himself ordained episcopally at the Restoration, but did so before he was required to. His 'An Hymne upon St Bartholomews Day' makes no reference to the two thousand clergymen who resigned their charges on St Bartholomew's day, 24 August 1662, rather than subscribe to the Act of Uniformity, which required that clergymen of the established church should declare their full assent to everything in the Prayer Book. He made the transition from Puritan to Prayer Book divine without visible signs of crisis. It is not certain whether he resided at Credenhill, a sparsely populated parish, but possibly during residence there he made the acquaintance of Susanna Hopton at Kington, some fifteen miles distant, and joined her religious circle. She is probably the 'friend of my best friend [i.e. God]' to whom his 'Centuries' are addressed.[1] In 1669

---

1. Traherne 1958, I, p. 2. The publication of Traherne's *Meditations on the Creation* as Hopton's by Nathaniel Spinckes in *A Collection of Meditations and Devotions* (1717) is an argument for their closeness; see Jordan 1982, pp. 218–25, for this and the confused attribution of *Daily Devotions*.

232

he was appointed chaplain to Sir Orlando Bridgeman, Keeper of the Great Seal, with whom, leaving Credenhill but not relinquishing his rectorship, he lived in London or at Bridgeman's country estate at Teddington, even after Bridgeman's expulsion from office in 1672. He died in October 1674.

Traherne published only *Roman Forgeries* (1673), under his own name, and, posthumously and anonymously, *Christian Ethicks* (1675). Most of the poems, the 'Centuries' and 'Thanksgivings' – the works upon which his reputation as a minor, eccentric and, for lack of other classification, Metaphysical writer rests – are the discovery of twentieth-century scholarship, a discovery also of late nineteenth-and early twentieth-century critical taste for visionary writers such as Blake. It is not that Traherne is not remarkable. But there are many remarkable writers who have not been taken up as he has, and only some compelling resonance of sensibility could have forced his work, not only from obscurity, but from anonymity into recognition in this century. In 1896, two anonymous manuscripts containing the 'Centuries' and some of his poems were picked up from a stall and attributed to Vaughan. Dissatisfied with this attribution, Bertram Dobell established that they were written by the author of *Christian Ethicks* and that that author was Traherne. He published the poems of the Dobell Manuscript in 1903 and the 'Centuries' in 1908. Another manuscript of poems, 'Poems of Felicity', was discovered in the Burney Collection in the British Museum by Idris Bell and published in 1910. These poems had been edited by Philip Traherne for publication but never published. It is evident from the twenty-two poems that appear in both manuscripts that Philip tinkered with his brother's poems with a view above all to suppressing their theological heterodoxy; the result is in the words of a modern editor 'irretrievably corrupt'.[2] But for forty of Traherne's poems we have no other text to go on. Further discoveries followed, notably in 1964 of 'Select Meditations', in 1982 of the 'Commentaries of Heaven' (rescued 'about 1967' from a burning rubbish dump in Lancashire but not identified at the time),[3] and in 1997 of 'The Ceremonial Law'.[4] Possibly when the latter two are edited and published Traherne may look rather different. Our concern, though, is with the poetry and that means chiefly the poems in the Dobell manuscript and 'Poems of Felicity'; apart from a few poems in *Christian Ethicks* the scattering of poems in the prose works is uninteresting.

---

2. Traherne 1991, p. xii.
3. Julia Smith, *DNB*.
4. Traherne 1997. For 'Commentaries of Heaven', see Julia Smith 1982, and for 'The Ceremonial Law' see Julia Smith and Laetitia Yeandle 1997, p. 17.

In a time of religious persecution, Traherne changed sides. Under the Commonwealth, episcopacy had been abolished and the Prayer Book forbidden in public worship. The Episcopalian Vaughan developed an apocalyptic religion out of his sense of persecution. During this time, Traherne was appointed to a living with the support of leading Puritan ministers.[5] At the Restoration, after a brief Presbyterian interim, it was the turn of the Episcopalians. The Cavalier Parliament passed the five acts known as the Clarendon Code between 1661 and 1665, which were designed to keep the formerly triumphant Puritans from power in Church and state, and indeed by the Five Mile Act of 1665 from non-episcopal education or religious services in the towns. Traherne was quick to conform to the restored episcopal church, and his friendship with Susanna Hopton and his chaplaincy to Bridgeman suggest that he found the social alliance of Church and landowning classes not uncongenial.

Was Traherne, then, a Vicar of Bray, one who changed his clerical coat according to the political weather? To so spiritual a man, the differences men fought over might have appeared unimportant. The spiritual and the cynical may behave in much the same way. Certainly if Traherne agonized over his loyalties, his writings bear little mark of it. It is only fair, however, to add that a number of distinguished bishops under Charles, such as John Tillotson and John Wilkins, had been non-episcopal churchmen under Cromwell. Uncomplicated allegiances, as the case of Marvell suggests, must have been hard and rare. After the Restoration, Traherne seems to have taken loyalty to the established form of religion as a duty. He welcomed the return of the monarchy and in a typically exuberant list includes bishops among such occasions for thanksgiving as 'Sacraments, Liturgy . . . Laws, Ecclesiastical Establishment of Tythes . . . Liberal Maintenance of our Saviours Clergy'.[6] Nevertheless he grew critical of Charles II.[7] Bridgeman, having been ejected from his Keepership of the Privy Seal in 1672 because he had opposed Charles's Declaration of Indulgence toward Catholics, became a symbol of Protestant opposition. Traherne's publication of *Roman Forgeries* in 1673, dedicated to Bridgeman, was not an innocuous publication of his BD thesis but support for Bridgeman's resistance to the dangerous solvents of Charles's policy of religious toleration.[8] Toward Protestant sectaries, on the other hand, there is evidence, at least from the company he kept, that Traherne, though impatient with dissent, was not in favour of

---

5. Julia Smith, *DNB*.
6. 'Thanksgivings', Traherne 1958, II, p. 296; all citations of Traherne are from this edition.
7. See Julia J. Smith 1988; Matar 1994.
8. Christopher Hill 1985, p. 228; Julia J. Smith 1988, p. 213.

persecution; Bridgeman, for example, had been involved in attempts to bring Presbyterians into the national church and supported indulgence of nonconforming Protestants.[9]

Putting his change of sides at the Restoration behind him, Traherne wrote within a wide tendency in the Church of England away from the controversial, dogmatic theology of the Civil War period toward a theology that appealed to universal principles. It is a far cry from the neoplatonic speculation of his poems to the Latitudinarian preaching of Tillotson and Edward Stillingfleet, but still Traherne's attempt to find saving truths in Plotinus and Ficino as well as in the Bible turns from revelation to universal principles that all can be rationally understood. His contemporaries the Cambridge Platonists were on the same tack.[10] Traherne, a solitary platonist at Aristotelian Oxford, pursues his ideas more adventurously than they do, but against the eccentric and original speculation of the poems should be placed the serious attempt in the 'Centuries' to give a rational account of such central Christian mysteries as the Atonement ('Centuries', II, 31–37). Traherne is not just a visionary but a persistent and candid thinker about the doctrines he was ordained to preach. He may harp on his favourite ideas with the relentlessness of an isolated mind, but his ideas are not foolish. For instance, trying to explain the Redemption, the bondage of the will and the freedom of a Christian, Traherne goes with a free mind directly to the heart of what so much theological labour had been spent on:

> What enabled Adam to lov God? Was it not that God loved him? What constrained him to be avers from God? Was it not that God was avers from him? When he was faln, he thought GOD would hate him, and be his Enemy Eternaly. And this was the Miserable Bondage that Enslaved him. But when he was restored; O the infinit and Eternal Change! His very lov to Himself made him to prize His Eternal Lov. I mean his Redeemers.
>
> ('Centuries', IV, 53)

Theologically Traherne's spirituality transcends doctrinal strife. That does not mean that it challenged the exclusiveness of the Restoration settlement. Bishops had been brought back for social and political reasons, and Traherne's attempt at a rational faith might find a place within that scheme

---

9.   Julia J. Smith 1988, pp. 208–10, and Julia Smith 1988, pp. 26–35, for Traherne's denunciation of Nonconformists and his association with those against persecution.
10. For Traherne's Latitudinarianism, see Christopher Hill 1985, p. 230; Marks 1966.

and leave church politics to politicians. In an odd way his spirituality also transcends the social strife let loose by the Civil War and entrenched in the social divisions of the Restoration.

Traherne's poetry of deprivation

Of all the Metaphysical poets, Traherne was born into the poorest circum-stances.[11] As an orphan and later as chaplain, his dependent position must have been brought home to him painfully. Oldham gives a memorable picture of a chaplain's servile state:

> Little the inexperienc'd Wretch does know,
> What slavery he oft must undergo:
> Who tho in silken Skarf and Cassock drest,
> Wears but a gayer Livery at best:
> When Dinner calls the Implement must wait
> With holy Words to consecrate the Meat,
> But hold it for a Favour seldom known,
> If he be deign'd the Honor to sit down.
> Soon as the Tarts appear, Sir *Crape*, withdraw!
> Those Dainties are not for a spiritual Maw:
> Observe your distance, and be sure to stand
> Hard by the Cistern with your Cap in hand:
> There for diversion you may pick your Teeth,
> Till the kind Voider comes for your Relief.[12]

Perhaps Bridgeman treated Traherne more civilly. Traherne was a bore. According to the preface to 'Thanksgivings', he was 'so wonderfully transported with the love of God to Mankind that those that would converse with him, were forced to endure some discourse upon these subjects, whether they had any sense of Religion or not'.[13] But Bridgeman may have noticed that Traherne was worth listening to all the same. Even so, the position cannot have been an easy one. Strikingly, the one ordinary human passion

---

11. But as Christopher Hill remarks (1985, p. 236), he was comparatively affluent as a churchman.
12. Oldham 1960, 'A Satyr Address'd to a *Friend*, that is about to leave University, and come abroad in the World', ll. 76–89; 'voider': a container into which the remains of the meal were cleared.
13. Traherne 1958, I, p. xxx.

that speaks out in Traherne's poetry is social envy and a sense of his own poverty:

7

Cursd and Devisd Proprieties,
With Envy, Avarice
And Fraud, those Feinds that Spoyl even Paradice,
Fled from the Splendour of mine Eys.
And so did Hedges, Ditches, Limits, Bounds,
I dreamd not ought of those,
But wanderd over all mens Grounds,
And found Repose.

8

Proprieties themselvs were mine,
And Hedges Ornaments;
Walls, Boxes, Coffers, and their rich Contents
Did not Divide my Joys, but shine.
Clothes, Ribbans, Jewels, laces, I esteemd
My Joys by others worn;
For me they all to wear them seemd
When I was born.

('Wonder', ll. 49–64)[14]

In many of Traherne's poems, the source of sin, what destroys the Edenic vision of the world, is custom, the way of the world, and in this Traherne agrees with the views of the Cambridge Platonists. More interestingly, in 'Dumnesse' he suggests that it is with language that social corruption enters. But in 'Wonder', the symbolic order takes the form of property, which transforms England's green and pleasant land into a social scene and decks the country by dividing it. Property robs us of paradise. This is a radical idea and one that had found voice in Winstanley and the Diggers in the Commonwealth period.[15] But Traherne's response is not utopian, revolutionary, or in any way social. He transcends the social order by a self-centred mental operation, or in 'Wonder' he says he did so as a child. It was not that his innocent eye was unaware of the social implications of walls and hedges and clothes, but that he was lord of all that he surveyed.

---

14. Cf. 'The Estate' by John Norris of Bemerton, a later Oxford platonist and chaplain, for a rather different appropriation of a rich man's property through the delighted eye.
15. See Christopher Hill 1985, pp. 233–35, on Traherne's affinities with Winstanley and the limitations of his 'Communism of the mind'.

By seeing he enjoyed the rich man's grounds as his own and took possession of those ornaments that assert privilege. What is interesting here is not the claim to enjoy everything spiritually but the naked expression of an appetite to possess – it is above all for such expressions of motive, at once naive and penetrating, that one values Traherne. The same spiritualizing of possessiveness can be seen at work in an autobiographical passage in 'The Third Century':

> The Citie seemd to stand in Eden, or to be Built in Heaven. The Streets were mine, the Temple was mine, the People were mine, their Clothes and Gold and silver was mine, as much as their Sparkling Eys Fair Skins and ruddy faces. The Skies were mine, and so were the Sun and Moon and Stars, and all the world was mine, and I the only Spectator and Enjoyer of it. I knew no Churlish Proprieties, nor Bounds nor Divisions: but all Proprieties and Divisions were mine: all Treasures and the Possessors of them.
>
> (III, 3)

He did not feel dispossessed by others' possession because he possessed the lot in his infantile gaze.

For Traherne, as for Wordsworth, the infant is a 'seer blest', but for Traherne, unlike Wordsworth, the infantile state can be regained by taking thought. The infant, as unfallen Adam, uncorrupted by social custom and property, is the model for his mature spiritual self. He transcends possessiveness, the cause of social division, by raising it to a spiritual power. Distinctly, though, it is with his spiritualized possessiveness as it was with his spiritualized theology: it does not seek to change the social order.

One should, of course, bear in mind that world loss as spiritual gain, poverty and plenty, desire for the infinite and the solipsistic condition of the lover of the One are all part of ancient and Renaissance traditions of neoplatonic thought from which Traherne draws. Nevertheless, it is hard not to hear a note of personal deprivation behind his spirituality, most directly perhaps in 'Poverty':

Poverty

As in the House I sate
Alone and desolate,
No Creature but the Fire and I,
The Chimney and the Stool, I lift mine Ey
Up to the Wall,
And in the silent Hall
Saw nothing mine

But som few Cups and Dishes shine
The Table and the wooden Stools
    Where Peeple us'd to dine: 10
    A painted Cloth there was
Wherin som ancient Story wrought
A little entertain'd my Thought
Which Light discover'd throu the Glass.

    I wonder'd much to see
    That all my Wealth should be
Confin'd in such a little Room,
Yet for more I scarcely durst presume.
    It griev' me sore
    That such a scanty Store   20
    Should be my All:
For I forgat my Eas and Health,
Nor did I think of Hands or Eys,
    Nor Soul nor Body prize;
    I neither thought the Sun,
Nor Moon, nor Stars, nor Peeple *mine*,
Tho they did round about me shine;
And therfore was I quite undon.

    Som greater things I thought
    Must needs for me be wrought,   30
    Which till my pleased Mind could see
I ever should lament my Poverty:
    I fain would have
    Whatever Bounty gave;
    Nor could there be
Without, or Lov or Deity:
For, should not He be Infinit
    Whose Hand created me?
    Ten thousand absent things
Did vex my poor and absent Mind,   40
Which, till I be no longer blind,
Let me not see the King of Kings.

    His lov must surely be
    Rich, infinit, and free;
    Nor can He be thought a God
Of Grace and Pow'r, that fills not his Abode,
    His Holy Court,
    In kind and liberal sort;
    Joys and Pleasures,
Plenty of Jewels, Goods, and Treasures,   50

(To enrich the Poor, cheer the forlorn)
    His Palace must adorn,
    And given all to me:
For till *His* Works *my* Wealth became,
No Lov, or Peace did me enflame:
    But now I have a DEITY.

'Poverty' is one of a number of poems in 'Poems of Felicity' that treat the experience of loss of an infantile edenic vision. Like many of the earlier poems in that collection and also those in the Dobell Manuscript, it starts from an incident in Traherne's spiritual autobiography. But the incident is more specifically localized than usual in his writing. The details of the room in the first stanza, though dull, vividly impress themselves, unlike the edenic generalities of lovely shining faces and streets paved with golden stones in 'Wonder'. That he places the fire, the chimney and the stool as creatures in the room along with himself speaks of his sunken state, his lapse out of the world where 'Peeple us'd to dine'. Equally the listless movement of his sentences through a stanza whose complications raise expectations of bright variety, only to disappoint them, conveys his dejection. This is particularly evident in the last five lines. After the inconsequentiality of what has gone before, one expects some significance to emerge from 'A painted Cloth there was / Wherin som ancient Story wrought'. But all one discovers is that the idle mind has been diverting itself. Following that, the trailing and oddly, if not wrongly, related qualifying clause in the last line is a happy stroke. Whether the light discovers the painted story or the thought, either must have been dim.

The first stanza shows that Traherne could write fine poetry, and whatever the evil effects of Philip Traherne's tinkering, he did not disturb his brother's mastery of the movement of the verse through a compex stanza or the attention of his imagination to his experience of deprivation. After that strong opening, 'Poverty' falls away, as is too often the case with his poems, including those in the Dobell Manuscript, where Philip Traherne cannot be blamed.

Like almost all his poems, 'Poverty' explains a firmly premeditated idea. Although it records what he thought at the time in the narrative past, it does not convey the experience of thinking, of evolving thought, of a new conversation with himself. Rather, in the second, third and fourth stanzas, Traherne rehearses snatches of old conversations, ideas about his wealth that he has developed more forcefully elsewhere. There is, of course, no reason why thought should be presented in the process of being thought in poetry. The excellence of Donne in that sort of writing does not rule out the excellence of Dryden in the measured exposition of ideas. Traherne's writing, however, aims at delivering ideas as if they were coming to him and the turns of his stanza are suited to that sort of immediate delivery. But his ideas are muffled; he gestures at thoughts he knows we have heard before and the concentration of mind in the first stanza is diffused by the second:

> For I forgat my Eas and Health,
> Nor did I think of Hands or Eys,
> Nor Soul nor Body prize.

The point of that, or at least the peculiar twist Traherne gives to the otherwise bland thought that one should be grateful for soundness of health and limb, can only be grasped by someone who remembers poems like 'The Salutation' and 'The Person', where he expresses his strange feeling for his body as a miracle. It makes little sense in itself to say that he 'was quite undon' because

> I neither thought the Sun,
> Nor Moon, nor Stars, nor Peeple *mine*,
> Tho they did round about me shine.

Nor does the italicizing of '*mine*' help, except in the light of poems like 'The Estate', 'The Amendment' or the 'The Improvement', where he explains how his possessions consist in viewing the world with the spiritual eye of childhood. At the same time his mind has wandered from the room in which he sits desolate to his general situation in the universe. The sun, moon, stars and people did not shine round him where he was sitting, but only inside his head. In this case the passing from outer to inner vision goes with a slackening of attention. The fluency of his verse and the simplicity and directness of his expression remain admirable in a way, but what Traherne wants to say is not really taking place in his words. And – what above all makes him a diffuse writer – he repeats himself: lines 19–21 say what he has just said in lines 15–18, and the repetition takes away from the weight of his utterance and from our feeling that what has been said might be got by heart.

Nevertheless, the first stanza makes 'Poverty' one of Traherne's most memorable poems. And that first stanza utters a feeling of deprivation too strongly for it to be just an idea.[16] At any rate the experience of deprivation resonates in his transcending of it and lends a human and social pathos to his spiritual triumphs, both in 'Poverty' and in other poems.

---

16. Margoliouth, in Traherne 1958, I, p. xxxiii, in fact suggests that the first stanza might describe a room in the inn kept by the Philip Traherne who possibly adopted him. For a vigorous defence of Traherne's poetry, see Dick Davies, in Traherne 1980, pp. 8–11.

The poetry of transcendence

In his 'Fourth Century', Traherne speaks about self-love with the boldness and oddity of someone who has thought things out for himself. He talks of himself in the third person as the friend of the person for whom he has written his book:

> He was a Strict and Severe Applier of all Things to Himself. And would first hav his Self Lov satisfied, and then his Lov of all others. It is true that Self Lov is Dishonorable, but then it is when it is alone. And Self endedness is Mercinary, but then it is when it endeth in oneself. It is more Glorious to love others, and more desirable, but by Natural Means to be attained. That Pool must first be filled, that shall be made to overflow. He was ten yeers studying before he could satisfy his Self Lov. And now finds nothing more easy then to lov others better than oneself.
>
> ('Centuries', IV, 55)

The consummation of self-love in the love of others is not a prominent theme in the poetry. But it occupies at least a prominent position in 'Goodnesse', the poem that ends the Dobell Manuscript, and it achieves fine expression in 'On Christmas-Day' in the middle of 'Poems of Felicity'. On the whole, though, his poems are occupied with the business of his ten years labour, how to satisfy his self-love, or, what perhaps amounts to the same thing, how to love himself. His means of loving himself is to look at himself looking: 'Talk with thy self; thy self enjoy and see: / At once the Mirror and the Object be' ('The Odour', ll. 53–54) – not just Narcissus but the pool that shows Narcissus to himself. It is seeing himself see that makes him divine to himself.

Traherne's thought is always radical. His original divine sense of himself was as an egg in the womb. In 'The Return', he declares, 'My early Tutor is the Womb'. But the startling and extended development of this idea is 'The Preparative':

1

My Body being Dead, my Lims unknown;
Before I skild to prize
Those living Stars mine Eys,
Before my Tongue or Cheeks were to me shewn,
Before I knew my Hands were mine,
Or that my Sinews did my Members joyn,
When neither Nostril, Foot, nor Ear,
As yet was seen, or felt, or did appear;
I was within
A house I knew not, newly clothed with Skin.

2

Then was my Soul my only All to me,
    A Living Endless Ey,
      Far wider then the Skie
Whose Power, whose Act, whose Essence was to see.
    I was an Inward *Sphere of Light,*
Or an Interminable Orb of *Sight,*
    An Endless and a Living Day,
A *vital Sun* that round about did *ray*
          All Life and Sence,
A Naked Simple Pure *Intelligence.*

3

I then no Thirst nor Hunger did conceiv,
    No dull Necessity,
      No Want was Known to me;
Without Disturbance then I did receiv
    The fair ideas of all Things,
And had the Hony even without the Stings.
    A Meditating Inward Ey
Gazing at Quiet did within me lie,
        And evry Thing
Delighted me that was their Heavnly King.

4

For *Sight* inherits Beauty, *Hearing* Sounds,
    The *Nostril* Sweet Perfumes,
      All *Tastes* have hidden Rooms
Within the *Tongue*; and *Feeling Feeling* Wounds
    With Pleasure and Delight: but I
Forgot the rest, and was all Sight, or Ey.
    Unbodied and Devoid of Care,
Just as in Heavn the Holy Angels are.
        For simple Sence
Is Lord of all Created Excellence.

5

Be'ing thus prepard for all Felicity,
    Not prepossest with Dross,
      Nor stifly glued to gross
And dull Materials that might ruine me,
    Nor fetterd by an Iron Fate
With vain Affections in my Earthly State
    To any thing that might Seduce
My Sence, or misemploy it from its use
        I was as free
As if there were nor Sin, nor Miserie.

6

Pure Empty Powers that did nothing loath,
Did like the fairest Glass,
Or Spotless polisht Brass,
Themselvs soon in their Objects Image cloath.
Divine Impressions when they came,
Did quickly enter and my Soul inflame.
'Tis not the Object, but the Light
That maketh Heaven; Tis a Purer Sight.
Felicitie
Appears to none but them that purely see.

7

A Disentangled and a Naked Sence
A Mind thats unpossest,
A Disengaged Brest,
An Empty and a Quick Intelligence
Acquainted with the Golden Mean,
An Even Spirit Pure and Serene,
Is that where Beauty, Excellence,
And Pleasure keep their Court of Residence.
My Soul retire,
Get free, and so thou shalt even all Admire.

Again one admires the fluency of Traherne's versification, the impetus of his ideas through his stanzas and from stanza to stanza, achieved by the simplest syntactical means, repetition and accumulation. So the first stanza runs through a series of subordinate temporal clauses, 'Before . . . Before . . . When . . .', until it reaches its main statement, which locates him inside his new skin. The second stanza amplifies the account of what he was 'then' mainly through an accumulation of descriptions in apposition.

The syntactical flow and cadence of his eloquence do not fail. But the thought falters. Until the end of the fourth stanza, Traherne develops his idea of the egg–'I'–eye as 'Heavenly king' with an astonishing display of intellectual fancy and ability to project himself into a strange, theoretical mode of being. But from stanza 5, he moralizes and conventionalizes his peculiar point of view and preaches moderation and detachment from the world. The sixth stanza has its charms, including a witty adaptation of lines from Suckling's jocularly libertine 'Song' to Cupid (quoted in the 'Introduction' p. 5): "'Tis not the meat, but 'tis the appetite / Makes eating a delight'.[17] This elegant perversity Traherne aptly seizes on for his own inverted

---

17. Traherne was so taken with these lines that he adapts them again in 'Desire', ll. 57–58.

purpose: "'Tis not the Object, but the Light / That maketh Heaven'. But on the whole the last three stanzas have let go of the development of his idea that the egg, with powers of sight, hearing, smell, taste, feeling in germ and as yet unlimited by taking in definite objects in the world, possesses the whole world and more in potentiality, as if a piano contained all piano music in a purer state than could ever be played on it. Unable to see anything, his eye sees only its own seeing and in that way, like the *autoeromenon*, the self-loving, unmoved mover of Aristotle, the egg becomes 'A Naked Simple Pure *Intelligence*'.

The sixth stanza treats how the 'Pure Empty Powers' of his senses soon turned to the created world and invested its objects with their divine radiance. That makes it possible to read the poem as if Traherne was thinking not so much of the egg as of an infant at the moment of birth, at the instant before its consciousness opens to things around it.[18] 'The Return' in 'Poems of Felicity' is equally ambiguous about whether a pre- or post-natal stage is in question. In any case, Traherne's imagination is much too theoretical to work up a remotely plausible or detailed account of life in the womb or of being born. Sexual generation never enters his poetry; generation, like the creation of the world from nothing, is divine. If he is thinking of an egg in 'The Preparative', it is an egg without a womb; if of an infant, it is of an infant without a mother (let alone a father). The love that, in Wordsworth's famous account in *The Prelude* of how a child comes to perceive the world, flows from the mother's eye, in Traherne emanates from the self-contemplating eye of the child itself. What interests Traherne is consciousness of consciousness, a state of mind that has gathered into itself all its powers and not yet put them forth into finite forms that might alienate it from itself, whether that state of mind is to be found in the egg or just the new-born child.

Few now can believe that pure consciousness is a workable idea. But Traherne's speculations are a wonderfully suggestive reduction of the tradition of philosophy that produced the Cartesian ego. Traherne is not to be prized as a philosopher. Rather, like Samuel Beckett, with his use of the ideas of the Cartesian Geulincx in his novel *Murphy*, Traherne shows his flair in imaginatively exploring the psychology of what it is to think like that. His pure consciousness is a fantasy, but the fantasy of someone

---

18. The usual interpretation, e.g. Clements 1964, is that Traherne is thinking of the new-born infant. The best argument for that is that 'The Salutation' has already dealt with coming to be from a state of non-being and so the sequence of autobiography of a consciousness in the Dobell MS will have moved on to the infant's first apprehensions of the world in preceding poems. But this leaves the self-contemplating of as yet empty faculties in 'The Preparative' unexplained and the argument from sequence founders. The Platonic doctrine of recollection, frequently invoked, does not help.

engaged as a human being, not just a dialectical machine, in his thoughts. More bizarrely, more radically and more tellingly than Vaughan in 'The Retreate', Traherne imagines a withdrawal into an ideal state as a regression or shrinking toward a seed point. And in 'The Preparative' anyway, his philosophic terminology plays aptly into the hands of his rapturous salutes to the divinity that lies in infancy. The paradoxical formulations for the infant eye require much the same bending of our ideas as the philosophical ones. 'I was an Inward *Sphere of Light*, / Or an Interminable Orb of *Sight*' awakens a rarefied play of sense that naturally runs into such philosophic notions as 'A Naked Simple Pure *Intelligence*' and enlivens their abstraction. The sort of concreteness to be found in 'Poverty' or in the description of the churchgoing congregation in 'On Christmas-day' – 'See how their Breath doth smoak' – is easily approved. But there is also linguistic vigour in the abstract reducing, stretching and rearranging of the world in 'The Preparative'.

'The Preparative', with its divinizing of the egg and its curious spiritual operations, is rarely discussed.[19] The well-known poems about entering a heavenly state of mind by becoming as a little child are more straightforward recollections of a paradisal sense of self and the world in early childhood:

> How like an Angel came I down!
> How bright are all things here!
> When first among his Works I did appear
> O how their GLORY me did crown?
> The World resembled his ETERNITIE,
> In which my Soul did walk;
> And evry Thing that I did see
> Did with me talk.

('Wonder', ll. 1–8)

The opening line of the stanza is striking in the manner Vaughan developed out of Herbert, and in the last two lines the way that things in their pristinity spoke to him in his unlanguaged state suggests the fascination of the newly awakened senses. For all its praise of infant sense, though, the senses are vaguely engaged in 'Wonder', as a stronger paradoxical version of the same theme in 'Dumnesse' brings out:

---

19. An exception is Clements 1964.

But Eys them selvs were all the Hearers there.
And evry Stone, and Evry Star a Tongue,
And evry Gale of Wind a Curious Song.

(ll. 60–62)

In 'Wonder', by contrast, everything is brightness, GLORY and ETERNITIE.

The splendour of this early vision of the world arises partly from its freshness uncorrupted by custom and particulary social custom introduced with language. Traherne is suspicious of conversation with people and trusts the intercourse of sense with things: 'By Novelty my Soul was taught' ('Right Apprehension', l. 35). But more is at issue than novelty. Already in his remembering his infant ideas of the world there is something self-reflexive in Traherne's thoughts and the radiance with which he sees things reflects on himself: they crown him with glory and he walks in eternity because his spirit sees them in a glorious and eternal fashion. There is implicit in this way of seeing the redounding of all things on himself that makes him the centre of the world and the mirror of its creator. So for example in 'My Spirit', he says that he dilated in seeing things to take things in so that he was at once present with them and they in him, – 'An Univers enclosd in Skin', as he puts it in 'Fulnesse' (l. 8). These transcendental optics turn the world itself into the act of its perceiver and all things become by simple seeing emanations of his spirit, as they are of the God that made them. By perceiving, by knowing the world, we take possession of the world and simultaneously, conscious of our knowledge, make ourselves divine. And it is God's design that we should be divinized in this way; this is the end for which he made all things. Such is the idea Traherne develops in 'The Improvement', a poem whose interesting idea is expressed with a woodenness that goes some way to explain the opinion that he is not so much a poet as a versifier of ideas like Henry More:

6

To bring the Moisture of far distant Seas
Into a *point*, to make them present here,
In *virtu*, not in *Bulk*; one man to pleas
With all the *Powers* of the Highest Sphere,
From East, from West, from North and South, to bring
The pleasing *Influence* of evry thing;

7

Is far more Great then to Creat them there
Where now they stand.

('The Improvement', ll. 31–38)

It does not seem to have struck Traherne, or the Renaissance platonists Pico or Charles de Bouelles, who expressed similar ideas, though not with Traherne's admirable literal-mindedness, that the virtual reality of the world in our minds is immeasurably less various, multifold and intricate than the world itself.

Self-divinizing is not the final stage of Traherne's spirituality. The self that reflects God reflects God back to himself; more arrestingly, the creation returns through Traherne's self-absorption in praise to God. The self that in Herbert could give nothing to God in return for everything, in Traherne can make a return from its own divinity.[20] But it must be added that the self has nothing to give apart from what it receives from God, though it does seem to have the free will to withhold its beams, to refuse to see the divine circulation of the world in Traherne's way and so deflect the current of love from itself as well as from God. In another uninspired and repetitive exposition of what should be an inspiring idea, Traherne asserts that

> Our Blessednes to see
> Is even to the Deitie
> A Beatifick Vision!

('The Recovery', ll. 8–10)

God is, accordingly, 'Undeified almost if once denied' (l. 20); he is condemned to 'Endless Pain . . . without relief' (ll. 28–30) – to hell, in other words – if he is not glorified by those who glorify themselves in glorifying him. Lines such as these have the blasphemous sound of genuine religious utterance, though they do not, unfortunately, make 'The Recovery' work as poetry.

For Traherne, the divine circulation of the world that regains paradise does not run just between the self and God. It does involve other selves. In writing his 'Centuries' for the friend of his friend, Traherne was, after all, trying to share his felicity with someone else. And as he says in 'Goodnesse',

> 1
> The Bliss of other Men is my Delight:
> (When once my Principles are right:)
> And evry Soul which mine doth see
> A Treasurie.

---

20. See Leimberg 1995–96, pp. 167–86.

> The Face of GOD is Goodness unto all,
> And while he Thousands to his Throne doth call,
>   While Millions bathe in Pleasures,
>   And do behold his Treasures
>   The Joys of all
>   On mine do fall
> And even my Infinitie doth seem
> A Drop without them of a mean Esteem.

It is not clear whether the happiness of others consists here in the Trahernian felicity of absorbing everything into oneself. Probably he would have been satisfied with the uninitiated happiness he sees his congregation take in God's overflowing into the world in the birth of Christ when they spruce themselves up for church in 'On Christmas-day':

> See how, their Bodies clad with finer Cloaths,
>   They now begin
>   His Prais to sing
>   Who purchas'd their Repose:
> Wherby their inward Joy they do disclose;
> Their Dress alludes to better Works than those:
>   His gayer Weeds and finer Band,
>   New Suit and Hat, into his hand
>   The Plow-man takes; his neatest Shoos,
>   And warmer Glovs, he means to use:
>   And shall not I, my King,
>   Thy Praises sing?

> (ll. 49–60)

This works as a homely illustration of his theory of social joy and also manages to ring out like a nativity ode. The people make their return for God's giving in the joy that expresses itself, not just as praise, but smarter dress. And seeing this, Traherne kindles and makes their joys his own, uttering his happiness in his celebration of Christmas.

The completion of Traherne's scheme of mirroring in the joy of others does not amount to a rich sociability. One can only admire, by contrast, how centrally Milton places human conversation of like with like in his vision of paradise. Traherne's paradise is a paradise for the watching eye. Looks for Traherne do not make up a mutual exchange. He wants to see others happy as if he stood apart from them, like God, even if at the same time he might be willing that they should similarly find pleasure in beholding him. Still it is an amiable conclusion that self-love should turn to benevolence, and not many seventeenth-century Christians thought freshly about how self might link up with other selves lovingly.

In outlining Traherne's ideas, I have passed over two important ways in which he views himself. The first is his celebration of his body, more strange for his extravagant, general idealizing of it in terms of the jewels and perfume he does not possess than for any specific physical sense of corporeality such as so remarkably comes out in Donne's 'Metempsychosis':

> These Hands are Jewels to the Ey,
> Like Wine, or Oil, or Hony, to the Taste:
> These Feet which here I wear beneath the Sky
> Are us'd, yet never waste.
> My Members all do yield a sweet Perfume;
> They minister Delight, yet not consume.

('The Odour', ll. 1–6)

It was Lord Herbert of Cherbury's vanity that his clothes smelled sweet when taken off his body and Henry More's '*that not only his own* Urine *had naturally the* Flavour of *Violets in it; but that his* Breast . . . *would . . . send forth flowery and* Aromatick Odours'.[21] Traherne is probably not making that sort of claim for his body but rather making a metaphor: a perfume gives off perfume without being consumed as the parts of his body function delightfully without being used up. Nevertheless he views his body with delight, almost in the sort of terms that a Petrarchan poet might praise his mistress. Something might be made of the way this body as love-object undergoes a sexual change and like his spirit becomes a bower of delights. But the important work of his imagination is to free bodily existence from the disparagement of the ascetic tradition in Christianity. Traherne's gospel is paradise now. He does not put off the regaining of paradise to a state beyond death. For him the corruption succeeding the Fall is all a matter of misapprehension; looked at in the right way the body, his body, streams with the glory of the eye that beholds it.

Traherne is particularly interested in the skin, the surface that bounds the self and divides the universe outside from the universe within, the universe that contains him physically from the universe that he contains spiritually. In 'An Hymne upon St Bartholomews Day', he asks, 'What Heavenly Light inspires my Skin[?]'. Bartholomew, who was martyred by being skinned alive, is often pictured carrying his skin over one arm and in the opposite

---

21. Edward Herbert 1900, p. 113; Ward 1710, pp. 123–24.

hand holding the knife that flayed him. Typically Traherne suppresses the cruelty of the Christian imagination. St Bartholomew is the patron of his skin because, for Traherne, the skin is sanctified by enclosing a spirit illuminated by enclosing the world beyond it:

> An Inward Omnipresence here,
> *Mysteriously* like His with in me stands;
> Whose knowledg is a Sacred Sphere,
> That in it self at once Includes all Lands.

(ll. 10–13)

The idea of being unconfined by the envelope of skin that encloses him and gives him physical form goes with a second way in which he characteristically views himself. He is divine because infinite:

> A Secret self I had enclos'd within,
> That was not bounded with my Clothes or Skin,
> Or terminated with my Sight, the Sphere
> Of which was bounded with the Heavens here:
> But that did rather, like the Subtile Light,
> Secur'd from rough and raging Storms by Night,
> Break throu the Lanthorns sides, and freely ray
> Dispersing and Dilating evry Way:
> Whose Steddy Beams too Subtile for the Wind,
> Are such, that we their Bounds can scarcely find.

('Nature', ll. 19–28)

The beautiful analysis of light untroubled by the turbulence of the air furnishes him with an analogy for the divine insatiableness of the mind that must go beyond nature and transcend the world it makes. In this it is like God, but also, at least in its restless striving for infinity, like Marlowe's Tamburlaine:

> Vast unaffected Wonderfull Desires,
> Like Inward, Nativ, uncausd, hidden fires,
> Sprang up with Expectations very strange,
> Which into New Desires did quickly change.

(ll. 39–42)

And so driven by a 'Soaring Sacred Thirst ('Desire', l. 53) to go beyond any definite thing, Traherne is moved to break out of the universe into the infinite space popularized by Henry More.[22] Such continual expansion of the self outwards corresponds with the retraction of his powers inwards to the indefinite potentiality of the egg, and in both ways he can reflect the inexhaustible potency of God.

Clearly there is a great deal to like about Traherne's self-centred religion. It is hard to see how his Christianity could be turned to persecution and it is free, moreover, from self-persecution, from the persecutory imagination that disturbs us in Herbert. Sin for Traherne is a wrong way of seeing the world and the fall of Adam has not irretrievably corrupted the human state: paradise can be regained on earth with the right principles and each of us can become an Adam – and an Adam, besides, who is God, more or less. All this is to spirit away the oppressive burden of more orthodox forms of seventeenth-century religion. But Traherne's liberation takes place only inside the individual's head, not in a communal utopian effort, and in retreat from society and custom. This is to give up the world in which we live with other people. Like Vaughan's retreat into liminal states, Traherne's divinizing of the self is really an absence, and he does not use that absence, in which he is charged spiritually, to turn back to the world and make a difference. The other people whose happiness he reflects, and even God, are not really other than himself in a rapturous condition. One wonders how he spoke to his parishioners, the exploited, the sick, the mourning, the bad.[23] Embarrassingly, Donne and Herbert, with their oppressive beliefs in original sin, in the impossibility of realizing heaven on earth, in the abasement of the human creature before its creator, have more to do with the life people live. Even the grotesque torments that Herbert sees as visited on him by God correspond more to our experience of things than Traherne's edenic vision. In one respect we may feel that Traherne's religion is not so much immaterial as baleful. In him the infinite appetite to possess is honorably harmless, but 'Vast unaffected strange Desires' that arouse 'Expectations very strange' have become so much the ruling impulse behind the accelerating transformation of the world through the agencies of capitalism and the technology of everyday life that few would not be in two minds about divinizing that Faustian aspect of the self. In our time we are more likely to value the earthly, solid stool and dishes in Traherne's room, sullenly resistant to vision and the reflection of infinity, than the marvellous possessions that come to him on his voyages in inner space.

---

22. See Nicolson 1950, pp. 73–79.
23. But see 'The Ceremonial Law' as reported by Smith and Yeandle 1997.

Traherne as Metaphysical

As for the Metaphysical quality of Traherne's verse, in a literal sense he is the most metaphysical of Metaphysical poets since only he puts forward a system of theological philosophy. Others play with or draw on metaphysical ideas in the course of talking to lovers or God or themselves, but only Traherne unfolds them as a way of attaining enlightenment. But if he is the only metaphysical poet, he is a Metaphysical too. His verse is mostly about himself and almost all about his inward life. Traherne's self, however, is a different affair from Donne's or Herbert's, or even Vaughan's. It is a thought creation. No doubt Donne or Herbert made themselves up partly in writing, but the selves they made up, however engaged with the spiritual or divine, however isolated or alienated, are still eminently the selves of men who live on earth among other people. Although both significant collections of Traherne's poems contain autobiographical sequences about his childhood, the child, except in 'Shadows in the Water' and 'On Leaping Over the Moon', is a theoretical exhibit, drawn out upon theosophical ideas, a blank as far as social identity goes. Traherne's poems illustrate a theology, where Donne's and Herbert's devotional poems are human attempts to live a life of prayer. All the same, as we have seen, Traherne's poetry gives out strong signs of his involvement in the world, even in his attempt to disengage himself from it. We may place his spiritual acquisitiveness and his spiritual self-regard alongside those marks of the peculiar interiorities of Metaphysical poets such as Donne's trouble with the world or Vaughan's retreat from it.

Traherne does not bring himself into his poems like Donne by self-dramatizing. Frequently the occasions of his poems are very general reflections, which move him to personal utterance. But probably his most successful poems start from what is presented as an experience, past or present, which he then analyses in his theoretical account of it, a pattern closer to Vaughan's procedure in some poems than to any other Metaphysical. Some of Traherne's experiences are really speculations:

> When silent I,
> So many thousand thousand yeers
> Beneath the Dust did in a Chaos lie,
> How could I Smiles or Tears,
> Or Lips or Hands or Eys or Ears perceiv?
> Welcom ye Treasures which I now receiv.

('The Salutation', ll. 7–12)

253

This is certainly an interesting imagining of becoming out of non-being, but smaller incidents perhaps make better poems. Two such, 'Shadows in the Water' and 'On Leaping Over the Moon', deal with illusions that are also the occasions of insights. Like certain incidents in *The Prelude* where a mischievous play in appearances suggests to Wordsworth a mysterious world spirit, the reflected world in a puddle or his brother's jumping over the reflection of the moon, illusions credited by the child, suggest spiritual truth to the no longer credulous adult Traherne.[24] Both of Traherne's poems are repetitious, and I believe that Philip Traherne has imposed a conventional intimation of an afterlife on the last stanza of 'Shadows in the Water', where Thomas was lost in wonder at the possibility of other worlds in infinite space or perhaps at the reflected inner world of the spirit. Still, both poems puzzle over the mysterious suggestiveness of the 'sweet Mistake' they treat. Unlike Vaughan, whose interpretation of his waterfall is commonplace, though his description is vivid, Traherne comes up with truly odd intimations from the specific things he starts out from. So, for example, his brother's experience of leaping over the moon in the stream (in fact he could no more jump over the moon's reflection than over his own shadow, but a bystander might think he did) leads into a series of dislocations of up and down, of heaven and earth, so that

> The Skies themselvs this earthly Globe surround;
>   W'are even here within them found.
>
> On hev'nly Ground within the Skies we walk.

(ll. 49–51)

The small disturbance of the ordinary view of heaven and earth is enlarged to a cosmic reversal of perspective and an etherealizing of life on earth. This is close to the paradoxical effects of more familiar sallies of Metaphysical wit. Indeed Traherne put the same thought in a more Metaphysical style in 'Adam':

---

24. Traherne was probably able to remember and make something of these experiences because he had read about illusions in Lucretius: 'A puddle no deeper than a finger's breadth, formed in a hollow between the cobblestones of the highway, offers to the eye a downward view, below ground, of as wide a scope as the towering immensity of sky that yawns above. You would fancy that you saw clouds far down below you and a sky and heavenly bodies deep-buried in a miraculous heaven beneath the earth' (*On the Nature of the Universe*, IV, 413, p. 105).

He was transported even here on Earth,
As if he then in Heven had his Birth:
The truth is, Heven did the Man surround,
    The Earth being in the middle found.

(ll. 37–42)

But in 'On Leaping Over the Moon', the absence of neatness and witty closure mean that the mind is more surprised by finding itself on the brink of new thoughts than entire master of itself.

'Shadows in the Water' and 'On Leaping Over the Moon' are only one sort of poem that Traherne wrote and successful only in part. Usually he writes not so much to illuminate specific experiences with spiritual implications as to situate himself in the scheme of the universe. Some of these situatings work splendidly. I have already spoken of the mind and language stretching of 'The Preparative'. A genuinely philosophic imagination is at work there.

Because Traherne produces himself through his ideas, his writing is more direct and expository than is usual among Metaphysical poets. In 'The Author to the Critical Peruser', he echoes Herbert's Jordan poems in calling for

No curling Metaphors that gild the Sence,
Nor Pictures here, nor painted Eloquence;
No florid Streams of Superficial Gems,
But real Crowns and Thrones and Diadems!

(ll. 11–13)[25]

But where Herbert calls for the simplicity and directness of sincerity, Traherne, perhaps attuned to the stylistic ideals of the Restoration, is concerned with transparency to truth. He does not wish to disguise or trick out his ideas in poetic fiction; the glory he sees is not a work of art. Still for all his protestation of plainness, Traherne is an eloquent writer. He can resort to analogy and simile. We have already looked at the comparison of the mind to a lantern in a storm (p. 251), an analogy as analytically surprising as Donne's and as harnessed to clear communication as some of Pope's in 'An Essay on Criticism'. In the following passage, the simile is as brilliant as the metaphors are insignificant:

---

25. Cf. 'The Person', where he protests against metaphor.

Drown'd in their Customs, I became
A Stranger to the Shining Skies,
Lost as a dying Flame.

('The Apostacy', ll. 60–62)

The chief figure of his style is paradox. Like all religious thought, Traherne's runs counter to the way of the world so that for him paradox is a natural and literal expression of his ideas. Here, his figures of speech are, like Vaughan's, at the same time insights. But his religious thought itself runs counter to traditional Christianity so that his paradoxes frequently turn on the reversal of ideas already paradoxical in themselves. While they are honestly come by in the course of thinking about himself and God (that should have emerged sufficiently in the numerous striking formulations already quoted), clearly Traherne had a way with arresting phrases as well as with arresting thoughts. Two further examples might be adduced. Developing a favourite thought that it is only an illuminated mind that sees truly as it looks around the world, he declares, 'To *walk* is by a Thought to go' ('Walking', l. 19). In 'The Demonstration', he explains his unorthodox view that God's helpless generosity needs his creatures' enjoyment of the world: 'In them he sees, and feels, and Smels, and Lives' (l. 71).

Much of Traherne's simplicity and directness is lame, all is prolix and his successes are not sustained. He is an extraordinary poet rather than a good one. His extraordinariness was probably made possible by his working to some extent in the line of Herbert and Vaughan. There are echoes of both. From Herbert there is not just the declaration of a plain intent in 'To the Critical Peruser', but also the lamentation, 'My Soul was full of Groans' ('Desire', l. 15), recalling Herbert's 'My breast was full of fears' ('Deniall') and groans in such poems as 'Sion' (l. 18), except that Traherne's groans are groans of insatiable desire, not of grief. From Vaughan there is the notion of the child as visionary. And to Vaughan's 'The Morning-watch' (quoted p. 190) he was probably indebted for this double simile for the obscuring of the light of heaven: 'As in the Air we see the Clouds / Like Winding Sheets, or Shrouds' ('The Demonstration', ll. 7–8). More generally, Traherne probably learned from both elder poets a way of exploring his relation to God in a collection of poems. For though only a part of each of his collections presents itself as autobiographical and his general reflections are occasioned by the development of a system of thought rather than the vicissitudes of his life with God, all his poems have a quality of personal effusion, if only through rapturous and celebratory exclamation at the way divinity communicates itself. In some ways Traherne was attuned to the history of his time and new currents of thought. But it was his isolation from contemporary metropolitan literary fashion, hostile to the eccentrically individual, together with his harking back to the inward turning mode of Herbert and Vaughan, that allowed him to make something new of an old way of writing.

Vera et viva Effigies
Johannis Cleeveland.

John Cleveland, from the frontispiece engraving to *Poems*, 1653. Bodleian Library,
University of Oxford.

CONCLUSION

Other forms of seventeenth-century wit

Two poets, both exemplars for Johnson of his race of Metaphysical poets, both good and one undervalued in this century, remain for summary treatment. John Cleveland (1613–58) and Abraham Cowley (1618–67) were famous exponents of the conceited style in their day, but neither came into favour with the vogue for Donne that Eliot's criticism and poetry encouraged. Twentieth-century taste has picked out chiefly the six poets I have discussed at length as its Metaphysicals because in one way or another each uses an elaborate manner to express an individual and peculiar inwardness. The curious and ingenious wit of Cleveland and Cowley, on the other hand, is a social style answerable to a common-sense view of things.

It may sound paradoxical to assert that a style so hyperbolical as Cleveland's is answerable to common sense:

> Hence ye fanastick Postillers in song,
> My text defeats your art, ties natures tongue,
> Scorns all her tinsil'd metaphors of pelf,
> Illustrated by nothing but her self.
> As Spiders travel by their bowels spun
> Into a thread, and when their race is run,
> Wind up their journey in a living clew,
> So is it with my Poetry and you.
> From your own essence must I untwine,
> Then twist again each Panegyrick line.
>
> ('The Hecatomb to His Mistress', ll. 1–16)[1]

---

1. All citations of Cleveland are from Cleveland 1967.

These lines boast that he will overgo ordinary hyperbolists, whose art of panegyric ransacks nature for comparisons; only praeternatural comparisons will serve his mistress; only by asserting her incomparable beyond even extraordinary comparisons can he speak of the ineffable object of his love. And yet despite so much tremendousness, we know where we are with Cleveland and his mistress. When Donne hyperbolizes in Songs and Sonnets, as for instance in 'Negative Love' or 'A Valediction: of Weeping', there is an effect of dislocation from the everyday world. Donne's utterances, when every allowance has been made for his habitual extravagance, bear the impress of an alienated experience of things. With Cleveland, by contrast, the wildness is just a fit of high spirits. Even the superbly grotesque comparison of himself to a spider is a social move, at once self-deprecating and self-aggrandizing: 'I am being absurd, but you could never be as amusingly absurd'. Like the flytings of the Scots makars, the 'Hecatomb' trounces opposition by aggressive brilliance. Cleveland limits himself to the competitive motive of a social game. When Donne in 'The Canonization' or Marvell in 'The Definition of Love' make superlative claims for their loves, their boasts have ambivalent undertones. Cleveland's feelings are always simple; only their expression is strange and difficult.

Cleveland's poems are collections of witticisms. But though he has no original or focused sensibility, his poems are often, like 'The Hecatomb' or 'Upon *Phillis* walking in a morning before Sun-rising' or 'The Antiplatonick', gracefully turned. Moreover the way in which he makes clever poetry out of straightforward feeling and conventional attitudes (he was ardently Royalist in verse and life) proved appealing.[2] Clevelandizing became a vogue, though it would take a fine nose to distinguish between Cleveland's influence and Cowley's on the taste for the far-fetched. From one or the other probably Marvell caught the trick of fantastic transformation. When Cleveland's Phillis walks,

> The trees like yeomen of her guard,
> Serving more for pomp than ward,
> Rank't on each side with loyall duty,
> Weave branches to inclose her beauty.
> The Plants whose luxurie was lopt,
> Or age with crutches underpropt;
> Whose wooden carkasses were grown
> To be but coffins of their owne;

---

2. For Cleveland's Royalism, see Loxley 1997, pp. 96–102, 121–23.

Revive, and at the generall dole
Each receives his antient soule.

('Upon *Phillis* walking', ll. 5–14)

Various points about the trees are pulled out into hyperbolical fictions around the charming woman: the trees grow in ranks, so they are a guard of honour, weaving their branches like swords crossed over the head of the honoured person; or they are aged and so cripples or even their own coffins (one notes the hyperbolical self-reflexive turn). We have seen this sort of panegyrical working up of details of a scene in 'Upon Appleton House'.

According to Aubrey, Cleveland was a friend of Samuel Butler. But his manner as a satirist is much simpler than Butler's. His most popular poem, 'The Rebell Scot', makes rough fun of the Scots for being hungry and coming into England to fight against their King for a meal. But in spite of a cannonade of witticisms ('Sure England hath the hemerods, and these / On the North Postern of the patient seize, / Like Leeches'), the satirist's attitude is uncomplicated honest indignation and contempt. In turning his flair for surprising comparisons to disfiguring the butt of his scorn, he shows no sensibility for the negative or involvement in a disturbing burlesque world.[3]

Dazzling display makes Cleveland an entertaining poet for a time. There is much more to Cowley. My notice of him will have to be brief and narrow in focus. The reader who wishes a more rounded treatment should go to Johnson's 'Life'.[4] Johnson's observations on the Metaphysicals, which seem to miss the point with Donne, are almost always just with Cowley. For him, Cowley was the significant Metaphysical, and the others were caught in relation to him as a tangle of wet branches shines in concentric rings round a streetlamp.

The Metaphysicals we have been considering at length all use an extravagant manner to communicate a singular experience. Even Herbert, the most gentlemanly and least wilful of them and, in a wholly admirable and disciplined sense, the most socialized, writes about supernatural visitings and communings of his heart with God; however much he puts himself on

---

3. But see Nigel Smith 1994, pp. 306–9, for Cleveland's 'zany word-games' and Loxley 1997. If we accept the ascription to Cleveland of the 'Epitaph on the Earl of Strafford', 'a poem unlike any of his genuine poems' (Cleveland 1967, p. xxxiv), then it must be said he could write altogether more seriously than I have suggested (see Gerald Hammond 1990, pp. 47–49). But according to the researches of Ann Sinnett on 'The Golden Remains of Dr Clement Paman', Harvard College MS. Eng. 1264, f. 41, it should be attributed to Paman, an attribution accepted by Davidson 1998, pp. 363, 547–48.

4. There is an admirable selection and introduction to his work in Cowley 1994.

Abraham Cowley, from a crayon drawing in the Library of Trinity College, Cambridge.
Courtesy of the Master and Fellows of Trinity College, Cambridge.

a footing with every Christian, there is something extraordinary about such discourse. And Marvell, for all his self-mockery, communicates distinctly odd privacies, even if we recognize them and are surprised by the sharpness of the recognition. Cowley, by contrast, situates himself in the shared world of men among other men. The character he presents is unassuming, convivial, with real sweetness – as Johnson put it, 'amiable'.[5] He is ambitious as a poet to be 'the *Muses Hannibal*' ('The Motto'), but his openness is engaging; he does not hug his ambition to himself with surly pride. He has his ecstasies, but these take a conventional form. He had read Longinus's *On the Sublime*, he was struck by classical, Renaissance and biblical accounts of mounting to the skies and does what is expected of a poet:

> I leave *Mortality*, and things below;
> I have no time in *Complements* to waste,
> > *Farewel* to' ye all in hast,
> > For I am *call'd* to go.
> A *Whirlwind* bears up my dull Feet,
> Th'officious *Clouds* beneath them meet.
> > And (Lo!) I *mount*, and (Lo!)
> How small the biggest Parts of *Earths* proud *Tittle* show![6]

Lo! indeed. His heroic fury is a social performance with a disarming air of naive surprise as he is snatched aloft from his friends like a baroque saint into the cumulo-nimbus. One feels he does not take his flight quite seriously or mean us to do so, and in comparison with Donne's 'Ecstasy', the result is not only not solemn and mysterious, but rather flat, if not bathetic. A similar flight, inspired by the Muse, claims to look prophetically into the future (as Virgil was thought to have done),

> > Where *Fates* among the *Stars* do grow;
> There into the close *Nests* of *Time* [thou, i.e. the Muse] do'st peep,
> > And there with piercing *Eye*,
> Through the firm *shell*, and thick *White* do'st spie,
> > *Years to come* a forming lie,
> Close in their *sacred Secondine* asleep,
> > Till *hatcht* by the *Suns* vital heat
> > Which o're them yet does *brooding* set
> They *Life* and *Motion* get,

---

5. Johnson 1952, I, p. 12; see also Hopkins and Mason, in Cowley 1994, p. xxvi.
6. 'The Extasie', st. 1. Citations of Cowley's poems (unless otherwise stated) are from Cowley 1905.

> And *ripe* at last with vigorous might
> Break through the *Shell*, and take their everlasting *Flight*.

> ('The Muse', st. 3)

This is myth-making. Unlike Donne and other Metaphysicals, who usually find the spiritual or supernatural disrupting or infusing the natural order, Cowley typically prefers an ordered cosmos in which the supernatural occupies the regions above and below the earth. So he needs a cosmic flight to spy into fate. But the way the sun is drawn into the nests of time by metaphoric exchange produces an effect of confused magnificence of which Donne might have been proud: the sun brings the future to being by measuring time, so its vital warmth can be supposed to incubate the eggs of fate, and perhaps there is a pun on 'set' appropriate to both the sun and fertilizing. But however magnificent the figure, it turns out rather disappointingly to be an allegory of a conventional idea, the poet as prophet.[7] Characteristically it is the idea that carries Cowley away. He cannot have imagined that he possessed or was possessed by the actuality and himself saw into the future. Even Cowley's idea of retreat, the occasion of so much peculiar inwardness in Marvell and Vaughan, is highly socialized. Informed by Horace, Virgil and Martial, his account of private and country life in his *Essays in Verse and Prose* is eminently a better sort of sociability and even solitude is more a retort to 'The Monster *London*' than a sinking into himself.

A lack of introspective depth need not be disabling to a poet. A lightness of touch in his wit, the absence of the curious strain and ambivalence prized in other Metaphysicals, allows Cowley to write very agreeably even when censorious. His address to London ends:

> Let but thy wicked men from out thee go,
>   And all the Fools that crowd the[e] so,
>   Even thou who dost thy Millions boast,
> A village less then Islington wilt grow,
>   A Solitude almost.[8]

The 'almost', in a poem praising solitude, half admits to having been immoderate in the desire to be alone and makes the last line comically smile and frown at once.

Not surprisingly, a poet who is always convivial, even in solitude, writes well to his friends alive or dead. His elegy 'On the Death of Mr Crashaw' is

---

7. See '*Sors Virgiliana*' in Cowley 1998, p. 13 and note; see also Johnson 1952, I, p. 6.
8. 'Of Solitude', st. 12, Cowley 1906, p. 397.

a particularly fine example of what he can do. On Crashaw's death at Loreto, he writes:

> *Angels* (they say) brought the fam'ed *Chappel* there,
> And bore the sacred Load in Triumph through the air.
> 'Tis surer much they brought thee there, and *They*,
> And *Thou*, their charge, went *singing* all the way.

Cowley's generosity and good sense come out admirably. He takes a sceptical view of the legend of the Virgin's house at Loreto and yet enters into Crashaw's imaginative etherealizing of sense. The alliteration on 'th' in the third and fourth lines assists in a splendid overbearing of rational objections with measured excess, which does not, however, obscure for him in the next paragraph the need to set down exactly how, as a Protestant, he can affirm that Crashaw's way to Loreto might be called angelic. Even when he appropriates Crashaw's manner by way of tribute, Cowley stands distinct from him. Where Crashaw, all fire and air, would simply have lost himself in the superhuman music, Cowley uses the magnificent figure of angelic transport to enlarge his admiration without surrendering consciousness of what humanly and reasonably may be said about his friend.[9] Lines such as these may have been what moved Pope to say of Cowley, 'I love the language of his heart'.[10] It is a heart that is the sounder for the rationality of the speaker.

Such claims cannot be made for Cowley's love poetry. *The Mistress* was probably modelled on Donne's Songs and Sonnets as a miscellany of love poems, and the echoes are certainly frequent. Above all, Cowley set out to equal Donne in the ingenuity of his conceits. But where Donne's ingenuities suggest an extravagant temperament and extravagant feelings, Cowley's suggest an equable temperament toying for some reason with unassertive feelings and the results are frigid. Donne's sort of love was unsociable. Yet it is not clear why Cowley could not adapt Donne's manner to the social amorousness to be found in Cleveland, Carew or Suckling.

For Addison, Cowley was the great exemplar of a vice of wit, 'mixed wit', and he drew his examples from *The Mistress*. 'Mixed wit' occurs when, in an analogy or metaphor, vehicle and tenor are run together with a sophistical effect.[11] In 'The Tree', Cowley's love is a flame (metaphor). He carves his love (metonymy) on a tree. The tree is withered by his flames (the vehicle operates literally, not metaphorically). This sort of sophistical wit was fully developed by Donne. In 'The Flea', the lovers are united because

---

9.   Trotter 1979, pp. 80–81.
10. 'First Epistle of the Second Book of Horace imitated', l. 78.
11. Addison 1965, p. 265.

the flea has sucked both their bloods (metonymy or synecdoche). It is therefore their marriage temple (metaphor). When the woman kills the flea, she
is guilty of the sacrilege of destroying a church (the vehicle is taken literally).
There are differences between Donne's practice and Cowley's. Donne's
figures are his own, whereas Cowley tortures a new fancy out of a stock
metaphor. Donne's conceits seem to be driven by a masterful argument,
while in Cowley the conceit seems to come first. The conceit, not the love
situation, is the source of his line of thought. Donne's conceits make longer
analogical flights; Cowley's aim at quicker, neater returns. But these differences do not explain the feebleness of Cowley's love poetry. In Marvell and
Crashaw, attenuations of Donne's bold style have their own vigour.

It is not Cowley's wit that is at fault. One need not share the Augustan
disapproval of mixed wit and its supple confusions. Besides, in a vein of wit
that should have met with Addison's approval Cowley writes with real
distinction. This is the metaphor or analogy that illustrates an idea with
clarity, elegance and force, a figure Pope cultivates in his *Essay on Criticism*.
Pope, in fact, reworked part of Cowley's 'Ode, of Wit':

> Yet 'tis not to adorn, and gild each part;
> > That shows more *Cost,* then *Art.*
> *Jewels* at *Nose* and *Lips* but ill appear;
> Rather then *all things Wit,* let *none* be there.
> > Several *Lights* will not be seen,
> > If there be nothing else between.
> Men doubt, because they stand so thick i' th' skie,
> If those be *Stars* which paint the *Galaxie.*

> ('Of Wit', st. 4)

> Some to *Conceit* alone their Taste confine,
> And glitt'ring Thoughts struck out in ev'ry Line;
> Pleas'd with a Work where nothing's just or fit;
> One *glaring Chaos* and *wild Heap of Wit*:
> Poets like Painters, thus, unskill'd to trace
> The *naked Nature* and the *living Grace,*
> With *Gold* and *Jewels* cover ev'ry Part
> And hide with *Ornaments* their *Want of Art.*
> . . .

> As Shades more sweetly recommend the Light,
> So modest Plainness sets off sprightly Wit.

> (*Essay on Criticism,* ll. 289–96; 301–302)

Pope's idea of nature and anxiety about disorder lend weight to his lines,
but Cowley's airy manner has an intellectual precision and concision that

Pope certainly did not better. Such wit goes with a kind of writing in which Cowley excelled, the exposition of ideas. The impressive poems in *The Mistress* are not expressions of love but poems analysing love and its attendant feelings and notions, poems such as 'Platonick Love', 'Against Hope' and 'For Hope'. Cowley writes with most assurance as a philosophical essayist in verse. The ideas of the Baconian movement of his time particularly lend themselves to his gifts, as in 'To the *Royal Society*', 'To Mr Hobs', 'The Tree of Knowledge' and 'Reason, the use of it in *Divine* Matters'.

Even those philosophical and scientific interests were convivial. During the Commonwealth and early Restoration, the critical movement of the mind was carried on by a close-knit group, and Cowley's intellectual interests went with his friendships with William Harvey, the discoverer of the circulation of the blood, Thomas Hobbes, the greatest political philosopher of his day, and Thomas Sprat, founding member and historian of the Royal Society; in him, advanced thinking combined with sociability.

Apart from Traherne, the Metaphysicals I have discussed at length did not generally take the propositional truth of their ideas into consideration. Alchemy, platonism, scholastic philosophy, were exploited figuratively for oblique expressions of desire or anxiety or involutions of these. But in some of Cowley, the mind is critically occupied with what may be truly affirmed. And less narrowly, he imagines a coherent universe and incorporates the science of his time into his imagining. So his translation of Virgil's Fourth Georgic fairly takes wing when it treats the secrets of nature, and wherever he can, he gives an up-to-date slant on Virgil's pictures. His imagination was kindled by optical effects and the analysis of light. He did not have a highly individual sensibility, and he was not a light mystic like Vaughan. The light he speaks of is a physical phenomenon, the subject of Isaac Newton's later inquiry into the spectrum. Here are two examples of his shining lucidity. In 'A *Reflection* made / From the false glories of a gay *reflected Bow*, / Is a more *solid* thing then [life]' ('Life and Fame', st. 1), life is a reflection of a reflection as the second bow of the rainbow reflects the first. In *The Davideis*, when David and Michol first see each other,

> Ev'en so (methinks) when two Fair *Tapers* come,
> From several Doors entring at once the Room,
> With a swift flight that leaves the Eye behind;
> Their *amorous Lights* into *one Light* are join'd.

> (Bk III, p. 343)

This analytic observation is worthy of Donne, but where he would have made it a figure for spiritual motion and interpenetration, Cowley with more simplicity and genial warmth leaves it as a figure for love at first sight.

267

Cowley's biblical epic, *The Davideis*, is unfinished. It is a heap of the magnificent and the trivial. He lacks the power to subordinate effects to an epic design, but he displays many other sorts of power in ill-organized prodigality, including the power to write vigorous political debate on the nature of kingship. I shall conclude with a passage that, having no bearing on the themes of conviviality or rational wit, will at least bring out the variousness of Cowley's gifts. It is a showy baroque set piece describing a picture of Lot's wife turning to a pillar of salt:

> No more a *Woman*, not yet quite a *Stone*.
> A lasting *Death* seiz'd on her turning head;
> One cheek was rough and white, the other red,
> And yet a *Cheek*; in vain to speak she strove;
> Her lips, though stone, a little seem'd to move.
> One eye was clos'ed, surpris'ed by sudden night,
> The other trembled still with parting light.
> The wind admir'ed which her hair loosely bore,
> Why it grew stiff, and now would play no more.
> To heav'en she lifted up her freezing hands,
> And to this day a *Suppliant Pillar* stands.
> She try'ed her heavy foot from ground to rear,
> And rais'd the *Heel*, but her *Toe's* rooted there.
> Ah foolish woman! who must always be,
> A sight more *strange* then that she turn'd to see!

(Bk III, p. 330)

The play of antithesis through his couplets, now one thing, now the other, captures the moment of change. One is reminded of Bernini's statue of Daphne becoming laurel. And then in the concluding couplet, with characteristic self-deflating amusement, Cowley turns from his display of virtuosity.

Metaphysical and Augustan

I do not intend to describe the historical development of the Augustan style, a subject at once complex and indefinite.[12] Yet I should offer some comment on what happened to writing in the Metaphysical style after the Restoration.

---

12. Leavis's account, based on the insights of Eliot's essays on 'The Metaphysicals' and 'Andrew Marvell' is 'The Line of Wit' (Leavis 1936); it is filled out in Walton 1955; see also Miner 1974.

Certainly Metaphysical poetry did not disappear with the advent of Charles II. Traherne was a Restoration writer, if largely unpublished. John Norris of Bemerton was still writing devotional poems in a manner influenced by Herbert and Crashaw in the 1680s, as was Edward Taylor in Massachussetts till 1725. And if Marvell's 'Garden' was written in the 1660s, possibly some of his other short non-satirical pieces were as well. Still it must be granted that Metaphysical writing rapidly became unfashionable. Butler, the crony of Cleveland, associated conceited styles with the Presbyterians and the Sectaries, with the politics of conscience and the inner light. In view of the fact that most Metaphysical poets were Royalist and anti-Puritan, this is a partisan twist.[13] Butler probably intended to typify what he saw as a general madness of the recent past with broad strokes. Presbyterians were mad, Sectaries were mad, enthusiasm and extravagant styles were mad and nice distinctions would spoil the fun. Cowley himself turned to more rationally accountable forms of wit, and Dryden, who Clevelandized absurdly on the death of Lord Hastings in 1649, by 1667 had come to a critically formulated rejection of Cleveland's kind of conceits.[14]

Interiority went out of fashion. Of course, it had never been the only or even the dominant character of writing about love or religion. But distinctly the prevailing social tone of Restoration writing ruled out private intensities. As a love poet, Rochester does not write a history of an emotion or I-centred dramatizings of mixed feelings. His feelings and his expression of them are uninvoluted. And while the contradictions of the character he bears as poet are fascinating, he speaks – plaindealer, scoundrel, man of feeling – more as a moralist or commentator on the social game of love than as someone caught up in its privacies. As for religious poetry, if we may take Dryden's *Religio Laici* or *Hind and the Panther* as representative, individual prayer gave way to public argument on the authority in religion. If the despair and repentance of the heroes of Milton's great poems witness against this generalization, it is easy to reply that Milton's achievement stands in splendid isolation.

As Cleveland and Cowley show, it was possible to write convivially in the Metaphysical style, but Cowley at least trimmed and disciplined its sportings. I shall conclude with a few observations on the Augustan reform of wit. These conform to the familiar story of how fancy was made more accountable to a rational examination of the world and how sensibility not only became less individual but more systematically developed in large public designs, as in Pope's reductions of unaccountable play of mind to spleen or the taste for dullness. Addison wrote a series of papers for the *Spectator* setting down

---

13. Butler 1967, pt 1, canto 1, ll. 65–234. See Keeble 1998, pp. 78–81, and cf. Parker 1670, p. 75, cited, Pooley 1980, p. 7.
14. 'An Essay of Dramatic Poesy' (1668), Dryden 1900, I, pp. 52–53.

what became received distinctions between true and false wit. The fifth (11 May 1711), the most substantial and original, starts with Locke's opposition between wit that draws resemblances and judgement that makes distinctions, and ends by suggesting that true wit may combine with judgement in turning distinctions with the neatness and surprise of antithesis.[15] Cowley had already arrived at the Augustan way of casting his thought in couplets into antitheses, though an antithetical gait never dominated his style. And neither his antitheses nor Dryden's aim at the sharp distinctions that Addison seems to have had in mind and Congreve's heroes use to set themselves up as masters of situations.[16] Cowley's, Dryden's and indeed Pope's general use of antithesis is more rhetorical than cognitive; it arranges thought in neat oppositions so that ideas may be communicated with elasticity and energy. In Dryden's 'For Lavish grants suppose a Monarch tame, / And more his Goodness than his Wit proclaim' (*Absalom and Achitophel*, ll. 385–86), it is not so much that goodness (good-nature) and wit (acumen) are being distinguished, as that the two key notions of Dryden's Davidic monarchy are being played off against each other by the scheming Achitophel to suggest that the King's good-nature is feeble-minded.[17]

Metaphysicals sometimes make a lot of play of binary oppositions, but they turn them toward paradox rather than antithesis: 'There should I see a sun, by rising set', 'Sommer in Winter. Day in Night!'. The oppositions are as broad as possible because Metaphysical paradoxes aim to suspend the natural order. In Augustan antitheses, where fineness of judgement is prized, oppositions are much narrower and less obvious. Nor did Augustans cultivate paradox. In Pope at any rate paradox is either bogus ('sleepless Lovers, just at Twelve, awake') or intentionally inane (as with the scissors that the Baron in *The Rape of the Lock* opens 'wide / T'inclose the Lock; now joins ... to divide' [III, 147–48]).

Paradox survived as a device of satirical irony. The conceit survived in the same way. The analogies between the reign of the biblical David and the reign of Charles II in *Absalom and Achitophel* (ironic, if not diminishing), between the epic and the concerns of the *beau monde* in *The Rape of the Lock*, between the epic again and the concerns of Grub Street in *The Dunciad*, bear a resemblance to Donne's ingenious procedures in 'The Flea'. Of course, these plays on the Bible or the epic are much more sustained and systematic

---

15. Addison 1965, pp. 266–67.
16. Pope uses antithesis to differentiate from envy and ill-nature Miss Blount's grief at leaving the parties in London: 'She sigh'd not that They stay'd, but that She went' ('Epistle to Miss Blount on her Leaving the Town after the Coronation'); see also the remarkable passage of self-analysis in 'Eloisa to Abelard', ll. 181–94.
17. Dryden 1962.

than any Metaphysical conceit, perhaps more like allegory, yet still delighting in incongruity, surprise and inversion.

Incongruous comparison was out of favour for serious purposes but flourished in burlesque. There is already a burlesque element in the non-satirical conceits of Marvell and certainly in his satirical ones, and also in Cleveland.[18] Butler made the incongruous comparison his special vein of burlesque humour: 'And like a *Lobster* boyl'd, the *Morn* / From *black* to *red* began to turn' (*Hudibras*, II, canto 2, ll. 31–32). In Donne, incongruous comparison suggests a mind jolted out of the way of the world and conventional orderings of experience. Butler's joke, by contrast, plays on a developed social ordering of things into high and low: sunrise occupies a dignified station, the cooking of lobsters in a kitchen a low one. To bring the two orders of things together at once is anarchic and confirms the norms that anarchy overturns. With much finer fun, Pope writes in *An Essay on Criticism*,

> 'Tis with our *Judgements* as our *Watches*, none
> Go just *alike*, yet each believes his own.

> (ll. 9–10)

Human judgement occupies a dignified station, a watch a trivial one. To compare consulting a watch with consulting one's judgement is delightfully to reduce human pretension, an effect enhanced by the suggestion of unsynchronized ticking brought out by the unusual run-over line and pauses.

Even mixed wit survived in burlesque form. In *The Dunciad*, the goddess Dullness

> beholds the Chaos dark and deep,
> Where nameless somethings in their causes sleep,
> 'Till genial Jacob, or a warm Third-day
> Call forth each mass, a poem or a play.

> (I, ll. 53–56)

Jacob Tonson, 'the leading publisher of his generation', was no doubt genial or good-natured in publishing rubbish, but there is a quibble on 'genial': Tonson is like Jacob, the father of the Children of Israel, in his generative power and incubates on Chaos a host of embryonic somethings. Dullness beholding Chaos is an allegory of the stupidity and uncreativity that Pope saw in contemporary literary culture. Tonson, part of that literary culture,

---

18.　See Leishman 1966, p. 215.

is part of the tenor signified by the allegorical vehicle. A piece of reality has invaded the allegorical fiction. Although the match is not exact, this shares with Cowley's flames of love in 'The Tree' a dissolving of the figurative frame into the figured to produce a fantastic event: Cowley's flames of love killed the tree; Pope's publisher has been taken over by demonic powers.

'The Taste of most of our *English* Poets, as well as Readers, is extremely *Gothick*', wrote Addison, meaning by '*Gothick*', 'extravagant and flimsy in conception'.[19] The incongruity, paradoxes and mixed wit of Metaphysical poets would all fall under this censure. Pope might indulge in this sort of Gothic, however, in his satirical anti-worlds. If we wish to speak of a line of wit between Metaphysical and Augustan, we might add that the Metaphysicals themselves were never more bizarre and fantastic than Pope in his perverse creations. And yet obviously something has been lost in the satirical Gothic. There Pope combines intellect and fancy, like the Metaphysicals I have discussed at length, but he does so for absurdity, while they, ranging more daringly, express a strained sense of being in the world arising from their highly individual quarrels with the world and with themselves.

---

19.   Addison 1965, p. 269.

BIBLIOGRAPHY

Primary

Addison, Joseph, 1965, *The Spectator*, 62 (11 May 1711), ed. Donald F. Bond, vol. 1, Oxford, pp. 263–70

Aubrey, John, 1949, *Brief Lives and Other Selected Writings*, ed. Anthony Powell, London

Beaumont, Joseph, 1967, *Psyche* (1648; 2nd edn, 1702), in *The Complete Poems of Joseph Beaumont*, ed. Alexander B. Grossart, 2 vols, New York (rept. of London, 1880 edn)

Benlowes, Edward, 1905, *Theophila* (1652), in *Minor Poets of the Caroline Period*, ed. George Saintsbury, vol. I, Oxford

Browne, Sir Thomas 1964, *Religio Medici and Other Works*, ed. L. C. Martin, Oxford

Burns, Robert, 1969, *Poems and Songs*, ed. James Kinsley, Oxford

Butler, Samuel, 1759, *Genuine Remains in Verse and Prose*, ed. R. Thyer, 2 vols, London

——, 1967, *Hudibras*, ed. John Wilders, Oxford

Carew, Thomas, 1949, *The Poems of Thomas Carew with his Masque* Coelum Britannicum, ed. Rhodes Dunlap, Oxford

Castiglione, Baldassare, 1959, *The Book of the Courtier*, trans. Charles Singleton, New York

Cleveland, John, 1967, *The Poems of John Cleveland*, ed. Brian Morris and Eleanor Withington, Oxford

Cowley, Abraham, 1905, *Poems*, ed. A. R. Waller, Cambridge

——, 1906, *Essays and Plays of Abraham Cowley*, ed. A. R. Waller, Cambridge

——, 1994, *Selected Poems of Abraham Cowley*, ed. David Hopkins and Tom Mason, Manchester

——, 1998, *Selected Poems of Abraham Cowley, Edmund Waller, John Oldham*, ed. Julia Griffin, Harmondsworth

Crashaw, Richard, 1957, *The Poems, English, Latin and Greek, of Richard Crashaw*, ed. L. C. Martin, 2nd edn, Oxford

——, 1970, *The Complete Poetry of Richard Crashaw*, ed. George Walton Williams, Garden City, N.Y.

Donne, John, 1610, *Pseudo-Martyr*, London

——, 1648, *Biathanatos, A declaration of that paradoxe . . . that Self-homicide is not so Naturally a Sinne, that it may never be otherwise*, London

——, 1930, *The Courtier's Library or Catalogus Librorum Aulicorum*, ed. Evelyn Mary Simpson, London

——, 1953–62, *The Sermons of John Donne*, ed. George R. Potter and Evelyn M. Simpson, 10 vols, Berkeley and Los Angeles

——, 1965, *John Donne: The Elegies and The Songs and Sonnets*, ed. Helen Gardner, Oxford

——, 1971, *The Complete English Poems*, ed. A. J. Smith, Harmondsworth

——, 1978, *The Divine Poems of John Donne*, ed. Helen Gardner, Oxford

——, 1990, *John Donne*, ed. John Carey, Oxford

Drummond, William, 1913, *The Poetical Works of William Drummond of Hawthornden*, ed. L. E. Kastner, 2 vols, Edinburgh

Dryden, John, 1900, *A Discourse Concerning the Original and Progress of Satire* (1693), in *The Essays of John Dryden*, ed. W. P. Ker, vol. II, Oxford

——, 1900, 'An Essay of Dramatic Poesy' (1667), in *The Essays of John Dryden*, ed. W. P. Ker, vol. I, Oxford

——, 1962, *The Poems and Fables of John Dryden*, ed. James Kinsley, Oxford

Greville, Fulke, 1968, *Caelica*, XXII, *Selected Poems*, ed. Thom Gunn, London

Herbert, Lord Edward, of Cherbury, 1900, *The Autobiography of Edward, Lord Herbert of Cherbury*, ed. Sidney Lee, New York

Herbert, George, 1941, *The Works of George Herbert*, ed. F. E. Hutchinson, Oxford

——, 1974, *The English Poems of George Herbert*, ed. C. A. Patrides, London

Herrick, Robert, 1956, *The Poetical Works of Robert Herrick*, ed. L. C. Martin, Oxford

Johnson, Samuel, 1952, *Lives of the Poets*, 2 vols, Oxford

Jonson, Ben, 1975, *The Complete Poems of Ben Jonson*, ed. George Parfitt, Harmondsworth

Lucretius, Carus Titus, 1994, *On the Nature of the Universe*, trans. R. E. Latham, Harmondsworth

Marvell, Andrew, 1964, *The Latin Poetry of Andrew Marvell*, trans. William A. McQueen and Kiffin A. Rockwell, Chapel Hill

——, 1971a, *The Poems and Letters of Andrew Marvell*, vol. I, *The Poems*, 3rd edn, ed. H. M. Margoliouth, rev., Pierre Legouis with E. E. Duncan-Jones, Oxford

——, 1971b, *The Rehearsal Transpros'd and The Rehearsal Transpros'd The Second Part*, ed. D. I. B. Smith, Oxford

——, 1972, *Andrew Marvell, The Complete Poems*, ed. Elizabeth Storey Donno, Harmondsworth

Milton, John, 1997, *John Milton: Complete Shorter Poems*, ed. John Carey, London

Montaigne, Michel, Sieur de, 1962, *Oeuvres Complètes*, ed. Albert Thibaudet and Maurice Rat, Paris

Oldham, John, 1960, *The Poems of John Oldham*, ed. J. M. Cohen, London

Ovid, 1982, *The Erotic Poems*, trans. Peter Green, Harmondsworth

Parker, Samuel, 1670, *Discourse of Ecclesiastical Politie*, London

Plato, 1993, *Phaedo*, trans. David Gallop, Oxford

Pona, Francesco, 1645, *Cardiomorphoseos sive ex Corde desumpta Emblemata sacra*, Verona

Rutherford, Samuel, 1727, *Christ Dying and Drawing Sinners to Himself*, 2nd edn, Edinburgh

Saint Teresa, 1957, *The Life of St Teresa of Avila*, trans. J. M. Cohen, Harmondsworth

Sidney, Sir Philip, 1962, *The Poems of Sir Philip Sidney*, ed. William A. Ringler, Oxford

Spenser, Edmund, 1910, *Edmund Spenser: The Minor Poems*, *The Poetical Works of Edmund Spenser*, vol. I, ed. Ernest de Selincourt, London

Suckling, Sir John, 1953, *Minor Poets of the Seventeenth Century*, ed. R. G. Howarth, London

Traherne, Thomas, 1958, *Centuries, Poems and Thanksgivings*, ed. H. M. Margoliouth, 2 vols, Oxford

——, 1980, *Selected Writings*, ed. Dick Davis, Manchester

——, 1991, *Selected Poems and Prose*, ed. Alan Bradford, Harmondsworth

——, 1997, *Select Meditations*, ed. Julia J. Smith, Manchester

van Veen, Otto, 1608, *Amorum Emblemata*, Antwerp

Vaughan, Henry, 1963, *The Works of Henry Vaughan*, ed. L. C. Martin, 2nd edn, Oxford

Voragine, Jacobus de, 1504, *Legenda . . . aurea*, Lyons

Walton, Izaak, 1927, *The Lives of John Donne, Sir Henry Wotton, Richard Hooker, George Herbert and Robert Sanderson*, ed. George Saintsbury, London

Ward, Richard, 1710, *The Life of the Learned and Pious Dr Henry More*, London

Zincgref, Julius Wilhelm, 1619, *Emblematicum Ethico-politicorum Centuria*, Heidelberg

Secondary

Aers, David, 1992, 'A Whisper in the Ear of Early Modernists; or Reflections on Literary Critics Writing the "History of the Subject"', in *Culture and History, 1350–1600: Essays on English Communities, Identities and Writing*, ed. David Aers, Detroit, pp. 177–202

Aers, David, and Gunther Kress, 1981, '"Vexatious Contraries": A Reading of Donne's Poetry', in *Literature and Society in England, 1580–1680*, ed. David Aers, Bob Hodge and Gunther Kress, Dublin and Totowa, pp. 49–74

——, 1994, '"Darke Texts Need Notes": Versions of Self in Donne's Verse Epistles', in *Critical Essays on John Donne*, ed. Arthur Marotti, New York, pp. 102–22

Allison, A. F., 1947, 'Some Influences in Crashaw's Poem "On A Prayer Booke Sent to Mrs M. R."', *Review of English Studies*, 23, 34–42

——, 1948, 'Crashaw and St François de Sales', *Review of English Studies*, 24, 295–302

Austin, Frances, 1992, *The Language of the Metaphysical Poets*, Basingstoke

Baker-Smith, Dominic, 1972, 'John Donne's Critique of true Religion' in *John Donne: Essays in Celebration*, ed. A. J. Smith, London, pp. 404–32

Bald, R. C., 1970, *John Donne: A Life*, Oxford

Beier, Nahla M., 1994, 'Irresolvable Dialectics: Donne's Sense of Disunity', *Explorations in Renaissance Culture*, 20, 127–41

Bennett, Joan, 1964, *Five Metaphysical Poets*, Cambridge

Bird, Michael, 1984, 'Nowhere but in the Dark: On the Poetry of Vaughan', *English*, 33, 1–20

Bradbrook, M. C., and M. G. Lloyd-Thomas, 1940, *Andrew Marvell*, Cambridge

Bradshaw, Graham, 1982, 'Donne's Challenge to the Prosodists', *Essays in Criticism*, 32, 338–60

Brooks, Cleanth, 1969, 'Marvell's "Horatian Ode"', *English Institute Essays*, 1947, in *Andrew Marvell: A Critical Anthology*, ed. John Carey, Harmondsworth, pp. 127–58

Bush, Douglas, 1962, *English Literature in the Early Seventeenth Century, 1600–1660*, 2nd edn, Oxford

——, 1969, 'Marvell's "Horatian Ode"', *Sewanee Review*, 60 (1952) in *Andrew Marvell: A Critical Anthology*, ed. John Carey, Harmondsworth, pp. 199–210

Camden, Vera J., 1983, 'Crashaw's Poetry: The Imagery of Bleeding Wounds', *American Imago*, 40, 257–79

Carey, John, 1978, 'Reversals Transposed: An Aspect of Marvell's Imagination', in *Approaches to Marvell: The York Tercentenary Lectures*, ed. C. A. Patrides, London, pp. 136–54

——, 1990, *John Donne: Life, Mind, Art*, 2nd edn, London

Chambers, Leland H., 1968, 'Vaughan's "The World": The Limits of Extrinsic Criticism', *Studies in English Literature*, 8, 137–50

Charles, Amy, 1977, *A Life of George Herbert*, Ithaca

Chernaik, Warren, 1983, *The Poet's Time: Politics and Religion in the Work of Andrew Marvell*, Cambridge

Christopher, Georgia B., 1973, 'In Arcadia, Calvin . . . : A Study of Nature in Henry Vaughan', *Studies in Philology*, 70, 408–26

Clarke, Elizabeth, 1997, *Theory and Theology in George Herbert's Poetry: 'Divinitie and Poesie Met'*, Oxford

Clements, A. L., 1964, 'On the Meaning and Mode of Traherne's Mystical Poetry: "The Preparative"', *Studies in Philology*, 61, 500–21

Coolidge, John S., 1965–66, 'Marvell and Horace', *Modern Philology*, 63, 111–20

Danielson, Dennis Richard, 1982, *Milton's Good God: A Study in Literary Theodicy*, Cambridge

Davidson, Peter, ed., 1998, *Poetry and Revolution: An Anthology of British and Irish Verse, 1625–1660*, Oxford

Davies, Julian, 1992, *The Caroline Captivity of the Church of England: Charles I and the Remoulding of Anglicanism, 1625–1641*, Oxford

Davies, Stevie, 1995, *Henry Vaughan*, Bridgend, Mid Glamorgan

Donno, Elizabeth Storey, ed., 1978, *Andrew Marvell: The Critical Heritage*, London

Duncan-Jones, Elsie, 1975, 'Marvell: A Great Master of Words', *Proceedings of the British Academy*, 61, 267–90

Duncan-Jones, Elsie Elizabeth, 1990, 'Who was the Recipient of Crashaw's Leyden Letter?', in *New Perspectives on the Life and Art of Richard Crashaw*, ed. John R. Roberts, Columbia and London, pp. 174–79

——, 1995, 'Marvell, R. F. and the Authorship of "Blake's Victory"', *English MS Studies*, 5, 107–26

Eliot, T. S., 1927, 'The Silurist', *The Dial*, 83, 259–63

——, 1932, 'Andrew Marvell', *Selected Essays*, London, pp. 292–304

——, 1963, *The Collected Poems*, London

Ellrodt, Robert, 1960, *L'inspiration personelle et l'esprit du temps chez les Poètes Métaphysiques Anglais*, 3 vols, Paris

Empson, William, 1935, *Some Versions of Pastoral*, London

——, 1953, *Seven Types of Ambiguity*, 3rd edn, London

——, 1984, *Using Biography*, London

——, 1993, *Essays in Renaissance Literature*, Vol. I, *Donne and the New Philosophy*, Cambridge

Everett, Barbara, 1972, 'Donne: A London Poet', *Proceedings of the British Academy*, 58, 245–73

——, 1979, 'The Shooting of Bears: Poetry and Politics in Andrew Marvell', in *Andrew Marvell: Essays on the Tercentenary of his Death*, ed. R. L. Brett, Oxford, pp. 62–103

Ferry, Anne, 1983, *The 'Inward' Language: Sonnets of Wyatt, Sidney, Shakespeare, Donne*, Chicago

——, 1993, 'Titles in George Herbert's "little book"', *English Literary Renaissance*, 23, 314–44

Fischer, Sandra K., 1983, 'Crashaw, Ste. Teresa, and the Icon of Mystical Ravishment', *Journal of Evolutionary Psychology*, 4, 182–95

Fish, Stanley E., 1972, 'The Dialectics of the Self in Herbert's Poetry', *Self-Consuming Artefacts: The Experience of Seventeenth Century Literature*, Berkeley

Fitter, Chris, 1992, 'Henry Vaughan's Landscapes of Occupation', *Essays in Criticism*, 42, 123–47

Flynn, Dennis, 1989, 'Donne and the Ancient Catholic Nobility', *English Literary Renaissance*, 19, 305–23

Foucault, Michel, 1979, *Discipline and Punish: The Birth of the Prison*, trans. Alan Sheridan, Harmondsworth

Freer, Coburn, 1979, 'Mirth in Funeral: Crashaw and the Pleasures of Grief', in *Essays on Richard Crashaw*, ed. Robert M. Cooper, Salzburg Studies in English Literature, 83, Salzburg, pp. 78–101

Gill, Roma, 1972, '"Musa jocosa mea": Thoughts on the Elegies', in *John Donne: Essays in Celebration*, ed. A. J. Smith, London, pp. 47–72

Gosse, Edmund, 1889, *The Life and Letters of John Donne*, 2 vols, London

Guibbory, Achsah, 1998, *Ceremony and Community from Herbert to Milton: Literature, Religion, and Cultural Conflict in Seventeenth Century England*, Cambridge

Hammond, Gerald, 1990, *Fleeting Things: English Poets and Poems, 1616–1660*, Cambridge, Mass.

Hammond, Paul, 1988, 'Dryden's Use of Marvell's "Horatian Ode"', *Notes & Queries*, 35, 173–74

——, 1998, 'Marvell's Sexuality', in *Andrew Marvell*, ed. Thomas Healy, Harlow, pp. 170–204

Harman, Barbara Leah, 1982, *Costly Monuments: The Representation of the Self in George Herbert's Poetry*, Cambridge, Mass.

Healy, Thomas F., 1986, *Richard Crashaw*, Leiden

Hesla, David H., 1971, *The Shape of Chaos: An Interpretation of the Art of Samuel Beckett*, Minneapolis

Hill, Christopher, 1985, *The Collected Essays*, vol. I, *Writing and Revolution in England*, Brighton

Hill, Geoffrey, 1991, *The Enemy's Country: Words, Contexture and Other Circumstances of Language*, Oxford

Hodge, R. I. V., 1973–74, 'Marvell's Fairfax Poems: Some Considerations Concerning Dates', *Modern Philology*, 5, 347–55

Hodgkins, Christopher, 1993, *Authority, Church and Society in George Herbert: Return to the Middle Way*, Columbia

Hutchinson, F. E., 1947, *Henry Vaughan: A Life and Interpretation*, Oxford

Jordan, Richard Douglas, 1982, 'Thomas Traherne and the Authorship of *Daily Devotions*', *Yale English Studies*, 12, 218–25

Keeble, N. H., 1982, *Richard Baxter: Puritan Man of Letters*, Oxford

——, 1990, '"I would not tell you any tales": Marvell's Constituency Letters', in *The Political Identity of Andrew Marvell*, ed. Conal Condren and A. D. Cousins, Aldershot, pp. 111–34

——, 1998, '"When Civil Fury first grew high, / And men fell out they knew not why . . .": *Hudibras* and the Making of History', *Literature and History*, 7, 70–87

Kelly, Kathleen, 1990, 'Narcissus in *Paradise Lost* and *Upon Appleton House*: Disenchanting the Renaissance Lyric' in *Traditions and Innovation: Essays on British Literature of the Middle Ages and the Renaissance*, ed. David G. Allen and Robert A. White, Newark, pp. 200–13

Kermode, Frank, 1969, 'The Argument of Marvell's "Garden"', *Essays in Criticism*, 2 (1952), 325–41, in *Andrew Marvell: A Critical Anthology*, ed. John Carey, Harmondsworth, pp. 263–64

Klause, John, 1994, 'Hope's Gambit: The Jesuitical, Protestant, Skeptical Origins of Donne's Heroic Ideal', *Studies in Philology*, 91, 181–215.

Knights, L. C., 1951, *Explorations*, Basingstoke

Lake, Peter, 1991, 'Lancelot Andrewes, John Buckeridge and Avant-garde Conformity at the Court of James I', in *The Mental World of the Jacobean Court*, ed. Linda Levy Peck, Cambridge, pp. 113–33

Lamont, William, 1990, 'The Religion of Andrew Marvell: Locating the "Bloody Horse"', in *The Political Identity of Andrew Marvell*, ed. Conal Condren and A. D. Cousins, Aldershot, pp. 135–36

Larkin, Philip, 1983, *Required Writing: Miscellaneous Pieces, 1955–82*, London

Lawrence, D. H., 1936, 'Introduction to these Paintings', *Phoenix: The Posthumous Papers of D. H. Lawrence*, ed. Edward D. McDonald, London, pp. 551–84

Leavis, F. R., 1936, *Revaluation: Tradition and Development in English Poetry*, London
——, 1968, 'The Responsible Critic, or the Function of Criticism at any Time' and a 'Rejoinder', *Scrutiny* (1953), in *A Selection from* Scrutiny, ed. F. R. Leavis, Cambridge, vol. 2, pp. 280–303, 308–16

Legouis, Pierre, 1928, *Donne, the Craftsman*, Paris
——, 1968, *Andrew Marvell: Poet, Puritan, Patriot*, Oxford

Leimberg, Inge, 1995–96, 'The Myth of the Self in Whitman's "Song of Myself" and Traherne's "Thanksgivings": A Hypothesis', *Connotations: A Journal for Critical Debate*, 5, 167–86

Leishman, J. B., 1966, *The Art of Marvell's Poetry*, London

Lennard, John, 1991, *But I Digress: The Exploitation of Parenthesis in English Printed Verse*, Oxford

Lewalski, Barbara Kiefer, 1979, *Protestant Poetics and the Seventeenth-Century Religious Lyric*, Princeton, N.J.

Loxley, James, 1995, ' "Prepar'd at Last to Strike in with the Tyde?" Andrew Marvell and Royalist Verse', *The Seventeenth Century*, 10, 31–62
——, 1997, *Royalism and Poetry in the English Civil War: The Drawn Sword*, London

Mackenzie, Donald, 1990, *The Metaphysical Poets*, Basingstoke

Marcus, Leah Sinanaglou, 1978, *Childhood and Cultural Despair: A Theme and Variations in Seventeenth Century Literature*, Pittsburgh

Marks, Carol L., 1966, 'Thomas Traherne and Cambridge Platonism', *Publications of the Modern Language Association*, 81, 521–34

Martz, Louis L., 1962, *The Poetry of Meditation: A Study of English Religious Literature of the Seventeenth Century*, rev. edn, New Haven

Matar, N. I., 1994, 'The Political Views of Thomas Traherne', *Hunterian Library Quarterly*, 57, 241–53

Maycock, A. L., 1938, *Nicholas Ferrar of Little Gidding*, London

McClung, William A., 1977, *The Country House Poem in English Renaissance Poetry*, Berkeley

Meres, Francis, 1598, *Palladis Thamia*, London

Miner, Earl, 1969, *The Metaphysical Mode from Donne to Cowley*, Princeton, N.J.

——, 1971, *The Cavalier Mode from Jonson to Cotton*, Princeton, N.J.

——, 1974, *The Restoration Mode*, Princeton, N.J.

Morrill, J. S, 1993, *The Nature of the English Revolution*, London

Newton, J. M., 1972a, 'What do we know about Andrew Marvell?', *Cambridge Quarterly*, 6, 32–42

——, 1972b, 'What do we know about Andrew Marvell?: Further Notes', *Cambridge Quarterly*, 6, 125–43

Nicolson, Marjorie Hope, 1950, *The Breaking of the Circle: Studies in the Effect of the New Science upon Seventeenth Century Poetry*, Evanston, Illinois, pp. 73–79

Norbrook, David, 1990a, 'Marvell's "Horatian Ode" and the Politics of Genre', in *Literature and The English Civil War*, ed. Thomas Healy and Jonathan Sawday, Cambridge, pp. 147–69

——, 1990b, 'The Monarchy of Wit and the Republic of Letters: Donne's Politics', in *Soliciting Interpretation: Literary Theory and Seventeenth Century English Poetry*, ed. Elizabeth D. Harvey and Katharine Eisaman Maus, Chicago, pp. 3–36

——, 1999, *Writing the English Republic: Poetry, Rhetoric and Politics, 1627–1660*, Cambridge

Norris, John, of Bemerton, 1871, *Poems*, ed. A. B. Grossart, London

Novarr, David, 1980, *The Disinterred Muse: Donne's Texts and Contexts*, Ithaca

Nowottny, Winifred, 1969, *The Language Poets Use* (1962), in *Andrew Marvell: A Critical Anthology*, ed. John Carey, Harmondsworth, pp. 314–16

Nuttall, A. D., 1980, *Overheard by God: Fiction and Prayer in Herbert, Milton, Dante and St John*, London

Oliver, Paul M. 1997, *Donne's Religious Writing: A Discourse of Feigned Devotion*, London

Palliser, Mrs Bury, 1870, *Historic Devices, Badges, and War-Cries*, London

Panofsky, Erwin, 1955, *The Life and Art of Albrecht Dürer*, 4th edn, Princeton, N.J.

Parfitt, George, 1992, *English Poetry of the Seventeenth Century*, 2nd edn, London

Patterson, Annabel, 1990a, 'Miscellaneous Marvell?' in *The Political Identity of Andrew Marvell*, ed. Conal Condren and A. D. Cousins, Aldershot, pp. 201–3

——, 1990b, 'All Donne', in *Soliciting Interpretation: Literary Theory and Seventeenth Century English Poetry*, ed. Elizabeth D. Harvey and Katharine Eisaman Maus, Chicago, pp. 37–67

——, 1991, 'John Donne Kingsman?', in *The Mental World of the Jacobean Court*, ed. Linda Levy Peck, Cambridge, pp. 251–72

Pebworth, Ted-Larry, 1992, '"Let me Here Use that Freedome": Subversive Representation in John Donne's "Obsequies to the Lord Harrington"', *Journal of English and Germanic Philology*, 91, 17–42

Petersson, Robert Torsten, 1970, *The Art of Ecstasy: Teresa, Bernini, and Crashaw*, London

Pooley, Roger, 1980, 'Language and Loyalty: Plain Style at the Restoration', *Literature and History*, 6, 2–18

Praz, Mario, 1958, *The Flaming Heart: Essays on Crashaw, Machiavelli, and Other Studies in the Relations between Italian and English Literature from Chaucer to T. S. Eliot*, New York

Pritchard, Allan 1983, 'Marvell's "The Garden": A Restoration Poem?', *Studies in English Literature*, 23, 371–88

Randall, Dale B. J., 1992, 'Once More to the G(r)ates: An Old Crux and a New Reading of "To His Coy Mistress"', in *On the Celebrated and Neglected Poems of Andrew Marvell*, ed. Claude J. Summers and Ted-Larry Pebworth, Columbia, pp. 47–69

Ricks, Christopher, 1978, ' "Its Own Resemblance" ', in *Approaches to Marvell: The York Tercentenary Lectures*, ed. C. A. Patrides, London, pp. 108–35

——, 1996, 'John Donne: Farewell to Love', *Essays in Appreciation*, Oxford, pp. 19–50

Røstvig, Maren-Sofie 1962, *The Happy Man*, 2 vols, Oslo

Schleiner, Louise, 1979, 'Song Mode in Crashaw', *Essays on Richard Crashaw*, ed. Robert M. Cooper, Salzburg Studies in English Literature, 83, Salzburg, pp. 145–68

Schoenfeldt, Michael, 1991, *Prayer and Power: George Herbert and Renaissance Courtship*, Chicago

Schwenger, Peter, 1974, 'Marvell's "Unfortunate Lover" as Device', *Modern Language Quarterly*, 35, 364–75

——, 1976, 'Crashaw's Perspectivist Metaphor', *Comparative Literature*, 28, 65–74

Shrapnel, S. E., 1971, 'The Poetry of Andrew Marvell in Relation to his Contemporaries and Contemporary History', University of Nottingham Ph.D. Dissertation

Shullenberger, William, 1993, 'Love as a Spectator Sport in John Donne's Poetry', in *Renaissance Discourses of Desire*, ed. Claude J. Summers and Ted-Larry Pebworth, Columbia, pp. 46–62

Singleton, Marion White, 1987, *God's Courtier: Configuring a Different Grace in George Herbert's Temple*, Cambridge

Smith, A. J., 1991, *Metaphysical Wit*, Cambridge

Smith, A. J., ed. 1975, *John Donne: The Critical Heritage*, London

Smith, Julia, 1982, 'Commentaries of Heaven', *Times Literary Supplement*, 19 March

——, 1988, 'Attitudes towards Conformity and Nonconformity in Thomas Traherne', *Bunyan Studies*, 1, 26–35

Smith, Julia, and Laetitia Yeandle, 1997, 'Felicity Disguisd in Fiery Words: Genesis and Exodus in a Newly Discovered Poem by Thomas Traherne', *Times Literary Supplement*, 7 Nov.

Smith, Julia J., 1988, 'Thomas Traherne and the Restoration', *The Seventeenth Century*, 3, 203–22

Smith, Nigel, ed., 1983, *A Collection of Ranter Writings from the 17th Century*, London

Smith, Nigel, 1994, *Literature and Revolution in England, 1640–1660*, New Haven

Sowerby, R. E., 1994, *The Classical Legacy in Renaissance Poetry*, London

Stein, Arnold, 1968, *George Herbert's Lyrics*, Baltimore

Strier, Richard, 1969, 'Crashaw's other Voice', *Studies in English Literature*, 9, 135–51

——, 1979, 'Herbert and Tears', *English Literary History*, 46, 221–47

——, 1983, *Love Known: Theology and Experience in George Herbert's Poetry*, Chicago

——, 1993, 'Radical Donne: "Satire III"', *English Literary History*, 60, 283–322

——, 1996, 'Donne and the Politics of Devotion', in *Religion, Literature and Politics in Post-Reformation England*, ed. Donna B. Hamilton and Richard Strier, Cambridge, pp. 93–114

Summers, J. H., 1954, *George Herbert: His Religion and Art*, London

——, 1970, *The Heirs of Donne and Jonson*, London

Sykes-Davies, Hugh, 1965, 'Text or Context', *Review of English Literature*, 6, 93–107

Trickett, Rachel, 1981, 'Henry Vaughan and the Poetry of Vision', *Essays and Studies*, 34, 88–104

Trotter, David, 1979, *The Poetry of Abraham Cowley*, London

Tuve, Rosemond, 1952, *A Reading of George Herbert*, London

Tyacke, Nicholas, 1990, *Anti-Calvinists: The Rise of English Arminianism, c. 1590–1640*, Oxford

——, 1993, 'Archbishop Laud', in *The Early Stuart Church, 1603–1642*, ed. Kenneth Fincham, Basingstoke, pp. 51–70

Vendler, Helen, 1975, *The Poetry of George Herbert*, Cambridge, Mass.

Vickers, Brian, 1989, 'Machiavelli and Marvell's "Horatian Ode"', *Notes & Queries*, 36:1, 32–38

Wallace, John M., 1968, *Destiny his Choice: The Loyalism of Andrew Marvell*, Cambridge

Wallerstein, Ruth C., 1959, *Richard Crashaw: A Study in Style and Poetic Development*, Madison

Walton, Geoffrey, 1955, *Metaphysical to Augustan: Studies in Tone and Sensibility in the Seventeenth Century*, London

Warren, Austin, 1939, *Richard Crashaw: A Study in Baroque Sensibility*, London

Watson, Graeme J., 1986, 'Political Change and Continuity of Vision in Henry Vaughan's "Daphnis. An Elegiac Eclogue"', *Studies in Philology*, 83, 158–81

White, Helen C., 1936, *The Metaphysical Poets*, New York

White, Peter, 1993, 'The *via media* in the Early Stuart Church', in *The Early Stuart Church, 1603–42*, ed. Kenneth Fincham, Basingstoke, pp. 211–30

Wiggins, Peter de Sa, 1982, '"Aire and Angels": Incarnations of Love', *English Literary Renaissance*, 12, 87–101

Wilcher, Robert, 1985, *Andrew Marvell*, Cambridge

——, 1992, 'Andrew Marvell and William Cartwright', *Notes & Queries*, 39, 462–63

Wilding, Michael, 1987, *Dragons Teeth: Literature in the English Revolution*, Oxford

Williamson, George, 1960, *Seventeenth Century Contexts*, London

Winters, Yvor, 1967, *Forms of Discovery*, Denver

Worden, Blair, 1981, 'Classical Republicanism and the Puritan Revolution', in *History and Imagination: Essays in Honour of H. R. Trevor-Roper*, ed. Hugh Lloyd-Jones *et al.*, London, pp. 198–200

——, 1987, 'Andrew Marvell, Oliver Cromwell, and the Horatian Ode', in *Politics of Discourse: The Literature of Seventeenth-century England*, ed. Kevin Sharpe and Steven N. Zwicker, Berkeley, pp. 147–80

Wordsworth, Jonathan, 1982, *Wordsworth and the Borders of Vision*, Oxford

Yeoman, Louise, 1995, 'The Devil as Doctor – Witchcraft, Wodrow and the Wider World', *Scottish Archives*, 1, 93–105

Young, R. V., 1982, *Richard Crashaw and the Spanish Golden Age*, New Haven

INDEX